Who Owns the Environment?

The Political Economy Forum

Sponsored by the Political Economy Research Center (PERC)
Terry L. Anderson, Series Editor

Common Sense and Common Law for the Environment: Creating Wealth in Hummingbird Economies
By Bruce Yandle

Enviro-Capitalists: Doing Good While Doing Well
By Terry L. Anderson and Donald R. Leal

Environmental Federalism
Edited by Terry L. Anderson and Peter J. Hill

Land Rights: The 1990s' Property Rights Rebellion
Edited by Bruce Yandle

The Political Economy of Customs and Culture: Informal Solutions to the Commons Problem
Edited by Terry L. Anderson and Randy T. Simmons

The Political Economy of the American West
Edited by Terry L. Anderson and Peter J. Hill

The Privatization Process: A Worldwide Perspective
Edited by Terry L. Anderson and Peter J. Hill

Property Rights and Indian Economies
Edited by Terry L. Anderson

Public Lands and Private Rights: The Failure of Scientific Management
By Robert H. Nelson

Taking the Environment Seriously
Edited by Roger E. Meiners and Bruce Yandle

Water Marketing: The Next Generation
Edited by Terry L. Anderson and Peter J. Hill

Who Owns the Environment?
Edited by Peter J. Hill and Roger E. Meiners

Wildlife in the Marketplace
Edited by Terry L. Anderson and Peter J. Hill

Who Owns the Environment?

EDITED BY
PETER J. HILL AND ROGER E. MEINERS

ROWMAN & LITTLEFIELD PUBLISHERS, INC.
Lanham • Boulder • New York • Oxford

ROWMAN & LITTLEFIELD PUBLISHERS, INC.

Published in the United States of America
by Rowman & Littlefield Publishers, Inc.
4720 Boston Way, Lanham, Maryland 20706

12 Hid's Copse Road
Cumnor Hill, Oxford OX2 9JJ, England

British Library Cataloging in Publication Information Available

Library of Congress Cataloging-in-Publication Data

Who owns the environment / Peter J. Hill and Roger E. Meiners,
editors.
    p.   cm. — (Political economy forum)
    Includes bibliographical references and index.
    ISBN 0-8476-9081-4 (cloth : alk. paper). — ISBN 0-8476-9082-2
(pbk. : alk. paper)
    1. Environmental law—Economic aspects. 2. Right of property—
Environmental aspects. I. Hill, Peter Jensen. II. Meiners, Roger
E. III. Series.
K3585.4.W5   1998
344′.046—dc21   98-19797
                                                         CIP

Printed in the United States of America

♾ ™ The paper used in this publication meets the minimum requirements of
American National Standard for Information Sciences—Permanence of Paper
for Printed Library Materials, ANSI Z39.48–1984.

Contents

Tables and Figures   vii

Acknowledgments   ix

Introduction   Property Rights and Externalities: Problems and
Solutions   xi
Peter J. Hill and Roger E. Meiners

Chapter 1   Private Property Rights as the Basis for Free
Market Environmentalism   1
Louis De Alessi

Chapter 2   Property Rights, the Environment, and
Economic Well-Being   37
Seth W. Norton

Chapter 3   Property Rights as a Natural Order: Reciprocity,
Evolutionary and Experimental Considerations   55
Vernon L. Smith

Chapter 4   The Common Law and the Environment: The
Canadian Experience   87
Elizabeth Brubaker

Chapter 5   Coase, Pigou, and Environmental Rights   119
Bruce Yandle

Chapter 6   Existence Value and Other of Life's Ills   153
Donald J. Boudreaux and Roger E. Meiners

Chapter 7   From Stakeholders to Stockholders: A View
from Organizational Theory   187
William J. Carney

v

Chapter 8   Habitat Preservation: A Property Rights
               Perspective   223
               Richard A. Epstein

Chapter 9   Viewing Wildlife through Coase-Colored
               Glasses   259
               Terry L. Anderson

Chapter 10   Cooperating on the Commons: Case Studies in
               Community Fisheries   283
               Donald R. Leal

Chapter 11   The Constitutional Protection of Private
               Property   315
               Richard E. Wagner

Index   337

About the Political Economy Forum and the Contributors   349

Tables and Figures

Tables

2.1 Measures of Property Rights   44
2.2 Property Rights and Environmental Performance
        Measures   47
2.3 Economic Growth and Environmental Performance
        Measures   49
2.4 Growth and Environmental Performance Measures for
        Developing Countries   50

Figures

3.1 Market Experiment   70
3.2 Two-Person Decision Tree   73
3.3 Ultimatum Game Results   77
3.4 Dictator Game Results   79
5.1 Coase, Pigou, and Regulation   122
5.2 Externality Analysis   124

Acknowledgments

As with every volume in the Political Economy Forum Series, the final product is a team effort that goes beyond the authors and editors. The captain of that team is Dianna Rienhart, who is responsible for PERC's desktop publishing process. She is the one who pays attention to detail and thus makes sure all the i's are dotted and t's are crossed. Her cocaptains are Michelle Johnson and Monica Lane Guenther, who assist with word processing, proofreading, and general project management.

The 1997 Political Economy Forum, "Who Owns the Environment?" was made possible by a grant from the E. L. Wiegand Foundation, Reno, Nevada, and the American Farm Bureau Federation, Park Ridge, Illinois. Without their investment in knowledge, the research represented in this volume would not have been possible.

We thank the authors for their cooperation in writing the papers and exposing their ideas to constructive criticism from participants at the 1997 forum held June 12–15. The final product between these covers owes much to the intellectual debate held at that forum.

Peter J. Hill
Roger E. Meiners

Introduction

Property Rights and Externalities: Problems and Solutions

Peter J. Hill and Roger E. Meiners

The past several decades have seen growing recognition that environmental concerns are essentially property rights problems. Property rights define who can take what actions respecting specific resources. Undesirable environmental results indicate that we need to examine the rules of the game that govern actions. Thus many scholars have come to think of institutional arrangements, or the structure of property rights, as the basis of environmental problems, rather than technological issues to be solved by regulatory fiat.

However, despite the agreement that the lack of well-defined and enforced property rights can lead to the overexploitation of air, water, and other resources, widespread disagreement still exists regarding aspects of the property rights paradigm. For instance, there has been little empirical work that relates the degree of property rights definition to environmental quality. Also, the suggestion that the lack of well-defined property rights is at the heart of environmental issues sheds little light on the form that property rights should take and who the owners of those rights should be. Recently, it has been argued that property rights to resources should be more widely distributed; all who are affected by the use of a particular resource should be stakeholders in that resource.

When property rights are not well defined and enforced, how should that problem be remedied and who should be responsible for better defining those rights? Where do property rights originate? Does it make sense to use the coercive power of government to create quasi rights through tax and subsidy programs? And, finally, what is the interface between markets and property rights? How do property rights relate to market signals and how do markets respond when property rights are attenuated?

In June 1997, PERC (the Political Economy Research Center) convened its eighth Political Economy Forum to discuss these issues. Participants met in Montana to discuss eight papers. These papers were refined on the basis of that dialogue, three more chapters were added, and this volume resulted. The forum did not reach a consensus on exactly how property rights can and should work, but there was considerable refinement of the concept of property rights and the importance of applying the property rights paradigm to tough environmental issues.

In chapter 1, Louis De Alessi provides an overview of the logic of the market process and the importance of property rights to that process. In chapter 2, Seth Norton examines different measures of property rights and presents empirical evidence relevant to the theoretical arguments of De Alessi. Norton finds that there is a strong correlation between stable, well-defined rights and economic growth. More important for our purpose, he also finds that these same rights lead, by various measures, to improved environmental quality. The common assertion that economic growth creates a worse environment is highly doubtful.

Vernon L. Smith takes up the issue of the origins of property rights in chapter 3. He argues that property rights are a part of the natural order. Experimental economics, a field pioneered by Smith, supports the hypothesis that human kind has both cooperative and competitive inclinations. Exchange results from the desire to capture the rewards from cooperating, but competition limits the forms that exchange can take. At the heart of exchange is a recognition of property rights. Smith details the lessons learned from numerous experiments that indicate that property rights are a part of the natural order. If property rights are, in a very substantial sense, natural, then one must ask how susceptible such rights are to change through government intervention.

In chapter 4 Elizabeth Brubaker extends the concept of property rights as an evolutionary order in her chapter on the common law. Canada and the United States both retained British common law when they became independent nations. The common law, in which property rights are integral, was presumed a part of the natural order required for a free people. Property rights were not created de novo but evolved over a very long time in response to problems among people that needed resolution. The common law yielded consistent rules that protected rights but imposed responsibilities so that the fruits of order could be enjoyed. Brubaker argues that the common law is often superior to statutory intervention in dealing with environmental problems in that it establishes, through trespass and nuisance doctrine, protection from what we now call environmental harms. In contrast to statutory law, common law makes no attempt to engage in explicit social, political, or economic engineering through the balancing of the costs and benefits of particular actions. Instead, it delineates rights and makes no judgment about whether the attenuation of these rights would lead to the maximization of some concept of social welfare.

Common law, with its rigorous strictures against taking actions that harm other people, might appear to stand in the way of numerous activities that would seem to be sensible to allow. For instance, as detailed by Brubaker, one small landowner who suffered $50 worth of harm from an adjacent factory could secure an injunction forcing the factory to close if it cannot stop polluting, even if it is generating several million dollars in benefits. However, this clear specification of rights allows markets to work. If the factory truly is worthwhile, then knowing the rights of its neighbors, it can afford to offer to purchase the right to impose some pollution on the landowner. It is this Coasian solution that Bruce Yandle takes up in chapter 5. He contrasts Ronald Coase's market approach under a rule of law to the interventionist position of A. C. Pigou. Yandle details why the institutional approach of Coase is superior to the institutional-free analysis of Pigou.

Donald J. Boudreaux and Roger E. Meiners in chapter 6 and William J. Carney in chapter 7 examine attempts to expand the concept of rights to include such concepts as existence value and stakeholders. Boudreaux and Meiners argue that the attempt to discover and codify existence values, in order to protect citizens against alleged externalities, is fraught with problems that cannot be solved and does not recognize the nature of markets or the law required for a free society. Carney suggests that evolution of successful business organizations leads to the conclusion that we need specific rights with respect to environmental assets, rather than expanding and diluting rights through the stakeholder concept. He proposes privatization of public lands in order to create more incentives to protect resources for the future, something less likely to happen when resources are subject to the nonforward-looking incentives of politicians and bureaucrats.

The next three chapters take up specific issues and property rights problems. In chapter 8 Richard A. Epstein argues that better social outcomes are achieved for endangered species if the Endangered Species Act follows the common law rules on property rights. In chapter 9 Terry L. Anderson uses a transaction cost approach to understand the difficulty of contracting for wildlife preservation, and in chapter 10 Donald R. Leal details how the tragedy of the commons can be avoided through community organizations. The latter two chapters refer to many real-world examples of private or community-based solutions to problems that are often presumed to be subject to a tragedy of the commons, thus requiring regulatory intervention.

Finally, Richard E. Wagner presents an overview in chapter 11 of the social coordination process, arguing that there are fundamentally two systems of property and two systems of pricing. He contrasts market pricing organized under the rules of private property with political pricing organized under the rules of common property. If market pricing and private property rights are to dominate, government must be constrained constitutionally in its ability to attenuate rights. However, democracy, by its very nature, makes such limits difficult. Wagner suggests institutional reforms and changes in ideology that are necessary to protect property rights and, thereby, the environment.

Chapter 1

Private Property Rights as the Basis for Free Market Environmentalism

Louis De Alessi

The market is a low-cost institution for organizing cooperation in production and exchange. In a market system, private property rights tie the welfare of individuals to the economic consequences of their decisions while freely fluctuating prices provide the information and the incentive to respond quickly and accurately to changes in circumstances. As a result, rights to the use of resources flow to their highest-valued uses, as judged by consumers, and the welfare of individuals depends on their success in making others better off through voluntary exchange. The presence of transaction costs and the absence of some private property rights, however, can inhibit voluntary exchange and give rise to external effects, including degradation of the environment.

The pollution of air and water, the exhaustion of fisheries and forests, and various actual, potential, or imagined environmental problems have encouraged wide-ranging conservation efforts. Unfortunately, conservationists have seldom combined good intentions with a working knowledge of economics, an understanding of statistical inference, a grasp of reliable data, and the skill to avoid fronting for special interest groups, including environmental activists. For decades many conservationists have pursued policies that do more harm than good and often work at cross purposes with the goals they claim to seek.[1]

An obvious example is the Endangered Species Act of 1973 (Epstein

This chapter draws on earlier work by the author (see De Alessi 1980, 1988, 1998) and benefits from comments by Michael L. De Alessi, Roger E. Meiners, Helen Peak, and Roberto M. Cid.

1

1998). This act restricts the use of land held to be inhabited by an endangered species but does not require either payment from those who benefit or compensation to those who are harmed. Fairness aside, failure to make those who benefit bear the cost provides the incentive to demand too many rights for conservation purposes, while the failure to compensate those who are harmed provides the incentive to make the habitat less attractive to actual and potential endangered species. In any case, the goal of saving all endangered species regardless of cost is not a useful guide to policy in a world in which resources are scarce and species are evolving.

The root causes of environmental problems, besides the search for rents[2] and the inability or unwillingness to think problems through, are reasonably clear: lack of private property rights and high transaction costs. Gordon (1954), marking the return of economists to a field that had become dominated by biologists and other natural scientists, showed that common ownership with open access removes the incentive to conserve a resource, such as a fishery, and eventually can lead to its exhaustion.[3] Scott (1955) quickly validated and extended Gordon's analysis. In a subsequent review of prevailing environmental policies, Gordon (1958, 110–11) found that "a great deal (perhaps the greater part) of what has been done in the name of 'conservation policy' turns out, upon subjection to economic analysis, to be worthless, or worse." He concluded that "It is the common property [open access] problem and the divergence between private and social costs and benefits that seem to be most worthy of the application of administrative and legal ingenuity" (Gordon 1958, 121).

Shortly thereafter, Coase (1960) published his classic essay on the problem of social cost. His analysis demonstrated that, in a neoclassical world of zero transaction costs and fully allocated private property rights, all parties to a potential trade must take into account the opportunity cost of the rights. As a result, rights flow to those uses in which they are most valuable; moreover, how resources are used is independent of their initial assignment.[4] These findings destroyed conventional wisdom, which had been given theoretical respectability by Pigou's (1920) standard work on welfare, that the party thought to harm others would not take that harm into account unless held liable or taxed an amount equal to the harm (Yandle 1998).[5]

Coase's analysis implies that there are no environmental problems if property rights are fully private and transaction costs are zero. Of course, some people might still wish for more pristine streams or cleaner air, but then people always want more of all things. Because resources are scarce, individuals must choose: they simply cannot have all the things that they desire.

In practice, transaction costs may be substantial and rights to the use of resources may not be wholly private. Transaction costs reduce the gains from trade and can inhibit exchange; in the limit, there is no trade. Property rights that are not fully defined, assigned to private users, and enforced are less amenable to exchange; in the limit, there is no trade. If trade is inhibited, individuals do not bear some of the economic (value) consequences of their decisions and thus lack the incentive to take them fully into account. The result is external effects, including environmental effects: some harmful, some beneficial, and many trivial.

Although the inference is tempting, it does not follow that all property rights should be private. Defining, assigning, and enforcing private rights is costly and individuals may choose other institutional arrangements, including communal ownership with auxiliary rules to control use (Field 1984; Ostrom 1990; Johannes 1992).

Analytically, a society's institutions establish the system of property rights by setting the constraints that limit the choices available (Alchian 1961). Because different systems of property rights typically set different constraints, they present individuals with different cost/reward structures and affect choices systematically. Accordingly, traditional economic theory can be used to explore the economic consequences of alternative institutional and contractual arrangements, including those adopted to control use of the environment (Smith 1998).

Extensive theoretical and empirical research has shown that taking account of transaction costs and the system of property rights is crucial in understanding how an economic system functions and grows (De Alessi 1980; Eggertsson 1990; North 1990; Rutherford 1994; Norton 1998). Much of the early work in the field focused on environmental problems (Gordon 1954; Coase 1960; Anderson and Hill 1975; Umbeck 1977; Libecap 1978), which still attract a great deal of interest (Yandle 1995; Endres 1996; Anderson and Hill 1997; De Alessi 1997b).

Nevertheless, discussions of environmental issues continue to be marred by a failure to understand the economic consequences of alternative systems of property rights. Proponents of central planning tend to compare the market as it actually works with the government as it would work under ideal circumstances (Demsetz 1969), neglecting the failure of political solutions (Buchanan 1988) and blaming private ownership for consequences that often are due to its absence (Brubaker 1998). Central planning, which is favored by many environmental groups and promoted under various guises, weakens or destroys private property rights and raises transaction costs while presenting insurmountable measurement and incentive problems (Boudreaux and Meiners 1998); even using the normative criteria of its proponents, central planning typically ends up doing more harm than good.

The market is simply an institution that facilitates voluntary transactions among individuals. In a market system, private property rights tie the welfare of individuals to the economic consequences of their decisions. Individuals are rewarded for their contributions to the welfare of others (rather than for rent seeking), for taking account of knowledge that is place and time specific (Hayek 1945), and for participating in the process of entrepreneurial discovery that promotes growth and adjustment to change (Kirzner 1997). Because the market is based on voluntary exchanges rather than coercion, it is also consistent with political freedom and individual liberty (Wagner 1998). The failure of central planning, including the extensive degradation of the environment in all the countries that have tried it, offers a lesson that is consistent with the U.S. government's track record in managing the environment (Anderson and Leal 1991) and offers a strong case for privatization (Carney 1998).

The logical starting point for addressing an environmental problem is to identify the institutions that give rise to it and then explore how they might be modified to yield a preferred outcome. The solution may lie in a more rigorous definition, assignment, and enforcement of private rights as well as in other techniques for lowering transaction costs and facilitating exchange, including the evolution of new institutional arrangements—such as the assignment of fishing rights to private, communal organizations—that establish or approach a market environment.[6]

This chapter explores the usefulness of the market in solving environmental problems. The topics covered include how institutions affect choices; how the market works and why its effectiveness depends on the existence of a well-established system of private property rights; the nature of external effects, including environmental problems; why the cost-reward structure embedded in central planning condemns it to failure; and how the market can be used to solve environmental problems.

Institutions and Choice

Economic theory provides a powerful set of tools for examining the evolution and economic consequences of alternative institutional and contractual arrangements, including the informal rules that arise from a society's customs and ethical values (De Alessi 1983). It even helps explain why and how certain norms of moral behavior arise, evolve, and interact with a society's formal institutions (Sethi and Somanathan

1996; Benson 1997). Before examining how institutions affect choices, it is useful to note the behavioral hypotheses that drive the analysis.

Behavioral Hypotheses

The working postulates of economics are few. Those concerning preferences assert that individuals seek a multitude of goals, such as health, knowledge, and the well-being of others, and that, at the margin, these goals are substitutable. Substitutability means that there is no hierarchy of wants and that individuals are willing to achieve a little less of any given goal, perhaps health, in order to achieve sufficiently more of some other goal, say an improved chance of survival for some endangered species. A final postulate about preferences asserts that as individuals achieve more of a goal, other things being the same, the personal value that they attach to further increments falls. These propositions apply to all goals and to all individuals, regardless of their role as decision makers and the economic system in which they live. For each individual, of course, at least some goals remain unfulfilled; without scarcity, there is no economic problem.

Goals are difficult to observe and distinguish from means. After all, individuals may care not only about ends, such as saving an animal species, but also about means, such as following due process. Moreover, what some individuals may view as ends others may view as means. Economists solve the ends–means problem by focusing on the demand and supply functions of the commodities that individuals use as inputs to pursue whatever goals they choose. Especially in the case of environmental issues, however, it is useful to keep the larger context in mind.

Even when individuals share the same goals, typically they assign them different weights and each individual has the incentive to advance those goals that he or she prefers. Accordingly, the decisions taken by a group, whether a family, a business firm, a government bureau, or some other collection of individuals, are best analyzed as the outcome of a decision process—and the institutions governing the process matter—in which members of the group pursue their own personal interests, including their view of what is best for other individuals and the group as a whole.

Individuals do not have identical preferences and constraints, and environmentalists do not have identical priorities. Because this diversity is reflected in the choices people make, economics focuses on the individual as the basic unit of analysis: the empirical evidence has shown that this approach yields better predictions or explanations of economic behavior. Although some individuals hold strong normative views either for or against individual values, positive economics—the analysis of choices subject to constraints—in principle is value-free.

Economics yields two major implications. First, individuals respond to a shift in constraints that change the rate at which they are able to substitute one commodity for another (the structure of relative prices) by consuming more of those commodities that have become relatively cheaper. Thus, the lower the cost (whatever the chooser has to forego) of any commodity (whatever the chooser views as a source of satisfaction), the more the chooser will consume: all demand curves are negatively sloped. For example, a fall in the cost of protecting a species will lead to more protection. Second, individuals respond to a shift in constraints that increase the opportunities available to them (an increase in income) by consuming more of all commodities.[7] For instance, citizens of wealthier countries exhibit a greater concern for a better environment.

How prices, including incomes, are set is determined by the system of property rights (Alchian 1967). To use economic theory for predictive purposes, therefore, it is necessary to establish how property rights affect constraints and, thus, the opportunities available to individuals.

Institutions and Property Rights

In a world of scarcity, individuals cannot satisfy all their goals or wants, including their personal wants for a better environment and a better society. Because individuals must compete with each other for the right to use the resources that are available, the fundamental economic problem within any society is to evolve a set of institutions for organizing cooperation, that is, for controlling competition and adapting to changes in circumstances.

The formal and informal institutions—statutory law, common law, and customs—of a society develop spontaneously as well as by design. Whatever their origin, they establish how individuals may behave, given a range of permissible alternatives (Alchian 1965). In other words, institutions establish how individuals are permitted to benefit and harm themselves and others. Institutions perform this function by specifying the rights that individuals may hold to the use of resources, to the stream of services (income or utility) that the resources yield, and to the transferability of these rights to others. For example, a manufacturer may legally harm competitors by making a higher quality product but not by lowering prices, staying open on Sundays, or dynamiting the competitors' plants. Similarly, farmers may legally kill varmints and their own chickens at any time, members of listed game species only at specific times, and spotted owls never.

Custom is also a powerful determinant of acceptable behavior, affecting and being affected by a society's institutions. For example, ethnic minorities bound by norms that proscribe the breach of contract often prosper in societies with weak legal systems (Landa 1981). In a system based on voluntary exchange, repeat transactions provide the incentive to observe contracts and, more generally, to invest in reputation. Indeed, Benson (1997, 271) argues that

> there is a property rights foundation to morality, or at least that private property rights and the institutions which evolve to induce the recognition of and secure those rights also create incentives to behave "morally." As private property rights and their supporting institutions evolve, incentives are created for individuals to behave cooperatively, ethically, and altruistically. On the other hand, institutions designed to produce involuntary transfers of wealth, and therefore, undermine the security of private property rights, also undermine the incentive to behave morally.

These comments suggest that environmental rules, whose enforcement can be spotty and costly, are more likely to achieve their goals if they are sanctioned by custom (Smith 1998).

The system of property rights specifies the constraints that limit the choices available to individual economic agents, including the sort of contracts that they may enter with one another. These constraints, acting through actual or imputed prices, determine how the harms and the benefits that flow from a decision are allocated between the decision maker and other members of society, establishing the costs and rewards associated with alternative choices. Thus, the system of property rights determines the expectations that individuals may form in their dealings with others.

All economic systems, including anarchy, capitalism, socialism, communism, and their various permutations and combinations, derive their distinguishing characteristics from their structure of property rights. Because they present individuals—via different sets of prices—with different opportunities to increase their welfare, including different opportunities to do good (as each chooser sees it), their economic consequences can be analyzed and compared using the standard tools of economic theory. Economics, however, does not provide value-free criteria for determining which institutions are preferable; that choice, like any other choice, ultimately depends on the normative values of the chooser.

Ownership Arrangements

In general, rights may be exclusive and voluntarily transferable (private), neither exclusive nor voluntarily transferable (common with open access), or exclusive but not voluntarily transferable (usufruct). Moreover, the rights pertaining to specific resources may be partitioned and bundled in complex combinations subject to frequent change (Anderson 1998). A review of the limiting types suggests the range of options available.

Common (Communal) Ownership

Rights to the use of resources may be held in common, that is, be neither exclusive nor transferable. One limit is open access: everyone in the group has the right to use the resource and capture its fruits on a first-come, first-served basis. Because individuals can establish private property rights in an open-access resource only by extracting it, they have little incentive to postpone capturing it and to invest in maintaining and developing it; the result is the tragedy of the commons. Relative to private ownership, individuals invest less in the habitat (for example, by building artificial reefs) and harvest the resource earlier and more intensively; they also invest more in the privately owned inputs, such as fishing boat and gear, used jointly in production. Open-access pasture lands, fisheries, hunting grounds, and forests typically are exploited more intensively and are more likely to be exhausted earlier in time.

Still, open access may be the best option if the value of a resource at the margin is sufficiently low. However, an increase in value, perhaps due to an increase in demand, or a fall in the cost of defining, establishing, enforcing, and exchanging private rights would provide more incentive to control use through auxiliary rules or privatization (Demsetz 1967). For example, early settlers in New England typically held some land in private and other land in a variety of communal arrangements (Field 1984). As the settlements flourished and land became more valuable, most of the commons gradually were privatized. Those few colonies in which all resources initially were held in common quickly vanished or began privatizing (Wright 1949).

Communal ownership with auxiliary rules to control use is a practical option if a resource is sufficiently valuable to justify the costs of organizing the group but not the costs of defining, establishing, enforcing, and exchanging private rights. Cooperative arrangements have worked well throughout the world in managing many resources, including mountain forests and meadows, water for irrigation, and fisheries (Ostrom 1990; Johannes 1992; De Alessi 1997b; Leal 1998).

For example, consider the solution observed in Törbel, a village in the Swiss Alps, nestled in terrain characterized by steep slopes, different microclimates determined by altitude and exposure to sunlight, and little precipitation (Ostrom 1990). For centuries, the villagers have held some land in private and used it to grow grains, hay, vegetables, fruit trees, and other crops. They also have held five different types of property in common: alpine grazing meadows, forests, "waste" lands, irrigation systems, and paths. Each type has its own set of rules for management, use, and transfer—including privatization, should that alternative become more valuable—and is controlled through a citizens' association.

The villagers hold much land in private. Why not all? The forests, in addition to providing wood, also protect the village from avalanches and help maintain the aquifer while the meadows at different altitudes provide pasture at different periods of the summer. Given the physical environment, land values in alternative uses, and existing technology, the villagers apparently concluded that transaction costs among many private owners were sufficiently high to make communal arrangements preferable.

Communal arrangements are used throughout Oceania to manage local reefs and lagoons, with control occasionally extending as far as the visible horizon (Johannes 1992). In the Solomons, reefs have been partitioned and allocated to individual families to grow giant clams for export; in Fiji, fishing grounds similarly have been partitioned and allocated to families with some sections allowed to lie fallow. In the Philippines, on the other hand, native rules to control the reefs were abrogated by the Spanish government at the time of conquest and open access allowed; today, 90 percent of the Philippine reefs are either dead or dying, often the result of fishing with dynamite and cyanide (De Alessi 1997a).

At some point, the value of a resource may rise enough or the cost of establishing private property rights fall enough that private ownership becomes viable. In Japan, a number of communal holdings have been privatized in response to increased land values (McKean 1986). In the United States, the introduction of barbed wire encouraged the development of private rights in western land by lowering the cost of enclosing it and enforcing exclusivity (Anderson and Hill 1975). More generally, the evolution of American institutions reflected the costs and benefits of defining and enforcing various kinds of property rights (Davis and North 1971), a point further illustrated by the development of private mineral rights in the West (Libecap 1978; Umbeck 1977).[8]

Private Ownership

In every society, the rights to the use of at least some resources are private, that is, exclusive and voluntarily transferable. Under this arrangement, the owner of the right has the exclusive authority to decide how the resource is used given a set of permissible alternatives; these usually exclude the right to affect the physical attributes of resources owned by others. The owner also has exclusive authority to receive the income generated by the resource and to transfer the property right to others at any mutually agreed price. Because individuals bear the full economic (value) consequences of their decisions, they have incentive to take them fully into account; in the limit, there are no external effects.

The authority to transfer rights implies the opportunity to establish a market for them. Rules that limit transferability, such as rules that control prices and other conditions of exchange, reduce the bundle of private property rights and diminish its usefulness.

The existence of a market in which private rights can be exchanged implies that future consequences are instantaneously capitalized into current transfer prices and reflected in owners' wealth. For example, the discovery of oil on some land increases the land's value as soon as the information becomes known, even though it may be years before any oil is extracted. In an open market, current prices reflect expectations regarding future events. Intermediaries cast dollar votes on behalf of future generations and bear the full value consequences of their decisions; if they are wrong, they lose wealth. In the political place, anyone can claim to speak for future generations without bearing the corresponding value consequences.

Private property means that individuals have the right to form voluntary contracts (transact) with others at any terms they choose within the institutional boundaries. With respect to business organizations, for example, they can choose to form single proprietorships, partnerships, corporations, cooperatives, or any other legal set of mutually agreeable contracts, including communal ownership and charitable foundations; moreover, they can choose to contract activities out or integrate them within their own firms. Private owners can choose to use their assets themselves, rent them or lease them to others, or give them away.

Usufruct Rights

Rights to the use and the income of some resources may be exclusive but not transferable. Unless this usufruct arrangement is formed voluntarily, rights do not flow to those individuals who have a comparative advantage in their use and their owners are unable to capitalize the future consequences of their decisions into current transfer prices. Among other implications, output will be smaller and investments in maintaining and developing the resource will be smaller and shorter-lived. An example may be helpful.

In Mexico, farmers who have been allotted land under the *ejido* program cannot sell or lease the land and can lose it if they do not work it for two consecutive years (De Vany 1977). The evidence shows that *ejidatarios*, relative to private owners of comparable land, make smaller investments in irrigation and other capital improvements, use more labor, and are less likely to grow crops with a long gestation period. Interestingly, they also have larger families to help work the land and retain usufruct rights while older members of the family seek more gainful employment elsewhere (De Vany and Sanchez 1979).

In a market system, many resources are rented or leased—both voluntary usufruct contracts. Renting and leasing, however, are limited by the possibility of opportunistic behavior. For example, farmers are more likely to lease land for growing wheat and other annual crops than for growing fruit trees and other crops with a long time to maturity. In the latter case, the cost of protection from opportunistic behavior often makes outright purchase cheaper; if leases occur, they are long-term and contain detailed provisions to limit opportunistic behavior by both parties. In an open market, individuals can choose the contract that best suits their circumstances.

State Ownership and Regulation

Rights to the use, income, and transferability of some resources may be held by the state and controlled by state employees according to whatever political procedures are currently acceptable. For example, in the United States the federal government owns much of the land in the western states: about 83 percent of Nevada, 64 percent of Utah, 62 percent of Idaho, 52 percent of Oregon, 49 percent of Wyoming, 47 percent of Arizona, and 45 percent of California (Lueck and Yoder 1997). The federal Bureau of Land Management alone administers 23 percent of the total area of the eleven far western states, including nearly 70 percent of Nevada and over 40 percent of Utah, and issues grazing and other permits; the evolution of the present arrangement is a textbook illustration of bureaucratic and private rent seeking (Libecap 1981).

Government regulation of individual choices means that specific rights—for example, the right to exclude certain groups or to charge prices above or below given limits—are transferred from other bundles (e.g., private or common) to the state. State employees then have the authority, following sanctioned political procedures, to decide how a right may be used.

The economic implications of government ownership and regulation are examined more carefully in a subsequent section. For the present, it is sufficient to note that these arrangements attenuate the link between the welfare of decision makers and the economic consequences of their choices—except as registered through bribes and the political process—with predictable consequences, including increased opportunities for rent seeking.

Partitioning of Rights

In practice, the rights to the use of many resources are partitioned: some private, some usufruct, some communal, and some state held. For example, a farmer may hold private rights to a parcel of land but choose to lease part of it to someone else, thereby giving up some of its uses; the terms of the lease may specify how the land may be employed as well as limit the farmer's ability to sell it and the lessee's ability to sublet it or exhaust it. A neighbor may have the usufruct right (easement) to beat a path through it, everyone in the community may jointly hold the (communal) right to dump smoke on it, and the state may own the right to build a road through it or regulate the characteristics of structures built on it. In a market system, voluntary partitioning of rights provides flexibility in their use, facilitating their combination into convenient bundles and easing their flow to higher-valued uses.

Rule of Law

Within any system of property rights, conflicts often arise regarding who has the right to do what. Contract law deals with conflicts regarding the partitioning of rights intended by the parties to an agreement while tort and nuisance laws deal with conflicts that arise when the choices made by owners of some rights impose harm on owners of other rights.

In common law jurisdictions, statute and common law have competed in addressing environmental problems. Common law, which allows people to contract around the rule, reduces the opportunities for rent seeking, adapts to local circumstances, affords protection often displaced by statutes, and buttresses an economic system based on private property rights (Yandle 1997; Brubaker 1998).

Institutions and Transaction Costs

Transaction costs, broadly defined as the costs of acquiring and processing information and of negotiating, forming, and policing contracts, affect and are affected by the system of property rights. The structure of transaction costs determines the choice of property rights, including the extent to which private rights are defined, allocated, enforced, and exchanged. The lower are these costs, the greater is the incentive to establish private rights and internalize harms (to avoid paying compensation) and benefits (to obtain compensation). Earlier examples, such as the privatization of communal land, are apt.

More generally, transaction costs are a key determinant of the organization of economic activity, helping to explain why some institutions exist and why, given the institutions, individuals choose to form particular contractual arrangements. For example, transaction costs help to explain why some activities are integrated within a firm and others are contracted out as well as why a firm, which is simply a nexus of contracts, takes different forms (Joskow 1988).

Although transaction costs help to explain why certain rights are not fully defined, assigned to private users, and enforced, other factors matter. Some individuals may prefer other ownership arrangements, such as a communal system, and are willing to forego other goals in exchange. Other individuals may fail to understand how alternative systems of property rights function, often confusing ideal systems and reality; central planning continues to have considerable appeal in spite of repeated and disastrous failures. Still other individuals may opt for other arrangements because they can use them to their own benefit, taxing the rest of the community to obtain more of the goals that they prefer—a key reason for the popularity of central planning.

The system of property rights, in turn, affects transaction costs. Institutions limiting ownership to usufruct rights, such as the *ejido* program in Mexico described earlier, set transaction costs in such rights at infinity. State ownership limits the opportunity and the incentive for employees of different state organizations to trade rights among themselves and with outsiders: transaction costs typically are prohibitive. Government regulation of business activity similarly limits private property rights and raises transaction costs by setting side conditions on market exchanges.

Markets, Production, and Consumption

Most people think of the market as a place where individuals buy and sell goods and services. It is analytically more useful as well as more accurate, however, to think of the market as a low-cost institution for organizing cooperation in production and consumption through voluntary exchange. How well individuals succeed in using the market to solve their society's economic problems depends on the extent to which the economic system relies on private property rights.

Markets

The fundamental economic problems of any society are when, how, and what to produce, how to distribute it, who bears the risk, and who decides. The solutions include setting priorities and ensuring that they are mutually consistent; acquiring and processing information; making relevant information available to those who decide; transmitting decisions to those who implement them; providing decision makers with the incentive to use information in the desired way; monitoring performance; and accomplishing all these and related activities in a world of uncertainty.

The market provides individuals, who are familiar with their own particular circumstances of time and place, with the opportunity to exchange rights to the use of resources and, through signals transmitted by prices, with the information and incentive to allocate these rights to their highest-valued uses. Thus, the market facilitates cooperation in economic activities and establishes a powerful mechanism for controlling competition; output is larger, and its composition and distribution are determined by the interplay of demand and supply. How well the market works depends on its openness, that is, on the absence of laws that limit the ability of individuals to form voluntary contracts, including the ability to enter and exit.

Central planning simply cannot solve a society's economic problems. Reasons for this failure include the incentive structure, which biases decisions and encourages rent seeking (McChesney 1997), and the loss of information inherent to the process of aggregation, which inevitably destroys information that is place and time specific for each individual affected (Hayek 1945).

Note that the issue is not planning, but who does it. Under central control, government employees do the planning and implement it through coercion but do not bear the resulting value consequences. Under a market system, private individuals—whether consumers, owners of rights, or managers of firms—make their own plans, implement them through voluntary exchanges with others, and bear the resulting economic consequences.

A comment on incentives may be helpful. Consider a race with attractive prizes for the first to finish. If all participants start at the same time and the race is over a short, level field, people will train to sprint and the best sprinter will win. If all participants start at the same time and the race is over a long course, people will train accordingly and the best long-distance runner will win. If participants can start whenever they wish, people will camp at the finish line and the one with the best skill in that competition will win. The rules of the game (system of property rights) reward those individuals who have a comparative advantage in playing the game according to those rules.

In an open market system, individuals are rewarded on the basis of the value of their contribution to the welfare of others as the latter see it. That is, the welfare of individuals is related to their success in cooperating with others in producing the kinds of commodities that people want and in adjusting their own consumption pattern in light of the wants of others. Unlike the political place, where individuals have only one vote and cannot express the intensity of their preferences, the market allows individuals to concentrate their dollar votes in pursuit of those goals that they value most.

How well the market works, other things being the same, depends on the extent to which the economic system rests on private property rights. Because private rights tie the welfare of individuals to the value consequences of their choices, they provide decision makers with the incentive to take these consequences into account by cooperating with others and specializing in those productive activities in which they have a comparative advantage; exchanging commodities with other individuals, so that each party ends up with a preferred consumption basket; and discovering new opportunities for gain, including technological and institutional innovations. The weaker the limits on private rights, including the limits imposed by government ownership and regulation, the stronger are individuals' incentives to increase their welfare through cooperation with others rather than through rent-seeking activities; and the better the market works.

Cooperation in Production and Consumption: Specialization and Exchange

Given limited resources, including limited means for converting inputs into outputs, individuals can increase their welfare through cooperation in production and consumption. Specialization in production allows individuals to concentrate their efforts on those activities in which they have a comparative advantage, including working with other individuals within the same and other firms, and results in a larger aggregate output. Exchange then allows individuals to consume a preferred combination of commodities, making others better off while fulfilling more of their own goals.

Exchange, of course, can occur in the absence of production. The necessary condition for exchange is that, at the margin, individuals attach different relative values to commodities. Differences in these subjective, marginal rates of substitution may occur because of differences in tastes or in the endowment of resources, including differences in natural skills, investment in human capital, and control over other assets. For trade to take place, however, the reasons why the subjective rates of substitution differ is irrelevant: all that matters is that they are different, thereby creating an opportunity for mutual gain.

The extent of trade, including whether it takes place at all, depends also on the constraints set by the system of property rights and the structure of transaction costs (Anderson 1998). As additional constraints are imposed to benefit special interest groups, the gains from cooperation are reduced; the incentives to specialize in production and consumption and to innovate are weakened. Aggregate output is smaller and the welfare of those individuals with a comparative advantage in the political place is increased at the expense of other members of society.

For example, the practices of the federal Bureau of Land Management enhance its survival and the welfare of its employees but inhibit the allocation of land to more productive uses (Libecap 1981). Thus, land use may be limited to grazing when it might be more valuable in other activities, grazing capacity may not reflect local conditions, and grazing fees may redistribute wealth from taxpayers to ranchers.

Prices are nothing more than coefficients of choice (Schumpeter 1934, ch. 6) and exist in every economic system. In a command system, the nominal price (the amount of currency given up) of a commodity frequently is a small portion of the real price (the opportunity cost), most of whose components are implicit: maintaining an information network to learn what is available where and when, waiting in line, bribing clerks and officials, and so on. In a market system, market prices reflect the rate at which individuals can actually exchange one bundle of rights for another. Because market prices are explicit, they can be observed more cheaply and provide a more effective guide to the allocation of resources.

Many conservationists either do not understand the role of prices in an open market system or do not find it advantageous to acknowledge it (Boudreaux and Meiners 1998). This observation is suggested by such things as a revealed preference for central planning (a choice presumably abetted by rent seeking) and by periodic forecasts of a coming crisis due to the exhaustion of some resource. These crises usually are based on taking the known stock of a finite resource, such as oil or timber, projecting its current rate of consumption into the future, and finding the date when the stock will run out. For very good reasons, however, such forecasts never materialize for privately owned resources.

Consider the case of oil deposits which, according to periodic doomsday predictions, should have been exhausted years ago. As the known stock is drawn down, individuals anticipate its extinction at some future date and the price of oil increases in the present. The prices of all commodities that use oil and its byproducts as inputs also increase, as do the prices of substitute inputs and outputs. These price increases offer entrepreneurs new possibilities for gain. Oil producers have incentive to search for new deposits; develop new techniques and apply known, higher-cost techniques for detecting new oil deposits and extracting more oil from old deposits; build roads, pipelines, and other means for tapping previously unprofitable deposits; and pursue a myriad of other strategies to increase the output of oil. Producers of commodities that use oil or its byproducts as inputs have incentive to use less of them, substituting other inputs, and to develop and adopt new techniques that economize on oil; for example, automobile manufacturers might build lighter cars with smaller engines using more exotic (more expensive) materials that are more fuel-efficient. Similarly, other manufacturers have incentive to develop new products that economize on oil, such as battery-powered cars. While all this activity is taking place on the supply side, the higher prices provide consumers with the incentive to shift their consumption toward commodities that use less oil and oil byproducts. Even if known oil deposits do not increase, the rate at which they are used up falls, giving time for the development of substitutes.

External Effects

In a neoclassical world of zero transaction costs, the way in which private rights to the use of resources are employed does not depend upon their initial assignment (Coase 1960).[9] Using the example of damage to crops by straying cattle, Coase showed that the number of cattle raised and the quantity of crops harvested are the same whether the rancher or the farmer is liable. The analysis is straightforward: the party who attaches the higher value to the right either holds it, foregoing compensation, or buys it, paying compensation; similarly, the individual who attaches the lower value to the right either sells it, receiving compensation, or fails to buy it, foregoing its use. Regardless of the initial assignment, both parties must take into account the opportunity cost of the right. Because individuals bear the full economic consequences of their decisions, they have incentive to take them fully into account; as a result, there are no external effects.

In practice, of course, transaction costs typically are positive and substantial. Because transaction costs reduce the gains from trade, they inhibit exchange; in the limit, there may be no exchange at all. As a result, not all the value consequences of a choice are brought to bear on the decision maker; there are external effects.

Coase's fundamental insight was to recognize the reciprocal nature of the problem raised by externalities:

> In the case of the cattle and the crops, it is true that there would be no crop damage without the cattle. It is equally true that there would be no crop damage without the crops. . . . If we are to discuss the problem in terms of causation, both parties cause the damage. If we are to attain an optimum allocation of resources, it is therefore desirable that both parties should take the harmful effect (the nuisance) into account in deciding on their course of action. It is one of the beauties of a smoothly operating pricing system that, as has already been explained, the fall in the value of production due to the harmful effect would be a cost for both parties. (Coase 1960, 13)

Conventional wisdom, buttressed by Pigou's (1920) classic work on welfare, held that state action was necessary to cope with external effects arising from market transactions. The state would reduce harmful externalities by taxing the agency causing them, such as a factory spewing smoke, and encourage beneficial externalities by granting subsidies. This approach, however, fails to recognize the reciprocal nature of the problem. As Coase (1960, 42) noted:

> Without the tax, there may be too much smoke and too few people in the vicinity of the factory; but with the tax there may be too little smoke and too many people in the vicinity of the factory. There is no reason to suppose that one of these results is necessarily preferable.

Under open market conditions, individuals have incentive to develop contractual and institutional arrangements for reducing external effects. For example, malls and shopping centers are designed to internalize many harms and benefits arising from adjacent independent stores. To the extent that these complexes spill external benefits and harms on the surrounding neighborhood, the developers have incentive to purchase adjacent land and sell it with suitable covenants, thereby internalizing the external effects and inducing all parties to take the relevant costs into account (Demsetz 1964). In an open market, firms that harm the environment can lose reputation and wealth as concerned consumers switch to more responsive producers (Yandle 1998). It is also important to recognize that not all conceivable transactions are worth completing for the same reason that not all conceivable commodities are worth producing: the demand curve is everywhere below the supply curve.

Still, transaction costs inhibit some exchanges. Typical examples arise when the number of individuals affected is small, and the incentive to engage in strategic behavior may lead them to miss a trade, or when the number of individuals affected is large, and the cost of organizing them is substantial (Boudreaux 1996). Even here, however, externalities may not exist or be trivial.

The Small-Numbers Case

In an open market with large numbers of buyers and sellers, individuals considering an exchange typically are price takers: sellers are unable to negotiate a price above the going market price and buyers are unable to negotiate a price below it. Under these conditions, the only option available is whether or not to trade at the going market price.

In the small-numbers case, say two parties, there is no single price. Instead, there is a set of prices ranging between the two personal price ratios that limit the gains from trade. At the lower limit one party, call it the seller, is just indifferent and the other party, call it the buyer, captures all the gains from trade; at the upper limit the buyer is just indifferent and the seller captures all the gains from trade. Because both buyer and seller have incentive to engage in strategic behavior, there is some probability that one or both may stake out positions that reduce or even prevent mutually beneficial trade (Smith 1998). An example might be the owner of a wetland and a conservationist bargaining over the right to maintain the wetland as a refuge for migratory species. The possibility of trade-inhibiting strategic behavior is enhanced in the case of repeat transactions. Here, one or both parties may seek to establish a reputation as hard bargainers in order to strike better deals in the future.

Empirically, there is no evidence that strategic bargaining has a visible effect on the allocation of resources. Among other considerations, bilateral monopoly is not a dominant market structure and the number of trades observed in the market is large by any reasonable standard.

More interesting, theoretical considerations suggest that strategic behavior need not hamper the allocation of resources to their higher-valued use even if it inhibits exchange. In the small-numbers case, Boudreaux (1996, 99) points out that "parties to mutually beneficial potential exchanges are not effectively barred from bargaining with each other. Buy and sell offers are made."

Boudreaux correctly emphasizes the importance of buy and sell offers. These offers establish the opportunities forgone by the parties to the potential exchange and, therefore, the costs of the choice. It does not matter whether the owners of the rights (such as the owners of some wetlands) refuse to sell them because they value them more than the amounts offered by the potential buyers or (the same thing) because they are pursuing a strategy designed to obtain a better price—if not now, then in the future from the same or other traders—and are prepared to invest (by foregoing gains from trade now) in building a reputation as hard bargainers.

In the small-numbers case, the presence of buy and sell offers assures the reciprocal nature of costs. It follows that resources flow to their higher-valued uses as perceived by the parties to the actual or potential exchange whether or not the rights actually change hands. There are no external effects.

The Large-Numbers Case

The large-numbers case is said to arise when many individuals wish to purchase a right from or sell a right to one or more individuals, and the costs of creating a market for the exchange (say by organizing the many) are too great. Typical cases are a factory spewing smoke over a large neighborhood (harm) or a rancher providing wetlands for migratory birds (benefit).

The initial consideration is whether an externality exists. For example, consider the developer of a large tract of land in an isolated area who builds a smoke-spewing factory and then sells the adjoining land to homeowners, say employees and providers of ancillary services. The harm occasioned by the smoke is reflected in lower land prices paid by homeowners and is taken into account by all parties to the exchange. The developer bears the full cost of the harm and the homeowners are fully compensated.[10] Thus, even though the smoke from the factory harms the property of many, there is no externality. Developments are common techniques for internalizing a broad range of external effects and handling the provision of public or collective goods (De Alessi 1986; Foldvary 1994).

Over time, of course, circumstances change. Having bought the land at a suitably lower price, the homeowners may subsequently claim to be harmed by the smoke and seek to use the political process to reduce the nuisance at others' expense and capture a gain. Or the homeowners may have become wealthier and wish to purchase more amenities, including a cleaner environment.

Presuming that an externality exists, the next consideration is whether it is relevant. Using Pareto efficiency criteria—which are not value-free—an externality is relevant if "the extent of the activity may be modified in such a way that the externally affected party, A, can be made better off without the acting party, B, being made worse off" (Buchanan and Stubblebine 1962, 374). Under this definition, Pareto equilibrium may exist even though one party is imposing marginal external harm on the other. Thus, without additional information, the observation of external effects is not sufficient to establish the desirability of some change in existing arrangements. According to Buchanan and Stubblebine (1962, 381), "The internal benefits [to the acting party] from carrying out the activity, net of costs, may be greater than the external damage that is imposed on other parties."

To continue with the smoke example, suppose that the factory does create a harmful externality. If the cost of reducing it is greater than the benefit—as judged by the parties to the potential exchange—then it is not relevant.

Whether a particular externality in fact is relevant, of course, cannot simply be assumed; it has to be established empirically. As discussed in more detail below, values (including costs) are subjective; as a result, a third-party observer cannot know the value that an individual attaches to a right, and the necessity of aggregating the preferences of the many makes valuation even more intractable. Indeed, it is not clear that an outside observer could even determine, in the absence of some market arrangement, which group of individuals attaches a higher value to the right: the consumers of the product of the smoke-emitting factory or the individuals living nearby.

To recap, suppose that transaction costs are zero and all property rights are fully allocated and privately held. Then rights are exchanged in the market and all harms and benefits are fully internalized. As transaction costs rise or constraints on private property rights become more binding, then gains from trade shrink, the extent of trade falls, and external effects appear and grow. At some point, the exchange of some rights ceases. These results are not necessarily undesirable: the externalities may not be relevant. The problem, of course, is how to deal with externalities that are relevant.

The Government Solution

Government decision makers do not bear the value consequences of their decisions (except through bribes and the political process). Thus, they have less incentive than private owners to take them into account and may be expected to generate substantial and pervasive externalities. Nevertheless, government intervention, either through ownership, regulation, or tax/subsidy schemes, continues to be a popular tool for dealing with externalities (Yandle 1995). Every level of government routinely promulgates rules to control the use of private rights, weakening the incentive of their owners to consider the value consequences of their decisions and fostering externalities. Growing evidence supports the theoretical implication that most regulations, including such hallowed programs as antitrust, do more harm than good (De Alessi 1995).

Government intervention is also exerted through more subtle means, including the redefinition of property rights. One example is the argument that animal and vegetable species have legal standing (Tribe 1974). If they do, then the obvious question is who represents their interests; presumably the courts would assign the property rights to government or a surrogate, possibly an environmental group. Another example is the public trust doctrine, which holds that some rights belong to the government who holds them in trust for the public (Sax 1970). Specific rights, whether currently held in private, in common, or some other arrangement, would be taken and assigned to the state to be managed by government employees according to political pressures. Other examples are stakeholders' rights (Carney 1998) and existence values (Boudreaux and Meiners 1998), which simply provide covers for rent-seeking activities.

The government solution is beset with difficulties. These include taking the relevant costs into account, measuring values, acquiring information, structuring incentives, controlling rent seeking, facilitating innovation and adjustment to change, and coping with the lack of value-free criteria for assessing the performance of alternative contractual and institutional arrangements.

Failure to Ensure Reciprocity of Costs

Taxing the owner of a smoke-emitting factory an amount equal to the harm caused would induce the harm to be taken into account and reduce the emission of smoke. Unless the nearby residents are taxed an amount equal to the costs incurred by the factory owner (the amount of the tax plus the additional costs of reducing emissions), however, they would lack the incentive to take these costs into account and move out of the area or take other precautions that would reduce the harm if doing so would entail lower costs than those incurred by the factory owner.

For instance, the market for pollution rights is expected to reduce the quantity of resources used in pollution abatement by inducing lower-cost producers to specialize in the task. The level of abatement, however, is set in the political place and the cost of abatement is not borne by those who benefit from it. As Coase (1960, 41) remarked, "A tax system which was confined to a tax on the producer for damages caused would tend to lead to unduly high costs being incurred for the prevention of damage."

Problem of Measuring Values

The (expected) value of an option to an individual is the present value of the stream of desirable consequences less the present value of the stream of undesirable consequences that the individual expects to experience (Alchian 1968). For example, spraying a field with a pesticide has the desirable consequence of reducing the population of harmful insects and yielding a larger crop; it has the undesirable consequences of reducing the population of some useful insects, contaminating the groundwater, and consuming labor and other resources.

Cost is the value of the next best option from the set of alternatives considered by the chooser. Without a choice, no opportunity is foregone and there can be no cost (Alchian 1968; Buchanan 1969). For example, the next best option considered by the farmer might be to introduce a natural predator of the harmful insects. This option has some desirable and undesirable consequences, and its net (positive) value—as judged by the farmer—is the cost of choosing the insecticide. Note that a rule holding the farmer liable for damage to others from contaminating the groundwater would be an undesirable consequence of using the insecticide; thus, it would reduce the value of that option but would not affect its cost, presuming that the natural predators did not contaminate the groundwater. Because values depend on the preferences of the chooser as well as on the alternatives and the consequences selected for consideration, they are wholly subjective and continually revised in response to new knowledge.

Market prices at best (for example, under equilibrium conditions in the absence of side provisions and corner solutions) reveal the value that individuals attach to an additional unit of a commodity. Market prices, however, do not reveal the value that an individual attaches to the inframarginal units; that is, they do not measure the gains from trade. Because prices measure values at the margin, they are very useful in guiding the allocation of rights from lower- to higher-valued uses. Precisely for that reason, however, they are not very useful for measuring total values.

Outside observers, say government employees, at best would know the expected higher-valued use after a trade was consummated. They would have no objective knowledge of the values that each actual or potential party to the exchange attached to the rights and to the next best opportunities, of the existence of side conditions (which often are implicit), of possible variations during the bargaining process in the values and alternatives considered by the parties, and of strategic behavior on the part of one or both parties (Boudreaux and Meiners 1998).

Problem of Knowledge and Local Circumstances

A great deal of information is local, linked to specific circumstances of time and place, and dispersed among many individuals; indeed, some information is simply impossible to convey. For example, a farmer—having taken account of the state of the crop, soil, weather, and other variables—may know when, what, and how much fertilizer to use without fully understanding the process involved, let alone being able to explain it to others.

Central planners necessarily deal with aggregate data. Because most of the information that is time and place specific is lost in the process of aggregation, decisions are based on incomplete and inaccurate knowledge.

Moreover, government controls typically apply to broad categories. For example, federal regulators have incentive to establish rules, such as water quality standards, that apply nationwide. But a rule that may make sense in a watershed or part of a watershed in one section of the country may make very little sense in another watershed.

Problem of Incentives

Government employees do not bear the full economic consequences of their decisions. Accordingly, they have incentive to take them into account only insofar as such consequences generate bribes, reverberate through the political process, or affect personal utility directly—for instance, because they yield a distribution of income that the decision maker prefers.

The extension of economic theory to public choices and a growing body of supporting evidence indicate that government officials adopt and implement policies designed to increase their own welfare, say by staying in office or increasing their power and wealth (McKean 1964; De Alessi 1980, 1995). Interestingly, such behavior seems independent of the ideology of the political party in power (Meltzer 1991).

Problem of Rent Seeking

Special interest groups have incentive to claim that an external effect is causing harm and seek to use the power of the state to achieve environmental or other goals that they deem desirable but are unable or unwilling to obtain otherwise. At the same time, government employees (such as politicians running for reelection) have incentive to supply—and stimulate the demand for—their services (McChesney 1997).

For example, let a group believe that a particular wetland should be preserved for the use of a migratory species. A market solution would be for the group to lease or buy the wetland and preserve it; government solutions would be to lobby the government to buy the wetland at taxpayers' expense or pass a law requiring the present owners to preserve the wetland at their own expense. Which option the group chooses depends in part upon the system of property rights, including the propensity of the legislatures and the courts to reassign (take) private rights without compensation.

Changes in the rules that make taking easier or more difficult have broad implications for conservation of the environment. Thus, a rule that allows taking without compensation to protect an endangered species provides landowners with the incentive to make the habitat less attractive to the species. In the long run, such a rule is counterproductive and divisive.

Problem of Adjusting to Change

Once established, government controls—whether exercised through ownership, regulation, or tax/subsidy schemes—are difficult to change. The reasons have already been noted: government employees lack the incentive and vested interests can mount powerful opposition.

The comparison of alternative institutional arrangements usually focuses on the respective static equilibrium conditions (consequences) expected to prevail. Such comparisons, however, at best reveal only part of the relevant information and may be grossly misleading (De Alessi 1997).

Individuals make choices in a world of uncertainty brought about by new knowledge, new institutional constraints, population dynamics, the vagaries of nature, and other phenomena. When there is an unanticipated change in circumstances, some individuals modify their choices and thereby help to nudge the economic system—subject to the constraints imposed by the structure of property rights and transaction costs—toward a new equilibrium. Long before that equilibrium is reached, however, changes in anticipations generate a shift toward another equilibrium. And so it goes. Equilibrium conditions, whether static or dynamic, based on an initial set of anticipations are seldom attained. As a result, the process for adjusting to unanticipated change matters.

An economic system based on private property rights transmits information quickly and inexpensively while it simultaneously provides individuals with the incentive to respond quickly and accurately. It also establishes the incentive to discover new and more productive ways to use resources, encouraging the introduction of new commodities, new production techniques, and new contractual arrangements that lower transaction costs and facilitate the internalization of external effects (Kirzner 1997). Neglecting the process of discovery and adjustment associated with alternative institutions biases the comparison in favor of bureaucratic solutions.

Problem of Benchmark

Suppose that all the problems just discussed somehow are solved and that the government decision maker has to choose among a set of alternatives that, as usual, entail different distributions of income. Unless the losers are fully compensated (as they see it), the choice necessarily involves a value judgment. There simply is no set of criteria that provides a value-free benchmark for aggregating individual gains and losses and for deciding whether the losses suffered by some individuals are greater or smaller than the gains enjoyed by other individuals (Boudreaux and Meiners 1998).

Current policies suggest that the criteria and interests of those with a comparative advantage in the use of political power dominate the decision process, which exhibits little concern for the protection of individual liberty and private property rights.

Problem of External (Unintended) Effects

The general problem of government-induced external effects has already been noted. Nevertheless, it seems useful to revisit it in the present context.

Like private owners, government employees often make decisions some of whose economic consequences are unintended and undesired. Unlike private owners, government employees are not subject to the control of the market and, except through bribes or political repercussions, do not bear the value consequences of their decisions. Accordingly, they have weaker incentive to take these consequences into account and to develop new institutional or contractual arrangements to internalize them. They do have the incentive, however, to blame allegedly undesirable events on the market and private ownership and seek to extend government control, thereby increasing their agencies' budgets and their own welfare.

Concluding Observations

The preceding comments suggest that government often is the problem. Welfare arguments for government intervention to reduce external harms typically neglect the desirability of having both parties take the relevant costs into account, the difficulty (impossibility?) of measuring values, the lack of information, the problem of incentives, and the absence of a value-free benchmark for comparing alternatives. Indeed, in many cases the case for government intervention simply provides the rhetoric used by special interest groups—including ranchers, timber companies, and environmental activists—to advance their own welfare at the expense of others. The next question, therefore, is how the market can be used to reduce or eliminate relevant externalities that matter.

Market Solution: Free Market Environmentalism

In the 1980s, when the failure of central planning to promote economic development became painfully obvious, much debate focused on "getting the prices right" (De Alessi 1988). The problem, however, was and always will be "getting the institutions right," that is, establishing a system that is capable of solving a society's economic problems in a world of change and uncertainty, recognizing that much relevant information is known only to the individuals affected and is time and place specific.

Different problems, including similar problems with different people or different times or different places, call for different solutions. Accordingly, focus should be on institutions that tie the self-interest of individuals to their success in solving these problems. Private property provides the link. The cornerstone of free market solutions is private property, which provides the right to form voluntary contracts and allows a variety of cooperative arrangements, including community-run organizations (Anderson 1998). Some illustrations may be helpful.[11]

The Straying Bison of Yellowstone

A herd of bison roams part of Yellowstone National Park during the summer and contiguous private ranches in Montana during the winter (Anderson and Leal 1991, 24–26). The bison consume grass and carry a virus, brucellosis, that can infect and lower the value of livestock; effectively, the bison pollute private lands. The park does not own the bison and thus is not liable for any damage that they may cause. The state of Montana does not own the bison either and so is not liable for any damage that they may cause, but apparently the state owns the right to kill (issue hunting licenses to kill) at least some of the bison who stray into Montana.[12]

One solution is to assign ownership of the bison to the park, making it liable for damages that the bison visit on ranchers (Anderson and Leal 1991). This arrangement would provide park officials with incentive to restrict the movement of the bison and address the virus problem.

Other market solutions offer a better structure of incentives. For example, the park could contract out management of the herd, including the provision of winter grazing. Depending on the size and location of ranches, individuals or coalitions of ranchers could bid for the contract to control grazing within the park in summer and outside the park in winter, deal with the virus, cull the herd, and so on. A better solution would be for the park to contract for the provision of bison to roam the park in summer, giving ranchers the incentive to own and manage the bison and resolving the conflict between livestock and bison. A still better (best) solution would be to privatize the park; several alternative techniques are available (Carney 1998).

The New Zealand Paua Fishery

Threatened with the extinction of the paua (abalone) fishery, New Zealand introduced Individual Transferable Quotas (M. De Alessi 1997b). Under this arrangement, government officials set the annual catch limit and assign a percentage of the catch to individual fishermen, who are allowed to trade the quotas in the market. Advantages include a limit on catch, the ability of lower-cost producers to specialize in fishing, and the incentive to invest in research and the habitat. When the program succeeded, however, outsiders obtained access to the fishing grounds through the political process (rent seeking) rather than through the purchase of quotas; until the practice stopped, the result was a drop in the value of paua fishing licenses and deterioration of the fishery.

A solution with a better incentive structure would be to assign (auction) the fishery to private interests, possibly a coalition of current fishermen.

The Marauding Elephants of Zimbabwe

Elephant populations have been decreasing in some parts of Africa but increasing in others, including Zimbabwe, Botswana, Namibia, and South Africa (Sanera and Shaw 1996, 134–35). A major problem has been poaching, which often is abetted by villagers whose crops can be destroyed overnight by elephant herds who wander outside the national park boundaries.

In Zimbabwe, villagers were assigned some private property rights in local elephant herds. When elephants are killed legally, villagers receive a share of the meat and of the income from the sale of the hide and ivory; they also receive a share of hunting fees. These property rights give villagers more incentive to protect the elephants from poachers and take other measures to maintain the herd.

Technological Innovation and Prospects for Privatization

A spectrum of technological innovations have substantially lowered the cost of defining, enforcing, and exchanging private property rights in many animal species, including some that migrate over broad areas (M. De Alessi 1997b). The following examples suggest the range of options available. Using sonar, the Integrated Undersea Surveillance System allows single whales to be tracked continuously without the aid of tags or radio beacons. New technologies have also lowered the cost of tagging (branding) and identifying various animals while satellites, using radio signals, allow tracking of tagged whales, manatees, bears, and other animals. Moreover, sonar and satellites can be used to fence sections of the oceans by monitoring the movement of ships: black boxes installed in ships can provide continuous monitoring while poachers can be detected and identified by the heat profile of their engines when they use extra power to tow nets.

A shift toward private ownership, including communal arrangements, would encourage the development of new technologies and new contractual arrangements that would result in better management of the environment.

Conclusions

The systems of property rights existing in different parts of the world, including the United States, yield some environmental consequences that one group or another considers undesirable. In some instances, all the parties affected agree that a problem exists and the debate focuses on what to do about it; an example might be air pollution in a particular location. In other instances, the debate centers on whether a problem exists, let alone what to do about it; an example might be an animal species threatened by extinction.

Environmental problems typically arise when property rights are not fully private and/or transaction costs are substantial. Under these conditions, individuals do not bear the full economic consequences of their decisions and thus lack the incentive to take them fully into account. The observation that some activity causes harm, of course, does not mean that it is undesirable. Those harmed may have been fully compensated or the costs of internalizing the activity, whether it generates harms or benefits, may be too great. The task then is to establish whether an externality exists, whether it matters (according to whose criteria?), and what to do about it.

Market solutions in a world of positive transaction costs and limited private property rights always appear to be inefficient when compared to the theoretical solutions of some ideal construct. It is also easy, and often convenient, to blame private ownership for external harms that in fact are due to the absence of private rights. The result has been a bias toward government control of various aspects of market behavior through government ownership and regulation, including mandated rules.

Government solutions, however, also fail to meet the ideal. They fail because they neglect a wide range of problems, such as incentives, information (including the measurement of values), and criteria for comparing alternatives. Typically, welfare arguments for government intervention simply provide the rhetoric used by special interest groups to advance their own goals.

Government solutions convert all decisions into political decisions. Incentives shift from the pursuit of cooperative activities that result in mutual gain to the pursuit of rent-seeking activities that result in the redistribution of wealth. There is overwhelming evidence that shifting decisions from the market to the political place—that is, from voluntary to coercive orders—yields a smaller aggregate output, encourages corruption, breeds dissent, and, of course, reduces liberty.

A strong case can be made for adopting simple rules to solve a society's increasingly complex economic problems (Epstein 1995). The cornerstone of such a rule system is private property, including self-ownership, voluntary exchange, and open markets. This approach to the solution of environmental problems would tie the welfare of individuals to their success in internalizing external harms and benefits, encouraging the development of new technologies and new institutional arrangements and the prompt adaptation to changes in circumstances. The problem, of course, is to design a suitable constitution (Wagner 1998).

Economic theory and empirical evidence indicate unequivocally that an economic system based on private property rights yields a larger output of goods and services, including better environmental protection and more effective social services, than a coercive system rife with rent seeking. The argument for adopting a system of private property rights, however, goes deeper than simple material considerations: fundamentally, it rests on the ethical and moral values of voluntary choices by free individuals.

Notes

1. A great deal of environmental nonsense is presented as scientific fact and taught in schools as part of a program to increase awareness of the environment (Sanera and Shaw 1996).

2. Including the incentive to take public positions that are politically correct (Kuran 1995).

3. A private owner has incentive to exhaust a renewable resource only if the opportunity cost of capital (the discount rate) exceeds the maximum rate of growth of the resource and if the resource can be harvested profitably to a point too low for its survival (Clark 1973).

4. The initial assignment of rights determines the distribution of wealth, which may affect the structure of demand and supply functions and, thus, the allocation of resources. The net effect, however, generally is small and unpredictable; arguably, it can be disregarded (Coase 1960).

5. Pigou's erroneous thinking continues to dominate environmental policies.

6. Government regulations frequently inhibit the evolution of new institutions for solving environmental problems. For example, in the United States, antitrust laws have been used to break up cooperative arrangements in shrimp fisheries (Johnson and Libecap 1982).

7. The usual caveats about inferior commodities apply. The more broadly a commodity is defined, the less likely that it is inferior.

8. Ostrom (1998) discusses in detail the characteristics of private and common property rights.

9. As noted earlier, the wealth effect generally can be disregarded.

10. The value of land used in the development (factory *and* homes) presumably is greater than its value in the next best use.

11. For a more complete discussion, see Anderson and Leal (1991).

12. Lueck (1989) provides an illuminating discussion of wildlife law.

References

Alchian, Armen A. 1961. *Some Economics of Property.* Santa Monica: Rand Corporation.

———. 1965. Some Economics of Property Rights. *Il Politico* 30(December): 816–29.

———. 1967. How Should Prices Be Set? *Il Politico* 32(June): 369–82.

———. 1968. Cost. In *International Encyclopedia of the Social Sciences,* vol 3. New York: Crowell, Collier, and Macmillan, 404–15.

Anderson, Terry L. 1998. Viewing Wildlife through Coase-Colored Glasses, this volume.

Anderson, Terry L., and Peter J. Hill. 1975. The Evolution of Property Rights: A Study of the American West. *Journal of Law & Economics* 18(1): 163–79.

Anderson, Terry L., and Donald R. Leal. 1991. *Free Market Environmentalism.* San Francisco: Pacific Research Institute for Public Policy and Westview Press.

Anderson, Terry L., and Peter J. Hill, eds. 1997. *Environmental Federalism.* Lanham, MD: Rowman & Littlefield.

Benson, Bruce. 1997. Institutions and the Spontaneous Evolution of Morality.

In *Values and the Social Order*, vol. 3: *Voluntary vs. Coercive Orders*, ed. Gerard Radnitzky. Aldershot, England: Avebury, 245–82.

Boudreaux, Donald J. 1996. The Coase Theorem and Strategic Bargaining. *Advances in Austrian Economics* 3: 95–105.

Boudreaux, Donald J., and Roger E. Meiners. 1998. Existence Value and Other of Life's Ills, this volume.

Brubaker, Elizabeth. 1998. The Common Law and the Environment: The Canadian Experience, this volume.

Buchanan, James M. 1969. *Cost and Choice: An Inquiry in Economic Theory.* Chicago: Markham.

————. 1988. Market Failure and Political Failure. *Cato Journal* 8(Spring/ Summer): 1–13.

Buchanan, James M., and William C. Stubblebine. 1962. Externality. *Economica* (new series) 29(November): 371–84.

Carney, William. 1998. From Stakeholders to Stockholders: A View from Organizational Theory, this volume.

Clark, Colin W. 1973. Profit Maximization and the Extinction of Animal Species. *Journal of Political Economy* 81(July/August): 950–61.

Coase, Ronald H. 1960. The Problem of Social Cost. *Journal of Law & Economics* 3(1): 1–44.

Davis, Lance E., and Douglass C. North. 1971. *Institutional Change and American Economic Growth.* Cambridge: Cambridge University Press.

De Alessi, Louis. 1980. The Economics of Property Rights: A Review of the Evidence. *Research in Law and Economics* 2: 1–47.

————. 1983. Property Rights, Transaction Costs, and X-Efficiency: An Essay in Economic Theory. *American Economic Review* 73(March): 64–81.

————. 1986. Leggi Ambientali e Valorizzazione Delle Aree [Environmental Law, Nuisance Law, and Land Development]. *Economia Pubblica* 16(June): 235–39.

————. 1988. How Markets Alleviate Scarcity. In *Rethinking Institutional Analysis and Development: Issues, Alternatives, and Choices,* ed. V. Ostrom, D. Feeny, and H. Picht. San Francisco: International Center for Economic Growth, 339–76.

————. 1995. The Public Choice Model of Antitrust Enforcement. In *The Causes and Consequences of Antitrust: The Public-Choice Perspective*, ed. Fred S. McChesney and William F. Shughart II. Chicago and London: University of Chicago Press, 189–200.

————. 1997. Value, Efficiency, and Rules: The Limits of Economics. In *Values and the Social Order*, vol. 3: *Voluntary versus Coercive Orders*, ed. Gerard Radnitzky. Aldershot, England: Avebury, 289–304.

————. 1998. Reflections on Coase, Cost, and Efficiency. In *The Economists' Vision*, ed. Bettina Monissen and James M. Buchanan. Frankfurt, Germany: Campus Verlag Frankfurt, 91–114.

De Alessi, Michael. 1997a. Holding Out for Some Local Heroes. *New Scientist* 153(March): 46, 48.

————. 1997b. Technologies of Sequestering and Monitoring Ocean Property.

In *Fish or Cut Bait!* ed. Laura Jones and Michael Walker. Vancouver, BC: Fraser Institute, 124–49.

Demsetz, Harold. 1964. The Exchange and Enforcement of Property Rights. *Journal of Law & Economics* 7(October): 11–26.

———. 1967. Toward a Theory of Property Rights. *American Economic Review* 57(2): 347–59.

———. 1969. Information and Efficiency: Another Viewpoint. *Journal of Law & Economics* 12(April): 1–23.

De Vany, Arthur S. 1977. Land Reform and Agricultural Efficiency in Mexico: A General Equilibrium Analysis. *Journal of Monetary Economics* (supplementary series) 6: 123–47.

De Vany, Arthur S., and Nicholas Sanchez. 1979. Land Tenure Structures and Fertility in Mexico. *Review of Economics and Statistics* 61(February): 67–72.

Eggertsson, Thráinn. 1990. *Economic Behavior and Institutions.* Cambridge: Cambridge University Press.

Endres, Alfred. 1996. Designing a Greenhouse Treaty: Some Economic Problems. In *Law and Economics of the Environment*, ed. E. Eide and R. van den Bergh. Oslo: Juridisk Forlag, 201–24.

Epstein, Richard A. 1995. *Simple Rules for a Complex World.* Cambridge: Harvard University Press.

———. 1998. Habitat Preservation: A Property Rights Perspective, this volume.

Field, Barry C. 1984. The Evolution of Individual Property Rights in Massachusetts Agriculture, 17th–19th Centuries. *Northeastern Journal of Agricultural and Resource Economics* 14(October): 97–109.

Foldvary, Fred. 1994. *Public Goods and Private Communities: The Market Provision of Social Service.* Aldershot, England: Edward Elgar.

Gordon, Scott H. 1954. The Economic Theory of a Common Property Resource: The Fishery. *Journal of Political Economy* 62(April): 124–42.

———. 1958. Economics and the Conservation Question. *Journal of Law & Economics* 1(October): 110–21.

Hayek, Friedrich A. 1945. The Use of Knowledge in Society. *American Economic Review* 35(September): 519–30.

Johannes, R. E. 1992. *Words of the Lagoon: Fishing and Marine Lore in the Palau District of Micronesia.* Berkeley: University of California Press.

Johnson, Ronald N., and Gary D. Libecap. 1982. Contracting Problems and Regulation: The Case of the Fishery. *American Economic Review* 72(December): 1005–22.

Joskow, Paul L. 1988. Asset Specificity and the Structure of Vertical Relationships: Empirical Evidence. *Journal of Law, Economics, and Organization* 4(Spring): 95–117.

Kirzner, Israel M. 1997. Entrepreneurial Discovery and the Competitive Market Process: An Austrian Approach. *Journal of Economic Literature* 35(March): 60–85.

Kuran, Timur. 1995. *Private Truths, Public Lies: The Social Consequences of Preference Falsification.* Cambridge: Harvard University Press.

Landa, Janet T. 1981. A Theory of the Ethnically Homogeneous Middleman Group: An Institutional Alternative to Contract Law. *Journal of Legal Studies* 10(June): 349–62.

Leal, Donald R. 1998. Cooperating on the Commons: Case Studies in Community Fisheries, this volume.

Libecap, Gary D. 1978. Economic Variables and the Development of Law: The Case of Western Mineral Rights. *Journal of Economic History* 38(June): 338–62.

———. 1981. *Locking Up the Range: Federal Land Controls and Grazing.* San Francisco: Pacific Institute for Public Policy Research and Ballinger Publishing.

Lueck, Dean. 1989. The Economic Nature of Wildlife Law. *Journal of Legal Studies* 18(June): 291–24.

Lueck, Dean, and Jonathan Yoder. 1997. Federalism and Wildlife Conservation in the West. In *Environmental Federalism*, ed. Terry L. Anderson and Peter J. Hill. Lanham, MD: Rowman & Littlefield, 89–131.

McChesney, Fred S. 1997. *Money for Nothing: Politicians, Rent Extraction, and Political Extortion.* Cambridge: Harvard University Press.

McKean, Margaret A. 1986. Management of Traditional Common Lands (*Iriaichi*) in Japan. In *Proceedings of the Conference on Common Property Resource Management, April 21–26, 1985.* Washington, D.C.: National Academy Press, 533–89.

McKean, Roland N. 1964. Divergences Between Individual and Total Costs Within Government. *American Economic Review* 54(May): 243–49.

Meltzer, Allan H. 1991. The Growth of Government Revisited. In *Perspectives on an Economic Future: Forms, Reforms, and Evaluations*, ed. Shripad G. Pendse. New York: Greenwood Press, 131–43.

North, Douglass C. 1990. *Institutions, Institutional Change and Economic Performance.* Cambridge: Cambridge University Press.

Norton, Seth. 1998. Property Rights, the Environment, and Economic Well-Being, this volume.

Ostrom, Elinor. 1990. *Governing the Commons: The Evolution of Institutions for Collective Action.* Cambridge: Cambridge University Press.

———. 1998. Private and Common Property Rights. In *Encyclopedia of Law & Economics*, forthcoming.

Pigou, A. C. 1920. *The Economics of Welfare.* London: Macmillan.

Rutherford, Malcolm. 1994. *Institutions in Economics: The Old and the New Institutionalism.* Cambridge: Cambridge University Press.

Sanera, Michael, and Jane S. Shaw. 1996. *Facts Not Fear: A Parent's Guide to Teaching Children About the Environment.* Washington, D.C.: Regnery.

Sax, Joseph L. 1970. The Public Trust Doctrine in Natural Resource Law: Effective Judicial Intervention. *Michigan Law Review* 68(January): 473–566.

Schumpeter, Joseph. 1934. The Nature and Necessity of a Price System. In *Economic Reconstruction.* New York: Columbia University Press, 170–76.

Scott, Anthony. 1955. The Fishery: The Objectives of Sole Ownership. *Journal of Political Economy* 63(April): 116–24.

Sethi, Rajiv, and E. Somanathan. 1996. The Evolution of Social Norms in Common Property Resource Use. *American Economic Review* 86(September): 766–88.

Smith, Vernon. 1998. Property Rights as a Natural Order: Reciprocity, Evolutionary and Experimental Considerations, this volume.

Tribe, Laurence H. 1974. Ways Not to Think About Plastic Trees: New Foundations for Environmental Law. *Yale Law Journal* 83(June): 1315–48.

Umbeck, John. 1977. A Theory of Contract Choice and the California Gold Rush. *Journal of Law & Economics* 20(October): 421–37.

Wagner, Richard E. 1998. The Constitutional Protection of Private Property, this volume.

Wright, Chester W. 1949. *Economic History of the United States*. New York: McGraw-Hill.

Yandle, Bruce. 1997. *Common Sense and Common Law for the Environment: Creating Wealth in Hummingbird Economies*. Lanham, MD: Rowman & Littlefield.

———. 1998. Coase, Pigou, and Environmental Rights, this volume.

———, ed. 1995. *Land Rights: The 1990s' Property Rights Rebellion*. Lanham, MD: Rowman & Littlefield.

Chapter 2

Property Rights, the Environment, and Economic Well-Being

Seth W. Norton

Alfred Marshall, the great English economist, made two observations about property rights. First, the importance of property rights has been undervalued by economists.[1] Second, property rights "have been inseparable from solid progress" (Marshall 1920, 40). Marshall's observations are borne out by the recent work of scholars who have developed operational definitions of property rights at the nation-state level. They have used these measures to examine the relationship between property rights and economic growth, concluding that property rights are an indispensable prerequisite for growth (Scully 1988 and 1992; Knack and Keefer 1995; Knack 1996; Keefer and Knack 1997; and Pejovich 1997). Other scholars have examined the relationship between economic growth and the environment, concluding that economic growth permits countries to produce greater output with less disturbance to the environment (Coursey 1992; Radetzki 1992). Thus, it appears that there is a strong relationship between property rights and environmental quality. This chapter examines that relationship.

Well-Defined Property Rights

Property rights, despite having a prominent place in philosophy, were largely ignored by the economics profession for nearly a half century after Marshall. Coase's celebrated paper on social cost changed that convention (Coase 1960). In its wake the economics of property rights has since become a central focus of contemporary economics (Barzel

37

1989; Demsetz 1967; Anderson and Hill 1975; North 1981 and 1990; Libecap 1989; Eggertsson 1990; Ellickson 1991).

As Yandle (1998) explains in his chapter in this volume, Coase's paper on social cost makes two key points: 1) if property rights are well defined and 2) transactions cost are zero, then wealth-maximizing behavior would result and economic agents would obtain the ideal use of resources. Subsequent research has moved in a host of directions, including examining the world when transactions costs are not zero (e.g., Libecap 1989) or delineating the relationship between certain types of transactions costs and the configuration of property rights (Barzel 1989). It is noteworthy that whatever the nature of transactions costs, it is still generally held that well-defined property rights are desirable. For example, patterns of common ownership that do not entail well-defined rights are shown to lead to less-desired outcomes (Hardin 1968; Libecap 1989). Thus, failure to assign property rights in grazing can lead to excessive grazing of a common field or failure to assign property rights in fishing can lead to overfishing (Gordon 1954; Eggertsson 1990).

Similarly, the economics of property rights generally presumes that economic systems that proscribe private property will have less desirable outcomes than economic systems that affirm private property. In a related vein, it is important to distinguish between attenuated property rights and partitioned property rights (Alchian 1989; Eggertsson 1990). Attenuated property rights means that ownership of resources does not exist or is ambiguous. For example, where fishing laws permit free entry into commercial fishing, the theory predicts that the absence of property rights in common fishing waters will result in ignoring the hatchery component of the fishing grounds and overfishing will occur, reducing the long-term stock of fish (Gordon 1954). In this case, the property rights to the common fishery are attenuated. Decision makers do not bear the full cost of their decisions and consequently tend to overuse the resource.

In contrast, partitioning of property rights means that different claims are assigned to different owners in situations where multiple or complex claims lead to the maximum value of certain resources (Leal 1998). For example, the bondholders of a corporation retain a property right to a fixed payment from the firm to be paid after all noncapital payments but prior to payments to stockholders. Stockholders obtain the right to claims on the residual cash flows to the enterprise after payments to the noncapital suppliers and payments to the bondholders have been made. The upshot of partitioning rights is that, unlike the attenuation of property rights, partitioning rights is a form of maximizing the value of resources by defining ownership to resources in complex but specific ways (Carney 1998).

Endogenous Property Rights

An important research stream in the property rights literature seeks to explain why well-defined property rights exist in some environments but not in others or why the definition of property rights take a particular form in a specific context. For example, Demsetz (1967) and Anderson and Hill (1975) view property rights as emerging and evolving in response to the benefits and costs associated with efforts dedicated to defining property rights. As the benefits to having well-defined property rights increase, we should expect to observe better-specified property rights, and indeed in the real world we do observe such patterns.

The endogenous property rights literature consists of two perspectives: the private ordering view and the legal centralist view. The private ordering view stresses the human tendency to adapt to environments and improve human well-being through mutually beneficial trading. However, this adaptation consists not just of goods, but also of the rules and procedures that are associated with the use and trade of economic goods (Ellickson 1991; Smith 1992 and 1998). The legal centrist view stresses the role of the state (including subsidiaries or subordinate arms of the state) in defining property rights (Hardin 1968; North 1981; Riker and Senedeker 1991).

Both perspectives have considerable merit. Clearly, nation-states do affect the configuration of property rights and the real world provides numerous examples of people designing mutually agreeable delineation of property rights through private contracting (Anderson 1998). However, these different perspectives are related to the degree of aggregation. The legal centrist view fits better with higher levels of aggregation. For example, the configuration of property rights at the nation-state level reflects the specifics of constitutional and nonconstitutional definition and enforcement of property rights as determined by macropolitical forces, including history and ideology. The private ordering of property rights within the nation-state reflects the human tendency to contract for mutually beneficial trade, but it also reflects the aggregate configuration of property rights. For example, a complex delineation of property rights for the suppliers of capital to a large firm is virtually impossible if the aggregate polity proscribes private ownership.

Thus, while both approaches are useful at both the smallest and greatest levels of aggregation, the legal centrist view would seem to have greater explanatory power at the highest levels of aggregation—

determining the ultimate configuration of property rights, while the private ordering view would have greater explanatory power at lower levels of aggregation—determining the configuration of property rights among decentralized economic agents, e.g., specialized consumers, the firm, suppliers to the firm, real estate, bond covenants, and such.

The Property Rights Growth Nexus

Both neoclassical growth models and empirical studies on growth are relevant to property rights.

Neoclassical Growth Models

The modern study of economic growth focuses primarily on abstract neoclassical growth models (Solow 1956; Nordhaus 1969). In these models, economic growth is a natural phenomenon occurring largely as savings increase and knowledge of technology diffuses across nations. Despite the elegance of the neoclassical growth models, a casual reading of history seems to suggest that something is wrong with these models, because most of the world remains underdeveloped and, presumably, most people prefer the amenities of life in a developed rather than an undeveloped environment.

Douglass North (1981 and 1990) addresses this anomaly by arguing that the neoclassical growth models (indeed all neoclassical models) omit important institutional details. North extends Coase's analysis by positing that more desirable outcomes occur in regimes where property rights are better specified than in regimes where property rights are poorly specified. Thus, North identifies the essential perquisites for growth—institutions that facilitate trade and investment by specifying the rights of buyers, sellers, investors, and inventors. Property rights affect incentives. The successful specification of property rights is one that provides incentives that encourage self-interested decision makers to make decisions that increase the value of resources.

Empirical Studies on Growth

In recent years a number of empirical studies have examined the causes of economic growth.[2] Some of these seem to corroborate neoclassical theory but many do not. Some of these studies include institutional variables that indicate that institutions are important. For example, Kormendi and Meguire (1985) find that civil liberties encouraged investment and economic growth. Scully (1988 and 1992) finds that polities that exhibited economic freedom and constitutional guarantees of property grew more rapidly than other polities. Barro (1991) and Barro and Sala-I-Martin (1995) find that a host of institutional variables affect growth. Knack and Keefer (1995), Knack (1996), Keefer and Knack (1997), and Pejovich (1997) find that institutional variables described as the "rule of law," "freedom of contract," and "economic freedom" are crucial forces behind economic growth at the nation-state level. Some scholars also integrate institutional variables into formal theories of economic growth (e.g., Rebelo 1991; Scully 1992), resulting in neoclassical type models of growth augmented by institutional or property rights types of variables.

Recent Measures of Property Rights

Property rights are not easily measured. At low levels of aggregation, contracts and implicit agreements must be examined (e.g., Joskow 1987). Consequently, careful case study approaches are appropriate, but such studies are, by definition, idiosyncratic and therefore difficult to use for aggregate comparisons.

The simplest measure of property rights at the aggregate level is the presence of meaningful constitutional law. That could be a formal document such as the United States Constitution or an unwritten but forcible legal tradition as in the case of the United Kingdom. The point simply is that without a meaningful framework for contracting, any specific contracts may be invalid or unenforceable if a new regime replaces the current one. Agreements made under the specter of revolution are not likely to be enforced and therefore are not credible. Accordingly, the presence of revolutions in nations means that property rights are ipso facto not well defined (Barro and Sala-I-Martin 1995). Thus, the absence of revolutions in a nation means that property rights are at least potentially enforceable. A measure of revolutions therefore is a subtle and important measure of the nonexistence of property rights, even if it is somewhat unconventional.[3]

More conventional and general measures of property rights at the nation-state level also exist. The early attempts to develop general measures of property rights for aggregate comparisons posed the difficulty of how to measure property rights when nation-states are simultaneously devising the legal means to define property rights and also devising redistributive policies that attenuate property rights. For example, Scully (1988 and 1992) used the Gastil (1987) property index to examine the relationship between property rights and growth. However, the Gastil index may be imprecise and too narrow in scope. Moreover, it does not clearly distinguish between different types of rights. It is important to note that some rights are negative or "protective," while other right are positive or "intrusive." Protective rights limit the government from arbitrary takings of private property. In contrast, intrusive rights generally entail redistributions of wealth that require taking property (or more commonly the periodic cash flows from private property) to finance the redistribution. For example, the "rights" to food, clothing, or medical care entail spending to provide for those rights. Gwartney, Lawson, and Block (1996, 14) note that: "Intrusive rights therefore conflict with economic freedom because such 'rights' imply that some have the right to the labor or possessions of others. In reality, alleged 'rights' of this type are simply disguised demands for the forced transfer of income and wealth." In short, Gwartney, Lawson, and Block recognize that intrusive rights represent an attenuation of property rights. Protective property rights are less well defined when such "rights" exist.

As an alternative, Gwartney, Lawson, and Block develop an index that measures property rights in a comprehensive sense and is consonant with emphasis on the principal of economic freedom implicit in much of the property rights literature. The index also overcomes the problem of blending protective and intrusive rights into one measure, a problem that early indices of property rights seemed to ignore. They state:

> The central elements of economic freedom are personal choice, protection of private property and freedom of exchange. Individuals have economic freedom when (a) property they acquire without the use of force, fraud or theft is protected from physical invasion by others and (b) they are free to use, exchange or give their property to another as long as their actions do not violate the identical rights of others. Thus, an index of economic freedom should measure the extent to which rightly acquired property is protected and individuals are free to engage in voluntary transactions. (Gwartney, Larson, and Block 1996, 12)

The index developed by Gwartney, Lawson, and Block explicitly recognizes the attenuation of property rights that can occur through other, supposedly non–property rights related events. For example, unstable monetary policy reduces the predictability of property values. The result is an attenuation of the value of assets for owners in regimes with such instability. In regimes with price control, these restrictions on price offerings by owners of assets also attenuate ownership rights. Similar arguments apply to government subsidies, high marginal tax rates, and protectionism.

The Gwartney, Lawson, and Block index entails ranking a broad sample of nations on seventeen dimensions composed of four categories related to property rights: money and inflation, government operations and regulations, takings and discriminatory taxation, and international exchange.

A third measure of property rights emphasizes the rule of law. In amplifying the meaning of his social cost paper, Coase (1988, 10) argues that the rule of law is a crucial prerequisite for the existence and well functioning of markets. Citizen and official support for the law means that contractual agreements are more likely to be honored and enforced. Knack and Keefer (1995) assert that the rule of law means that private property will not be expropriated and consequently incentives exist for owners to improve the value of their assets via further investment leading to economic growth. Knack and Keefer use the *International Country Risk Guide* (ICRG), which measures inter alia the extent of the rule of law across countries as an operational definition of property rights.

Holmes, Johnson, and Kirkpatrick (1997) also provide a comprehensive crossnational index of freedom for the Heritage Foundation and the *Wall Street Journal*. This study uses ten measures of "economic freedom." It is similar in spirit and content to the Gwartney, Lawson, and Black index. The study is made annually but coverage only started in 1994. The primary advantage of the Heritage study is that one of the ten categories is explicitly the protection of private property rights. This narrow measure of property rights definition may be closer to the connotation of property rights that most readers of Coase use.

A summary of these measures of property rights—their definitions and sources—is shown in table 2.1. The various definitions in the table indicate the richness of the property rights concept and provide a basis for empirical analysis of the effects of alternative property rights specifications.

Property Rights and Growth

The property rights measures have been the subject of a number of tests. For example, Gwartney, Lawson, and Block (1996) examine the growth patterns based on their rankings. In one comparison they found that the growth rate in per capita gross domestic product (GDP) for countries with high rankings on their index averaged 2.4 percent for 1980–94 and 2.6 percent for 1985–94, while the growth rate for countries with low rankings on their index averaged a −1.3 and −1.6 for the same periods (Gwartney, Lawson, and Block 1996, 93–94). More-

Table 2.1
Measures of Property Rights

Source	Time Period	Description of Measures
Barro and Lee (BL)	1960–1984	Number of revolutions per year averaged over period
Gwartney, Lawson, and Block (GLB)	1975–1995	Categories of protective rights
International Country Risk Guide (ICRG)	1984	Law and order tradition
Heritage Foundation (HER)	1997	Right to private property

Sources: BL: as referenced in note 3; GLB: Gwartney, Lawson, and Block (1996); ICRG: Political Risk Services (1984); HER: Holmes, Johnson, and Kirkpatrick (1997).

over, they found a statistically robust relationship between their index and economic growth.

Empirical analysis by Knack and Keefer (1995), Knack (1996), and Keefer and Knack (1997) show that the rule of law and related measures of business risk provided by the international country risk guide indicate that the absence of the rule of law is associated with diminished economic growth.

Beach and Davis (1997) also provide evidence that the Heritage index statistically relates property rights categories with differential rates of growth. Their findings show that countries that are economically free had an average annual per capita GDP growth rate of 2.88 percent for the 1980–93 period, while the mostly free, mostly not free, and repressed had average growth rates of 0.97 percent, -0.32 percent and -1.44 percent, respectively, for the same period (Beach and Davis 1997, 9).

In summary, recent evidence is unambiguous. Property rights and its related construct, the rule of law, and the more general category, freedom from property rights attenuation, are all positively related to economic growth. Their absence leads to economic stagnation and decline.

The Growth/Environmental Nexus

The literature on property rights strongly suggests that well-specified property rights increase economic growth. Growth in turn expands economic opportunities for citizens in growing economies. If environmental amenities are a normal good (i.e., increased income increases consumption rates), then economic growth should lead to a cleaner environment. As Eggertsson (1990) points out, small changes in property rights can lead to large changes in economic growth. Accordingly, it seems that the implementation of well-specified property rights should solve the problems of poverty and the environment.

There are some counter arguments. Some empirical research (Grossman and Krueger 1994 and 1995) shows that as poor countries grow, the amount of certain types of pollution (e.g., sulfur dioxide emissions) increases, although at higher levels of income pollution falls. Some researchers also argue that economic growth threatens the long-term viability of the earth (Arrow et al. 1995).

The responses to these counter arguments emphasize several points. First, there is clear evidence that affluent nations choose to increase the quality of life by reducing environmental degradation. A clean environment is highly income-elastic after some modest threshold (Coursey 1992; Radetzki 1992). There is therefore no obvious inconsistency with property rights promoting growth and environmental well-being simultaneously in a long-term perspective.

Second, while the empirical record does not address the possibilities of long-run sustainable growth consistent with the world's limited resources, at least one major compendium on that question suggests growth and the earth's limited resources are compatible for any conceivable time frame (Simon 1995). Moreover, while growth-enhancing policies may not always lead to enhanced environmental quality, there is precious little systematic evidence that curbing growth will necessarily lead to enhanced environmental quality. A convincing story should clearly document the alleged environmental advantages of economic stagnation.

Third, some literature claims that the range of environmental stress induced by economic growth is limited to a small range of countries with modest per capita wealth (Radetzki 1992). Moreover, the limited failures for growth to accompany improved environmental conditions may simply stem from poorly specified property rights as poor countries incur modest growth (Radetzki 1992). In that case, improving property rights should strongly limit environmental degradation as well as stimulate growth.

Some Fragments of Evidence

The relationship between property rights, economic growth, and environmental quality can be examined by using the measures of property rights described above and looking at several measures of well-being that are sensitive to environmental conditions as well as economic growth. Table 2.2 contains the means of the measures. Water is the proportion of a country's population with access to safe water in 1990. Sanitation is the proportion of the population with access to sanitation in 1990. Life expectancy is life expectancy at birth averaged between 1965 and 1985. Deforestation is the annual percentage decline in woodlands from 1981 to 1990, and growth is average annual growth in per capita GDP between 1960 and 1985.

Subsamples of the Barro and Lee data set that represent strong property rights (the upper one-fifth to upper one-third of the property rights distribution) and weak property rights (the lower one-fifth to one-third of the property rights distribution) are shown in table 2.2. Bilateral comparisons of the subsamples can be made by examining the means for each environmental performance measure. For example, the absence of revolutions during the 1960–85 time period is associated with strong property rights, while nation-states in the upper third of the distribution of revolutions are associated with weak property rights. Comparing access to safe water, the data show that roughly 90 percent of the population in nations with strong property rights have access to safe water, while only about 60 percent of the population in nations with weak property rights have access to safe water.

Examining the difference in access to sanitation provides an even stronger contrast. Examining other property rights measures leads to similar conclusions for access to safe water and sanitation. The smallest gap is the Gwartney, Lawson, and Block index where the gap is roughly 26 percentage points for access to safe water. Comparison tests for the differences in proportions indicate that the differences in access to safe water and sanitation are statistically significant for all bilateral comparisons.

Large gaps in life expectancy at birth are also present for all the measures of property rights. The smallest gap is roughly fifteen years for the Barro and Lee measure while the largest gap is almost twenty years for the Heritage property rights measure. Indeed, examining the life expectancy data leads to the conclusion that substantial utility must be generated to citizens in nations that have well-defined property rights. Means tests for all the property rights categories indicate that these differences are statistically significant.

The deforestation data provide some provocative comparisons. Critics of market economies sometimes argue that markets lead to overuse of natural resources. The data in table 2.2 show that deforestation is greater in nations with weak property rights as opposed to nations with strong property rights. (Note that for this measure a lower value is the

Table 2.2
Property Rights and Environmental Performance Measures

Property Rights Sample	Source	Performance Measures				
		Water	Sanitation	Life Expectancy	Deforestation	Growth
Total Sample		71.38	64.97	58.30	.606	.032
		(25.08)	(32.64)	(11.16)	(1.23)	(.034)
		113	95	119	109	117
Strong	BL	90.00**	91.80**	67.81**	.336	.045**
		(15.93)	(15.12)	(9.01)	(1.61)	(.038)
		32	25	32	28	36
Weak	BL	59.77	49.49	52.26	.911	.022
		(25.27)	(30.24)	(9.03)	(1.20)	(.032)
		39	35	41	35	39
Strong	GLB	90.05*	85.63*	68.92**	.574	.049**
		(15.12)	(23.52)	(6.97)	(1.36)	(.041)
		20	16	25	23	26
Weak	GLB	63.76	53.15	52.33	.448	.021
		(21.9)	(30.35)	(8.09)	(.895)	(.024)
		21	20	23	21	22
Strong	ICRG	97.57**	98.90**	71.41**	−.065**	.059**
		(5.30)	(3.03)	(4.69)	(.642)	(.041)
		21	19	24	20	24
Weak	ICRG	59.20	47.79	52.33	1.52	.006
		(17.21)	(21.71)	(4.60)	(1.16)	(.010)
		15	14	15	12	16
Strong	HER	95.45**	95.33**	69.19**	−.027**	.055**
		(9.01)	(10.12)	(5.96)	(1.09)	(.044)
		22	18	27	22	26
Weak	HER	54.00	40.10	49.83	.915	.015
		(21.46)	(30.19)	(8.97)	(.953)	(.025)
		26	20	28	20	21

*Difference in proportion or mean between strong rights and weak rights is significant at the .05 level.

**Difference in proportion or mean between strong rights and weak rights is significant at the .01 level.

Note: The numbers in parentheses are standard deviations. The third row in each sample is the number of observations for the sample. Water is the percentage of the population with access to safe water in 1990. Sanitation is the percentage of the population with access to sanitation in 1990. Life expectancy is an average of 1965 and 1985 life expectancy at birth. Deforestation is the annual percentage of woodlands lost between 1981–90. Growth is the average annual rate of growth in per capita GDP, 1960–85.

Sources: Property rights measures: table 2.1; environmental performance measures: World Bank (various years).

preferred outcome.) In three of the four measures, the rate of deforestation is greater for the weaker specification of property rights. For example, in countries with weak property rights as measured by the rule of
law (ICRG), the average annual reduction in forest woodlands was 1.52
percent, whereas the same measure for nations with strong property
rights as measured by the rule of law had an average annual reduction
in forest woodlands of −0.065, i.e., forest woodlands increased during
this period. Comparison of means tests indicate that for the ICRG and
Heritage (HER) measures the distinction is clearly statistically significant. In the Barro and Lee (BL) data, the distinction is marginally significant (t = 1.57). In the case of the Gwartney, Lawson, Block (GLB)
measure, the deforestation rate is higher for the strong property rights
countries, but the difference is not statistically significant. In short,
strong property rights do not increase deforestation and may actually
decrease deforestation.

Finally, the data in table 2.2 show that growth rates in per capita GDP
are also substantially higher where property rights are well defined and
comparison tests indicate that all the differences are statistically significant. The smallest magnitude is the Barro and Lee measure and there
the growth rate in the strong property rights regime is roughly twice the
growth rate for countries in the weak property rights category. The
Heritage measure provides a growth rate that is three times greater in
the strong property rights regime as opposed to the growth rates in the
weak rights regime. The differential between strong rights and weak
rights growth rates is nearly tenfold for the rule of law version (ICRG)
of property rights measures. In short, the data in table 2.2 indicate that
strong property rights are associated with better environments and
greater economic growth.

Table 2.3 provides an alternative view of the growth/environment
nexus. Low-growth countries are ones with annual per capita GDP
growth rates averaging less than 1 percent per year, while countries
with a high growth rate are those averaging more than 4.5 percent per
year. The subsamples constitute approximately the upper and lower
third of the sample distribution.

The data in table 2.3 show that over 30 percent more of the populations enjoy access to safe water in high-growth countries compared to
low-growth countries. The access to sanitation is in the same direction
but the gap is even greater. The percent of the population in high-
growth countries enjoying access to sanitation is twice that of low-
growth countries. Life expectancy is over thirteen years greater in the
high-growth countries than low-growth countries. Deforestation is over
four times greater in low-growth countries. Comparisons of proportions
and means tests indicate that all these distinctions are statistically sig-

Table 2.3
Economic Growth and Environmental Performance Measures

Sample	Environmental Performance Measures			
	Water	Sanitation	Life Expectancy	Deforestation
Total Sample	71.38	64.97	58.30	.606
	(25.04)	(32.55)	(11.29)	(1.27)
	113	95	119	109
High Growth	84.64*	83.91*	63.61*	.195**
	(19.84)	(23.46)	(8.86)	(1.22)
	28	22	27	21
Low Growth	53.13	40.30	50.14	.941
	(21.95)	(25.46)	(9.21)	(1.37)
	32	23	32	27

*The difference in proportion or mean between high growth and low growth is significant at the .01 level.

**The difference in proportion or mean between high growth and low growth is significant at the .1 level.

Note: For variable definitions, see table 2.2. Numbers in parentheses are standard deviations. The third row in each sample is the sample size.

Sources: Growth measures: Barro and Lee data set (see Barro and Sala-I-Martin 1995, 330–32); environmental performance measures: World Bank (various years).

nificant at conventional levels. In short, bifurcating the data by growth reinforces the impressions evident in table 2.2. Property rights and growth appear to be good things in terms of simple measures of environmental quality.

The Case of Developing Countries

To examine the proposition that economic growth encourages environmental degradation at low levels of per capita wealth, the measures in table 2.3 are replicated in table 2.4 only for countries with per capita GDP less than $5,000 in 1985. The high-growth countries in this subset of low-income countries have safer water and better sanitation, although the gaps are not as large as in the data set representing all countries. Deforestation is actually higher in the high-growth countries, although the difference is not statistically significant.

It is important to note that life expectancy is approximately ten years greater for the more rapidly growing low-income countries, and the difference is statistically significant. Therefore, even if some measures

Table 2.4
Growth and Environmental Performance Measures for Developing
Countries

Sample	Water	Sanitation	Life Expectancy	Deforestation
		Performance Measures		
Total Sample	61.83	53.07	53.67	.877
	(22.30)	(29.91)	(9.03)	(1.26)
	82	69	86	81
High Growth	68.09*	62.28*	56.82**	.963
	(20.38)	(26.68)	(5.60)	(1.53)
	22	18	22	19
Low Growth	48.04	35.74	46.90	.689
	(21.55)	(24.44)	(7.49)	(1.90)
	24	19	24	19

*The difference in mean or portion is significant at the .1 level.
**The difference in mean or portion is significant at the .01 level.
Note: The total sample consists of all countries in the data set with per capita GDP in 1985 less than $5,000. Low growth and high growth are approximately the lower and upper 30 percentiles, respectively.
Source: World Bank (various years).

of pollution, such as SO_2 emissions, are greater at low-income levels (Grossman and Krueger 1995), other benefits of growth such as better health care or nutrition can offset negative consequences and leave the average citizen better off. Longer life expectancy and increased access to safer water and better sanitation for people in developing countries indicate that this is the case.

Summary and Conclusions

Alfred Marshall's assertions regarding property rights seem correct. Notwithstanding the prodigious research on property rights in the wake of Coase's social cost paper, the failure to pursue systematic analysis of human well-being and the configuration of property rights until recently attests to the economics profession's undervaluation of property rights. Moreover, Marshall's point regarding the necessity of property rights for "solid progress" is unambiguously supported by the data presented above.

The economics of property rights suggests that human well-being should be greater in regimes where the state creates a configuration of property rights that allows economic agents to contract reasonably freely and with general predictability regarding ownership and contract enforcement. In such regimes, the human tendency to contract for property rights in wealth-enhancing ways should be amplified. Economic growth should increase in such regimes and the opportunities to improve environmental amenities should also increase pari pasu. The main theoretical and empirical caveats deal with possible growth-induced environmental degradation at moderate levels of per capita wealth.

Recent scholarship provides specific methods to evaluate these working hypotheses. Several measures of aggregate property rights exist and permit us to examine the relationship between property rights, growth, and simple measures of environmental quality. The data presented above show that environmental quality and economic growth rates are greater in regimes where property rights are well defined than in regimes where property rights are poorly defined. Therefore, property rights and growth should be viewed, at least in several respects, as favorable to environmental quality and conservation of resources. At a minimum, a Pavlovian reaction against the natural concomitants of strong property rights—markets and economic growth—is unwarranted. More to the point, the specification of strong aggregate property rights appears to have an important place in improving human well-being.

Notes

1. See Marshall (1920). Frank H. Knight (1971, 319–20) also recognized the importance of property rights:

> The facts of progress will be seen to have an intimate connection with the very institution of private property. In an unprogressive society private property in the modern sense of the term need not exist. The social justification of private ownership is that the coupling of control of resources with the enjoyment of the fruits of their use is supposed to give an incentive to the use of the goods effectively in production.

However, Marshall's observation that property rights have been undervalued by economists seems to apply even to Knight because his discussion of private property is but an oblique reference in a work that contains extensive discourse on nearly every other aspect of the free enterprise system.

2. See, for instance, Baumol, Nelson, and Wolff (1994) and Barro and Sala-I-Martin (1995) for a summary of many of these studies.

3. I shall refer to this data set as Barro-Lee as it was developed by Robert J. Barro and Jong-Wha Lee. It is available on disk from Ms. Ingrid Sayied, Economics Department, Harvard University, Cambridge MA. The data set is described in Barro and Sala-I-Martin (1995, 330–32).

References

Alchian, Armen A. 1989. Property Rights. In *The Invisible Hand: The New Palgrave*, ed. John Eatwell, Murray Milgate, and Peter Newman. New York: Norton, 232–38.

Anderson, Terry L. 1998. Viewing Wildlife through Coase-Colored Glasses, this volume.

Anderson, Terry L., and P. J. Hill. 1975. The Evolution of Property Rights: A Study of the American West. *Journal of Law & Economics* 18(1): 163–79.

Arrow, Kenneth, Bert Bolin, Robert Costanza, Partha Dasgupta, Carl Folke, C. S. Holling, Bengt-Owe Jansson, Simon Levin, Karl-Götsn Mäler, Charles Perrings, and David Pimentel. 1995. Economic Growth, Carrying Capacity, and the Environment. *Science* 286: 520–21.

Barro, Robert J. 1991. Economic Growth in a Cross Section of Countries. *Quarterly Journal of Economics* 196: 407–43.

Barro, Robert J., and Xavier Sala-I-Martin. 1995. *Economic Growth*. New York: McGraw-Hill.

Barzel, Yoram. 1989. *Economic Analysis of Property Rights*. Cambridge: Cambridge University Press.

Baumol, William J., Richard R. Nelson, and Edward N. Wolff. 1994. *Convergence and Productivity*. Oxford: Oxford University Press.

Beach, William W., and Gareth Davis. 1997. The Index of Economic Freedom and Economic Growth. In *1997 Index of Economic Freedom*, ed. Kim R. Holmes, Bryan T. Johnson, and Melanie Kirkpatrick. Washington, D.C.: Heritage Foundation, and New York: Wall Street Journal, Dow Jones & Company, 1–13.

Carney, William J. 1998. From Stakeholders to Stockholders: A View from Organizational Theory, this volume.

Coase, Ronald H. 1960. The Problem of Social Cost. *Journal of Law & Economics* 3(1): 1–44.

———. 1988. *The Firm, the Market, and the Law*. Chicago: University of Chicago Press.

Coursey, Don. 1992. The Demand for Environmental Quality. Department of Economics, Washington University, St. Louis.

Demsetz, Harold. 1967. Toward a Theory of Property Rights. *American Economic Review* 57(May): 347–59.

Eggertsson, Thráinn. 1990. *Economic Behavior and Institutions*. Cambridge: Cambridge University Press.

Ellickson, Robert C. 1991. *Order without Law: How Neighbors Settle Disputes*. Cambridge: Harvard University Press.

Gastil, Raymond. 1987. *Freedom in the World*. Westport, CT: Greenwood Press.

Gordon, H. Scott. 1954. The Economic Theory of a Common Property Resource: The Fishery. *Journal of Political Economy* 62(April): 124–42.

Grossman, Gene M., and Alan B. Krueger. 1994. Environmental Impacts of a North American Free Trade Agreement. In *The U.S.–Mexico Free Trade Agreement*, ed. P. Garber. Cambridge: MIT Press, 165–77.

————. 1995. Economic Growth and the Environment. *Quarterly Journal of Economics* 112: 353–78.

Gwartney, James, Robert Lawson, and Walter Block. 1996. *Economic Freedom of the World, 1975–1995.* Vancouver, BC, Canada: Fraser Institute.

Hardin, Garrett. 1968. The Tragedy of the Commons. *Science* 162: 1243–48.

Holmes, Kim R., Bryan T. Johnson, and Melanie Kirkpatrick, eds. 1997. *1997 Index of Economic Freedom.* Washington, D.C.: Heritage Foundation, and New York: Wall Street Journal, Dow Jones & Company.

Joskow, Paul. 1987. Contract Duration and Relationship-Specific Investments: Evidence from Coal Markets. *American Economic Review* 77: 168–85.

Keefer, Philip, and Stephen Knack. 1997. Why Don't Poor Countries Catch Up? A Cross- National Test of an Institutional Explanation. *Economic Inquiry* 35: 590–602.

Knack, Stephen. 1996. Institutions and the Convergence Hypothesis: The Cross-National Evidence. *Public Choice* 87: 207–28.

Knack, Stephen, and Philip Keefer. 1995. Institutions and Economic Performance: Cross-Country Tests Using Alternative Institutional Measures. *Economics and Politics* 7: 207–27.

Knight, Frank. 1971. *Risk, Uncertainty, and Profit.* Chicago: University of Chicago Press.

Kormendi, Roger C., and Philip C. Meguire. 1985. Macroeconomic Determinants of Growth. *Journal of Monetary Economics* 16: 141–63.

Leal, Donald R. 1998. Cooperating on the Commons: Case Studies in Community Fisheries, this volume.

Libecap, Gary. 1989. *Contracting for Property Rights.* Cambridge: Cambridge University Press.

Marshall, Alfred. 1920. *Principles of Economics*, 8th ed. London: Macmillan.

Nordhaus, William D. 1969. An Economic Theory of Technological Change. *American Economic Review* 59: 18–28.

North, Douglass C. 1981. *Structure and Change in Economic History.* New York: Norton.

————. 1990. *Institutions, Institutional Change and Economic Performance.* New York: Cambridge University Press.

Pejovich, Svetozar. 1997. Property Rights and Technological Innovation. In *The Economics of Property Rights,* ed. Svetozar Pejovich. Cheltenham, UK: Edward Elgar, 193–205.

Political Risk Services. 1984. *International Country Risk Guide.* East Syracuse, NY.

Radetzki, Marian. 1992. Economic Growth and the Environment. In *World Bank Discussion Papers, International Trade and Development*, ed. Patrick Low. Washington, D.C.: World Bank, 121–34.

Rebelo, Sergio. 1991. Long-Run Policy Analysis and Long-Run Growth. *Journal of Political Economy* 99: 500–21.

Riker, William H., and Itai Senedeker. 1991. A Political Theory of the Origin of Property Rights: Landing Slots. *American Journal of Political Science* 35: 951–69.

Scully, Gerald W. 1988. The Institutional Framework and Economic Development. *Journal of Political Economy* 96: 652–62.

———. 1992. *Constitutional Environments and Economic Growth*. Princeton: Princeton University Press.

Simon, Julian L. 1995. *The State of Humanity*. Cambridge, MA: Blackwell.

Smith, Vernon L. 1992. Economic Principles in the Emergence of Humankind. *Economic Inquiry* 30: 1–13.

———. 1998. Property Rights as a Natural Order: Reciprocity, Evolutionary and Experimental Considerations, this volume.

Solow, Robert C. 1956. A Contribution to the Theory of Economic Growth. *Quarterly Journal of Economics* 70: 65–94.

World Bank. Various years. *World Development Report*. Washington, D.C.

Yandle, Bruce. 1998. Coase, Pigou, and Environmental Rights, this volume.

Chapter 3

Property Rights as a Natural Order: Reciprocity, Evolutionary and Experimental Considerations

Vernon L. Smith

A property right is a guarantee allowing actions to occur within the guidelines defined by the right. We automatically look to the state as the guarantor against reprisal when rights are exercised by rights holders. But property rights predate nation-states. This is because social exchange within stateless tribes, and trade between such tribes, predate the agricultural revolution of a mere ten thousand years ago—little more than an eye blink in the time scale for the emergence of humanity. Both social exchange and trade implicitly recognize mutual rights to act, which are conveyed in what we commonly refer to as "property rights." In what sense are such rights "natural"? The answer, I think, is to be found in the universality, spontaneity, and evolutionary fitness value of reciprocity behavior. Reciprocity in human nature (and prominently in our closest primate relative, the chimpanzee) is the foundation of our uniqueness as creatures of social exchange, which we extended to include trade with nonkin and nontribal members long, long before we adopted herder and farmer lifestyles.

This chapter is about evolutionary, anthropological, and experimental concepts and data as they relate to reciprocity behavior and the property rights implicitly defined by such behavior. Evolution, or the concept of

I am indebted to P. J. Hill and Roger Meiners, directors of the 1997 Political Economy Forum, for assigning me a title that I would not have hit upon myself, but which inspired me to bring together some evidence and ideas on questions that have long puzzled and troubled me.

natural selection, enters the picture because it is a good bet that reciprocity is *innate* in human nature, as it is in the common and "pygmy"
(bonono) chimpanzees. Anthropological and archaeological considerations are important in my thesis because they provide the record for the
changing human tool-making industry from antiquity to contemporary
hunter-gatherer cultures. Assorted laboratory experiments shed light on
the puzzle implicitly contained in Adam Smith's only two full-length
books: Why is human nature simultaneously both self-regarding and
other-regarding? The broad sweep of this chapter renders impractical
an in-depth treatment of each of the key background topics.[1]

The Two Faces of Adam Smith

Adam Smith published just two complete books in his lifetime. Two
quotations convey the essential themes in each of these classic works.

> It is not from the benevolence of the butcher, the brewer, or the baker, that
> we expect our dinner, but from their regard to their own interest. . . . This
> division of labor . . . is not originally the effect of any human wisdom,
> which foresees and intends that general opulence to which it gives occa-
> sion. It is the necessary, though very slow and gradual, consequence of a
> certain propensity in human nature which has in view no such extensive
> utility; the propensity to truck, barter, and exchange one thing for another.
> (Smith [1776] 1909, 19, 20)

> How selfish soever man may be supposed, there are evidently some princi-
> ples in his nature, which interest him in the fortune of others, and render
> their happiness necessary to him, though he derives nothing from it except
> the pleasure of seeing it. (Smith [1759] 1976, 9)[2]

The juxtaposition of these two statements lays bare what would appear to be directly contradictory views of human nature held by Adam
Smith. This has long been noted and perhaps helps to account for the
greater notoriety of the *Wealth of Nations* in both popular and academic
discourse. Thus, as observed by Jacob Viner (1991a, 250), "Many writers, including the present author at an early stage of his study of Smith,
have found these two works in some measure basically inconsistent."

These two views are not inconsistent, however, if we recognize that
a universal propensity for social exchange is a fundamental distinguishing feature of the hominid line, and that it finds expression in both
personal exchange in small-group social transactions, and in impersonal
trade through large-group markets. Thus, Smith had but one behavioral
axiom, "the propensity to truck, barter, and exchange one thing for

another," where the objects of trade I interpret to include not only goods but also the content of what he called sympathy, that is, "generosity, humanity, kindness, compassion, mutual friendship and esteem" (Smith [1759] 1976, 38). As can be seen in both the ethnographic record and in laboratory experiments, whether it is goods or favors that are exchanged, they bestow gains from trade that humans seek relentlessly in all social transactions. Thus, Adam Smith's single axiom, broadly interpreted to include the social exchange of goods and favors across time, as well as the simultaneous trade of goods for money or other goods, is sufficient to characterize a major portion of the human social and cultural enterprise.

The Origins of Trade: Reciprocity, Hunter-Gatherer Sharing, and the Market Economy

It is useful in discussing reciprocity and trade to look first at chimpanzee communities and then at several non-Western human communities.

Reciprocity in Chimpanzee Communities

Humans and modern chimpanzees—biologically our closest cousin with whom we share 98.4 percent of the same DNA—are believed to have branched off from a common ancestor about 5 to 6 million years ago (Diamond 1992, 15–31). Our chimp relative, more than any other nonhuman primate, shares with us a remarkable sophistication in social organization (de Waal 1989 and 1996), but I want particularly to emphasize the chimp capacity to engage in acts of reciprocity, both positive and negative (McCabe, Rassenti, and Smith 1996). By positive reciprocity, I mean individual A responds, nonsimultaneously, with like acts, when individual B has transferred goods or favors to A. Such behavior is common among the chimps studied by de Waal at the Yerkes Regional Primate Research Center and the Arnheim Zoo. Thus, the number of food transfers in each direction are positively related to those in the opposite direction: "if A shared a lot with B, B generally shared a lot with A, and if A shared little with C, C also shared little with A." Also, "grooming affected subsequent sharing: A's chances for getting food from B improved if A had groomed B earlier that day" (de Waal 1996, 153, 245–46).

Negative reciprocity occurs when individuals are punished for "cheating" on a social exchange; i.e., failing to return positive reciprocity to those that have provided it to them. Negative reciprocity is the endogenous policeman in social exchange that defines natural property rights systems. Positive reciprocity, or "reciprocal altruism" (Trivers 1971), is subject to invasion by selfish free riders. Hence the importance of negative reciprocity to punish free riders, as an implicit transaction or enforcement cost of positive reciprocity. The evolutionary psychologist Leda Cosmides (1989) reports a large number of psychology experiments motivated by the hypothesis that for social exchange our minds contain specialized mechanisms for cheater detection on social contracts, as opposed to general purpose content-free rules of reasoning that allow one to naturally make judgments as to how to falsify statements of the form "if P, then Q." The falsificationist logic requires one to look for P, not Q evidence. Cosmides (1989) reports that people in a large number of decision tasks do very poorly in solving such problems unless the description of the task is recognizable in the benefit and cost format of a social exchange or contract. In the latter cases people's natural tendency toward cheater detection enabled them to do much better in such problem-solving exercises than in other cases requiring reliance on the general logic of falsifying, "if P, then Q" statements.

Negative reciprocity is also observed in ape communities. The primatologist, de Waal, contrasts two chimps, Gwinnie and Georgia, who were very stingy (free-riding) sharers, with Mai and Walnut, who shared readily with many others. "Gwinnie, Georgia, and other stingy personalities encountered far more threats and protestations than generous sharers such as Mai and Walnut" (de Waal 1996, 160). Group expression of negative reciprocity was particularly intense, as well as prominently delayed, in the following incident of "breaking the rules."

> One balmy evening, when the keeper called the chimpanzees inside, two adolescent females refused to enter the building. The rule at Arnheim Zoo being that *none* of the apes receive food until *all* of them have moved from the island into their sleeping quarters, the chimpanzees actively assist with the rule's enforcement: latecomers meet with a great deal of hostility from the hungry colony.
>
> When the obstinate teenagers finally entered, more than two hours late, they were given a separate bedroom so as to prevent reprisals. This protected them only temporarily, however. The next morning, out on the island, the entire colony vented its frustration about the delayed meal by a mass pursuit ending in a physical beating of the culprits. Needless to say, they were the first to come in that evening. (de Waal 1996, 89)

Apes also appear to understand exchange, or at least have no difficulty interpreting intent when something is offered by a human in return for retrieving an object. For example, someone leaves an item, such as a screwdriver, behind in the ape enclosure. "One of its inhabitants will quickly grasp what we mean when we hold up a tidbit while pointing or nodding at the item. She will fetch the tool and trade it for the food" (de Waal 1996, 147).

That apes consciously engage in reciprocity is hardly proved by any of these studies (skeptics are not hard to come by), but clearly the observations are consistent with reciprocity as a hypothesis and inconsistent with the null alternative of random interactions. But among humans much of our reciprocity behavior is subconscious, as is much of what we learn. We acquire almost the whole of our natural language ability in the preschool years, age three to five, without formal instruction, when we learn algorithms to add "s" to form regular noun plurals, "ed" to form the past tense of regular verbs, and that you can say teeth-marks but never claws-marks, mice-infested but never rats-infested. This is because, in English, compound words are always formed out of root or stem words stored in one's mental dictionary—words that are not generated by an algorithm. Thus teeth-marks, rat-infested, tooth-mark and gay-bashing are natural compounds generated by our brain, but rats-infested and gays-bashing are not. Hence, compounds are always formed from singular regular nouns or irregular plurals. The irregular plurals like men and mice are words that we memorize as exceptions to the rule of adding "s" to form a plural. The instinct of the three-year-old is to say that two mans came to the door, we correct her and she eventually learns that men is the irregular plural of man. But she has the logic dead right; that plurals are formed algorithmically out of root singulars.

We learn these algorithms without instruction from mom or our English teacher and without memory of learning them, because it is the way the brain works (Pinker 1994). That the modularity of the brain allows subconscious learning is proved in experiments with amnesiacs, who are taught a new task, which they subsequently perform with skill, but have no memory of having learned it (Knowlton, Mangels, and Squire 1996).[3]

Reciprocity and the Origins of Human Trade

For at least 2.5 million years—the earliest dated stone tools (Klein 1989, 163; Semaw et al. 1997)—our hominid ancestors lived as tool-making hunter-gatherers in small extended families and tribes. Some of our brethren still live as hunter-gatherers whose lifestyles have been intensively studied by ethnologists for a century (Boas 1897), providing clues as to what life in the Paleolithic period might have been like. It is only in roughly the last 10,000 years that most of our ancestors abandoned this traditional lifestyle beginning in the Near East, first by domesticating sheep about 10,500 years ago, then about 9,500 years ago

by growing various grains that had been gathered by foraging technologies developed much earlier. Similar independent changes occurred in
North America and the Far East. Although this agricultural revolution
accelerated a previous tendency to a more sedentary life, and greater
dependence on trade through specialization, the origins of trade are far
older, going back 50,000 to 100,000 years, and perhaps much earlier.

The key to understanding our long "propensity to truck, barter and
exchange" is to be found, I think, in our evolved capacity for reciprocity, which formed the foundation for social exchange long before there
was trade in the conventional economic sense. All humans, in all cultures, engage in the trading of favors. Although the cultural forms of
reciprocity are endlessly variable, functionally, reciprocity is universal.
We do beneficial things for our friends, and implicitly we expect beneficial acts in kind from them. In fact this condition essentially defines
the difference between friends and nonfriends. We avoid close relationships with those who do not reciprocate. You invite me to dinner and
two months later I invite you to dinner. I lend you my car when yours
is in the shop and on another occasion you offer me your basketball
tickets when you are out of town. Close friends are not conscious of
"keeping accounts," and the fact that we are in a trading relationship is
as natural as it is subconscious and taken for granted. Once either of
two friends become conscious of asymmetry in reciprocation, the
friendship may become threatened. People who persistently have trouble forming and maintaining friendships are subclinical sociopaths who
fail to possess a subconscious capacity and intuition for reciprocity.
Prisons contain a disproportionate share of a population's sociopaths
(Mealy 1995).

Exchange among the Aché of Paraguay

Extant hunter-gatherer societies without a monetary system commonly cooperate through multilateral social exchange. The Aché of Par-
aguay are a case in point. Hunting is predominantly a responsibility of
adult males whose principal game target is the collared peccary, and
this high-variance product of the hunt is shared widely across the entire
tribe. Gathering is predominantly a preoccupation of adult females and
children. The product has low variance and is shared only within the
nuclear family. As such, these are rational exchange institutions in that
the higher potential enforcement cost of wide sharing is matched with
the greater benefits of pooling infrequent lumpy supplies over a larger
group. Unlucky hunters are assured of meat for their families, and in
return give up their claim to others when they are successful. But some
hunters are consistently more successful than others, and since there is

intertribal mobility, they would be expected to leave if not adequately compensated. One hypotheses was that the better hunters spent less time hunting, taking their pay in leisure, but the research results showed that the superior hunters spent more, not less, time hunting. They also shared meat disproportionately outside the immediate family. An explanation was suggested by the observation that they gained increased access to extramarital mates but also enjoyed a higher survivorship of their children, both legitimate and illegitimate, from tribal nurturing inputs (Kaplin and Hill 1985; Hawkes 1990). The greater reproductive success of superior hunters would also have selected heritable traits tending to improve tribal hunting skill.

Gift Exchange with the Eskimo

That trade can be hypothesized to have grown directly out of social or gift exchange is illustrated by the individual's negotiating stance in many extant hunter-gatherer tribes. Consider the trading procedures that accompanied an exchange by the Greenland Eskimo at the turn of this century. Peter Freuchen, the first Caucasian to establish a permanent trading post at Thule, describes the multiday process of striking an agreement with a man and his wife who arrive with a sled-load of fox skins (Freuchen 1961). First, there is denial that he even has any skins because he is such an incompetent hunter. Then, he generally denigrates the quality and condition of any skins that he might have. They are unworthy objects in comparison to the fine merchandise in Freuchen's post. Finally, inspection is allowed, and Freuchen heaps praise on the hunter's supply of fine skins. But the man insists that the skins are "too poor" for him to accept pay. But Freuchen wants to show his gratitude through his "poor" gifts. Ultimately, there is endless examination of the post's merchandise, which of course is insisted by the trapper to be of far greater value than what is on the sled. Eventually a deal is consummated, which can be interpreted as a mutual exchange of gifts, each side receiving a far more valuable gift from the other than provided by self. So, the gains from exchange are enormous for each side, and the inevitable deal was struck, but it was necessary to embed it in a verbal process that is the inverse of what your automobile dealer and you go through when you trade in your used car for a new one.

Kinship, Trade, and Self-Enforcing Property Rights

These considerations suggest the hypothesis that positive reciprocity as voluntary social exchange originated in the nuclear family where close kin relationships allowed gene survivorship even if reciprocation was weak, while simultaneously making it easier to detect free-riding and allowing it to be more easily punished. Since the tribal society is essentially an extended family with kin relationships continuing to have some force, the model of family reciprocity is expanded in a wider circle. The genius of trade was to allow the gains from social exchange to be extended beyond the reach of the family and the tribe. That it might initially have involved kin relationships has been emphasized by Dalton (1977) who observed from ethnographic studies that young nubile women were exchanged between tribes as a mechanism for purchasing peace and political stability, thereby creating an environment conducive to the intertribal exchange of private goods but also public goods like unmolested rights to trade routes, crests, technical knowledge, and ceremonial functions. Hence, the first extensions of trade beyond the tribe continued to rely on nepotism. This would have been efficient insofar as it reduced reliance on negative reciprocity to constrain the violation of implicit contracts.

Once a continuing trading relationship is established across time, the reciprocal benefits of exchange provide the foundation for self-enforcing property rights. Suppose you make ceramic pots and I make spears—both predate agriculture: ceramics appear at least 27,000 years ago (Klein 1989, 376) while recent finds establish a wood spear industry and big game hunting at the astonishingly early date of 400,000 years ago (Thieme 1997, 807). Once we establish a trading relationship, you become dependent on my spears and I become dependent on your ceramic products, because both are perishable and both require specialized human capital. Consequently, we each have a stake in protecting the other's property rights. If either of us plays the game of "steal," rather than the game of "trade," that ends the trading relationship and thereby the gains from exchange. It is also natural for us to form a pact to defend our common interest against external nomadic marauders. The same incentives carry into the agricultural revolution, except now you grow corn, I grow pigs, and we exchange our respective surpluses beyond immediate home consumption needs.[4]

And at some point, some uncomprehending "genius" invented something that would be called "money," and reciprocity is broken free of the double coincidence of wants for particularized commodity pairs. Trading based on gift exchange is now totally relieved of any need to keep track of who owes who what. As reported by Lee (1968a, 21–22), the cultural traditions of !Kung bushman villages are nightmares of incessant talk about dividing the meat from hunting.

The Mind in Prehistory: Implications for Property Rights in the Natural Order

Steven Mithen (1996) identifies three phases in the early evolution of mind. First, the mind is dominated by a general-purpose intelligence for learning and decision-making rules. This intelligence mediates behavior based on experience in all domains of behavior. But those who rely on such general-purpose intelligence "can only produce relatively simple behavior—the rate of learning would be slow, errors would be frequent, and complex behavior patterns could not be acquired" (Mithen 1996, 68). As I understand the argument, it would be analogous to learning to play the piano by never being able to advance beyond the stage of consciously thinking about each note, and then executing the play of each note in sequence. Obviously, the concert pianist could not perform, as is typical, via any such conscious process. Child development studies indicate that up to the age of about two years this is the way the young infant's mind works with language and object manipulation. Subsequently, specialized modules, such as language, become key to the developmental process (Greenfield 1991). If such modules exist in the first stage, their operation is not evident.

Second, the mind is characterized by multiple specialized intelligences, which supplement general intelligence; each operates on some specific domain of behavior, but each functions in relative isolation from the others. Since we are talking about the evolutionary environment of our ancestors—hunter-gatherers—there are at minimum three such prominent forms of specialized intelligence, corresponding to intuitive knowledge of psychology, biology, and physics.

Intuitive, or folk, psychology takes the form of social intelligence on which interaction with other humans is based, and must include "mind reading" modules (see next section) for detecting intentions, and a shared attention mechanism. Biological knowledge takes the form of natural history intelligence, which provides the intuitive understanding of the natural world needed to function as a hunter-gatherer, such as knowledge of seasonal plants and seeds that can be gathered, and knowledge of animal behavior and vulnerabilities. Finally, there is technical intelligence of the kind needed to fashion artifacts of stone, bone, and wood including slings and spears for throwing. The atlatl, for throwing spears, requires an intuitive grasp of the physics of leverage and moment arms.

Although modern linguistics uses the concept of specialized innate language modules, it also involves integrating knowledge from the other specialized modules and, by definition, is really part of phase three (Mithen 1996, 68–70).

Third, the mind is capable of integrating the operations of the various specialized intelligences with a seamless free flow of information between the behavioral domains. Now we have experience gained in one domain informing behavior in another domain. An example would be where a hunter's specialized knowledge of prey behavior informs the design of weapons tailored to exploit vulnerabilities in that behavior. For a gregarious herding animal that gathers at a watering hole, approach is simplified and short thrusting spears, or darts, may suffice for harvesting. But for a seal taken at a blowhole cut through the Arctic ice, the spear had better have a barbed point and a long cord attached to retrieve the injured game.

The above model applied to what is known about chimpanzee behavior shows rather clearly that chimps rely on general intelligence, and a single fairly well-developed specialized module, social intelligence, but have very poor knowledge of technology and their natural history environment. Chimps are tool makers; they use sticks for retrieving honey or ants, leaves for sponges to gather ants or water or to clean themselves, and stone hammers and anvils to crack nuts. But all their tools are made of single components, and there have been no technical advances in thirty years of chimp observation. Moreover, it is a struggle to impart what knowledge they have to the next generation. It is a misconception that apes "ape" (imitate) well. Juveniles, watching their mothers, have great difficulty learning to place a nut on an anvil and hitting it with a hammer. They are adults before learning the task, which requires four years of exposure and practice.

Their natural history knowledge is good for foraging known environments but very poor for new environments where intuition plays a prominent role. Creativeness is not their forte. But their social intelligence is another matter. They not only have detailed knowledge of their allies and friends but are creative in the use of Machiavellian deception to achieve their ends. But their social skills are not integrated with the other specialized intelligences. Their accomplished ability to persuade (and deceive) others does not carry over to the teaching of tool use, or to better organize foraging in an unfamiliar environment (Mithen 1996, 74–84).

The archeological record suggests that the first stone tool makers (*Homo Habilis*) possessed technical and natural history knowledge superior to that of the apes just described, and very high social intelligence, but like apes relied heavily on general intelligence with the specialized intelligences poorly integrated and interconnected.

With the arrival of *Homo Erectus*, 1.8 million years ago, technology, social organization, and knowledge of natural history all show increased sophistication, but it is remarkable how little major innovation occurs from 1.8 to 0.1 million years ago. Thus, tools with multiple components are not part of the record, although single component manufacturing technology is greatly improved. Cognitive fluidity—the work of the modern mind—seems to be conspicuously absent. This in spite of a period of rapidly expanding brain size beginning about 500,000 years ago, and including Neanderthals with brains as large or larger than ours, who appear about 150,000 years ago and survive as late as 30,000 years ago. "The most persuasive evidence of a cognitive barrier between social and technical intelligence is the absence of any artifacts used for body decoration, such as beads and pendants" (Mithen 1996, 139).

If language first evolved as a complement to social intelligence, then the evidence for increased social skill beginning with the first tool maker is consistent with the finding that *H. Habilis* has bumps inside the crania corresponding to a well-developed Broca's area—one portion of the brain associated with speech. Neanderthal brain casts suggest a modern neural structure, Broca's and Wernick's areas. The discovery of a Neanderthal's hyoid bone that is virtually identical to that of modern humans shows that the vocal tract and larynx gave them the capacity for modern language.

But there was no big bang in the archeological record documenting the emergence of the modern mind. This did not happen until the time period 60,000–30,000 years ago, some 40,000 years after the arrival of our immediate Cro-Magnon forefathers, the sole survivors of the bushlike hominid tree. They were marked by the making of bone artifacts and the placing of animal parts into human burials, both new forms of behavior 100,000 years ago, but otherwise nothing visible happens until the explosion in art, religion, technology, and the occupation of Australia beginning 60 millennia ago. "My explanation of the big-bang of human culture is that this is when the final major redesign of the mind took place . . . the specialized intelligences of the Early Human mind no longer had to work in isolation" (Mithen 1996, 153–54). Capacities that had appeared first in a narrow context became extended into other domains. We see body adornment, tailored clothes, fine sculpture, breathtaking cave art a mile from the entrance, tools with numerous and intricate component parts, atlatls to leverage the arm for spear throwing, arrows for bows that exploit energy storage principles, and so on.

With this big bang came an explosion in tangible property, particularly after about 40,000 years ago: boats, houses, villages, sledges, atlatls, bows and arrows, sculpture, jewelry, sewn clothing, seed-grinding stones, storage and boiling vessels, kilns for firing clay and, most important, the domesticated wolf to aid in hunting.[5] Gathering had earlier focused on seeds and plants that could be eaten while on the move from camp to camp; now, many of the gathered materials were inedible without boiling, grinding, or soaking. With the growth in personal paraphernalia, life is necessarily more sedentary. This unprecedented expansion of personal property and real estate would have generated a demand for complex property rights and contracting arrangements. Neighbors were near and more permanent. Long-term relationships and trade would have given each a stake in protecting the property rights of others—the new reciprocity for defense and specialization, the latter limited only by the extent of the market, and vice versa.

Modern civilization is born, forged from the genetic and experiential endowment accumulated prior to 50,000 years ago. From this springboard, declining stocks of big game and humankind's vast and sophisticated knowledge of seeds, eggs, plants, and animal behavior, the domestication of sheep and the planting of grain was as inevitable as night following day, waiting only for a decline in the opportunity costs of herding and planting. But a few pockets of tribal societies remain to the present day. As noted by a Kalahari desert !Kung tribesman, in one of those pockets, when asked why he did not farm like his neighbors, "Why should we plant when there are so many mongongo nuts in the world?" (Lee 1968b, 33).

Suddenly, our Cro-Magnon ancestors learned to learn on an unprecedented scale, with intuitive modular knowledge of folk biology, physics, and psychology fluidly affecting each other and mediated by large front lobe executive activity.

Evolutionary Psychology and "Mind Reading": Implications for Property Rights as Natural Order

Humphrey (1976a) was the first psychologist to argue that human consciousness evolved to equip us for strategic interaction in social transactions. Being conscious of self and aware of one's own thoughts and desires enabled one to read the minds of—predict the behavior of—others from their words and actions. This capacity, however, is largely intuitive and need not be consciously calculating: as you read this essay, images form in your mind as to what must have been in mine when I wrote it. We know that complex behavior is possible in the absence of conscious awareness, or memory of it. Petit mal seizures constitute a disorder of the brain in which a person suffers sudden loss of higher brain stem functions. The victims lose conscious experience but continue their activities, which can include complex behavior like playing the piano. Similar behavior has been indicated in experiments with amnesiacs. Consciousness must therefore be associated with modules, or mental mechanisms in the brain that are distinct from other mental mechanisms.

Most of what we know and can do we learned without conscious awareness or memory of the learning. How vision constructs images of the external world in the brain is something we have no conscious awareness of. The same is true for natural (spoken) language. But some things are not learned naturally, they require conscious applications of mental activity, as when we learn left from right or to play the piano (although some can play "by ear" and never learn to read music), or what a Nash equilibrium is. This last can be hard to learn or to understand, yet Nash outcomes can nevertheless be achieved by experimental subjects who know nothing of the equilibrium logic.

Evolutionary psychologists argue that your mind is like a Swiss army knife, which is composed of numerous computational modules specialized for particular functions that are context-dependent and domain-specific—modules for vision, language, cheater detection, friend-or-foe detection, and so on. A controversial question is whether there are innate modules that govern our reciprocity behavior. Thus, it has been said that, "all we do in life is discover what is already built into our brains. While the environment may shape the way in which any given organism develops, it shapes it only as far as preexisting capacities in that organism allow. Thus the environment *selects* from the built-in operations; it does not modify them" (Gazzaniga 1992, 2–3). I don't know if these things are true, but the last decade has uncovered evidence for genetic causes or predispositions in a long series of maladies and behaviors that were once thought to be a product of the environment, culture, or upbringing. When I was growing up everything was thought to be like the Thurber cartoon depicting a woman being interrogated by the authorities, with a body on the floor alongside a pistol. The caption, "Well, you see, the story *really* goes back to when I was a teensy-weensy little girl" (Thurber 1943, 156). One thing, however, seems clear: we cannot rule out the hypothesis that what we inherit in nature is a major, if not the only, factor in the reciprocity norms traditionally thought to be the product of culture. Major modifications of fruit fly behavior have been manipulated by controlled experiments in sexual selection (Rice 1996). Some ten thousand years of controlled breeding of dogs has yielded an astonishing range of behavioral capacities that have been shown experimentally to have heritable components (Scott and Fuller 1965).

The standard economics and social science model of the mind, contrary to the above, is that it is like a general-purpose logic machine. All decision tasks, regardless of context, constitute maximization problems subject to external constraints whether from the physical environment or the reaction functions of other agents. This is what we teach as economists. Furthermore, as we all know, it is hard to teach—it does not come naturally—and many students give up, unable to learn it. But that does not mean they will fail to function effectively in social and economic exchange in life or in a laboratory experiment. This is because people have natural intuitive mechanisms—modules that serve them well in daily interchanges—enabling them to "read" situations and the intentions and likely reactions of others without cognitive analysis.

Awareness of our own mental phenomena is what permits us to "mind read," that is, infer the mental states of others from their actions or words. Baron-Cohen (1995, 31–58) hypothesizes that our mind reading ability utilizes such modules as an "intentionality detector" (ID) and a "shared attention mechanism" (SAM) that provide inputs to a "theory of mind mechanism" (TOMM). The ID is concerned with inferring the intentions of another, like "she is hungry," a dyadic relation, while SAM is triadic: "Mary and I both see the onrushing car." The more sophisticated capacity of the TOMM enables us to know that another person can have a false belief. This is what makes deception, bluffing, double crossing, and so on, possible in strategic interaction. The "pretend" play of young children, as well as various experimental tests, make it plain that humans by about age four years develop a fully operational TOMM. But not every child and adult has an intact TOMM, and in some even the SAM is faulty. These are people afflicted with autism.

A diagnostic test for autism is the "Smarties Test." Smarties are a British candy like M&Ms. Show a Smarties box to a three- to four-year-old child, and ask him what he thinks is in the box. He says, "candy." Now let him look inside the box, which in fact has been emptied of candy and filled with pencils, and tell the child that you are going to ask the same question of the next child that enters the room. You then ask the subject what the next child will think is in the box. A normal preschooler is most likely to reply "candy," or "Smarties," while an autistic child is most likely to reply "pencils." The autistic child is not aware of mental phenomena in others.

Yet autistics can have normal, even superior, intelligence as measured by standard IQ tests. Their natural language ability is intact, normal, even superior. (The vast majority of mentally retarded children, for example those with Down's syndrome, when they are at the equivalent three- to four-year-old developmental stage, have no difficulty passing the Smarties test, have good natural language ability, but do very poorly on IQ and other intelligence tests.) As adults autistics can learn to predict how others will act in particular circumstances by simply calling on a vast library of memorized experiences, as in the case of Temple Grandin. She has a Ph.D. in agricultural science, but she has no intuitive sense of others' actions in social situations (Sacks 1993–94). She reports feeling like "an anthropologist on Mars." The technical language of science is easy for her, while social language is completely nonintuitive—jokes, irony, allusions, and metaphors are beyond her natural instincts.

The implications of all this for the theme of this chapter are straightforward. Normal human beings, and even those with various, and substantial, limitations on their general intelligence, have intact mental modules that enable them to be intuitively aware of mental phenomena in others. This enables me to see not only the value to me of possessing certain rights to act (property rights), but also to know intuitively the value of such rights for others. Hence, your rights have indirect value to me insofar as they enable us to enjoy the fruits of specialization and to mutually share the resulting gains through exchange. This evolved social capacity appears to be a normal part of the development of the human mind; it is as much a part of the natural order as being hungry and requiring that hunger to be satisfied.

The Experimental Record Shows that Human Nature is Both Self-Regarding and Other-Regarding

We next examine the experimental record as it relates to noncooperative behavior in markets, and cooperative behavior in some two person interactive games.

Noncooperative Behavior Makes Impersonal Markets Work

The puzzle implicit in the two great works of Adam Smith is whether, why, and how cooperation and noncooperation (classical competition) can coexist. We have seen that even in our two closest chimp relatives what clearly coexists is positive and negative reciprocity. But these behaviors are complementary: positive reciprocity needs the negative side to keep free-riders from invading a population of reciprocating altruists, which we have called social exchange. This is not precisely what Adam Smith was talking about. He was talking about the juxtaposition of positive reciprocity and self-loving or noncooperative behavior. Why do these coexist? Noncooperative behavior is the absence of positive reciprocity, not negative reciprocity, which incurs private cost to punish defection from offers to cooperate. The key is to distinguish impersonal market exchange from personal social and economic exchange, and to understand that efficiency in the former is based on noncooperative behavior while efficiency in the latter requires reciprocity.

First, we illustrate the long-standing experimental result that "self love" as expressed in a market of impersonally interacting agents simultaneously maximizes the individual's return, given the self-loving behavior of everyone else, and maximizes the aggregate gains from exchange. Agents both maximize the size of the pie and maximize their share against the maximizing behavior of all others, as per the teaching in the *Wealth of Nations* and technically first established by Cournot in 1838 when the number of agents, N, becomes large. (Cournot invented the idea of a noncooperative equilibrium, but because of the sociology of our profession, we call it a Nash equilibrium.)

Figure 3.1 plots the contracts in an experiment using the double auction institutional rules of trade that are universal the world over in commodity, financial, and derivatives markets; buyers announce bids to buy, sellers announce offers to sell, or asks (in this case in an electronic exchange), a new bid has to be higher than the standing last (and best) bid while a new offer must be below the standing last offer. This yields a bid/ask spread that can only become smaller until a contract occurs, either with some buyer accepting the standing ask or some seller accepting the standing bid.

The supply and demand schedules on the left are induced into the

Figure 3.1
Market Experiment

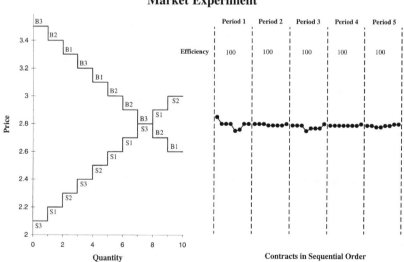

market by assigning value steps to individual buyers (three buyers, B1, B2, and B3 as shown), and cost steps to individual sellers (S1, S2, and S3). Each buyer knows only her own values, and similarly for the sellers. No subject sees what is shown in figure 3.1, although each can observe the bids, offers, and contracts as they occur in real time.

Efficiency, computed as the percentage of the consumer plus producer surplus that is realized by all subjects, always tends to approach 100 percent over time, as claimed implicitly in the *Wealth of Nations*: surplus is the wealth created by the exchange made possible by the existence of the market in figure 3.1. This is measured by the triangular area in figure 3.1 between the supply and demand schedules and to the left of their intersection. Furthermore, at the competitive equilibrium, achieved by the close of period one in continuous repeat trading (price = $2.80; quantity = 8) in figure 3.1, each buyer and seller is maximizing his or her profits, which are paid in cash by the experimenter. Each contract price on the right pairs a buyer and a seller, with the buyer paid in cash the difference between his or her value for the unit bought and the contract price; the seller is paid in cash the difference between the contract price and his or her cost for the unit sold.

But It Is Reciprocity Behavior that Makes Personal Exchange Work

Figure 3.2 shows a two-person extensive form game tree studied by McCabe, Rassenti, and Smith (1996). Starting at the top of the tree, player 1 moves right or down. Then 2 moves left or right, then 1 moves, and so on. The game stops when a payoff box is reached giving 1 the upper amount, and 2 the lower amount, in dollars. Thus, if 1 moves right at the top the game stops and 1 earns $7, while 2 earns $14. There are usually twelve people in the room, each paired anonymously at random with one other person randomly assigned to be player 1 or 2. Each sits at a computer terminal, and decisions are made by clicking the mouse on an arrow corresponding to each possible move (not shown). Each person sees all payoffs, and all moves in sequence. If player 1 moves down at node x_1, then 2 determines whether play will occur in the right or left branch of the tree.

In the discussion to follow we will call the left side the reciprocity branch of the tree. The right side will be referred to as the noncooperative branch. To see why, apply the principles of backward induction and maximization in the self-interest to the right branch starting at node x_8. If 1 is at x_8 the self-interested move is right yielding payoffs ($3, $6) to players (1, 2) respectively. At node x_6, 2 can see that since ($3, $6) is the consequence of moving down, it is in his own interest to move right, yielding ($8, $8). At x_4, player 1, seeing these subsequent consequences, will choose down. Hence, using backward induction, assuming each player always chooses a dominant payoff move for himself and expects the other to do likewise, the logical outcome of a right branch move at node x_2, by 2, is ($8, $8). The same analysis applied to the left branch yields the outcome ($12, $6). Hence, at x_2 a self-interested player 2 will choose right, which in turn implies that 1 will move down at x_1 ($8 is better than $7 for 1). So, game theoretic analysis, based on self-interested noncooperative play, predicts that player 1 will move down at x_1, and player 2 will move right at x_2, yielding the outcome ($8, $8).

But there is a cooperative interpretation based on reciprocity that argues for a left move by 2 at x_2. Why? If player 2 moves left at x_2, it can be interpreted as expressing 2's intention to achieve ($10, $10) on the left; in effect 2 is telling 1, "Look, we can both do better at ($10, $10) on the left than ($8, $8) on the right. Indeed, I obviously would not be moving left, if I expected you to defect at x_3 by moving down. Also, note that if you do move down at x_3, I can punish you for this action by moving down at x_5, and thus not accommodate your attempt to collect $12 at my expense." This is, of course, an interpretation based on conscious calculation, while actual play may be intuitive and not fully calculating. The threat interpretation is also not credible; i.e., in a single play of the game, it is never in player 2's interest to incur the cost of punishing 1 for failing to cooperate. But the reciprocity hypothesis asserts that some people will be preprogrammed to engage naturally in acts of positive reciprocity, and some in acts of negative reciprocity, *even under conditions of anonymous interaction.* We would expect reciprocity to be common in face-to-face negotiation (for example, Hoffman and Spitzer 1985), and for this reason we control for it using anonymity, which gives the noncooperative game theoretic outcome a more favorable prospect by controlling for social communication. Think of left branch play as an exercise in trading favors. Player 2 offers to favor player 1 with $10 (cooperation) expecting player 1 to reciprocate by returning the favor.

The move results for thirty pairs of subjects are indicated on each leg of the decision tree, and the conditional outcomes are shown adjacent to each payoff box. Thirteen of the thirty subject pairs play in the left reciprocity branch, and seventeen in the right noncooperative branch of the tree. Of the thirteen left-branch moves at x_2, eleven (84.6 percent) reciprocate with left moves at x_3. Of the two defections at x_3, one achieves the dominant strategy outcome, and one is punished. On the right branch, conditional on being in that branch, the [$8, $8] outcome is nearly certain (the conditional probability is 0.941). The data strongly

Figure 3.2
Two-Person Decision Tree*

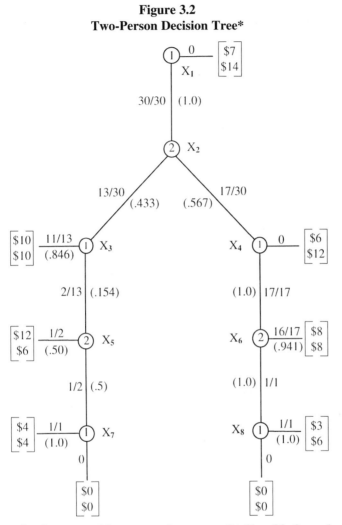

*Extensive form tree with moves and outcomes for N = 30. On each choice leg appears the number of pairs relative to the total arriving at the previous node. Conditional probabilities are shown in parenthesis.

reject the game theoretic hypothesis that all subjects will follow noncooperative strategies. With equal strength we reject the hypothesis that all interactions will be based on reciprocity. The sample suggests that under strict anonymity somewhat less than half the population consists of types who expect offers of cooperation to be reciprocated, and the rest are types who do not, given the payoff alternatives specified in figure 3.1.

Another interpretation is that in a single play using inexperienced subjects, left-branch play occurs because of poor understanding of the game. This interpretation is contrary to two observations:

1. Subject 2s, based on subsequent play frequencies, obtain an expected profit of $9.23 by moving left at x_2—over $1 more than if they reached the $8 outcome on the right. Hence, left play cannot be dismissed as an "irrational" mistake. On balance, player 2s act as if they expect their player 1s to be good mind readers, and in fact player 1s tend predominantly to be good mind readers and to reciprocate.
2. McCabe, Rassenti, and Smith (1996) replicated the above experiment under the following "repeat single play" condition: there are sixteen people in the room and each player is matched exactly once with every other player in the room. Hence, each subject plays the game once in each role, player 1 or player 2, with fifteen distinct counterparts. Three sessions were run for a total of $3 \times 8 = 24$ observational pairs. By playing in each role, subjects have an opportunity to better see and understand the hazards of play in the left branch of the tree. But instead of learning to avoid reciprocity, and the risk of defection, the frequency of left branch play increases to 58.6 percent (from the 43.3 percent observed above), while the conditional frequency of the cooperative outcome is observed to be 63.2 percent.

Consequently, the propensity for play in the reciprocity branch appears to be a deliberate, stable, and profitable strategy for over 40 percent of the population even under the unfavorable conditions of anonymity.

Earned Property Rights: Effect on Outcomes in Ultimatum and Dictator Games

Suppose you have acquired a specific right. You might have obtained it by accident, as if it were awarded by a flip of a coin, or you might have done something to earn it. Will such circumstances affect recognition of your right by others? Will it affect your willingness to take advantage of the right? Hoffman and Spitzer (1985) found it necessary to develop an answer to these questions as part of their seminal experimental study of Coase bargaining (Yandle 1998; Anderson 1998). According to Coase's argument, if two parties are capable of harming each other but can negotiate, they will strike an efficient bargain, whichever party (termed the "controller" in the experiment) has the legal right to inflict damage. The experimental results overwhelmingly confirm this prediction. The subjects, however, who are the controllers, always failed to extract the full individually rational share of the bargaining surplus as predicted by game theory. Thus, two bargainers negotiate face to face for sharing $14, with the controller having the right to collect $12 if an agreement is not reached. Both parties know this. With an external option of $12, the controller should never settle for less; i.e., the joint objective would be to negotiate a split of the $2 difference. Instead, the bargainers tend strongly to share the $14 equally, which has been interpreted as due to a "fairness" norm.

Hoffman and Spitzer (1985) hypothesized that subjects do not consider an asymmetric property right to be legitimate if it is awarded by a coin flip as in their experiments. Consequently, they replicated all their experiments with a new treatment: the right to be the controller was awarded to the subject who won a pregame of skill ("nim") before the bargaining experiment. More than two-thirds of the controllers now obtain at least $12, whereas under the random assignment none did.

That an earned property right is considered natural and legitimate has also been demonstrated by Hoffman et al. (1994) in their study of ultimatum game bargaining. In this game, two individuals, matched anonymously in a room with twelve people, bargain over the allocation of ten one-dollar bills between them, using the following rules: one person, selected by a process described below, is the proposer, who makes an offer of $x(0 \leq x \leq \$10)$ of the bills to the other person; the responder either accepts or rejects x. If it is rejected each person receives zero dollars; if it is accepted the responder will be paid $x and the proposer $(10 - x)$. The game theoretic solution is for the proposer to offer the minimum unit of account, $1, and for the responder to accept—accept because one dollar is better than nothing, and the proposer, seeing that this is the case, will not need to offer more. The experiment normally uses an instructional procedure in which the people in the room are randomly matched into pairs, and one person is randomly chosen to be the proposer. The instructions also inform each subject that $10 has been "provisionally allocated to each pair" and that their task is to "divide" the $10. In these circumstances, replicated by many researchers, the observed most frequent offer is x = $5 with a mean offer somewhat in excess of $4, a clear violation of the game theoretic prediction. The explanation usually offered for this tendency toward an equal split of the $10 is "fairness" although it is not clear how this can be an explanation since "fairness" is a name for the equal splitting that is observed (Kahneman, Knetsch, and Thaler 1986). It seems strange to think that one has "explained" an observation by giving it a transparent name. The real question is, "Why are people fair?" Equal splitting has also been explained as due to "manners," but why is it considered mannerly; i.e., where do such manners come from? (Camerer and Thaler 1995). A more generous interpretation of "fairness" is that it is utilitarian; as implied by the earlier quotation from *The Theory of Moral Sentiments*, the proposer gets pleasure from giving the respondent a sizable share of the money. But even here we can ask why humans might be constituted to derive such pleasures; i.e., what are the evolutionary functions served by such a constitution?

I and my coauthors report ultimatum game results that question the "utility for other" interpretation. Taking our cue from Hoffman and Spitzer (1985), we conjectured that part of the observed generosity of proposers was the fact that their property right was both ambiguous and "illegitimate." Ambiguous because the standard instructions state that the $10 has been "provisionally allocated to each pair." Also, the right to be the proposer is acquired by chance, and the task is to "divide $10," which suggests sharing. In these circumstances the proposer's right to act in a self-interested manner may not be recognized as legitimate within the implicit rules of the game, and the proposer may not feel justified in taking advantage of the right. These considerations suggest that context-dependent expectations, that derive directly from "mind reading," not utility for another's reward, may be involved in the outcome.

Reported below are ultimatum game experiments, using anonymous pairing of subjects, under three treatment conditions. To control for the effect of experience N = 30 distinct subject pairs participated under each treatment; each pair participated once and only once in one of the treatments.

(1) *Random entitlement; divide $10.* In this treatment we replicated the instructional procedures used previously (Kahneman, Knetsch, and Thaler 1986; Forsythe et al., 1994). The results were statistically equivalent to those reported by Forsythe et al.

(2) *Earned property right entitlement; divide $10.* The instructional procedures are like those in (1) except a general knowledge test consisting of ten questions is administered. The twelve subjects in the room are then ordered by test score from highest to lowest (ties are broken in favor of those finishing earlier). The top six are paired with the bottom six, and the former are assigned the role of proposers. All are told that the former as a group have *earned* the right to be proposers.

(3) *Property right entitlement; exchange.* The transaction is now formulated as an exchange between a seller (proposer) and a buyer (responder) in which the seller chooses a price, x = 0, 1, 2, . . . 10 dollars. As in (2) the pregame test determines who is a seller and who is a buyer. The buyer can then either buy or not buy. If he buys, the buyer's profit is $(10 − x) and the seller's profit is x. If he does not buy, each gets zero profit. Hence, the game is identical to one in which a proposer offers 10 − x to the responder. But the setting is that of an exchange. In this context, we hypothesized that the seller (proposer) would offer less than under treatment (2), because the right of sellers to move first and quote an advantageous price is considered to be a legitimate right in addition to its having been earned.

The results are shown in figure 3.3. The amounts offered on the horizontal axis, at each cumulative frequency level on the vertical axis, decrease as we move from the baseline replication (1) through (2), and (3). As predicted, offers are less generous under the earned property right entitlement conditions than in the random entitlement, divide $10 baseline; and when the earned property right is combined with ex-

Figure 3.3
Ultimatum Game Results

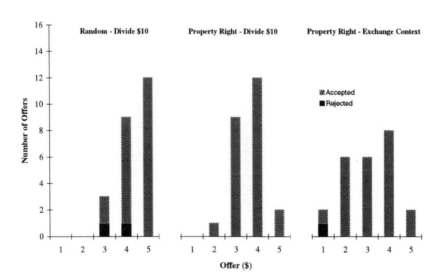

change, offers are still less generous. Also of particular interest is the fact that the overall percentage of rejected offers does not increase significantly as we move from (1) to the other treatments. This is consistent with the hypothesis that proposers expect to offer less with no increase in the probability of rejection, and that this is compatible with responder expectations. Each correctly "reads" the mind of the other.

In terms of the theme in this chapter both proposers and responders in ultimatum games take account of the conditions under which rights to act have been conveyed. In particular a person with a legitimate right believes he/she can use that right in a more self-regarding manner than when the right is ambiguous, ill-defined, or illegitimate, and others (responders in this case) agree with, or respect, these beliefs of the rights holder (Boudreaux and Meiners 1998).

Dictator Game

In the dictator game, the right of the responder to reject the proposer's offer is eliminated. Now the offer yields the proposer $(10 - x) for certain and the equilibrium offer is zero. The dictator game was used by Forsythe et al. to test the hypothesis that fairness alone drove proposer generosity in the ultimatum game; i.e., if one offers x > 0 because of fairness then nullifying the strategic component—the prospect of rejection—should not alter the amounts offered. In fact dictator game offers are much lower than ultimatum game offers showing that, as noted by Forsythe et al., the self-interest is alive and well—proposers take into account the strategic prospect that their offer may be rejected. But dictators still give substantial positive amounts (in Forsythe et al., 80 percent of the dictators give $1 or more, and their distribution of offers is statistically replicated by Hoffman, McCabe, and Smith 1996, 654).

We summarize two of the dictator game treatments reported by Hoffman et al. (1994):

(1') *Random entitlement; divide $10.* This is the same as (1) above except that the responder cannot veto the proposer's offer.
(2') *Double blind condition.* Dictators and recipients are recruited to separate rooms: fifteen in room A and fourteen in room B. The dictators are in room A, and one subject is chosen to monitor the experiment. This assures the subjects that one of them will verify that there exists a room B with fourteen recipients. Common instructions are read in both rooms. Fourteen opaque, unmarked envelopes are in a box in room A; twelve contain ten one-dollar bills and ten blank sheets of paper cut to the size of a

dollar bill; two contain twenty blank sheets of paper. Hence, all are the same thickness. Each subject, in order, chooses an envelope, goes to the back of the room and sits down in front of a large privacy box, leans inside the box, opens the envelope, and pockets ten pieces of money and paper in any combination from zero to ten pieces of money (or paper), reseals the envelope, drops it in a second box, leaves the room and the building. When all have finished, the monitor takes the box of envelopes to room B, sits outside, and calls the roster of names, one at a time from room B. Each person opens the envelope, and the monitor records the number of one-dollar bills it contains on a plain white sheet of paper containing no names.

Consequently in (2), no one, including the experimenter, the monitor, nor any one who subsequently sees the data, can know how much money each person in room A left in the envelope. The two dummy envelopes with no money still guarantee this condition even if no subject in room A leaves any money in the envelope. Giving is thus blind with respect to all but the giver. In all other dictator (and ultimatum) game experiments, the experimenter knew each decision for purposes of making payments. The double blind conditions remove all social context in the sense of providing complete privacy.

The results are charted in figure 3.4. The double blind treatment dra-

Figure 3.4
Dictator Game Results

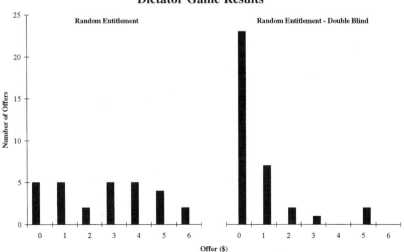

matically lowers the offer distribution relative to the standard reported
dictator game experiments Now 64 percent give nothing, while 84 percent give 0 or $1. In random entitlement/divide $10, 18 percent give
nothing, while 36 percent give 0 or $1.

This supports the claim of those who argue for "the social function
of intellect" (Humphrey 1976b). It is consciousness that enables mind
reading, reciprocity, and all social interaction to be intuitively meaningful. Other-regardingness comes from the requirements of, and the need
for, social exchange. Take away all social context—no others can
know—and we see the maximal expression of purely self-regarding behavior.

Conclusion

The puzzle that humans are simultaneously other-regarding and self-
regarding, that they are relentless in seeking gains from exchange, and
that the apparent inconsistency in the two faces of Adam Smith—
sentimental and competitive behavior—is resolved (I claim) by making
the distinction between personal and impersonal exchange. Smith,
being an astute observer, could see that exchange was a positive sum
game leading to specialization and wealth creation limited only by the
extent of the market. He also saw that humans were capable of kindness
and compassion in their ordinary daily interactions, a contrary observation that he could not just leave unattended with the statement of how
it is that we get our dinner from the butcher, baker, and brewer. But
this beneficence he attributed to design by the great director of nature,
Providence, the judge of hearts, and so on. It is not clearly connected
in Smith's thinking with the informal social exchange of favors and
goods, from which markets ultimately appear to have arisen. Smith's
explanation of beneficence was utilitarian—the ultimate conversation
stopper—not expectational through exchange across time (positive reciprocity), as implied by the statement that man is interested in the fortune and happiness of others, "though he derives nothing from it except
the pleasure of seeing it"—pleasure indeed, I would argue, from the
expectation of reciprocal benefits. Try *never* returning like benefits to a
friend, and see how long your friendship will run on her other-regarding
utility! Friends don't do that to friends. But to the Scotch moral philoso-
pher it was just too much to see in gifts, the hidden benefits of gifts in
return. Smith never asked why, outside of Divine design, otherwise
selfish humans derived nothing from beneficence to others "except the
pleasure of seeing it."

Besides the theorem on specialization and markets, Smith's other incredible insight was that every individual in making the annual revenue of society as great as he can "neither intends to promote the public interest, nor knows how much he is promoting it." This is because the behavioral processes underlying the theorem operate subconsciously "like an invisible hand" on the economic agent who consciously seeks only his own gain. This is also half the equation that helps us to see why this same agent is prone to *distrust the market and interfere with it*. After all, "By pursuing his own interest he frequently promotes that of the society more effectively than when he really intends to promote it" (Smith [1776] 1909, 351).

Here is the other half of that equation: we are able to appreciate, or at least can come more easily to understand and become consciously aware of, the benefits of social exchange. Intuitive, innate, or subconscious as is our reciprocity in friendships and the polite initial treatment of strangers (whom our friend-or-foe detector does not sense as a "foe"), people easily believe—in spite of Smith's warning—that doing good accomplishes good *because that is our experience in friendships*. By this reading we are led to qualify slightly the conclusion of Viner who endeavored "to show that the *Wealth of Nations* was a better book because of its partial breach with the *Theory of Moral Sentiments*, and that it could not have remained, as it has, a living book were it not that in its methods of analysis, its basic assumptions, and its conclusions it abandoned the absolution, the rigidity, the romanticism which characterize the earlier book" (Viner 1991b, 88).

It is true that Smith failed to put the two books together into a single coherent system of thought. This made him vulnerable to Viner's criticism. But careful observer that Smith was, he was right to insist that the earlier book was concerned with important features of the human condition that should not be ignored. From the perspective of contemporary data and insights, I think we can now see the faint outlines of a single system based on the "propensity to truck, barter, and exchange" interpreted more broadly than seems to have been intended by Smith.

This single system, I have argued, served to underpin the implicit development of property rights by early humans. This is because social exchange within tribal extended families cannot be viable without mutual recognition of rights to act. If A gives help, favors, food, or objects to B, B must recognize his own obligation to fulfill A's right to something in return, somewhere, sometime, if the relationship is to be maintained. This is the foundation of human social behavior, of bilateral associations, friendships in particular, and friendship in general. But social exchange requires not only positive reciprocity—trading favors—but also negative reciprocity, the endogenous policeman whereby failures to reciprocate are punished with unkind acts in which

A reminds B of his or her obligations. Without negative reciprocity, reciprocating altruists invite invasion by free riders.

As humans we are born social exchangers, much as we are born to learn naturally, without being taught, any language we hear spoken around us, which language becomes the communication basis of social exchange. In this sense the property rights that support these spontaneous exchange systems are natural, and it is natural for formalized societies to embody such rights in legal codes that mirror the vast human experience captured in exchange practices.

Notes

1. In addition to the references in the text below, the reader is referred to my earlier economic anthropology papers (Smith 1975 and 1993); and for the experimental economics and evolutionary psychology perspective, see Hoffman, McCabe, and Smith (1996 and 1997) and Smith (1996).

2. Although *The Theory of Moral Sentiments* was Smith's first book, it was extensively and importantly revised and republished only a few weeks in advance of his death (Viner 1991a, 249). In this sense it represented his later, mature, thinking.

3. For a review, also see Squire and Knowlton (1996).

4. See discussion and references by Louis De Alessi, this volume.

5. That all dogs descend from the wolf has long been consistent with the fact that the earliest evidence of domesticated canines comes from Europe. Although all feral species of the genus *Canis* can interbreed, this seemed to rule out the jackal, whose range is limited to Africa, and the coyote, a new world canine. Very recently the study of mitochondrial DNA sequences documents the wolf origins of the dog and the likelihood that there were several independent lines of descent from the wolf suggesting repeated genetic exchange between dogs and wolves (Vilà et al. 1997).

References

Anderson, Terry L. 1998. Viewing Wildlife through Coase-Colored Glasses, this volume.

Baron-Cohen, Simon. 1995. *Mindblindness.* Cambridge: MIT Press.

Boas, Franz. 1897. The Social Organization and the Secret Societies of the Kwakuit Indians. In *Report of the U.S. National Museum for 1895.* Washington, D.C.

Boudreaux, Donald J., and Roger E. Meiners. 1998. Existence Value and Other of Life's Ills, this volume.

Camerer, Colin, and Richard Thaler. 1995. Ultimatum and Dictator Games. *Journal of Economic Perspectives* 9: 239–40.

Cosmides, Leda. 1989. The Logic of Social Exchange: Has Natural Selection Shaped How Humans Reason? Studies with the Wason Selection Task. *Cognition* 31: 187–276.

Dalton, George. 1977. Aboriginal Economies in Stateless Societies: Interaction Spheres. In *Exchange Systems in Pre-history*, ed. J. Erickson and T. Earle. New York: Academic Press.

De Alessi, Louis. 1998. Private Property Rights as the Basis for Free Market Environmentalism, this volume.

de Waal, Frans. 1989. *Chimpanzee Politics*. New York: Harper and Row.

———. 1996. *Good Natured*. Cambridge: Harvard University Press.

Diamond, Jared. 1992. *The Third Chimpanzee*. New York: Harper Collins.

Forsythe, Robert, Joel Horovitz, N. Savin, and Martin Sefton. 1994. Replicability, Fairness and Pay in Experiments with Simple Bargaining Games. *Games and Economic Behavior* 6: 347–69.

Freuchen, Peter. 1961. *Book of the Eskimos*. Cleveland: World Publishing.

Gazzaniga, Michael. 1992. *Nature's Mind*. New York: Basic Books.

Greenfield, P. M. 1991. Language, Tools, and Brain: The Ontogeny and Phylogeny of Hierarchically Organized Sequential Behavior. *Behavioral and Brain Sciences* 14: 531–95.

Hawkes, Kristin. 1990. Showing Off: Tests of an Hypothesis about Men's Foraging Goals. *Ethnology and Evolutionary Biology* 12: 29–54.

Hoffman, Elizabeth, Kevin McCabe, Keith Shachat, and Vernon Smith. 1994. Preferences, Property Rights and Anonymity in Bargaining Games. *Games and Economic Behavior* 7: 346–80.

Hoffman, Elizabeth, Kevin McCabe, and Vernon Smith. 1996. Social Distance and Other-Regarding Behavior in Dictator Games. *American Economic Review* 86: 653–60.

———. 1997. Behavioral Foundations of Reciprocity: Experimental Economics and Evolutionary Psychology. Economic Science Laboratory, University of Arizona, January. Forthcoming in *Economic Inquiry*.

Hoffman, Elizabeth, and Matthew Spitzer. 1985. Entitlements, Rights and Fairness: An Experimental Examination of Subjects' Concepts of Distributive Justice. *Journal of Legal Studies* 14: 259–97.

Humphrey, Nicholas. 1976a. *Consciousness Regained*. Oxford: Oxford University Press.

———. 1976b. The Social Function of Intellect. In *Growing Points in Ethology*, ed. P. Bateson and R. Hinde. Cambridge: Cambridge University Press, 303–17.

Kahneman, Daniel, Jack Knetsch, and Richard Thaler. 1986. Fairness and the Assumptions of Economics. *Journal of Business* 59 (pt. 2): 5285–300.

Kaplin, Hillary, and Kim Hill. 1985. Food Sharing among Ache Foragers: Test of Explanatory Hypotheses. *Current Anthropology* 26: 223–46.

Klein, Richard G. 1989. *The Human Career*. Chicago: University of Chicago Press.

Knowlton, B., J. Mangels, and L. Squire. 1996. A Neostriatal Habit Learning System in Humans. *Science* 273: 1399–402.

Lee, Richard. 1968a. Eating Christmas in the Kalahari. *Natural History*, December.

———. 1968b. What Hunters Do for a Living, or How to Make Out on Scarce Resources. In *Man the Hunter*, ed. R. Lee and I. DeVore. Chicago: Aldine, 30–48.

McCabe, Kevin, Stephen Rassenti, and Vernon Smith. 1996. Game Theory and Reciprocity in Some Extensive Form Bargaining Games. *Proceedings National Academy of Science* 93: 113421–28.

Mealy, Linda. 1995. The Sociobiology of Sociopathy: An Integrated Evolutionary Model. *Behavioral and Brain Sciences* 18: 523–99.

Mithen, Steven. 1996. *Prehistory of the Mind*. London: Thames and Hudson.

Pinker, Steven. 1994. *The Language Instinct*. New York: William Morrow and Co.

Rice, William R. 1996. Sexually Antagonistic Male Adaptation Triggered by Experimental Arrest of Female Evolution. *Nature* 381: 232–34.

Sacks, Oliver. 1993–94. A Neurologist's Notebook: An Anthropologist on Mars. *New Yorker*, December 27 and January 3.

Scott, John P., and John L. Fuller. 1965. *Genetics and the Social Behavior of the Dog*. Chicago: University of Chicago Press.

Semaw, S., P. Renna, J. W. K. Harris, C. S. Feibel, R. L. Bernor, N. Fesseha, and K. Mowbray. 1997. 2.5 Million-Year-Old Stone Tools from Gona, Ethiopia. *Nature* 385: 333–36.

Smith, Adam. (1759) 1976. The Theory of Moral Sentiments. Reprinted in *Liberty Classics*, ed. D. D. Raphael and A. L. Mactie. Indianapolis: Liberty Press.

———. [1776] 1909. Wealth of Nations. Reprinted in *Harvard Classics*, vol. 10, ed. C. J. Bullock. New York: P. F. Collier.

Smith, Vernon L. 1975. The Primitive Hunter Culture, Pleistocene Extinction and the Rise of Agriculture. *Journal of Political Economy* 83: 727–55.

———. 1993. Humankind in Prehistory: Economy, Ecology, and Institutions. In *The Political Economy of Customs and Culture*, ed. Terry L. Anderson and Randy T. Simmons. Lanham, MD: Rowman & Littlefield, 157–84.

———. 1996. Puzzle Solving: Reciprocity, Reasoning and Behavior. In *Foundations of Research in Economics: How Do Economists Do Economics?* ed. Steven Medema and Warren Samuels. Cheltenham, UK: Elgar, 216–26.

Squire, L., and B. Knowlton. 1996. Memory, Hippocampus, and Brain Systems. In *The Cognitive Neurosciences*, ed. Michael Gazzaniga. Cambridge: MIT Press, 625–837.

Thieme, H. 1997. Lower Paleolithic Hunting Spears from Germany. *Nature* 385: 807–10.

Thurber, James. 1943. *Men, Women, and Dogs*. New York: Dodd, Mead, and Co.

Trivers, R. L. 1971. The Evolution of Reciprocal Altruism. *Quarterly Journal of Biology* 46: 35–57.

Vilà, Carles, P. Savalainen, J. Maldonado, I. Amorim, J. Rice, R. Honeycutt, K. Crandall, J. Lundeberg, and R. Wayne. 1997. Multiple and Ancient Origins of the Domestic Dog. *Science* 276: 1687–89.

Viner, Jacob. 1991a. Adam Smith. In *Essays on the Intellectual History of Economics*, ed. Douglas A. Irvin. Princeton: Princeton University Press, 248–61.
———. 1991b. Adam Smith and Laissez Faire. In *Essays on the Intellectual History of Economics*, ed. Douglas A. Irvin. Princeton: Princeton University Press, 85–113.
Yandle, Bruce. 1998. Coase, Pigou, and Environmental Rights, this volume.

Chapter 4

The Common Law and the Environment: The Canadian Experience

Elizabeth Brubaker

When the Canadian government proposed entrenching property rights in the Constitution in 1991, the mainstream environmental community expressed virtually unanimous opposition. Career environmentalists objected that stronger rights would weaken government's authority to legislate and would shift undue power to the judiciary. Further, they asserted that property rights would confer a right to pollute. Such concerns betrayed an ignorance of government's role in environmental degradation and a profound misunderstanding of legal history. For centuries, property rights have empowered people to protect the environment. More often than not, it has been the legislated erosion of property rights that has allowed industries to pollute.

This chapter reviews the ancient roots of contemporary property rights and traces their evolution, influenced by English and American legal decisions, in Canada. It describes the ways in which concerned citizens have used their property rights to clean up and to prevent pollution. It then chronicles successive governments' efforts to replace the common law with statutes and regulations governing the environment. Lastly, it recommends restoring strong property rights in order to return control over environmental degradation to those most directly affected by it.

This chapter draws from my book, *Property Rights in the Defence of Nature* (London and Toronto: Earthscan Publications Ltd., 1995). Copyright © 1995 by Elizabeth Brubaker.

Common Law Property Rights

In all Canadian provinces except Quebec, property rights come from the English common law—the unwritten or customary law that from medieval times has governed the rights and responsibilities of property owners. England passed the common law down to her colonies, including Canada. Both federal and provincial governments have often overridden it with their own statutes and regulations. Where they have not done so, however, the common law continues to apply.

The common law is court-made law. Judges, rather than politicians, created and refined it. In the Middle Ages, local custom often determined a judge's decision. As decisions were recorded and made available to other judges, legal custom began to replace local custom. Judges followed previous decisions, or precedents, thus entrenching a number of legal principles.

Until 1949, Canadian courts hearing property disputes were legally obligated to follow the laws as revealed by English courts. Although Canadian courts have since gained independence from their British counterparts, they often continue to look to English precedents when deciding cases. American judicial decisions have also, although to a lesser degree, influenced Canadian courts. Loyalists settling in Upper Canada, bringing with them an understanding of American law, may have influenced the early Canadian legal system (Flaherty 1981, 22, 26). Of greater influence was the similarity of the legal challenges facing the two countries. Canadian judges could look to American cases without violating their obligation to follow English precedent if no English cases applied to the situation at hand (Risk 1981, 108).

Because both English and American cases helped form Canadian property law and continue to influence its development, this chapter discusses cases from all three countries. While different in certain respects, American common law is very similar to Canadian common law; the legal history of the countries, and their moves favoring regulation, are much the same (see Yandle 1997).

Under the common law, people have very strong property rights: They have the right to both use and enjoy their property. Balancing this right, however, is a responsibility not to interfere with others' rights to use and enjoy their property. This responsibility dates back to the English law of the mid-thirteenth century. Henry of Bracton, a judge and prominent legal scholar of that era, wrote that "no one may do in his own estate any thing whereby damage or nuisance may happen to his neighbor." Bracton, whose writings provided a foundation for later nuisance law, noted that a landowner could not, in raising a pond, flood his neighbor's land; nor could he divert a watercourse and deprive his neighbor of water (Lauer 1963, 65–68).

This principle became embodied in a maxim that has governed common law decisions since being coined by an English court in 1611: "Use your own property so as not to harm another's." Clearly, the maxim has profound environmental implications. It was one of the important legal concepts applied in seventeenth-century air pollution cases (Harvey 1990, 518). By the eighteenth century, the famous jurist William Blackstone cited the maxim as "the rule" in English law (Blackstone [1765–1769] 1876, 3:191). Nineteenth-century courts continued to accept the maxim as a given. One British law lord summarized the law as it stood in 1885:

> Prima facie no man has a right to use his own land in such a way as to be a nuisance to his neighbour, and whether the nuisance is effected by sending filth on to his neighbour's land, or by putting poisonous matter on his own land and allowing it to escape on his neighbour's land, or whether the nuisance is effected by poisoning the air which his neighbour breathes, or the water which he drinks, appears to me wholly immaterial.
>
> If a man chooses to put filth on his own land he must take care not to let it escape on to his neighbour's land. (*Ballard v. Tomlinson* 1885, 126)

The maxim also applied in Britain's North American colonies, where courts invoked it frequently.[1] Deeply ingrained in our legal history, it influences Canadian courts to this day.

If a victim of pollution convinces a court that, on the balance of probabilities, his property is being harmed by another's actions, the court will likely issue an injunction. It will order the defendant to refrain from acting in a particular way or, in some cases, require it to take specific action. At one time, certain courts had no choice but to issue injunctions. Not until 1858 did the British Parliament empower Chancery courts to award damages in lieu of injunctions. Ontario's 1877 Judicature Act gave Ontario courts the same power. The courts, however, remain hesitant to exercise their authority in this realm.

A number of factors have contributed to the courts' reluctance to substitute damages for injunctions. Judges have long understood that many injuries cannot be monetized. How, one law lord wondered, can someone prove the exact quantity of pecuniary loss he has sustained? What, for example, is the value of a business's lost customers (*Imperial Gas Light and Coke v. Samuel Broadbent* 1859, 243)? Only victims themselves can know what value they place on a good night's sleep or how much money they would be willing to accept for breathing foul air. When a judge or jury awards damages, however, the victims do not determine the amount. Substituting damages for an injunction therefore amounts to forcing the victim to sell his property rights at a price set by the court. It amounts, in short, to giving a defendant the power of expropriation.

In contrast, injunctions allow the victim to negotiate his own price. If his environment is priceless, he may insist that the polluter stop harming it. Alternatively, he may bargain away his rights or reach a compromise that benefits both him and the polluter. Whatever the result, the decision will be arrived at freely and fairly and will reflect the values and circumstances of both parties (Yandle 1998).

Furthermore, only injunctions can prevent the recurrence of property rights violations. In allowing damages to replace injunctions, courts in effect license continuing wrongs—a role they generally reject. A British judge warned in 1894 that the Court must not become "a tribunal for legalizing wrongful acts. . . . [T]he Court has always protested against the notion that it ought to allow a wrong to continue simply because the wrongdoer is able and willing to pay for the injury he may inflict." His colleague added that a court should substitute damages for an injunction only if the injunction would be oppressive and the injury was small and could be easily estimated and compensated by money (*Shelfer v. London Electric Lighting* and *Meux's Brewery v. London Electric Lighting* 1894, 311, 315–16, 322–23). With some important exceptions, the judges' successors have paid them heed. Injunctions remain the favored remedy in Canadian property rights cases, especially where trespass or a violation of riparian rights has occurred, and generally, but somewhat less categorically, in nuisance cases (Nedelsky 1981, 301–3; Sharpe 1983, 6, 180–201; Estrin and Swaigen 1993, 108–10). A discussion of each of these categories of property rights violations follows.

Trespass

Under the common law, it is a trespass to place anything upon someone else's property or to cause anything to be placed there by wind, water, or other means. A trespass occurs against the person in possession of the invaded land. If a tenant is in possession of the land at the time of the trespass, it is normally he rather than the owner who should sue (Hailsham 1985, 45:637, 639).

Any intrusion onto another's land—whether by people, floodwaters, structures, or pollutants—constitutes a trespass. The common law forbids even harmless trespasses. A 1765 decision, for example, noted that a person could be subject to an action for trespass, "though the damage be nothing," for merely "bruising the grass and even treading upon the soil" (*Entick v. Carrington* 1765, 1066). More than a century and a half later, a judge in Manitoba echoed that decision, explaining, "every invasion of private property, be it ever so minute, is a trespass" (*Boyle v. Rogers* 1921, 706). The common law remains unchanged on this point. In 1978, organic farmers won a trespass case against a company that sprayed their land with pesticides as part of the New Brunswick government's program to control spruce budworm in the province's forests. In finding that the spraying constituted a trespass, the judge explained the law as follows:

> To throw a foreign substance on the property of another, and particularly in doing so to disturb his enjoyment of his property, is an unlawful act. . . . This of course does not involve any question of whether or not the spray may have been toxic or nontoxic, because even to have thrown water, or garbage, or snow, or earth tippings, or any substance on the property would equally have amounted to an act of trespass. (*Friesen v. Forest Protection* 1978, 162)

In its early days, trespass law helped people combat the diverse environmental problems of an agrarian society, from straying livestock to seeping privies. An eighteenth-century judge explained the law's virtually physical character: "The law bounds every man's property, and is his fence" (*Star v. Rookesby* 1711, 295). More recently, people have adapted the law of trespass, using it to protect themselves or their land against more elusive encroachment by industry. The Alberta Supreme Court held in 1976 that fly ash and sawdust from a lumber company constituted a trespass against a nearby motel. In a decision that indicates that the common law could play a major role in controlling air pollution, the court explained that it is a trespass to cause any noxious substance to cross the boundary of another's land (*Kerr v. Revelstoke Building Materials* 1976, 137).

Trespass law has had to evolve to accommodate modern technologies. Courts have wrestled with the question of how far property rights extend above and below the land. A thirteenth-century maxim guided early common law cases: "A landowner owns everything from the sky to the depths." More recent cases have narrowed the scope of ownership and determined that airspace is public domain; air traffic far above the ground that is transient and does not directly interfere with the use of peoples' property does not constitute a trespass. As one judge noted, however, a low-flying aircraft might indeed commit a trespass (*Didow v. Alberta Power* 1988, 612). As a general rule, rights to airspace extend only as far as is necessary to protect the use and enjoyment of one's land and structures (Hailsham 1985, 45:632).

Another question facing the courts, as ancient trespass laws evolve to suit contemporary circumstances, is whether an invasion need be tangible to constitute a trespass, and if so, how to define tangibility. Traditionally, courts restrained only sensible, visible invasions—invasions by a tangible mass that could be seen by them in evidence. However, modern science, enabling courts to verify the presence of invisible pollutants, has vastly expanded potential applications of trespass laws. Some courts, relaxing traditional requirements, have found invisible gases and microscopic particulates to be trespasses. In the most frequently cited cases, the invisible trespasses have damaged property (*McDonald v. Associated Fuels* 1954; *Fairview Farms v. Reynolds Metals* 1959; *Martin v. Reynolds Metals* 1959, 1960). As noted above, however, traditional trespass law allows a landowner or tenant to sue whether or not he has suffered any harm. Conceivably, then, courts could define trespass to include any measurable invasion, any scientifically detectable emission, regardless of its effect.[2]

It is impossible to know what balance the courts will strike in their efforts to preserve common law principles while preventing scientific advances from pushing trespass law to unworkable extremes. At a minimum, trespass law remains a powerful tool for protecting oneself against visible encroachments. And where it fails as a remedy for environmental wrongs, nuisance law, which has traditionally dealt with less material infractions, may succeed.

Nuisance

Blackstone broadly defined nuisance as "anything done to the hurt or annoyance of the lands, tenements, or hereditaments of another" (Blackstone [1765–1769] 1876, 3:190). Two centuries later, where the common law still applies, an interference with the use or enjoyment of property remains a nuisance for which an owner or tenant can sue. Blackstone's definition, however, was overly inclusive: Stopping a nuisance, unlike a trespass, requires proof of harm. Furthermore, unlike trespass law, nuisance law does not deal with trivial matters. Courts are reluctant to address minor infractions necessarily resulting from everyday practices; they are guided by the notion that everyone benefits from relaxing standards to allow people to carry on common activities. An English judge explained in 1862:

> It is as much for the advantage of one owner as of another; for the very nuisance the one complains of, as the result of the ordinary use of his neighbour's land, he himself will create in the ordinary use of his own, and the reciprocal nuisances are of a comparatively trifling character. The

convenience of such a rule may be indicated by calling it a rule of give and take, live and let live. (*Bamford v. Turnley* 1862, 33)

Nuisance law nonetheless prohibits an infinite variety of environmental harms. People have used it to protect themselves from pesticide sprays, smoke, soot, steam, dust, fumes, and other air pollutants. Road salt has been successfully challenged under nuisance law, as have leaking oil tanks and seeping privies. Foul smells are often found to be nuisances, as are noise and vibrations from commercial and industrial operations. In the 1920s, one judge went so far as to say, "Pollution is always unlawful and, in itself, constitutes a nuisance" (*Groat v. Edmonton* 1928, 532).

Courts have also found less tangible interferences, as varied as aesthetic blight and the casting or obstruction of light, to be nuisances. People have invoked nuisance law to keep countless undesirable commercial operations, from gas stations to houses of prostitution, out of their neighborhoods (Ellickson 1973, 719, 721, 734). In 1910, the Supreme Court of Washington issued an injunction against a tuberculosis sanitarium that caused nearby residential properties to depreciate in value. According to the court, "The question is, not whether the fear [of tuberculosis] is founded in science, but whether it exists; nor whether it is imaginary, but whether it is real, in that it affects the movements and conduct of men. Such fears are actual, and must be recognized by the courts as other emotions of the human mind" (*Everett v. Paschall* 1910, 880).

Industry has long tried to defend its nuisances on the grounds that they are in the public interest. Manufacturers reiterate the number of people employed, and utilities cite the essential services provided. Although no longer always the case, courts have traditionally refused to consider such social factors. They have instead stressed the sanctity of minority rights and refused to condone activities, whatever their presumed value, that would override them. As Blackstone explained, "So great . . . is the regard of the law for private property that it will not authorize the least violation of it; no, not even for the general good of the whole community" (Blackstone [1765–1769] 1876, 1:109–10).

A famous nuisance case of the nineteenth century illustrates the law's refusal to accommodate public needs at the expense of individuals. The case concerned Birmingham, England, which in 1851 had built a large sewer that disgorged into the Tame River. The owner of a downstream estate sued, complaining that the resulting pollution aggravated disease, killed fish, and prevented cattle from drinking from the river and sheep from being washed in it. Birmingham did not deny that dumping sewage was highly offensive. It argued, however, that the Court should allow continued pollution in the name of the public good:

[T]he evil that must ensue if the Court should interfere would be incalculable . . . Birmingham will be converted into one vast cesspool. . . . The deluge of filth will cause a plague, which will not be confined to the 250,000 inhabitants of Birmingham, but will spread over the entire valley and become a national calamity. The increase of population, inseparable from the progress of a nation in industry and wealth, is attended of necessity by inconvenience to individuals against which it is in vain to struggle. In such cases private interests must bend to those of the country at large. (*Attorney-General v. Birmingham* 1858, 224)

The judge who heard the case dismissed the argument as an "extreme proposition . . . of remarkable novelty." He was not, he explained, a public safety committee; his function was simply to interpret the law and to define who has what rights. Once the plaintiff's right to enjoy a clean river was established, the court should grant an injunction, regardless of its consequences: "it is a matter of almost absolute indifference whether the decision will affect a population of 25,000, or a single individual carrying on a manufactory for his own benefit" (*Attorney-General v. Birmingham* 1858, 224, 225). The judge added that if an injunction would produce considerable injury, the court would, "by way of indulgence," give Birmingham an opportunity to stop its nuisance before restraining its activity. But if the city failed to stop the nuisance, it would be up to Parliament—rather than the court—to allow it to continue: "If, after all possible experiments, they cannot drain Birmingham without invading the Plaintiff's private rights, they must apply to Parliament for power to invade his rights" (*Attorney-General v. Birmingham* 1858, 225–26).

In the following century, the courts returned time and again to the themes that informed the Birmingham case: the sanctity of individuals' property rights and the inappropriateness of overriding them. The courts, it was said, should not weigh a nuisance's cost to an individual against the social costs of shutting down a polluting industry. They should simply determine where property rights lie and enforce them. Any balancing of interests should be done—if at all—by the legislature.

When an electric company protested in 1894 that restraining its steamy, noisy, vibrating generating station would leave London's streets and buildings in darkness, the court refused to sacrifice an individual's rights for the public's convenience: "Neither has the circumstance that the wrongdoer is in some sense a public benefactor (e.g., a gas or water company or a sewer authority) ever been considered a sufficient reason for refusing to protect by injunction an individual whose rights are being persistently infringed." Consideration of the public good, the court explained, would be better left to Parliament: "Courts of Justice are not like Parliament, which considers whether proposed works will be so beneficial to the public as to justify exceptional legislation, and the deprivation of people of their rights with or without compensation" (*Shelfer v. London Electric Lighting* and *Meux's Brewery v. London Electric Lighting* 1894, 316).

In an 1899 case regarding the effects of asphalt excavation on neighboring property, the British Privy Council granted a restraining injunction despite its possible impact on the community. It rejected the defense of the public good with the following comments: "It was said that digging for pitch was the common industry of La Brea, and that if an injunction were granted the industry would be stopped altogether. . . . Whatever the result may be, rights of property must be respected, even when they conflict, or seem to conflict, with the interests of the community." Any overriding of property rights, the court explained, would be up to the government rather than the court: "If private property is to be sacrificed for the benefit of the public, it must be done under the sanction of the Legislature" (*Trinidad Asphalt v. Ambard* 1899, 602–3).

Over the years, Canadian courts have occasionally strayed from this reasoning, ruling that the public good—in the guise of industrial development, economic growth, job creation, or other community benefits—required them to override the property rights of individuals. Fortunately, such decisions have been exceptions to the rules. The Ontario High Court noted in 1984 that "the defence of 'general benefit of the community' . . . is not available in answer to a claim for nuisance. There has been consistent rejection of that notion by the highest Canadian courts" (*Buysse v. Town of Shelburne* 1984, 740). Five years later a Canadian Supreme Court judge confirmed the courts' reluctance to override common law property rights. "The courts," he said, "strain against a conclusion that private rights are intended to be sacrificed for the common good" (*Tock v. St. John's Metropolitan Area Board* 1989, 651).

Polluting industries also frequently try to defend themselves by claiming that their actions are reasonable. The "defense of reasonable use" seems to mean something different to every polluter. It can mean that the disputed activity is ordinary and lawful, or, given the location, appropriate. It can mean that a business has taken great care and caution, having installed the most modern machinery available and having operated it responsibly. Or it can be industry's way of urging the courts to balance competing interests and find reasonable compromises among them. Although contemporary courts occasionally heed the defense, they have traditionally refused to consider whether a disputed activity is reasonable.

A 1915 case in which a Toronto resident claimed that a blacksmith's operation in his neighborhood constituted a nuisance exemplifies the courts' reluctance to consider the reasonableness of an activity. The fact that the smith did his work "in a usual and reasonable fashion" did not influence the trial judge: "If the defendant has caused a nuisance to the plaintiff, it is of course no defence to say that he is making a reasonable use of his premises in the carrying on of a lawful occupation." On appeal, a higher court judge agreed. "It is," he said, "of no importance" (*Beamish v. Glenn* 1916, 13, 18).

The defense of reasonable use again failed in a 1952 nuisance case against a foundry in Ontario whose emissions damaged the finish on cars in a nearby lot. Citing an authoritative legal text, the judge explained, "He who causes a nuisance cannot avail himself of the defence that he is merely making a reasonable use of his own property. No use of property is reasonable which causes substantial discomfort to others or is a source of damage to their property" (*Russell Transport v. Ontario Malleable Iron* 1952, 728).

The issue also arose in a 1990 nuisance suit against an Ontario steel products company. The steel company had argued that its operations were reasonable in its particular neighborhood. The judge responded that other industrial activity in the mixed use neighborhood could not justify the nuisance, which would offend the typical resident: " 'Unreasonableness' in nuisance law is when the interference in question would not be tolerated by the ordinary occupier." To support his opinion, the judge relied on, among other sources, a respected law text: "It is not enough to ask: Is the defendant using his property in what would be a reasonable manner if he had no neighbour? The question is, Is he using it reasonably, having regard to the fact that he has a neighbour?" (*340909 Ontario Ltd. v. Huron Steel Products* 1990, 645, 644).

Courts have also rejected two other defenses that industries have put forward time and again: that either their responsibility for small fractions of greater environmental problems or their operations' long histories justify continued pollution. The existence of numerous sources of pollution has not prevented courts from ruling against one particular source. An early example can be found in a 1851 English case regarding a brickmaker's pollution. The defendant tried without success to excuse his brick burning on the grounds that others also polluted the local air. But, the judge responded, the plaintiffs had not objected to these more remote operations. And even if they were nuisances, they would "not form a reason why the defendant should set up an additional nuisance.

There is no ground, I think, for inferring a licence to him" (*Walter v. Selfe* 1851, 435).

Almost one hundred years later, when a foundry in Ontario tried to defend itself against a florist's nuisance suit on the grounds that other industries contributed to the offending pollution, the court would not be moved. Other pollution, the chief judge explained, is no defense:

> even if others are in some degree polluting the air, that is no defence if the defendant contributes to the pollution so that the plaintiff is materially injured. It is no defence even if the act of the defendant would not amount to a nuisance were it not for others acting independently of it doing the same thing at the same time. (*Walker v. McKinnon Industries* 1949, 767)

In Canada, nuisances can be stopped even when they predate the people complaining of them. For example, in an 1896 case concerning a stable in a residential neighborhood of Montreal, the defendant objected that since the plaintiff had acquired the neighboring property after the stable's construction, he had no right to complain. The court dismissed this argument: "This circumstance as to the date of the respondent's acquisition of title can make no difference in his rights to object to the nuisance" (*Drysdale v. C. A. Dugas* 1896, 25).[3]

Even a long-established operation may lose its right to pollute if a new neighbor complains about it. Although the Ontario Malleable Iron Company had been doing business since 1907, and its predecessors had operated a foundry on the property since 1876, a court restrained its harmful emissions in 1952. The chief justice refused to consider that the plaintiff company had chosen to locate beside the foundry. He noted that only after two years in business had it become aware of the damage. And regardless, he added, citing a well-known legal commentary, "It is no defence that the plaintiffs themselves came to the nuisance." On this subject the chief justice also cited a much earlier decision: "whether the man went to the nuisance or the nuisance came to the man, the rights are the same" (*Russell Transport v. Ontario Malleable Iron* 1952, 728, 729).

Riparian Rights

From nuisance law has evolved a separate branch of the common law that riparians—people who own or occupy land beside lakes and rivers—can enlist to protect water. Under the common law, riparians have the right to the natural flow of water beside or through their property, unchanged in quantity or quality.[4] This simple provision has enabled farmers, mill owners, manufacturers, absentee landlords, fishermen, and titled aristocrats alike to protect themselves and the environment from water diversions or abstractions and from a host of pollutants including coal mine discharges, pulp and paper mill wastes, sanitary sewage, storm-water runoff, salt, and oil.

During the second half of the nineteenth century and the first half of the twentieth century, riparian rights played a crucial role in preserving and restoring lakes and rivers throughout much of Britain and North America. Riparian law remains a powerful force in Great Britain. There, the Anglers' Conservation (formerly Cooperative) Association fights water pollution by defending the property rights of riparians and fishermen in county courts. The association has brought some 2,000 actions since its founding in 1948; it has lost only two (Bate 1993, 52–54; Bate 1994, 14).

In Canada's western provinces, where riparian law would have impeded mining and irrigation, statutes have governed water allocation since the late nineteenth century, although riparians may retain rights to clean water (Harvey 1990, 523). Even in Atlantic Canada and Ontario, where riparian rights theoretically remain in place, provincial governments have in recent decades overridden essential elements of riparian rights with statutes and regulations governing water (Percy 1988, 72; Lucas 1990, 20). Furthermore, for various reasons including the financial risks entailed in court cases and the courts' possible reluctance to frustrate industry, Canadians now rarely enforce even those riparian rights that haven't been overridden by statutes (Sharpe 1983, 197–98; Canadian Environmental Law Research Foundation 1986, 112; Percy 1988, 75). Where they continue to exist and are enforced, however, riparian rights remain powerful tools for environmental protection.

Under the common law, riparians may use an unlimited amount of water for "ordinary" purposes, which traditionally included only domestic and subsistence agricultural activities. More recently, courts have stretched the meaning of ordinary to encompass waterpower, provided that the power is used on the riparian land, or even, in some industrial areas, manufacturing (Campbell et al. 1974, 481; McNeil and Macklem 1992, 2). In most jurisdictions, riparians may use additional water for certain reasonable "extraordinary" purposes, such as irrigation or manufacturing, connected with their property. Courts have debated the reasonableness of various activities, with one of the strictest definitions of unreasonable being "any user which inflicts positive, repeated, and sensible injury upon a proprietor above or below" (*Ellis v. Clemens* 1891, 230). Reasonable or not, riparians do not have a right to divert water for use off their property.

A riparian's right to use water confers no right to abuse it. Extraordinary water users may not interfere with other riparians' property rights:

They must return the water to the watercourse substantially undiminished in quantity and quality. As early as 1858 the courts determined that a tanner in Lower Canada must not block the River Yamaska's flow to a downstream mill; they found that the tanner had the right to hold back water to propel his tannery's wheels and machinery—an extraordinary use—only if "he does not thereby interfere with the rights of other proprietors" (*Miner v. Gilmour* 1858, 870). Similarly, in deciding an 1893 case against a Scottish mining company, one British law lord noted, "I am not satisfied that a riparian owner is entitled to use water for secondary [i.e., extraordinary] purposes, except upon the condition that he shall return it to the stream practically undiminished in volume and with its natural qualities unimpaired" (*John Young v. Bankier Distillery* 1893, 696).

Riparian law is extraordinarily potent, prohibiting any noticeable change in the water's quality. In the Scottish case noted above, a distiller obtained an injunction preventing an upstream coal mine from discharging hard water into a stream; while still pure and drinkable, the stream was no longer fit for the manufacture of whiskey. Twenty years later, a New Brunswick court ruled against an iron company whose operations discolored the Nepisiquit River (*Nepisiquit Real Estate and Fishing v. Canadian Iron* 1913). More recently, at the behest of a fishing club and a local landowner, a British court restrained upstream industries whose thermal pollution killed fish (*Pride of Derby v. British Celanese* 1952).

Riparians can sue polluters to protect their rights even if they have suffered no evident harm; once interference with a riparian right is established, damage is presumed. In fact, riparians who can demonstrate that a proposed activity will likely violate their rights may act before water has been polluted or diverted. In 1970, a riparian living in northern Ontario demonstrated the law's prophylactic effect by going to court to prevent a speed boat regatta planned by the Rotary Club. She feared that sixty racing boats would contaminate the lake upon which she lived. The judge issued an order forbidding the races, explaining that the plaintiff's riparian rights entitled her "to the flow of water through or by her land in its natural state" (*Gauthier v. Naneff* 1970, 101). By polluting the lake—regardless of whether the pollution caused any harm—the planned races would violate her property rights. In such a case, said the judge, the court should grant an injunction as a matter of course.

Riparians' rights to water substantially undiminished in quality and quantity by other riparians exist whether or not they use the water, and whether or not its alteration interferes with any of their activities. That a Trinidadian landowner in one 1918 case put to no use whatsoever either the river flowing through his property or the property itself didn't prevent the court from recognizing his right to the natural flow of the river (*Stollmeyer v. Trinidad Lake Petroleum* 1918). The law thus enables riparians to prevent polluters from establishing the right to carry on long-standing activities (a "prescriptive" right) that might interfere with future water uses.

As with nuisance law, under riparian law existing water pollution does not justify further pollution. Courts have not cared that, because a dozen other industries polluted a river, restraining one would not restore the water's purity. If every polluter could defend himself on the ground of existing pollution, the reasoning goes, riparians could never repair the environment. The issue arose in an early twentieth century case against a New York salt manufacturer accused of depleting a creek's flow and contaminating it with salt. The company tried to defend itself on the grounds that a dozen other salt works also diminished and polluted the creek. The judge, however, found that others' contribution to the problem in no way lessened the defendant's obligation; if anything, it increased it:

> The fact that other salt manufacturers are doing the same thing as the defendant, instead of preventing relief, may require it. "Where there is a large number of persons mining on a small stream, if each should deteriorate the water a little, although the injury from the act of one might be small, the combined result of the acts of all might render the water utterly unfit for further use; and, if each could successfully defend an action on the ground that his act alone did not materially affect the water, the prior appropriator might be deprived of its use, and at the same time be without a remedy." (*Strobel v. Kerr Salt* 1900, 148)

Nor, under traditional riparian law, may polluters violate an individual's rights in order to promote a greater good, be it private or public. As with nuisances, courts long refused to consider the economic or social costs of prohibiting water abstraction, diversion, or pollution; they ruled against companies that had invested considerable capital in their works, those that employed hundreds of people, and those representing a region's leading—sometimes only—industries. Likewise, municipalities frequently failed to convince the courts to allow polluting sewage disposal systems in the name of the greater good. The courts, however, generally made one concession to the public interest: They delayed injunctions in order to give industrial and municipal polluters time to clean up.

American cases have provided some of the most interesting decisions about conflicts between individuals and the so-called public good. A case in 1900 against a paper mill in Indiana whose wastes polluted a creek illustrates the courts' traditional refusal to balance private economic factors when choosing a remedy. In issuing an injunction against further pollution, the Indiana court refused to weigh the paper mill's $90,000 construction costs against the plaintiffs' material damages, which amounted to just $250. The court noted that the creek's condition constituted a nuisance that caused damages "immeasurable by a pecuniary standard." In this context, the size of the company's investment was irrelevant:

> The fact that [the] appellant has expended a large sum of money in the construction of its plant, and that it conducts its business in a careful manner and without malice, can make no difference in its rights to the stream. Before locating the plant the owners were bound to know that every riparian proprietor is entitled to have the waters of the stream that washes his land come to it without obstruction, diversion, or corruption, subject only to the reasonable use of the water, by those similarly entitled, for such domestic purposes as are inseparable from and necessary for the free use of their land; and they were bound, also, to know the character of their proposed business, and to take notice of the size, course, and capacity of the stream, and to determine for themselves, and at their own peril, whether they should be able to conduct their business upon a stream of the size and character of Brandywine creek without injury to their neighbors; and the magnitude of their investment and their freedom from malice furnish no reason why they should escape the consequences of their own folly. (*Weston Paper v. Pope* 1900, 721)

A dozen years later, in a similar New York case, a judge who refused to consider the financial burdens an injunction would place upon a pulp mill explained, "It has always been the boast of equity that any substantial injustice might be corrected by it to even the humblest suitor, and that the financial size of such a suitor's antagonist was not important" (*Whalen v. Union Bag & Paper* 1911, 393). The New York high court later confirmed that balancing an injunction's great cost to the pulp mill against the plaintiff's relatively small injury would be unjustified: "Although the damage to the plaintiff may be slight as compared with the defendant's expense of abating the condition, that is not a good reason for refusing an injunction. Neither courts of equity nor law can be guided by such a rule, for if followed to its logical conclusion it would deprive the poor litigant of his little property by giving it to those already rich" (*Whalen v. Union Bag & Paper* 1913, 806).

Canadian courts have reached the same conclusions. In fact, the courts' refusal to consider an injunction's economic impact on a defendant remained so common that, according to the judge in the above-mentioned case against a proposed Rotary Club regatta, "It is trite law that economic necessities of the defendants are irrelevant in a case of this character" (*Gauthier v. Naneff* 1970, 103).

So, too, have courts refused to consider the *public* costs of their injunctions. In rejecting the public good as a justification for water pollution, judges have frequently soared to inspiring rhetorical heights. Behind the rhetoric have been some of the most powerful environmental protection decisions in common law history. In the New York salt case previously discussed, the manufacturer tried to defend its polluting ways in the name of the public good. Salt manufacturing, it averred, was the region's leading industry. The defendant alone employed more than one hundred men and women. To shut it down—to say nothing of the dozen other salt mines that might be subject to similar actions— would harm the public interest. But the Court of Appeals judge objected. Requiring the interest and convenience of the individual to give way to the general good, he warned, "would amount to a virtual confiscation of the property of small owners in the interest of a strong combination of capital" (*Strobel v. Kerr Salt* 1900, 145).

In defending individual rights against the interests of industry the judge cited an early coal mining decision:

> It was urged that the law should be adjusted to the exigencies of the great industrial interests of the commonwealth, and that the production of an indispensable mineral . . . should not be crippled and endangered by adopting a rule that would make colliers answerable in damages for corrupting a stream into which mine water would naturally run. . . . The consequences that would flow from the adoption of the doctrine contended for could be readily foretold. Relaxation of legal liabilities and remission of legal duties to meet the current needs of great business organizations, in one direction, would logically be followed by the same relaxation and remission, on the same grounds, in all other directions. One invasion of individual right would follow another, and it might be only a question of time when, under the operations of even a single colliery, a whole countryside would be depopulated. (*Strobel v. Kerr Salt* 1900, 146)

The judge acknowledged that a higher court had, in the name of the community interest in natural resource development, overturned this decision, but noted that "[c]ourts of the highest standing have refused to follow the Sanderson Case" and that "its doctrine was finally limited by the court which announced it" (*Strobel v. Kerr Salt* 1900, 147).

The judge then launched into his own passionate defense of individual rights:

> The lower riparian owners are entitled to a fair participation in the use of the water, and their rights cannot be cut down by the convenience or neces-

sity of the defendant's business. . . . While the courts will not overlook the needs of important manufacturing interests, nor hamper them for trifling causes, they will not permit substantial injury to neighboring property, with a small but long-established business, for the purpose of enabling a new and great industry to flourish. They will not change the law relating to the ownership and use of property in order to accommodate a great business enterprise. According to the old and familiar rule, every man must so use his own property as not to injure that of his neighbor; and the fact that he has invested much money and employs many men in carrying on a lawful and useful business upon his own land does not change the rule. (*Strobel v. Kerr Salt* 1900, 147–48)

Most Canadian courts continue to uphold the tradition of placing individual rights before the public good. When considering the above-mentioned bid to cancel the Rotary Club's speed boat regatta, the judge hearing the case refused to allow his respect for the Rotary Club's mission—to raise money for its work with crippled children—to influence his decision. "It is unfortunate," he said, "that in the circumstances of this case the rights of a riparian land proprietor come into conflict with the laudable objects of a charitable pursuit formulated and prosecuted with sincerity and dedication. . . . None the less, the most honourable of intentions alone at no time can justify the expropriation of common law rights of riparian owners" (*Gauthier v. Naneff* 1970, 103).

In the absence of a specific law to the contrary, even government itself cannot justify violating people's property rights to clean water in the name of the public good. As one judge explained at the end of the nineteenth century:

I know of no duty of the Court which it is more important to observe and no power of the Court which it is more important to enforce than its power of keeping public bodies within their rights. The moment public bodies exceed their rights, they do so to the injury and oppression of private individuals, and those persons are entitled to be protected from injury arising from the operations of public bodies. (*Roberts v. Gwyrfai District Council* 1899, 614–15)

Similarly, in his decision on a 1928 challenge to the storm sewage disposal practices of Edmonton, Alberta, a Supreme Court judge acknowledged that the city represented the collective rights of its ratepayers, who required sewers. "But these rights," he explained, "are necessarily restricted by correlative obligations. Although held by the municipalities for the benefit of all the inhabitants, they must not—except upon the basis of due compensation—be exercised by them to the prejudice of an individual ratepayer" (*Groat v. Edmonton* 1928, 533). The judge echoed the decision from an early sewage disposal case: "whatever the consequences, and much as the result may cause inconvenience, the principle must be upheld that, unless Parliament otherwise decrees, 'public works must be so executed as not to interfere with private rights of individuals' " (*Groat v. Edmonton* 1928, 534).

Riparian rights, protecting lakes and rivers from obstruction, diversion, and corruption, complete the trio of property rights most commonly used in the defense of nature. Together, trespass, nuisance, and riparian rights have effectively empowered people to preserve or restore clean land, air, and water—*too* effectively, apparently, for governments, which have worked assiduously to undermine property rights and the environmental protection they have fostered.

The Erosion of Common Law Property Rights

Governments and, to a lesser degree, courts have weakened common law property rights. Through statutes, regulations, and judgments, they have modified liability rules, eroding victims' rights to obtain injunctions against harmful activities and allowing pollution that the common law traditionally forbade.

The Defense of Statutory Authority

For centuries, governments have overridden or modified the common law with statutes and regulations. All too often, legislatures have made laws legalizing trespasses, nuisances, and violations of riparian rights, thereby indemnifying polluters from liability under the common law. As one judge explained, "The Legislature is supreme, and if it has enacted that a thing is lawful, such a thing cannot be a fault or an actionable wrong" (*Canadian Pacific Ry. v. Roy* 1901, 389). Governments have thus given polluters who are challenged in court a prized defense: the defense of statutory authority.

Courts, in determining whether governments have indeed indemnified particular activities, generally distinguish between permissive and mandatory statutes. Under the former, which maintain industries' discretion over operating methods and locations, industries are expected to act in conformity with private property rights and cannot claim the defense of statutory authority. For example, a company's obligation to maintain a highway cannot justify its use of damaging road salt when instead it could have used a harmless deicing agent. Similarly, the right to generate electricity does not authorize a company to create a nuisance; it must choose a generating method and location that will not interfere with others' property rights.

It is when the harm is an *inevitable* consequence of a legislatively authorized activity that a polluter can claim the defense of statutory authority. In mandating an activity or authorizing something to be done in a specific manner or location, the reasoning goes, the legislature sanctions all of its unavoidable consequences, including those that would have previously been forbidden. This is based on the principle of law that "he who grants something is deemed to also grant that without which the grant would be worthless."[5] Without legislative protection from liability, people would retain their right to challenge in court the inevitable results of statutorily authorized activities; legal actions could lead to injunctions against offending activities, thus thwarting the will of the legislature. Not surprisingly, legislators have written the laws— have set the rules governing the courts, in other words—so as to avoid that outcome.

Two judges of the Supreme Court of Canada have recently questioned the wisdom of the inevitability test, and with it the value of the defense of statutory authority. Chief Justice Dickson concurred with Justice La Forest that inevitability itself should not excuse exemption from tort liability. The fact that an operation will inevitably damage some individuals does not explain why those individuals should be responsible for paying for that damage. "Arguments about inevitability," the judges agreed, "are essentially arguments about money. . . . '[I]nevitable' damage is often nothing but a hidden cost of running a given system." Their conclusion? "The costs of damage that is an inevitable consequence of the provision of services that benefit the public at large should be borne equally by all those who profit from the service." The judges added that requiring the body that provides a service to bear the costs of its operations could serve as a valuable deterrent: "if the authority is to bear the costs of accidents . . . it may realize that it is more cost effective to forestal[l] their occurrence" (*Tock v. St. John's Metropolitan Area Board* 1989, 645, 646, 647, 648). Unfortunately, the judges do not seem to have succeeded in weakening the almost universal respect that the defense of statutory authority has enjoyed for more than two hundred years.

Although government-authorized nuisances are as old as the rights they violate, they long remained exceptions to the rule. Government-sanctioned property rights violations became more common in the late eighteenth century when American state legislatures passed a series of Mill Acts in order to promote their favored form of economic development. Designed to encourage the construction of mills and to protect mill owners from expensive lawsuits, they permitted the owners to flood neighboring lands. Although they provided for monetary compensation, they deprived victims of the rights to injunctions, punitive damages, or self-help actions that they would have otherwise enjoyed under the common law (Horwitz 1992, 47–51).

British acts of that era likewise protected certain ventures from common law liability. As early as 1792, the courts determined that the public interest warranted indemnifying some public works authorized by Parliament. As the chief justice explained in that year, without liability exemptions "every Turnpike Act, Paving Act, and Navigation Act would give rise to an infinity of actions. . . . Some individuals suffer an inconvenience under all these Acts of Parliament; but the interests of individuals must give way to the accommodation of the public" (*British Cast Plate Manufacturers v. Meredith* 1792, 1307).

Some of the most dramatic early illustrations of statutory authority can be found in the British, American, and Canadian laws protecting railway companies from common law liability. Railways, the first of which were chartered in Britain in the late 1820s, mushroomed in the following decades; the British Parliament authorized the construction of more than four hundred between 1844 and 1846. As steam locomotives became commonplace, their noise, vibration, and smoke, along with the danger of fires set by escaping sparks, became frequent problems. Lawsuits involving nuisances caused by trains were common. It rapidly became apparent, however, that the legislation authorizing the railways had overridden people's common law rights to stop such nuisances. Those harmed could not expect the courts to issue injunctions against the railway companies; in fact, unless the legislation so provided, they couldn't even count on being financially compensated for their losses.

Rex v. Pease, an 1832 English case in which users of a highway complained that the noisy, smoky locomotives on an adjacent railway line alarmed their horses and caused accidents, established the extent to which governments had immunized railway companies from liability for the damages they caused. The railway company defended itself on the grounds that Parliament, in authorizing its operations, undoubtedly took into consideration—and therefore tacitly authorized—the nuisances caused by steam locomotives. It likely did so, the company added, because locomotives served a public interest by facilitating the cheap transport of coal; the benefits of highway use, in short, should "be sacrificed to the greater public benefit derived from the undertaking" (*The King v. Edward Pease* 1832, 370). The court agreed that Parliament had, without qualification, authorized both the construction of the railroad parallel to the highway and the use of locomotives upon it. Although Parliament must have known that the railroad would inconvenience highway travelers, it had failed to impose any duty to screen the railway or to otherwise lessen its impacts. One could reasonably presume, therefore, that "the Legislature intended that the part of the public which should use the highway should sustain some inconvenience for the sake of the greater good to be obtained by other parts of the public in the more speedy travelling and conveyance of merchandise along the new railroad" (*The King v. Edward Pease* 1832, 371).

The courts confirmed the validity of the railroads' defense of statutory authority in *Vaughan v. Taff Vale Railway*, an 1860 case against a company whose sparking locomotive had set fire to a woods. The judges who heard that case agreed that they could not hold the company responsible for the fire. As one explained, "although the use of a locomotive engine must have been accounted a nuisance unless authorized by the legislature, yet, being so authorized, the use of it is lawful, and the defendants are not liable for an accident caused by such use without any negligence on their part" (*Vaughan v. Taff Vale Railway* 1860, 1355).

Four years later Horatio and Mary Brand filed a now-famous claim against the Hammersmith and City Railway Company, whose trains traveled the rails beside their property. The railroad's vibrations reduced the value of their house and gardens and ensured that they would command a reduced rent in the future. When the Brands requested compensation for their losses, the lower court ruled against them, explaining that Parliament, in expressly authorizing the use of locomotives, had overridden the common law and its protection of individuals' property rights. The statutes that replaced the common law did not stipulate that the companies must compensate for the effects of their operations. Requiring the railway company to compensate the Brands would therefore interfere with the power conferred upon it by the legislature.

The House of Lords upheld this decision after a spirited hearing at which some law lords argued that the Brands deserved compensation and others insisted that compensation was inappropriate since the legislature had not provided for it. Most agreed that in the absence of statutory authorization, the railway's vibrations would have constituted a nuisance that neighbors could have enjoined. No longer could the Brands sue for nuisance, however. As one justice explained:

if the Legislature authorizes the doing of an act (which if unauthorized would be a wrong and a cause of action) no action can be maintained for that act, on the plain ground that no Court can treat that as a wrong which the Legislature has authorized, and consequently the person who has sustained a loss by the doing of that act is without remedy, unless in so far as the Legislature has thought it proper to provide for compensation to him. (*Hammersmith and City Railway v. G. H. Brand* 1869, 196)

Rex v. Pease, he said, had decided the matter back in 1832; *Vaughan v. Taff Vale* had followed. Huge sums had been invested in railways on the strength of those decisions. And so, regardless of those original decisions' soundness, they ought to now be considered the law.

One law lord did point out the inequity of this reasoning. Mr. Baron Bramwell could not imagine that a company would be allowed to increase its profits by refusing to compensate the victims of its nuisances. Arguments about the necessity of creating nuisances, he protested, were really arguments about costs. For example, a railway company intent on preventing fires might station employees along its tracks to prevent sparks from igniting nearby grass. Since doing so would cost a considerable sum, the company would find it cheaper to simply risk starting fires. But there was no reason that the company—and ultimately the fare-paying passengers who benefitted from the system—should not bear those risks and costs:

> Admitting that the damage must be done for the public benefit, that is no reason why it should be uncompensated. It is to be remembered that that compensation comes from the public which gets the benefit. It comes directly from those who do the damage, but ultimately from the public in the fares they pay. If the fares will not pay for this damage, and a fair profit on the company's capital, the speculation is a losing one, as all the gain does not pay all the loss and leave a fair profit. Either, therefore, the railway ought not to be made, or the damage may well be paid for. (*Hammersmith and City Railway v. G. H. Brand* 1869, 191)

The law lord failed to persuade his colleagues or to modify the well-established thinking on the issue of statutory authority.

Hammersmith v. Brand was to be extensively cited over the years, including in a 1901 case brought against the Canadian Pacific Railway Company for a fire set by sparks from one of its locomotives. In that case, CPR acknowledged that under common law it would have been liable for damages caused by fires that its trains started. It argued, however, that in authorizing the use of locomotives, Parliament had also authorized the use of fire and the occasional accidental escape of sparks. It claimed that Parliament had, in other words, indemnified railroad companies against the anticipated and inevitable results of using locomotives. The Privy Council agreed. "[I]t would be a repugnant and absurd piece of legislation," the lord chancellor suggested, echoing *Hammersmith v. Brand*, "to authorize by statute a thing to be done, and at the same time leave it to be restrained by injunction from doing the very thing which the Legislature has expressly permitted to be done" (*Canadian Pacific Ry. v. Roy* 1901, 388).

Statutes authorizing property rights violations now abound. Their forms are legion. Often the statutes shield a single polluter or an entire industry by ordering courts to substitute damage awards for injunctions. Ontario's government started protecting favored polluters from injunctions in 1885 in response to a riparian's legal challenge to sawmills that deposited their wastes in the Ottawa River. Concerned that the lawsuit could shut down the polluting mills, the legislature passed a law ordering judges to weigh the lumber trade's economic importance against the plaintiff's injury before granting an injunction (McLaren 1984). In 1921, the Ontario government extended protection from injunctions to the copper and nickel mining and smelting industry, passing a law forbidding courts to hear cases about sulphur fumes. Instead, an arbitrator appointed by the government would award damages; in no circumstances would the arbitrator issue injunctions (Dewees and Halewood 1992). Three decades later, in response to a Supreme Court decision against a polluting pulp mill, the Ontario government decreed that the mill's downstream victims would have to be content with damage awards rather than an injunction. Five years later, again in response to a successful court case, the government likewise protected the operators of sewage treatment plants across the province.

By now, in Canada and in the United States, virtually no major polluter operates without some kind of statutory protection. Farmers benefit from laws that exempt them from liability for odors, noises, and dust that would, under the common law, constitute nuisances. The designers and manufacturers of nuclear power plants enjoy the protection of federal laws releasing them from any financial liability resulting from a nuclear accident—even if the accident is caused by their negligence or willful wrongdoing.

In case after case, regulations and standards governing emissions, odors, and noise levels have made it easier—and cheaper—for industries to pollute. Polluters have long understood that they benefit from regulation. As one industry advisor noted, "No industry offered the opportunity to be regulated should decline it. Few industries have done so" (Owen and Braeutigam 1978, 2). The legislative erosion of traditional common law property rights has provided enormous subsidies to polluting industries. Manufacturers have been allowed to use others' property for free, or at greatly reduced costs. The costs, of course, have not disappeared simply because polluters have not had to bear them. Instead, they have been externalized: The victims of pollution have been forced to underwrite the activities that harm them. This redistribution of costs is in effect a redistribution of wealth, typically from individuals to industry (Ellickson 1973, 694–99; Horwitz 1992, 70, 100–101).

While the erosion of property rights may have helped some industries to thrive, those industries have often been unviable, harming the economy as a whole as well as the environment. And they have often survived at the expense of more promising industries that have failed to secure special regulatory treatment. Furthermore, in relieving polluters from responsibility for the consequences of their actions, governments have removed a strong incentive for environmentally responsible behavior. Under a common law liability regime, it is in an industry's financial interest to avoid harming others. Otherwise, it may face injunctions or large damage awards. Experience in diverse fields confirms that strict liability increases incentives for responsible behavior. Stricter product liability laws in the United States have led to the improved safety of many products. Similarly, increased medical malpractice premiums have changed doctors' practices (Trebilcock and Winter 1993, 11).[6]

Conversely, immunizing people or industries from risk and responsibility decreases their level of care. After Quebec adopted a no-fault automobile insurance system in 1978, automobile fatalities rose; Australia's no-fault scheme similarly increased fatalities. Likewise, industries that, thanks to government regulation, do not bear the costs of environmental destruction are unlikely to invest adequately in systems that preserve clean air, land, and water (Trebilcock and Winter 1993, 10, 22).

The public seems blissfully unaware of the perverse results of much environmental regulation. Environmentalists habitually call for further government intervention to stop pollution. Nobel economist Ronald Coase explained that most economists share that approach:

> When they are prevented from sleeping at night by the roar of jet planes overhead (publicly authorized and perhaps publicly operated), are unable to think (or rest) in the day because of the noise and vibration from passing trains (publicly authorized and perhaps publicly operated), find it difficult to breathe because of the odor from a local sewage farm (publicly authorized and perhaps publicly operated) and are unable to escape because their driveways are blocked by a road obstruction (without any doubt, publicly devised), their nerves frayed and mental balance disturbed, they proceed to declaim about the disadvantages of private enterprise and the need for Government regulation. (Coase 1960, 26)

More than three decades later, those concerned about the environment continue to cling to the illusion that our land, air, and water can only be saved by further government action. Far too few yet realize the extent to which government-made laws and regulations, designed to protect particular industries and promulgated in the name of the public good, are environmental culprits (Yandle 1997).

Compromise in the Courts

Governments aren't the only ones who have eroded common law property rights. The courts themselves have modified both the rules governing liability and the remedies available to those whose rights have been violated, diminishing people's power to oppose environmental degradation. Various courts in the United States have been willing to modify the common law to accommodate industrial concerns (Horwitz 1992). While British and Canadian courts have maintained more conservative views, even they have sporadically made concessions to industrialization (Risk 1981, 122; Nedelsky 1981, 281–310).

The most important concession has concerned whether the character of a neighborhood in which an activity occurred should influence its legality. In 1865, a British law lord suggested a compromise. He distinguished between nuisances resulting in personal discomfort and those resulting in material injury or financial harm. Courts, he said, should consider the character of the neighborhood only in the former cases:

> If a man lives in a town, it is necessary that he should subject himself to the consequences of those operations of trade which may be carried on in his immediate locality, which are actually necessary for trade and commerce, and also for the enjoyment of property, and for the benefit of the inhabitants of the town and of the public at large. If a man lives in a street where there are numerous shops, and a shop is opened next door to him, which is carried on in a fair and reasonable way, he has no ground for complaint, because to himself individually there may arise much discomfort from the trade carried on in that shop. But when an occupation is carried on by one person in the neighbourhood of another, and the result of that trade, or occupation, or business, is a material injury to property, then there unquestionably arises a very different consideration. . . . [T]he submission which is required from persons living in society to that amount of discomfort which may be necessary for the legitimate and free exercise of the trade of their neighbours, would not apply to circumstances the immediate result of which is sensible injury to the value of the property. (*St. Helen's Smelting v. William Tipping* 1865, 1486)

The compromise as laid down in that case was accepted in both England and Canada; it still applies today. Courts continue to distinguish between nuisances resulting in "mere" personal inconvenience, discomfort, or annoyance and those causing actual damage to health or property. The former, unless substantial, may be justified by the character of the neighborhood in which they occur. The latter, in contrast, readily entitle a complainant to his remedy. In 1989, two Canadian Supreme Court judges summarized the law as follows:

The courts attempt to circumscribe the ambit of nuisance by looking to the nature of the locality in question and asking whether the ordinary and reasonable resident of that locality would view the disturbance as a substantial interference with the enjoyment of land. . . . [T]hese criteria find their greatest application in cases where the interference complained of does not consist of material damage to property but rather interference with tranquility and amenity. . . . In the presence of actual physical damage to property, the courts have been quick to conclude that the interference does indeed constitute a substantial and unreasonable interference with the enjoyment of property. (*Tock v. St. John's Metropolitan Area Board* 1989, 639–40)

Reversing the Trend

The simple rule that one may not interfere with his neighbor's use or enjoyment of his property has protected the environment from an endless variety of insults for more than seven hundred years. Only in the last two hundred years have governments extinguished, in any systematic way, people's common law rights to be free of harm. In Canada, this trend has escalated over the course of the last fifty years, as governments have assumed greater control over polluting activities. The environmental consequences have been devastating.

Our challenge is to reverse the trend. We must restore strong property rights, thereby returning authority over resource uses and other environmental changes to those most directly affected by them. We must make it possible for the victims of pollution to once again use trespass, nuisance, and riparian law to prevent or to clean up the pollution of their land, the air above it, and the water running by or through it.

Property rights are not the best tool to solve every contemporary environmental problem. As a general rule, high transaction costs resulting from unavailable information, costly negotiations, or other factors reduce the common law's effectiveness in fighting pollution. When many people suffer minor, cumulative damages from many small polluters, no individual has an incentive to sue; each costly suit would bring inconsequential relief. No one, for example, could sue every smog-producing driver that passes his home, and suing one or two would not measurably clear the air. Such cases call for government regulations that, in reducing emissions from numerous minor sources, make a major difference in air quality. However, the need for finely tuned regulations in specific cases does not diminish the need for stronger property rights that will empower individuals to address many of the most serious environmental threats facing them.

As discussed by Wagner (1998), it is far more difficult to restore property rights than it is to erode them. Both those with preexisting rights and those with newer rights now have legitimate—but nonetheless conflicting—interests in the ways property is used and affected by others' uses. Whose rights should take precedence, who deserves compensation, and the source and form of that compensation are questions that both governments and courts will have to grapple with for years.

It will, in contrast, be far easier for governments to decide that new laws and regulations will not further override people's property rights. When authorizing industries' activities in the future, governments should specify that they are maintaining their citizens' common law rights and not legalizing trespasses, nuisances, or violations of riparian rights. Conditions protecting the rights of potential victims to sue were common in nineteenth-century England, where early sanitation statutes specified that they did not legalize nuisances or other unlawful acts and where the Gas Clauses Act stated that in carrying on their works, gas manufacturers could not injure surrounding land.[7] Inserting such conditions into contemporary laws would benefit the environment immensely.

Furthermore, although Canadians missed the opportunity in 1991 to enshrine property rights in the constitution, constitutional reform is by no means off the political agenda. Including property rights in the constitution's Charter of Rights and Freedoms would more formally secure them. As centuries of case law so clearly demonstrate, secure property rights provide both citizens and the environment with immeasurable protection.

Notes

1. See Horwitz (1992, 32, 102) for a discussion of the frequency with which eighteenth-century American courts invoked the maxim and its decline in the nineteenth century.

2. For further discussion of this problem and a possible solution, see Rothbard (1990, 250–54). Rothbard suggests that if trespass is defined as an interference with one's exclusive use of one's property, many intangible invasions—which would not so interfere—would not constitute trespasses. Magnet (1977, 291) suggests that contemporary courts may be less willing than their traditional counterparts to treat trifling interferences as trespasses.

3. Although this case originated in Quebec, the chief justice of the Supreme Court of Canada cited another justice's observation that "the English and French law on the subject of nuisance are exactly alike" (*Drysdale v. C. A. Dugas* 1896, 23).

4. Legal scholars disagree about who has riparian rights. According to Rueg-

geberg and Thompson (1984, 4), riparian rights "belong only to those who own the banks of rivers, lakes or other bodies of water." Similarly, Percy (1988, 73) explains that "the riparian doctrine restricts water rights to those who own property that adjoins a body of water." Others define riparians more broadly. According to McNeil and Macklem (1992, 1), "Every person who is in lawful possession of land adjacent to water, whether as a freeholder, leaseholder or in some other capacity, has riparian rights." Campbell et al. (1974, 479, 480) straddle the issue, suggesting first that the riparian "doctrine provides occupiers of land bordering a natural stream (riparian land) with certain rights to the use and flow of water" but later mentioning "rights which are incidental to the ownership of land."

5. For an extensive discussion of this issue, see the Supreme Court decision in *Tock v. St. John's Metropolitan Area Board* (1989). In her decision for the majority, Justice Bertha Wilson reviewed the case history of the defense of statutory authority and stated the principles to be derived from it. She distinguished between the inevitable results of legislation that imposes a duty or confers a specific authority and the results of legislation that confers a discretionary authority. Only the former, she concluded, have been statutorily authorized.

Justice Wilson noted disapprovingly that some recent cases have not followed these principles. "[T]he inevitable consequences doctrine is now being applied without regard to the type of statutory authority conferred on the public body," she warned. "In my view," she concluded, "to the extent that some of the more recent cases are inconsistent with the early principles, they should not be followed" (*Tock v. St. John's Metropolitan Area Board* 1989, 634, 635). The *Tock* decision has been followed in at least seven cases since and has been considered in several others. For commentary on the extent to which the decision has narrowed the defense of statutory authority, see Harvey (1990, 522) and Rankin (1991, 30–31).

6. For more on the deterrent value of liability, see Wright and Linden (1980, chapter 1) and Bardach and Kagan (1982, 271–83).

7. See Brenner (1974, 423). One law establishing sewage works is described in *Pride of Derby v. British Celanese* (1952, 164). The 1901 Derby Corporation Act, while establishing sewage disposal works, had specifically prohibited nuisances: "The sewage disposal works constructed . . . shall at all times hereafter be conducted so that the same shall not be a nuisance and in particular the corporation shall not allow any noxious or offensive effluvia to escape therefrom or do or permit or suffer any other act which shall be a nuisance or injurious to the health or reasonable comfort of the inhabitants of Spondon."

The Gas Clauses Act is described in *Hammersmith and City Railway v. G. H. Brand* (1869, 222).

Similarly, an order in connection with England's Electric Lighting Act, specifying that "Nothing in this order shall exonerate the undertakers from any indictment, action, or other proceedings for nuisance in the event of any nuisance being caused by them," is discussed in *Shelfer v. City of London Electric Lighting* and *Meux's Brewery Company v. City of London Electric Lighting* (1894, 290).

References

Bardach, Eugene, and Robert A. Kagan. 1982. *Going by the Book: The Problem of Regulatory Unreasonableness.* Philadelphia: Temple University Press.

Bate, Roger. 1993. English and Welsh Rivers: A Common Law Approach to Pollution Prevention. Master's thesis, Cambridge University.

———. 1994. Water Pollution Prevention: A Nuisance Approach. *Economic Affairs* (April): 13–14.

Blackstone, William. [1765–1769] 1876. *The Commentaries on the Laws of England.* Adapted to the Present State of the Law by Robert Malcolm Kerr. London: John Murray.

Brenner, Joel Franklin. 1974. Nuisance Law and the Industrial Revolution. *Journal of Legal Studies* 3(2): 403–33.

Campbell, Richard S., Peter H. Pearse, Anthony Scott, and Milan Uzelac. 1974. Water Management in Ontario—An Economic Evaluation of Public Policy. *Osgood Hall Law Journal* 12(3): 475–526.

Canadian Environmental Law Research Foundation. 1986. An Overview of Canadian Law and Policy Governing Great Lakes Water Quantity Management. *Case Western Reserve Journal of International Law* 18(67): 109–53.

Coase, Ronald H. 1960. The Problem of Social Cost. *Journal of Law and Economics* 3(1): 1–44.

Dewees, D. N., with Michael Halewood. 1992. The Efficiency of the Common Law: Sulphur Dioxide Emissions in Sudbury. *University of Toronto Law Journal* 42: 1–21.

Ellickson, Robert C. 1973. Alternatives to Zoning: Covenants, Nuisance Rules, and Fines as Land Use Controls. *University of Chicago Law Review* 40(4): 681–781.

Estrin, David, and John Swaigen. 1993. *Environment on Trial: A Guide to Ontario Environmental Law and Policy*, 3d ed. A project of the Canadian Institute for Environmental Law and Policy. Toronto, ON: Edmond Montgomery Publications Limited.

Flaherty, David H. 1981. Writing Canadian Legal History: An Introduction. In *Essays in the History of Canadian Law*, ed. David H. Flaherty. Toronto, ON: University of Toronto Press and the Osgoode Society, 3–42.

Hailsham, Lord, of St. Marylebone. 1985. *Halsbury's Laws of England*, 4th ed. London: Butterworths.

Harvey, Christopher. 1990. Riparian Water Rights: Not Dead Yet. *Advocate* 48(July): 517–24.

Horwitz, Morton J. 1992. *The Transformation of American Law 1780–1860.* New York: Oxford University Press.

Lauer, T. E. 1963. The Common Law Background of the Riparian Doctrine. *Missouri Law Review* 28(1): 60–107.

Lucas, Alastair R. 1990. *Security of Title in Canadian Water Rights.* Calgary: Canadian Institute of Resources Law.

Magnet, Joseph Eliot. 1977. Intentional Interference with Land. In *Studies in Canadian Tort Law*, ed. Lewis Klar. Toronto, ON: Butterworths, 287–323.

McLaren, John P. S. 1984. The Tribulations of Antoine Ratté: A Case Study of the Environmental Regulation of the Canadian Lumbering Industry in the Nineteenth Century. *University of New Brunswick Law Journal* 33: 203–59.

McNeil, Kent, and Patrick Macklem. 1992. *Aboriginal, Treaty and Riparian Rights in the Moose River Basin: The Potential Impact of the Ontario Hydraulic Plan . . . Task Five: Riparian Rights in the Moose River Basin.* A report prepared for the Moose River/James Bay Coalition and submitted as evidence in the Environmental Assessment Hearing into Ontario Hydro's Demand Supply Plan.

Nedelsky, Jennifer. 1981. Judicial Conservatism in an Age of Innovation. *Essays in the History of Canadian Law*, ed. David H. Flaherty. Toronto, ON: University of Toronto Press and Osgoode Society, 281–322.

Owen, Bruce M., and Ronald Braeutigam. 1978. *The Regulation Game: Strategic Use of the Administrative Process.* Cambridge: Ballinger.

Percy, David R. 1988. *The Framework of Water Rights Legislation in Canada.* Calgary, AB: Canadian Institute of Resources Law.

Rankin, Murray. 1991. An Environmental Bill of Rights for Ontario: Reflections and Recommendations. Discussion paper, January.

Risk, R. C. B. 1981. The Law and the Economy in Mid-Nineteenth-Century Ontario: A Perspective. In *Essays in the History of Canadian Law*, ed. David H. Flaherty. Toronto, ON: University of Toronto Press and the Osgoode Society, 88–131.

Rothbard, Murray. 1990. Law, Property Rights, and Air Pollution. In *Economics and the Environment: A Reconciliation*, ed. Walter E. Block. Vancouver, BC: Fraser Institute, 233–79.

Rueggeberg, H. R., and A. Thompson. 1984. *Water Law and Policy Issues in Canada.* Vancouver, BC: Westwater Research Center.

Sharpe, Robert. 1983. *Injunctions and Specific Performance.* Toronto, ON: Canada Law Book Limited.

Trebilcock, Michael, and Ralph Winter. 1993. *The Impact of the Nuclear Liability Act on Safety Incentives in the Nuclear Power Industry.* Exhibit 967 in *Energy Probe et al. v. The Attorney General of Canada.* Toronto, ON: Energy Probe.

Wagner, Richard E. 1998. The Constitutional Protection of Private Property, this volume.

Wright, C. A., and A. M. Linden. 1980. *Canadian Tort Law: Cases, Notes & Materials*, 7th ed. Toronto: Butterworths.

Yandle, Bruce. 1997. *Common Sense and Common Law for the Environment.* Lanham, MD: Rowman & Littlefield.

———. 1998. Coase, Pigou, and Environmental Rights, this volume.

Cases Cited

Attorney-General v. Borough of Birmingham (1858), 4 K. &. J. 528, 70 E. R. 220 (V. Ch.)

Ballard v. Tomlinson (1885), 29 Ch. D. 115

Bamford v. Turnley (1862), 3 B. & S. 66, 122 E. R. 27 (K. B.)

Beamish v. Glenn (1916), 36 O. L. R. 10

Boyle v. Rogers, [1921] 2 W. W. R. 704 (Man. K. B.)

British Cast Plate Manufacturers v. Meredith and Others (1792), 4 T. R. 794, 100 E. R. 1306

Buysse et al. v. Town of Shelburne (1984), 6 D. L. R. (4th) 734

Canadian Pacific Ry. Co. v. Roy (1901), C.R. [12] A.C. 374 (P.C.)

Didow et al. v. Alberta Power Limited, [1988] 5 W. W. R. 606 (Alta. C.A.)

Drysdale v. C. A. Dugas (1896), 26 S. C. R. 20

Ellis v. Clemens (1891), 21 O.R. 227

Entick v. Carrington (1765), 19 St. Tr. 1030 (C.P.)

Everett v. Paschall, 61 Wash. 47, 111 P. 879 (1910)

Fairview Farms Inc. v. Reynolds Metals Co., 176 F. Supp. 178 (D. Or. 1959)

Friesen et al. v. Forest Protection Limited (1978), 22 N. B. R. (2d) 146 (S. C. Q. B.)

Gauthier et al. v. Naneff et al. (1970), [1971] 1 O.R. 97 (H. C. J.)

Groat v. City of Edmonton, [1928] S. C. R. 522

Hammersmith and City Railway Company v. G. H. Brand and Wife (1869), L. R. 4 H.L. 171

Imperial Gas Light and Coke Company v. Broadbent (1859), 7 H.L.C. 600, 11 E.R. 239

Kerr et al. v. Revelstoke Building Materials Ltd. (1976), 71 D. L. R. (3d) 134 (Alta. S.C.)

The King v. Edward Pease and Others (1832), 4 B. &. Ad. 30, 110 E. R. 366

Martin v. Reynolds Metals Co., 342 P. 2d 790 (Or. 1959), cert. denied, 362 U.S. 918 (1960)

McDonald et al. v. Associated Fuels Ltd. et al., [1954] 3 D. L. R. 775 (B. C. S. C.)

Miner v. Gilmour (1858), 12 Moo. P.C. 131, 14 E. R. 861

Nepisiquit Real Estate and Fishing Company, Limited v. Canadian Iron Corporation, Limited (1913), 42 N. B. R. 387 (Ch.)

Pride of Derby and Derbyshire Angling Association Ld. and Another v. British Celanese Ld. and Another (1952), [1953] 1 Ch. 149 (C.A.)

Roberts v. Gwyrfai District Council, [1899] 2 Ch. D. 608

Russell Transport Ltd. et al. v. Ontario Malleable Iron Co. Ltd. (1952), 4 D. L. R. 719 (Ont. H.C.)

St. Helen's Smelting Co. v. Tipping (1865), 11 H. L. C. 642, 11 E. R. 1483

Shelfer v. City of London Electric Lighting Company (1894) and *Meux's Brewery Company v. City of London Electric Lighting Company* (1894), [1895] 1 Ch. 287

Star v. Rookesby (1711), 1 Salk. 3. 335, 91 E. R. 295 (K. B.)

Stollmeyer and Others v. Trinidad Lake Petroleum Company Limited, and Others, [1918] A.C. 485 (P.C.)

Strobel et al. v. Kerr Salt Co., 164 N.Y. 303, 320, 58 N. E. 142, 51 L. R. A. 687, 79 Am. St. Rep. 643 (N.Y. Ct. App. 1900)

340909 Ontario Ltd. v. Huron Steel Products (Windsor) Inc. and Huron Steel Products (1990), 73 O.R. (2d) 641 (H. C. J.), aff'd (1992), 10 O.R. (3d) 95 (Ont. C.A.)

Tock et al. v. St. John's Metropolitan Area Board (1989), 64 D. L. R. (4th) 620

Trinidad Asphalt Co. v. Ambard, [1899] A.C. 594 (P.C.)

Vaughan v. Taff Vale Railway Company (1860), 5 H. & N. 679, 157 E. R. 1351 (Ex.)

Walker v. McKinnon Industries Ltd., [1949] 4 D. L. R. 739 (Ont. H.C.), aff'd [1950] 3 D. L. R. 159 (Ont. C.A.), aff'd [1951] 3 D. L. R. 577 (P.C.)

Walter v. Selfe (1851), 4 De G. & S. 315, 20 L. J. Ch. 433

Weston Paper Co. v. Pope et al., 155 Ind. 394, 57 N. E. 719, 56 L. R. A. 899 (1900)

Whalen v. Union Bag & Paper Co., 145 App. Div. 1, 129 N.Y. Supp. 391 (1911), 208 N.Y. 1, 5, 101 N. E. 805 (1913)

John Young and Company v. Bankier Distillery Company and Others, [1893] A.C. 691 (P.C.)

Chapter 5

Coase, Pigou, and Environmental Rights

Bruce Yandle

When I was a sophomore in high school, back in 1949, a buddy in my homeroom had a wonderful after-school job. He worked for the local paper mill located on a large river that flowed through our town. My friend's job seemed simple enough, and it paid well. Each day, he sat on the bank of the river near the mill's discharge point and sampled the river water, dutifully recording the level of dissolved oxygen and other chemical characteristics.

Consider these facts: The Ocmulgee River was a common-access resource. Discharge from the mill was potentially harmful to fish as well as to the general ambiance of that part of middle Georgia, of which there was very little in the immediate section of the river where the mill was located. Several downstream communities obtained drinking water from the river, and a large number of farms operated along the banks of the river. Bear in mind that this was years before the federal government seriously entered the water pollution control business. At the time, there were no federal statutes guarding the nation's rivers and streams, and there were few rigorous state statutes.

Flash back to the time when the mill was being planned. Suppose an economist was given these facts about the Ocmulgee River and told that a paper mill was to be sited so that it could discharge oxygen-consuming waste into the river. Suppose further that the economist was asked to analyze the situation, offer a policy for siting the mill, and comment on the practical aspects of adopting the policy proposal as a general rule. Most economists, such as Tom Tietenberg (1992, 51–69) would

---

This chapter draws on my book, *Common Sense and Common Law for the Environment* (see Yandle 1997).

consider two primary theoretical approaches for analyzing the problem. The first approach involves an externality analysis, where the paper mill pollutes the river, imposing an unwanted cost on society, a cost that does not enter the mill owners' profit calculations. This is the problem of social cost.

Following this line of inquiry, failure to consider the external cost leads to too much paper and too little environmental quality. This economist would be using an analytical framework developed by A. C. Pigou (1920), a noted British economist whose works were published in the early twentieth century. Pigou argued that pollution generates a social cost that should be dealt with by the central government. He proposed a system of taxes, bounties, and regulations for resolving the problem. Most likely, the economist using this framework would call for some form of effluent taxes or regulation to control the mill's discharge.

The second approach likely taken by an economist considers the paper mill and others who wish to consume or enjoy water quality as part of a competitive market where people bargain for the use of rights to scarce property. This analysis has nothing to do with polluters' imposing cost on society, but everything to do with competing demands for use of an asset. If rights to the asset are defined and assigned to members of the river-basin community, then those planning to build the paper mill must bargain with the rightholders to determine just how much, if any, they will discharge into the river. If the rights are held by the mill, then the existing communities along the river must bargain with the mill owner for rights to water quality. Again, bargaining determines the amount of discharge to the river.

This approach relies on the work of Nobel Laureate Ronald H. Coase (1960), who established a different way of thinking about the problem of social cost. Using this framework, an economist might recommend a meeting of the mill owners and others who have access to the river. After organizing the parties, negotiations would ensue. If existing river users owned water-quality rights, the mill would have to buy the rights in order to discharge specified amounts of waste. If the mill had the right to pollute, existing river users would have to buy water quality from the mill, paying the mill to limit its discharges.

Having offered two options and moving to make a recommendation, the economist would consider the practical aspects of the two approaches. Pigou's approach will likely miss the mark. Information is costly to assemble. It is impossible to determine the optimal amount of discharge for thousands of industrial dischargers located along hundreds of rivers and streams, a difficulty Pigou recognized late in his career. F. A. Hayek describes Pigou's misgivings this way:

Perhaps even more instructive is the case of the late Professor A. C. Pigou, the founder of the theory of welfare economics—who at the end of a long life devoted almost entirely to the task of defining the conditions in which government interference might be used to improve upon the results of the market, had to concede that the practical value of these theoretical considerations was somewhat doubtful because we are rarely in a position to ascertain whether the particular circumstance to which the theory refers exist in fact in any given situation. Not because he knows so much, but because he knows how much he would have to know in order to interfere successfully, and because he knows that he will never know all the relevant circumstances, it would seem that the economist should refrain from recommending isolated acts of interference even in conditions in which the theory tells him that they may be sometimes beneficial.[1]

What about Coase? While the Coase solution theoretically handles the information problem, because the parties involved are the decision makers, it can fail because of transaction costs that emerge if thousands of people along a river are expected to bargain with multiple dischargers. The pure Pigou and Coase options are difficult to apply in the real world. This suggests two possibilities: (1) the mill will locate and do nothing to affect its discharge or (2) the troubled community will call on government to regulate, hoping that most of the inherent difficulties will be overcome. Given the options, regulation will take the day. Coase gets the Nobel Prize and academic recognition for having developed a powerful approach for analyzing social cost; Pigovians seem to have won the policy battle by default.

We should not be too quick in naming Coase the loser in a contest he did not enter. He was not developing an environmental policy prescription. Quite the contrary, Coase explains how an appropriate interpretation of market forces relying on a rule of law could eliminate the need for specialized statutes for handling "the problem of social cost," which includes environmental issues. In doing so, he calls attention to institutions that evolve for reducing the inevitable costs that are generated in communities. Government regulation is just one of the many approaches that might be taken. The cost of organizing and running the various institutions dictates which, if any, approach might be utilized.

Evidence of the record of Coase's intellectual influence is seen in the count of citations to his 1960 article, which is shown in figure 5.1. This shows the annual count of citations to "The Problem of Social Cost" for the years 1966–1995. Included in the figure are citations to Pigou's *The Economics of Welfare*. The citation data are superimposed on a count of *Federal Register* pages for the same years. The data mapping suggests several things. First, Pigou's influence on academics seems to operate at a steady state. There is no evidence that Pigovians were

Figure 5.1
Coase, Pigou, and Regulation

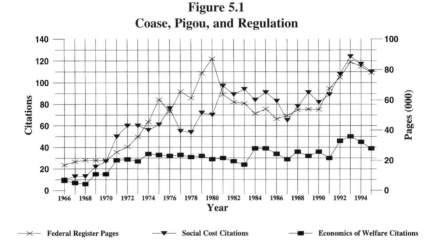

 — legend: Federal Register Pages · Social Cost Citations · Economics of Welfare Citations

responding to the growth of regulation occurring around them. The Coase citations indicate the reverse. References to his ideas seem to be a reaction to the growth of the regulatory state. There is a systematic relationship between Coase citations and new pages of federal rules. Coase challenges command-and-control regulation. Pigou's influence seems to be narrow and focused; his prescriptions are in harmony with the rise of the regulatory state.

How This Chapter Is Organized

This chapter seeks to make a broader interpretation of Coase, one that considers the full market process, not just analyses of cattle and corn, chiropractors and confectioners. Getting to that point requires us to focus on the prescriptions offered by Pigou and Coase, using the traditional interpretation. The next section of the chapter begins with a discussion of externalities, the problem that motivated Pigou's analysis. The implications of the Pigou prescription are examined. The absence of property rights considerations and Pigou's implicit assumption that politicians will seek to serve the public interest are shown to be major flaws in Pigovian proposals for centralized regulation.

Section three focuses on Coase's proposal for managing unintended harmful side effects, which was his way of describing externalities. The focus here is on property rights, private law, and the market process. Pigou sees public law and regulation as the remedy; Coase looks to the market process where private law, courts, and judges are driven toward efficient solutions. This section emphasizes the bargaining interpretation of Coase and the accompanying transaction costs. A broader interpretation of Coase, which starts with transaction costs and may avoid direct bargaining, calls for an examination of the full market process, one that includes customs, traditions, and other market forces.

Section four of the chapter looks to these broader market forces for solutions that go beyond command-and-control (Pigou) and direct bargaining (Coase). The discussion makes the point that firms and organizations subject to market forces will not likely engage in costly polluting activities. Pigou-type externalities will be minimized without Pigovian remedies and without Coasean bargaining. But some firms and organizations are immune to important disciplinary forces of the market. These require some form of external control. Chief among these are government enterprises. It is here that Pigovian logic must be applied. The final section offers some concluding thoughts.

Externalities and Pigou

The classic externality story is often presented in terms of an upstream discharger and a downstream receiver of unwanted wastes.

The Externality Story

When a paper mill discharges waste into a stream, it is possible that a cost is imposed on downstream water rightholders or others who care about the river. These costs are often called negative externalities. For the externality to be recognized at law, the costs must be imposed on a rightholder and be of sufficient size for an objective observer to recognize them. But the term externality is often applied to a much broader category of events; it is commonly used to describe any undesirable outcome that springs from human activity. Under this broad interpretation of the term, pipe smokers impose negative externalities when they puff away on the streets of Washington, D.C., even when no one is walking near them. The noise from ascending and descending aircraft generates externalities, and women who wear a spray of perfume may be dousing a room with externalities. The same may be said about retail stores that provide "too much" air conditioning in the summer or "too much" heat in the winter. As Boudreaux and Meiners (1998) suggest in the discussion of existence value, just the thought to some of a paper mill discharging waste to a river beclouds an otherwise pleasant moment, even if they never expect to see the river. Under this rubric, externalities are ubiquitous.

A tighter and more operational definition asks that we consider relevant costs when we examine an externality. Buchanan and Stubblebine (1962) ask if the effects being considered cause recipients to alter their behavior or in some way engage in activities designed to mitigate a loss of happiness and well-being. This distinction between relevant externalities, those that impose marginal costs worth removing—as revealed by actions being taken by affected parties—and irrelevant externalities, those that do not, in some ways separates those who would side with Pigou from others who prefer Coase.

A simple externality analysis is usually shown in terms of an abstract supply and demand diagram, such as the one in figure 5.2. Let the supply curve represent a paper mill's cost of producing and shipping paper products. The supply curve captures all costs paid by the mill owners. Costs include labor, rent, interest on borrowed money, electricity, supplies—everything that has to be purchased to produce paper. The curve's upward slope indicates that it is more costly to produce more paper in a given time period. Notice that the cost of using a river for

Figure 5.2
Externality Analysis

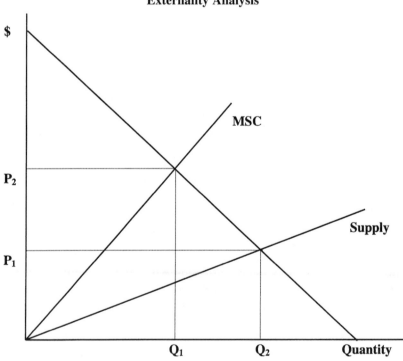

waste disposal was not mentioned when listing the costs embodied in the supply curve, and for good reason. No one sends a bill for using the river; the river is a commons.

The demand curve in the figure captures the value of different amounts of paper to consumers who purchase the product. The demand curve tells us that the mill must lower its price if it wishes to sell more paper in a given week or month. The demand curve also illustrates the reverse—the higher the price, the less paper will be sold.

The market clearing price for paper, P_1, is shown in the figure. At that price, the mill covers the additional cost of producing the last unit, and the amount produced equals the amount demanded. At P_1 we have an equilibrium. Meanwhile, the mill is discharging waste that imposes costs on downstream landowners. The cost imposed on downstream landowners is not captured in the supply curve, unless the downstream landowners send a bill that must be paid. And since those downstream hold no claims to the river, they cannot send bills.

There is a second upward sloping line, MSC, in figure 5.2 that captures *all* of the costs of producing paper, including the externality (cost) imposed downstream. MSC stands for marginal social cost and includes the costs shown in the supply curve plus the external costs associated with each additional unit of paper produced. The amount of externality is equal to the vertical distance between the supply curve and MSC.

This traditional display of external cost shows an equilibrium point where MSC crosses the demand curve that corresponds to a higher price than P_2. If the mill owners had to bear the cost of the externality, the owner would charge a higher price for paper and produce and sell less of it. (P_2Q_1 would be the equilibrium.) If the externality is left unattended, too much paper will be produced, and its price will be too low. The "too much paper" outcome is called a *market failure* by many economists. Market failure means that prices and costs generated through the market process have not captured the costly effects of the pollution discharge from the mill. Analysts following the Pigovian tradition argue that government action is required in such instances.

A. C. Pigou Enters

The analysis of market failure described in figure 5.2 was extensively discussed in the 1920s by A. C. Pigou (1920, 183–94), who went on to prescribe a solution to the problem. Pigou spoke in terms of social and net product, instead of social and private marginal cost, but the meaning is the same. Pigou offers air pollution as an example of divergence: "Smoke in large cities inflicts a heavy uncharged loss on the community, in injury to buildings, vegetation, expenses for washing clothes and cleaning rooms, expenses for the provision of artificial light, and in many other ways" (Pigou 1920, 184). In a footnote, typical of current efforts to justify stricter air pollution standards, Pigou refers to a 1920 report of the British Departmental Committee on Smoke and Noxious Vapours Abatement, which cites a Pittsburgh, Pennsylvania, study that estimates the cost of smoke nuisance to be approximately four British pounds per head (Pigou 1920, 184).

Pigou's solution for too much pollution calls on government actions: "It is, however, possible for the State, if it so chooses, to remove the divergence in any field by 'extraordinary encouragements' or 'extraordinary restraints' upon investment in that field" (Pigou 1920, 192). Skipping over the truly difficult matter of "if it so chooses," he indicates that taxes and bounties are the most obvious restraints that might be used, leaving open the possibility of using command-and-control regulation. Command-and-control emerges soon thereafter when Pigou addresses conditions of urban life. Here he asserts:

> No "invisible hand" can be relied on to produce a good arrangement of the whole from a combination of separate treatments of the parts. It is therefore necessary that an authority of wider reach should intervene to tackle the collective problems of beauty, of air and light, as those other collective problems of gas and water have been tackled. (Pigou 1920, 195)

If because of high transaction costs, local communities fail to act in their self interest, Pigou (1920, 195) indicates that "power [should be] given to the appropriate department of the central Government to order them to take action." An authoritarian, command-and-control regime is as much a part of the Pigovian prescription as taxes and bounties.

Pigou's prescription for government enhancement of welfare extended a public finance tradition in economics that overlooked the purpose and function of the legal/cultural environment that supports and surrounds all market transactions. In discussing divergences between social and private cost, Pigou never mentions the role played by private law, customs, and traditions. Property rights are never discussed. He, like many later economists, performed the analysis in an institutional vacuum.

We should not be overly critical of Pigou for focusing so closely on analysis and so little on existing institutions. Failure by economists to focus on the rich role played by institutions is not uncommon, even today. Pigou's work was done in the tradition of early twentieth century neoclassical economists. Adam Smith's fascination with the realities of the market had long since been forgotten. The neoclassical economists were much like builders of increasingly complex and ornate clocks who seldom asked if their clocks could tell (predict) time. Portraying problems in the abstract terms of the differential calculus was, at the margin, considered more important than discovering the way the world worked. This passion for analysis contributed to the myopic development of powerful theories that enabled Coase and others to call the hand of the theory builders.[2]

From today's retrospective advantage, we can readily see how Pigou's failure to be concerned with predicting or explaining the way the world really worked led him to call for political solutions for those problems where the "invisible hand" seemed crippled. But his inability or failure to account for the functioning of the legal environment led him, perhaps unwittingly, to call for collective solutions for controversies that could have been, and were, settled by private law and other less formal ways.

Writing long before the discovery of Public Choice, Pigou saw government as an exogenous force, unconnected to unbridled market forces. Pigou implicitly saw government as being neutral and efficiency-bound at worst and benevolent at best. There is clearly no recognition that government enterprises could become the worst polluters and the least likely to respond to the spur of competition. To cap it all off, Pigou seems to assume that information can be obtained at no cost. Pigou armed the state with an appealing, informed, and logical analysis, and dignified market intervention and regulation, and armed future generations of political favor seekers with a kind of Old Testament interpretation of how to make the world a better place. If enough rules are written and enforced, better things will emerge, especially for well-organized interest groups.

Taken at face value, Pigou's influence on the economic analysis of public policy seems to be astounding. Today, there are taxes on oxides of carbon and nitrogen in Scandinavian countries, effluent charges in Germany, the Netherlands, and France, emission and effluent fees operating across Latin and South America, bottle taxes across the United States, emission taxes on industry in California, and various fuel taxes in many states that attempt to adjust for smog production (Brannlund 1995; Egenhofer 1996). In each case, public authorities can claim to be adjusting for market failures; they are attempting to place a price on environmental use. Every industrialized country has taken the Pigovian approach in a larger sense. Centralized command-and-control is found more often than taxes and bounties. But it is ludicrous to credit Pigou with all this. As far back as recorded history carries us, we find "Pigovian" solutions at play. Pigou did not invent the regulatory state. His work simply provided a dose of academic credibility that supports the natural tendency of people to seek power over the lives of others.

Applying the Prescription

Intellectual credibility is surely important, especially for those who seek to empower the state. And when credibility is added to apparent simplicity, the Pigovian approach is almost unbeatable. Consider the simplicity. To rid the world of unwanted externalities, just calculate the correct tax (the difference between P_2 and P_1 in figure 5.2), impose it on polluters, and all will live happily ever after. Reflection on the task at hand replaces apparent simplicity with obvious complexity. Think of the information that must be gathered to accomplish this feat. Reference to figure 5.2 reminds us of the difficulty in determining the appropriate tax with any degree of precision. Somehow government authorities must estimate the demand for paper and the prices people are willing to pay for different amounts of output. When that is done, an assumption falls in place—the estimated demand curve will not change.

Next, as Macaulay (1972) notes, the politician must have an estimate of the amount of damage imposed on people downstream. Estimating damage in the absence of market-generated information is no simple matter. For example, what if a person downstream can take actions to avoid the harm of dirty water by moving to another location at a cost of $5,000, yet the estimate of damage without taking offsetting action is $10,000? It is the $5,000 damage that should be relevant to the policy maker, not the $10,000. But the $10,000 estimate is easier to obtain than the $5,000 estimate. If the tax is based on $10,000, the paper mill and its customers will pay more than the social cost of producing paper. The river will be too clean.

The situation becomes even more complicated when there are many receivers of waste, and each one assigns a different level of harm to the water pollution. As the scale of control increases, information cost rises exponentially. Consider the complication that comes when a national government attempts to set an appropriate tax for each producer that pollutes water, and all users of their products, and all downstream water users to take care of multiple externalities across a vast geographic area with many rivers.

These difficulties are found in efforts by Mexico and Colombia to implement Pigovian effluent fees for controlling water pollution (World Bank 1996, 30–33). Mexico's system of pollution charges has been in place since 1991, but little has been accomplished. Due to the complexities of setting fees based on damages or cost of cleanup, the government sets a charge based simply on volume of wastewater discharged, neglecting completely the amount of pollutants in the waste stream. The program's recognized failure is attributed to high monitoring and enforcement costs. Opposition from industry based on competitiveness arguments has also taken its toll. On the other hand, Colombia has attempted to take a true Pigovian approach, at least in terms of the country's official program. The Colombian statute requires that pollution taxes be based on estimates of damages somehow related to people, property, and the environment. Again, the Colombian statute seems to say the right thing, but practice is something else. Simply put, the institutional basis for determining appropriate fees and for monitoring and enforcing compliance are lacking. From 1974 to 1994, only $116,000 was collected from a potential revenue base of $90 million (World Bank 1996, 31).

Pigovian Taxes and Moving Targets

Suppose all the technical complications could be resolved and government officials could determine the appropriate per-unit tax, individually tailored and imposed on the harmful waste discharged by all paper mills and other producers. Would the problem be solved? There are two answers to the question. At a technical level, the answer is yes. But in a world of human action, the answer is no. What then is the problem?

Think for a moment about the forces that generate the call for taxation. Politicians are concerned when constituents complain about pollution. Concerned citizens want cleaner rivers. They have no way of knowing what the optimal pollution should be; they just want cleaner water. When the politicians impose a tax on polluters, the constituents are understandably pleased. Let the polluter pay; it only makes sense.

But once the appropriate tax is calculated and imposed, some level of pollution continues to make its way into rivers. Reference to figure 5.2 reveals a nonzero pollution outcome. All along, the friends of the environment have not been charged directly for their enjoyment of the river. When the river becomes cleaner, they continue to receive benefits at no higher cost to themselves.

People who live along affected rivers come and go, and many environmentalists never actually see the river, but tax-paying paper mills have a way of staying put. When the price of something we value is zero, we tend to want a relatively large amount of it. Economics tells us that we seek to consume the valued resource until the last unit consumed is approximately equal to the value of what we give up in exchange for the unit. A zero price goes with zero enjoyment of the last unit. With pollution still in the water, though it be the optimal amount approved by Professor Pigou, the mobile population along rivers—and environmentalists in other regions—will likely call for more pollution control, which means a higher tax or some form of regulation.[3] Of course, political action is not costless, so the concerned population may not clamor for complete elimination of pollution, but that outcome is clearly the more desirable one from their standpoint. Unless the Pigovian solution calls for zero discharge, the solution tends to be politically unstable. A reading of the Federal Water Pollution Control Act of 1972 clearly communicates this point. The statute called for *zero* pollution in the nation's rivers and streams by 1985. That goal obviously was not and cannot be met. But that goal, and only that goal, which everyone had to know was an impossibility, satisfied the dedicated environmentalists who influenced the writing of the statute.

The One-Sided Solution

What we have here is a commons problem with a one-sided solution. There is a demand for water quality, which is scarce but unrationed. Part of the demand relates to industrial production. Paper mills want to discharge waste into the river to produce paper. People along the river wish to enjoy nature's bounty. Thus, there is competition for use of the commons. If one group, say the paper mills, is required to pay a price for using the commons, we can predict that their use will decline. But the competing groups, including political action groups, will lobby for more control yet want to pay nothing directly. They understandably want to expand their use of the commons. The one-sided solution leaves an unstable outcome. In contrast, when all users of the environment pay recognized rightholders for the benefits they receive, the environment is protected by the system of rights. When only one group pays, the rights system tends to break down again. A commons is a commons so long as a group of users has free access. As Louis De Alessi (1998) points out, a policy that fails to ensure reciprocity of costs will fail to solve environmental problems.

The Political Economy of Pigovian Taxes

Imposing a tax on the polluter offers a centralized approach to the pollution problem. It is possible, but highly doubtful, that Pigovian taxes can be found that reflect a best effort by politicians to deal exclusively with environmental costs. But the political economy of the situations raises serious doubts about the frequency of such outcomes in a majoritarian democracy. The logic for taking a pessimistic view reflects assumptions about politicians: Politicians want to keep their jobs; they seek to serve the interests that support them.

Think for a moment about Pigovian taxes and the interest groups that might favor or oppose them. Then, consider the relative strength of organized interest groups and their ability to provide meaningful support to politicians who seek to serve the public interest by pricing away external costs. Some environmental organizations would likely support Pigovian taxes. Perhaps downstream landowners who believe the taxes will improve their lot will lend their support.[4]

But not all environmental organizations support taxes on pollution. Some believe that setting a price on pollution accepts pollution as a legitimate feature of life, which is repugnant to many committed environmentalists. Among supporters of the Pigovian way, we should also throw in a few economists who like the idea of putting prices on environmental use. But industries seldom favor taxes that increase the price of their products; they are likely to alert consumers of their products that could become more costly, urging the consumers to join an antitax parade. We are left with relatively weak support for the politician who simply seeks to serve the public interest by imposing the "efficient" tax on polluters. But the story doesn't end here. Politicians who seek to serve other interests may still push for taxes that wear the clothing of Pigou.

The special interest theory of politics claims that politicians will, more often than not, take actions that provide well-identified benefits to narrowly defined special interest groups. Suppose producers of corn and corn products discover that they can also produce ethanol, a substitute for gasoline. Suppose that ethanol is asserted to be cleaner burning than petroleum-based gasoline. The ethanol producers organize and seek special tax treatment for their fuel. Instead of asking for a higher tax on gasoline, they ask for a subsidy or a lower tax on ethanol-based fuels. The larger the subsidy or smaller the tax, the lower will be the relative price of ethanol. The market for ethanol will expand, and ethanol producers capture the benefits of a Pigovian-type tax that claims to deal with externalities.

Similar logic can be applied to taxes placed on the sulfur content of fuels, such as coal and oil. Producers of natural gas, hydropower, and other substitutes for carbon-based fuels will appreciate a tax that reduces the relative price of their products. They may support a Pigovian tax on carbon.

Another theory of political behavior says that politicians constantly seek new sources of revenue that can be spent to serve interest groups that favor the politicians. Citizens generally favor taxes that are placed on someone other than themselves. This seems to be the case even though consumers ultimately pay all taxes, one way or another.[5] A tax that seems to address a pollution problem generates revenues that can be spent on politically popular activities. The revenue maximizing politician, who wants funds to spend on unrelated projects, may support Pigovian taxes, even though the support is not based on environmental considerations. Along these lines, consider the Organization for Economic Cooperation and Development's (OECD) description of amendments modifying the "Polluter-Pays Principle" in the Netherlands:

> These amendments resulted in a replacement of the five previous charges by *one general fuel* charge as well as the abandonment of other charges theoretically allowed for in legislation but never applied. Approximately two-thirds of this charge has the character of a surtax on the mineral oil excise duties; the other third has the character of a levy. Although this charge is considered a product charge in [their] report, its meaning is much broader because of the general financial characteristics of this instrument, i.e., financing the majority of the Ministry's expenses for its environmental programme. (OECD 1989, 58)

The OECD reports a similar conclusion on the French system of water pollution fees: "The French charge system is purely revenue raising, intended to finance the year-to-year expenditures by the six responsible Agences Financieres de Bassin" (OECD 1989, 37). In recent discussions of Pigovian taxes in the European Union, revenue hungry politicians were assisted by some environmental economists who argue that Pigovian taxes can replace taxes that currently fall on labor, thereby increasing employment while simultaneously improving environmental quality, yielding a so-called "double dividend" (Egenhofer 1996, 1).

By combining public interest, special interest, and revenue-maximizing theories of political behavior, we can expand the support base for Pigovian taxes. Along with some environmental organizations, receivers of pollution, and a few economists, we can also expect support for such taxes from producers of competing products and politicians who seek to reduce the tax burden that falls directly on citizens. This gives a much stronger case for Professor Pigou's tax plan.

Coase and Market Forces

Ronald Coase focused tightly on the Pigovian solution and arrived at a very different way of looking at the same pollution problem, as well as every other problem of social cost. Assuming a system of well-specified property rights, his analysis led him to conclude that were it not for transaction costs, that is, the costs parties incur in dealing with one another, there would be no pollution problem. Yes, there would be pollution, but the amount would be agreed upon voluntarily by producers and receivers of pollution.

The Mill, the River, and the Downstream Community

The Coasean story, like that of Pigou, can be told in terms of a paper mill located on a remote river—a common-access resource—that seeks to minimize the cost of producing paper. The location of the mill is not a random occurrence. The river is an important input to the production process. The river provides water used in producing paper and then provides carriage for waste discharged from the production process. In other words, the mill operators value the river. Indeed, they probably paid a premium for the land because of the river.

Like all production inputs, use of the river is determined by its cost to the mill. If river use comes without a bill—a common-access resource—the mill will use more water. Production theory tells us that all the previous units of water used provide positive, but declining, benefits. This outcome can be easily visualized where the mill's demand for the river's assimilative and waste transportation capacity is labeled marginal benefit. The marginal benefit curve slopes downward, indicating that the initial benefits are relatively large. If river use is free, the mill will tend to discharge waste to the point where the net marginal benefit is zero.

The value of the river to the mill is determined by what the mill would have to do if the river disappeared. The mill would still require water for its production process and would still have to get rid of its waste products, which means that some kind of disposal system would be built or alternate location chosen. The imaginary marginal benefit curve is the inverse of a rising marginal cost curve. Benefits denied are costs incurred. Remember that it is very costly for the mill to reduce its discharge to zero, but the first units of waste it removes are relatively cheap.

Now suppose people live downstream from the mill in a remote location on the outer fringe of a large city. It is a charming location, set on hills that slope down to the river. The spot was carefully selected by a developer who constructed a community complete with recreational facilities and a boat dock. As explained by Rinehart and Pompe (1997), developers assign value to riparian land, even though the adjacent stream or ocean is a common-access resource. Wealth-maximizing developers will build and locate condominiums to maximize the value of the complete environmental package. In our terms, the real estate developer estimates the marginal benefits of the unpolluted river that passes the downstream development, and like all marginal benefits these diminish as the development expands. Since units of the river can be consumed at no additional cost to the developer, the developer will construct units until the last unit built derives zero benefit from the river's location. Similarly, the homeowners will use the river up to the point where the net marginal benefit is zero. Any denial of benefits imposes a cost on the development. If the river deteriorates slightly, there is relatively low cost, but if the entire river disappears or becomes a waste dump, then the imposed costs reach their upper limit.

At the outset of this story, the paper mill imposes no cost on the downstream community; the waste discharged to the river is assimilated at it moves downstream. The downstream community is aware that the mill exists somewhere upstream but is not bothered by the mill's operation. Everything is fine until the mill increases its production, which comes when demand for its product increases. Increased production taxes the assimilative capacity of the river. Eventually, with rising demand for paper and more daily discharge, the river begins to deteriorate. Now, we move to the downstream community.

People who live in the community gather on weekends to enjoy swimming, fishing, and boating. On one of these happy occasions, residents, much to their distress, see odd colors in the water, notice a peculiar odor, and then see a few dead fish. Their getaway from the city has been invaded by pollution. Some of the marginal benefits enjoyed previously have been taken away. Costs are imposed on the community. The mill enjoys 100 percent discharge of wastes; the community is gradually losing its previous 100 percent of the river's value. Expansion of water quality for the community means reducing discharge by the mill, and vice versa. Use of the river by the mill produces value in the form of lower cost quantities of paper. Use of the river by the community produces value in the form of lower cost quantities of residential life. There is scarcity. Coase reminds us that tradeoffs are inevitable. Is paper production more valuable than water quality to the community? The next part of the story addresses this question.

Finding a Property Rights Solution

Suppose it is election time; a candidate seeking a seat in the House of Representatives hears about the voters who live along the river and makes an appointment to visit. The community is pleased to hear from the politician. They have a problem they hope the politician will solve.

On the evening of the politician's visit, she is asked to talk about her platform. After telling about her desire to cut taxes, improve welfare programs, reduce red tape, and make the streets safer for citizens, she stops to take questions. A member of the community rises and asks the big questions: "Where do you stand on the environment? Have you seen the polluted mess outside?"

The politician will, no doubt, say that if she is elected, she will sponsor a bill that gives environmental rights to communities like this one. No polluter should have the right to destroy the environment. There will be no more indiscriminate discharge of waste, if she is elected.

Having given the right answer, the politician receives support from members of the community. True to her word, she sponsors a river protection act that contains the details she promised to the community. The act becomes law; the community celebrates, and the paper mill cuts its emissions to zero. The mill incurs a high cost for handling its waste in another way. The community, on the other hand, has reclaimed its original level of water quality. With zero discharge affecting the community, the community owners enjoy marginal benefits of zero. The marginal benefit to the mill of being allowed to discharge a small amount of waste is larger than zero. There are potential gains from trade. This is where transaction costs enter the picture. If those costs are small enough, the mill operator may be able to entice the community to accept a little waste in the community's river. Remember, the federal statute transferred ownership to the community.

Suppose the mill operator calls a key member of the community and asks: "Would you allow us to discharge some waste into your river?" An emotional response might not be repeatable. After all, the community has just recovered from the days when pollution practically destroyed the local environment. But a more dispassionate analysis may yield another response. Suppose the mill operator says: "We will be happy to pay you for each unit we discharge. Our records of discharge will be monitored by a certified environmental engineer. If we violate the contract, you can haul us into court." Since the marginal benefits of discharge to the mill, across some zone of discharge, are larger than the marginal losses sustained by the community, the mill operator can pay enough to purchase some discharge rights from the community.

For the sake of our analysis, suppose the community agrees to sell the mill some discharge rights. They use the funds generated to make community improvements that are worth more to them than the slight deterioration of the river. As transfers are made between the two parties, the action generates an outcome where the marginal benefits of discharge to the mill are equal to the community's loss of benefits caused by the discharge. Since the outcome is based on voluntary agreement between the affected parties, economists call it an optimal outcome. We recognize that the cost of transacting had to be small enough, given the value of the potential gains, to allow the water-rights trading to take place.

The solution is based on several important institutional traits. Of key importance, property rights to the river were assigned to one of the trading parties and the rights were enforced by statute. The statute allowed for exchange between parties, so long as all affected parties agreed to the outcome. Finally, the mill operator agreed to an enforceable contract based on outcomes assured by a third-party auditor. We are now halfway into the Coase analysis. Coase's crucial point is yet to be made.

Return to the politician who visited the riverside community and promised to pass a property rights statute if elected, but let us revise the story. There was another politician running for office who did not visit the community. He visited the paper mill. This politician spoke to a gathering of mill employees and managers and told them that their future was threatened by a group of unreasonable environmentalists who wanted to shut down an American factory and destroy free enterprise. To the sound of cheers and applause, the politician said: "If you send me to Washington, I will make it safe to produce paper in this country. I will push through a statute that gives rights to use rivers and streams to all firms that produce valuable products for the marketplace." The mill operators and its employees' union offer their support for the campaign. This politician defeated the candidate who supported environmental rights for the downstream community.

When the new statute was passed that opened the valves of America's polluting industries, paper mill operators gave a sigh of relief. They had been concerned about the possibilities of demonstrations and petitions; they could now use the river, pollute, and relax. Members of the downstream community install air conditioners and odor reducing devices and build fences to block the view of the dead fish in the river. Recall that the mill received little benefit for the last units of waste it discharged, and the community suffered considerable harm as the river reached its biological death. There are obvious gains from trade, if the community can entice the mill to reduce its discharge by some small amount.

Let a spokesman for the community call the mill operator and say: "We despise what you are doing, but the river is yours. Would you consider reducing your waste by a small amount? Just take out the big chunks. We will pay you for each unit of waste removed." Reflection on the previous analysis tells us again that the community can outbid the mill for water quality to a point. The value to the community of cleaner water is likely to be higher than the cost to the mill of alternative effluent disposal. In fact, it is to the same point that was reached when the community owned the river, and the mill was doing the bidding.

Coase's Insights

In telling this story, it is natural that we sympathize more with one party than the other. Most people relate more to the community that had enjoyed water quality until the mill spoiled it. Others relate to the mill and its employees that had enjoyed the use of the river until the community moved in and complained. The point, however, is not to argue one side or the other, but to see that each party imposed costs on the other. This is one of Coase's key points. Externalities flow both ways because costs and benefits flow both ways. There is no such thing as a one-sided externality problem.

The final key point in the story relates to the outcome generated when the two parties engaged in trade. The outcome is the same, no matter which party holds the rights. The deeper implication of this outcome relates to the value of the two activities. Bidders for more valuable use of the river are able to outbid the less valuable uses. Put differently, the low-cost avoider of the problem makes the largest adjustment. In addition, the system is forward-, not backward-looking. Instead of looking at the current users and finding solutions that fit the needs of existing technologies and plans, the more dynamic approach encourages all users to focus on the future: What is the lowest-cost way to organize my use of the environment? Can I find a new approach that enables me to bid more for the resource? Putting it this way makes another point: Trade based on property rights brings a solution that minimizes society's costs for managing valuable water quality.

Coase and Common Law Rules

The stylized river story, which seeks to present the essence of Coase's bargaining model, yields some interesting insights but leaves a concern that in many cases one will not find two well-identified and organized groups such as the paper mill and community that can bargain at such low cost. The world is just too complicated for this to happen. Does high bargaining cost leave us with no other alternative but to return to Pigou? Coase addresses this question in a retrospective of his 1960 article:

> It would not seem worthwhile to spend much time investigating the properties of [a world with zero transaction costs]. What my argument does suggest is the need to introduce positive transaction costs explicitly into economic analysis so that we can study the world that exists. This has not been the effect of my article. (Coase 1988, 15)

There is obviously far more to the story.

Coase was not analyzing a world of zero transaction costs, nor were those in the academic community who were inspired by his contribution. While he did not emphasize its crucial role, his discussion was

based on common law—informal, judge-made law that focuses on contracts, torts, and property. His challenge to Pigou really involved the
legal environment, not the economic analysis of pollution. As explained
by Elizabeth Brubaker (1998), common law protection of environmental rights has an ancient heritage. At the time of Pigou's analysis, England had long operated under rules of common law where downstream
holders of riparian rights could bring suit for damages if their rights
were taken. Property rights formed the basis for common law rules. If
a paper mill discharged wastes into a river that flows by land owned or
occupied by other people, it was possible for the dirty water to reduce
the value of the land, reduce the quality of fishing, or just make life
miserable, that is, infringe on the landowner's common law rights.[6] The
common law caused a common-access resource, the river, to be treated
like private property. With common law in place, it is not necessary for
anyone to own the river. Property rights were an explicit component of
common law.

At common law, a plaintiff (downstream water user) must demonstrate damages to obtain relief in court. Loose assertions about environmental quality and the need to protect it will not do the job. Ownership
of damaged property or loss of recognized rights must be shown. Information relevant to the harm must be provided. The common law protects rightholders—those who seek to preserve the environment as they
want it and those who wish to use it for production—from being dis-
rupted by those who simply do not like what they see.

Unlike the remedy offered by the Pigovian solution, remedies based
on common law are two-sided. If a downstream landowner has invested
in land, expecting to receive a predictable level of water quality, he has
incurred a cost that relates to his demand for environmental quality. He
has paid for environmental rights. That takes care of one side of the
commons problem. Investment in land that carries riparian rights pre-
cludes other investments that might be made with the same funds; the
landowner is bearing an opportunity cost for environmental quality.

Under common law, to avoid litigation a mill operator who desires to
degrade water quality by discharging waste must first gain the approval
of the downstream rightholder, that is, purchase environmental rights
(Davis 1971). That takes care of the other side of the problem. Having
purchased rights, the mill owner bears the opportunity cost of environmental quality he seeks to use. If the landowner held some rights after
selling some water quality rights to the mill, then the rights still being
held carry an opportunity cost. In any case, both transacting parties are
bearing the cost of their environmental preferences. Coase's famous
bargaining solution may require very little direct bargaining. The envi-

ronmental bargain is a part of land transactions and credible threats of common law suits discipline the market process.

How far can the market process carry us in resolving environmental problems? If property rights are defined and enforced, will all meaningful spillover problems disappear? The theory answers affirmatively; as explained in the next section, market forces generate a wide variety of beneficial responses. Still, the political economy provides liability protection and common law shields that limit the reach of the law. Laissez-faire and the rule of law will guard environmental assets. If we are to apply laissez-faire, we must first clear the way.

The Broader Market Process and the Environment

The earlier discussion of Pigovian taxes and regulation was based on the assumption of market failure. Somehow the polluter was able to discharge waste without paying a penalty at least as large as the cost imposed on people downstream. But what about my friend who worked after school for the paper mill? Is there something here that speaks to market failure and the motivation of firms to protect environmental assets?

The paper mill that employed my friend was owned by Mead Corporation, a company headquartered in Ohio. The mill was located in middle Georgia. Why might Mead spend money to monitor water quality in a distant river? Is it possible for the desires of people along a river in Georgia to be systematically communicated to the headquarters of a firm in Ohio? And how would those expenditures be shown in figure 5.2? Recall that the firm's supply curve did not capture all the cost of producing paper. The wages paid to my friend and the cost of running the laboratory for analyzing river water are included in the supply curve. Logic tells us that these payments narrow the gap between private and social cost. Indeed, if water quality monitoring completely eliminates costs that might be imposed downstream, the gap disappears. The supply curve is marginal social cost.

Most likely, the paper mill took precautionary actions because of a combination of forces. Common law rules formed one force. The mill owners did not want to be sued by downstream landowners. Law suits are costly and the firm's reputation as a good citizen is at stake. Firms like Mead have made large investments in their brand name, or brand name capital, and they seek to get a return on those investments. The larger the firm's customer base and the more extensive its product line, the larger the reputational risk that comes from pollution or any other action viewed as improper in the eyes of consumers. Some consumers of Mead products will punish the firm if its brand name becomes tarnished.

Examples of Market Forces

The power of consumer response to information that links a firm to environmental degradation is seen in recent activities undertaken by the Geneva, Switzerland, International Organization for Standardization, which issues voluntary standards for manufacturers. Best known for its ISO-9000 standards that relate to manufacturing quality control, ISO has also developed environmental management standards (ISO-14000) that require a fully integrated management approach aimed at eliminating pollution. To qualify for any ISO standard, a firm must develop costly plans and stand periodic audits to assure that its programs are functioning effectively.

Home Depot, a major national seller of building supplies, requires all of its suppliers to be ISO-14000 certified. The firm's action reflects its perception of consumer interests. If consumers want more assurance that manufacturers are taking steps to reduce pollution, the market process seems destined to deliver. Other firms, including Hitachi, adopt ISO standards for all plant operations worldwide. Multinational firms sometimes show more concern for environmental quality in distant locations than do the people in those locations. Indeed, firms such as Ford Motor Company and Procter & Gamble apply U.S. environmental standards when building and operating plants in other countries.

With voluntary ISO environmental management approach gaining ground, we might expect to see a competitive response from EPA. After all, the rise of more effective voluntary standards poses a threat to EPA's well-established monopoly on environmental regulation. EPA is now embracing and attempting to influence the ISO-14000 process, which has become increasingly popular with state regulatory agencies (*State Environmental Monitor* 1997). The EPA has provided grants to eight state environmental regulatory agencies to learn more about the prospects of ISO-14000 and to blend into the program EPA's definitions of pollution prevention and regulatory compliance.

Another story of efforts to satisfy consumers and protect reputational capital is found in the saga of McDonald's efforts to provide "environmentally correct" packaging for its many hamburger and sandwich products (National Pollution Prevention Center 1995). In the 1970s, McDonald's responded to environmentalists' concerns about timber cutting for paper production by switching from a paper hamburger carton to a polystyrene clamshell. Concerned about its public image, the firm made the switch after obtaining the results of a thorough full-cycle study by the Stanford Research Institute. The study attempted to take into account the full environmental consequences—cradle to grave—of providing paper or plastic containers. Shortly after McDonald's made the conversion, scientists sounded the alarm about the chlorinated fluorocarbons (CFCs) used as a blowing agent in producing polystyrene. The CFCs were linked to destruction of the ozone layer (Harvard Business School 1993). With its highly visible 12,400 restaurants in 59 countries and 18 million daily store visits by customers in the United States, McDonald's was fearful about the loss of its reputation for providing high quality, clean, and safe products.

Environmental groups placed pressure on the firm to do something about the clamshell, labeling the company McToxic. In response, McDonald's installed incinerators at a number of its restaurants to eliminate all solid waste. The firm was then labeled McPuff. Wrestling with the public image problem, McDonald's then developed regional polystyrene recycling centers, which were made available to other firms that lacked recycling capability. All along, however, pressure kept building for the firm to eliminate polystyrene. The former paper container began to look more attractive.

Finally, when schoolchildren nationwide—the heart of the firm's market—were guided into the fray by environmental interest groups, McDonald's threw in the towel. Working with the Environmental Defense Fund, a large environmental group, the firm conducted more research, developed other recycling programs, pressured its suppliers to do the same, and finally adopted a paper container. With that, the pressure ended, and the blemish on the firm's reputation was removed. It is still not clear that paper is environmentally superior to polystyrene. The full-cycle analysis of paper versus polystyrene, which takes into account energy costs, natural resource use, and final disposal, is just not convincing. Paper products do not degrade in landfills. Polystyrene does. In addition, the discarded plastic provides a liner that helps to prevent leaching from landfills. Transaction costs are positive. In any case, reputations matter, and market forces do cause nationally prominent firms to become very sensitive to environmental issues.

Another example of how market forces generate demands for improved environmental management is seen in a golf course certification program developed by the Audubon Sanctuary Program.[7] In this case, Audubon put its brand name at risk. The environmental problem relates to the heavy use of pesticides, herbicides, and fertilizers used to provide the near-perfect greens desired by golfers. When combined with the heavy use of irrigation and sprinklers, use of concentrated chemicals can lead to contamination of surface and groundwater. In the absence of other constraints, golf course operators have an incentive to go after the last weed when manicuring their courses. The incremental cost of chemicals is low, and the perceived value of extended lush fairways is high.

In an effort to provide better information to golf course operators, the Golf Course Superintendents Association developed a stewardship strategy, which provided guidelines for chemical use and information on alternative ways to provide improved greens. Then, in 1990, the Audubon Sanctuary staff began to work with the U.S. Golf Association to improve environmental quality. The effort led to the Audubon certification program. Golf course operators who see value in having the Audubon seal of approval petition Audubon and document the details of their environmental management program. The documentation includes information on chemical use, water conservation, and maintenance of wildlife habitat. Audubon Sanctuary staff work with golf course managers to improve overall environmental management. A similar effort is underway for advanced planning and certification of new golf courses. Managers of certified golf courses display the Audubon logo and in some cases provide each golfer with a flyer telling about their environmental practices. The cooperative effort is voluntary and the steps being taken to protect environmental assets are evidence of market forces at work in a positive transaction cost world.

Market forces deliver environmental protection in yet other less complex ways. Campbell Soup Company pays a premium for tomatoes with low nitrate residues, which gives farmers an incentive to reduce their use of chemical fertilizers. Campbell Soup is apparently responding to concerns expressed by those who buy its food products or is acting in advance of the kind of criticism they know could arise.

Investors in the stock of polluting firms are also interested in the environmental behavior of firm managers. Managers who are careless with rivers and other features of the environment may also be careless when producing and delivering products. Profit maximization implies careful use of all resources over time. Investors generally assign negative value to news of law suits that affect firms in their portfolios. Common-law actions are not viewed positively. Negative reactions lead to sell orders, which cause stock prices to fall. When stock prices fall, the managers of affected firms find it more costly to obtain additional capital; investors can punish polluting firms. The firm's reputation, fear of common-law suits, and investor monitoring give three reasons for polluting firms to discipline their behavior.

Recent work on requirements that U.S. firms provide annual data on the number of pounds of more than six hundred chemicals emitted from their plants illustrates how financial markets react to news about pollution. Konar and Cohen (n.d.) gathered data on the annual listing of emissions, known as the Toxic Release Inventory, and matched the data to the discharging firms listed on major U.S. stock exchanges. Using financial markets analysis to isolate the effects of an event on the movement of specified stock portfolios relative to the market as a whole, the researchers found that firms associated with chemical releases on the annual list experienced systematic losses in share values. Looking at data for a later period, the researchers found that firms that suffered the largest reductions in share values reduced their emissions significantly in the next period. In other words, financial market monitoring matters.

Eco-labeling of consumer products by independent organizations may be seen as yet another approach for reducing the cost of bargaining for improved environmental quality (Thomas 1997). Now popular outside the United States, eco-labeling programs operate in Austria, Canada, Denmark, Finland, France, Germany, Iceland, Japan, the Netherlands, Norway, Sweden, and several Asian countries. Generally developed and administered by quasi governmental organizations, eco-labeling programs, which are voluntary, require interested producers of specified consumer products to provide detailed technical information on the environmental impact of the manufacture, consumption, and final waste disposal of their products, in some cases requiring a full life-cycle environmental impact analysis. Firms that successfully satisfy requirements of the granting authority, and who agree to stand periodic random audits, receive contract authority to affix a highly recognized label on their products and in their advertisements. Ideally, eco-labeling enables uninformed buyers to make better consumption choices, thereby sending market signals that promote an additional element of market competition.

While eco-labeling may induce producers to take efficient steps toward internalizing the cost of environmental use, there is a downside to such programs. Domestic producers seem to have a systematic advantage over their international counterparts in obtaining eco-label authority. Part of the advantage stems from the development of criteria to be used in judging the relative merits of products, which are inherently technical and therefore subject to special interest influence. In addition, governmental authorities, such as the European Union, have moved to harmonize and institutionalize the eco-labeling process (European Council Regulation 1992). What began as a quasi competitive use of market forces to provide consumer information could become a part of an unyielding bureaucratic process that chills international competition.

There is one last motivation that nudges factory managers in the direction of providing better care for the environment. Factory managers and employees generally live near the vicinity of the factory; some will likely live downstream. If the pollution that spews from a factory contaminates drinking water supplies and in other ways diminishes the quality of life for employees, the managers and owners will eventually bear some of the cost. The extent to which this concern causes managers to reduce pollution nudges the firm's supply curve closer to the marginal social cost curve. Some firms require managers to live next to their plants to help demonstrate their environmental commitment.

Protection of reputational capital, avoidance of common-law suits, fear of investor punishment, and concern for community yield a set of forces that can push profit-hungry management in the direction of environmental protection. But even the most diligent factory managers can fail to protect environmental assets. There will be spills and accidents that impose unwanted costs on downstream owners and citizens. Environmental insurance provides a standard approach for managing this risk, yet insurance carries costs and imposes special demands on clients. Standard commercial insurance for environmental risks requires periodic inspections of facilities, training programs for employees, and other accident-reducing steps to be taken. When firms take all the actions mentioned and also purchase insurance to cover environmental liabilities, the associated costs become embodied in the firm's supply curve. This moves the curve all the closer to marginal social cost and the elimination of "market failure."

How Reliable Are Market Forces?

It is obvious that some industrial firms will take actions to protect common-access resources, like rivers, but how reliable are these forces? Will all firms respond to the forces we have just discussed? Or are some firms more responsive than others?

Our theory-based discussion spoke of common-law suits, reputation, investor monitoring, community protection, and insurance as motivating factors. The motivation related to cost avoidance, or profit maximization. Those motivations will be weakest for polluters that are not challenged by market forces: publicly owned sewage treatment plants and hospitals, military and defense establishments, and all governmental units. Indeed, the threat of common-law suits is completely missing for public units; they enjoy immunity from such actions. Brand name reputation carries less weight, since many public units are monopolies that do not compete directly for consumer patronage. There is no stock market monitoring of the United States Army that punishes it for inflicting groundwater damage at one of its bases, and most public units carry no environmental insurance. All else equal, publicly owned and operated facilities will be less careful with the environment than privately owned units. Evidence of this tendency is reported in a 1995 survey of the hazardous waste cleanup challenge faced by federal government agencies (Council on Environmental Quality and Office of Management and Budget 1995). The Department of Energy has 10,000 potentially contaminated sites; the Department of Defense more than 21,000; the Department of the Interior some 26,000; and the U.S. Department of Agriculture, some 3,000 (Council on Environmental Quality and Office of Management and Budget 1995, 17). The federal survey indicated that as much as $389 billion would be required over the next seventy-five years to address the problem (Council on Environmental Quality and Office of Management and Budget 1995, 32).

The public sector pollution problem is also seen in U.S. urban areas where cities do not feel the spur of common-law liability, brand name capital, and capital market monitoring. Recently, an Atlanta-based organization called the Upper Chattahoochee Riverkeeper, which was formed for the purpose of monitoring the Chattahoochee River, reported a number of water quality violations by the City of Atlanta that involved uncontrolled discharge of raw sewage into the river (Seabrook and Helton 1997). Upper Chattahoochee Riverkeeper is one of 3,000 grassroots river conservation groups now working nationwide to monitor and improve water quality.[8]

Relying on dedicated volunteers, Riverkeeper has blown the whistle on the city of Atlanta, which is paying a $20,000 daily fine to the state of Georgia because of permit violations associated with city-operated sewage treatment plants. Paradoxically, the same issue of the newspaper that told of Riverkeeper's effort reported on actions by the Georgia legislature to provide immunity to the Atlanta Hawks basketball arena and the Atlanta Housing Authority in meeting a moratorium on sewage discharge (*Atlanta Constitution* 1997). Riverkeeper, a private group, is monitoring water quality and seeking to discipline government. The government is seeking to increase its pollution while trying to placate Riverkeeper. Professor Pigou prefaced his proposal for government action with the words "if it so chooses." He would not like the way the real world works.

Looking further, we can conclude that private firms that do not need brand name capital or public reputations and that are privately owned will not experience as much of the force of the market for reputational and financial capital. These are likely to be less responsive to environmental concerns than their market-exposed counterparts. All of the factors that push in the direction of environmental protection rely heavily on actions taken by consumers, investors, or private citizens. If none of these are concerned about pollution, the management of firms will

likely show little concern if there are not clearly established rights to
the use of the environment.

Rising Incomes and Private Action

Can we depend on consumers and widely dispersed citizens to demonstrate concern for environmental quality? Based on research and casual observation, we know that income has a great deal to do with
environmental concern. The higher the level of income, all else equal,
the more people value the environment. Rising income is one of the
most important forces leading to environmental cleanup. At the low
income end of the social spectrum, people do their best to provide the
basic necessities to their families. Food, shelter, and basic health are
assigned far more importance than improving water and air quality. In
the lowest income cases, life expectancies are too short to reap the
benefits of a cleaner environment. As income rises and basic necessities
are provided, individuals become more concerned about the world in
which they live. Longevity increases, and with longer expected life-
times, people become more concerned about avoiding environmental
diseases that have long gestation periods. In addition, the environment
where they will spend their retirement years becomes more relevant.
Natural resources, parks, forests, and scenic beauty become more important.

Empirical research on the linkage between income growth and environmental quality supports the hypothesis that economic growth leads
to improvements in environmental quality (Norton 1998). Using data
on air quality, income, and other variables for a sample of 42 countries,
Grossman and Krueger (1991) isolated the relationship between levels
of income and levels of pollution. Income levels in the sample were as
low as $1,000 annually and as high as $17,000. The results of their
statistical modeling indicate that environmental quality falls in the earlier stages of industrialization when per capita incomes are less than
$5,000 annually. After that, environmental quality systematically rises
with income growth. Other research on income growth and environmental quality for developed countries indicates that a 1 percent increase in income leads to a 2.5 percent increase in the demand for
environmental improvements (Coursey 1992).

Research by Rinehart and Pompe on beach and resort development,
which reviewed the treatment of amenities and natural resources across
several decades, supports the view that higher incomes generate more
environmental protection (Rinehart and Pompe 1997). They find that
developers now assign significant importance to the complete environmental package when building new resort communities. Trees, species

habitat, wetlands, natural beach access, and wide expanses of beach-front are carefully preserved to enhance property values. The relationship between income growth and demand for environmental quality, the income elasticity of demand, is about the same for Mercedes and BMW automobiles. This implies that richer is better, especially for the environment.

Firms that locate in higher-income communities face a higher likelihood of common-law suits and complaints over pollution than will firms that locate in lower-income communities. We should expect similar levels of attention to be paid by investors in the shares of stocks of polluting firms. Reputational capital will be more important and therefore riskier in higher-income communities.

Consideration of these market forces helps us to understand why nature seems to have been mistreated in early industrial periods, and why improvements came in later periods. Critics of the reliability of market forces often point out that in past periods, say during the industrial revolution, the rivers were despoiled, forest land denuded, and air quality was allowed to deteriorate. They suggest that any relaxation of government regulation of the environment today would lead to similar outcomes. The effects of rising incomes, shorter work weeks, and longer life expectancies on the demand for environmental quality imply that command-and-control regulation is less important today than twenty or thirty years ago. At the same time, we find that community attention to environmental concerns is found most frequently in higher-income countries and regions, giving politicians added incentive to act. In short, both market and political forces are fed by rising incomes.

When the "market failure" story is fleshed out with institutional detail, market failures tend to disappear, at least for a large category of firms. Any pollution that remains leads us to speculate that the cost of eliminating that part may be greater than the resulting benefits. Human ingenuity, the mainspring of the market process, constantly drives toward elimination of relevant costs, but any path taken will itself be costly. In that sense, there is a supply of and demand for solutions to problems like pollution. When the value of taking one more step is greater than the cost, the next step will be taken. But there is always friction in every system, whether it be mechanical or social. In this case, the friction is transaction costs. People have to organize, communicate, make agreements, and enforce them, and all this is costly. If transaction costs were eliminated, the world would be a very different place.

Externalities, Pigou, and Coase: Final Thoughts

This chapter has discussed pollution as a negative externality—unwanted costs that can be imposed on unwitting parties who have no direct voice in the polluter's decision. Two very different approaches to the problem have been described. Pigou's solution spoke of market failure and the need for a central authority to fine-tune markets so that the appropriate level of pollution would emerge. This approach called for collection of complicated and rapidly changing information, translating the information into a tax or regulation, and imposing the tax or rule on the polluter. This chapter considered some of the problems with this approach and indicated that in spite of the problems, Pigovian taxes continue to be debated and used.

Following Pigou, the chapter turned to the Coasean analysis of the same problem. Instead of speaking of market failure, this analysis looked to markets for the solution. Where transaction costs are low and property rights are clearly assigned, the market process can lead to an optimal solution. The Coase solution takes a decentralized, process approach where parties involved in the problem assemble their own information and use it in formulating contracts, just as in any other market. The Coase solution is dynamic. If conditions change, the parties can revise their agreement in the next contracting period. They do not have to wait for elections and changes in national statutes.

In its barest form, the Coasean approach seems to fit small numbers cases where people involved in a problem can transact, an issue discussed by De Alessi (1998) in this collection. The Pigovian approach seems to fit larger numbers cases, where there are just too many parties to rely on contracts and trading. But before jumping to conclusions about the relative merits of the two approaches, we should recognize that large numbers cases can become smaller numbers when the large numbers form associations, clubs, or firms, such as river basin associations.

In thinking about Coase versus Pigou, we should also recall the purpose of Coase's investigation; he wanted to understand a world in which transaction costs are positive. When we investigate that world, a rich array of quality assurance devices are observed. Rules of liability and common law rules form a minor part of that world. Brand name capital, capital market monitoring, concern for community, and third-party monitoring form a major part. These are evidence of positive transaction costs that limit direct Coasean bargaining. Among the world players are governments and other organizations that are immune to the spur of competition and have no need for quality assurance. It is this part of the world that Pigou was really addressing. It is government itself that must be controlled with government regulation.

At first blush, suggesting that government should focus on itself, imposing command-and-control regulation on government enterprises and leaving the unfettered forces of the market to deal with private firms and individuals, seems itself to be a Pigovian prescription. The recommendation implicitly assumes that a centralized authority managed by wise welfare-maximizing economists will rule the day. Yet if Public Choice theory has taught anything, it is that government is endogenous to the political economy. Barring benevolent dictatorships, there is no ruling authority. Process alone determines outcomes, and it is in analyzing process that Coase has the advantage over Pigou.

To avoid the Pigovian trap, we must focus on first principles, constitutional rules that recognize privately arranged property rules of the sort discussed by Richard Wagner (1998). When the rule of law is accepted by consensus, the role of government become clear. Government has a constitutional duty to protect property rights and accordingly to manage its own affairs so the unwanted costs are not imposed on citizens. When fundamental constitutional protections are compromised by the politics of expediency, we find ourselves at sea without an anchor. Instead of pleading for Pigovian solutions that compromise constitutional property rights protection, we should call for a constitutional order that minimizes the need for Pigovian approaches and maximizes the domain for Coasean bargaining.

We live our lives in a world formed by statutes and rules. There is tension between the rule of law and rule by politics. Property rights and the market process affect and are affected by the political forces as they play through the larger social system. Political initiatives inspired by purposeful interest groups encounter the untamed forces of the market where contracts and property rights dictate outcomes. New institutions for protecting environmental assets that emerge from the market encounter the raw forces of politics and an entrenched bureaucracy. Each day, a new world emerges from these encounters. Part of the outcome we observe is Coasean; another part is Pigovian. Underlying it all is a system of property rights that continues to evolve. Both Coase and Pigou help us to understand this evolutionary process that generates an ever-changing definition of environmental rights.

Notes

1. Hayek (1969, 264). In his discussion, Hayek refers to A. C. Pigou's 1954 article, "Some Aspects of the Welfare State," *Diogenes* 7: 6.

2. Hayek (1969, 123) expresses grave concern about the tendency for economists and other scientists to become overspecialized: "But nobody can become a great economist who is only an economist—and I am even tempted to add that the economist who is only an economist is likely to become a nuisance if not a positive danger."

3. This second round of pressure is referred to as post-equilibrium bargain-

ing (Turvey 1963; Cordes 1981). Opinion surveys regularly indicate that the public thinks more needs to be done about the environment, even where improvements have been so great that there is little evidence of any problem.

4. Page 3 of "Notes from the Environmental Grantmakers Association Meeting" held February 3–4, 1997, Embassy Row Hotel, Washington, D.C., included the following statement: "Pollution taxes are an ideal way to deal with pollution. It raises money and can be sold as a market mechanism."

5. An interesting exception to this is found in the failure to pass of a November 1996 Florida referendum on placing a one penny per pound tax on sugar produced by Florida sugar firms for the avowed purpose of mitigating the effects of pollution in the Florida Everglades. The tax, which would have raised an estimated $37 million annually, would have been lightly felt by many people. A campaign opposing the tax pointed out that Florida sugar cane growers were already paying $233 to $322 million annually of $685 million being spent by state government to deal with the problem (Blumel 1996).

6. Common-law rules provide owners of land adjacent to a stream the right to beneficial use of an uninterrupted supply of water of undeteriorated quality. If water quality has been *unreasonably* reduced by an upstream user, the holders of riparian rights have a cause of action against the polluter.

7. On this, see Golf Course Superintendents Association (1996a and 1996b); Costa (1996, 176).

8. Conversation with Chad Smith, spokesman for American Rivers, May 12, 1997. American Rivers is a national umbrella organization with 20,000 members that coordinates and promotes the activities of the grassroots organizations.

References

Atlanta Constitution. 1997. Panel Passes Exemption for Arena's Sewers, March 19, B-2.

Blumel, Philip. 1996. *Is the Proposed Sugar Tax a Good Thing?* James Madison Institute, Tallahassee, FL, October.

Boudreaux, Donald J., and Roger E. Meiners. 1998. Existence Value and Other of Life's Ills, this volume.

Brannlund, Runar. 1995. Where Have Eco-Taxes Worked? The Swedish Experience. Presentation at the Center for European Policy Studies, Brussels, Belgium, December.

Brubaker, Elizabeth. 1998. The Common Law and the Environment: The Canadian Experience, this volume.

Buchanan, James M., and William Craig Stubblebine. 1962. Externality. *Economica* 29(November): 371–84.

Coase, Ronald H. 1960. The Problem of Social Cost. *Journal of Law & Economics* 3(1): 1–44.

———. 1988. *The Firm, the Law, and the Market*. Chicago: University of Chicago Press.

Cordes, J. J. 1981. The Relative Efficiency of Taxes and Standards. *Public Finance* 36: 339–42.

Costa, Bob. 1996. Golf and the Environment: Initiating Change. *Golf Course Management.* Lawrence, KS: Golf Course Superintendents Association of America, February, 136.

Council on Environmental Quality and Office of Management and Budget. 1995. *Improving Federal Facilities Cleanup.* Report of the Federal Facilities Cleanup Group, Washington, D.C., October.

Coursey, Don. 1992. The Demand for Environmental Quality. Department of Economics, Washington University, St. Louis, MO.

Davis, Peter N. 1971. Theories of Water Pollution Litigation. *Wisconsin Law Review* 3: 738–81.

De Alessi, Louis. 1998. Private Property Rights as the Basis for Free Market Environmentalism, this volume.

Egenhofer, Christian. 1996. *Applying Economic Instruments in EU Environmental Policy: Challenges, Experiences and Prospects.* Business Policy Report No. 2. Brussels: Center for European Policy Studies, September.

European Council Regulation (EEC). 1992. *Official Journal of the European Communities*, March 23.

Golf Course Superintendents Association of America. 1996a. Environmental Activists Tee Off. *Golf Course Management* (February): 22–40.

———. 1996b. *The Audubon Cooperative Sanctuary Program for Golf Courses* [cited 8 October 1997]. Available on the Internet from www.gcsaa.org.

Grossman, Gene M., and Alan B. Krueger. 1991. Environmental Impacts of a North American Free Trade Agreement. Working Paper 3914. National Bureau of Economic Research, Cambridge, MA.

Harvard Business School. 1993. *Du Pont Freon Products Division (A).* Harvard Business School Case 9–389–11. Boston, MA, October 18.

Hayek, F. A. 1969. *Studies in Philosophy, Politics and Economics.* New York: Simon and Schuster.

Konar, Shameek, and Mark A. Cohen. N.d. Information as Regulation: The Effects of Community Right to Know Laws on Toxic Emissions. *Journal of Environmental Economics and Management,* forthcoming.

Macaulay, Hugh H. 1972. Environmental Quality, the Market, and Public Finance. In *Modern Fiscal Issues*, ed. Richard Bird and John G. Head. Toronto: University of Toronto Press, 187–224.

National Pollution Prevention Center. 1995. *McDonald's/EDF: Case Study.* Ann Arbor, MI, March.

Norton, Seth. 1998. Property Rights, the Environment, and Economic Well-Being, this volume.

Organization for Economic Cooperation and Development. 1989. *Economic Instruments for Environmental Protection.* Paris: OECD.

Pigou, A. C. 1920. *The Economics of Welfare.* London: Macmillan.

Rinehart, James R., and Jeffrey J. Pompe. 1997. Entrepreneurship and Coast Resource Management. *Independent Review* 1(Spring): 543–59.

Seabrook, Charles, and Charmagne Helton. 1997. A Fine Mess: Sewage Runoff
  Puts City Up the Creek, Again. *Atlanta Constitution*, March 19, 1.
State Environmental Monitor. 1997. USEPA Gives Eight States ISO 14000
  'Management System' Grants. Washington, D.C.: Inside Washington, May 5,
  19–20.
Thomas, Stacie. 1997. Eco-Seals as Market-Based Incentives for Improving the
  Environment: Promises, Pitfalls, Opportunities, and Risks. Center for Pol-
  icy & Legal Studies, Clemson University, Clemson, SC.
Tietenberg, Tom. 1992. *Environmental and Natural Resources Economics*. New
  York: HarperCollins.
Turvey, Ralph. 1963. On Divergences between Social Cost and Private Cost.
  Economica 30(August): 309–13.
Wagner, Richard E. 1998. The Constitutional Protection of Private Property,
  this volume.
World Bank. 1996. *Market Based Instruments for Environmental Policymaking
  in Latin American and the Caribbean: Lessons from Eleven Countries*. Wash-
  ington, D.C.: World Bank.
Yandle, Bruce. 1997. *Common Sense and Common Law for the Environment:
  Creating Wealth in Hummingbird Economies*. Lanham, MD: Rowman & Lit-
  tlefield.

Chapter 6

Existence Value and Other of Life's Ills

Donald J. Boudreaux and Roger E. Meiners

The fact that the world is not "efficient" at all times bothers economists who see, perhaps depending on whether they are optimists or pessimists, unexploited gains or costs imposed on others. This concern is exemplified by work drawing upon the notion that all parties can be made better off, at no cost to anyone, by Pareto-enhancing (efficiency) moves. Why all such moves do not occur has been blamed, in part, on market imperfections. Bator (1958) and others instructed a generation of economists that the primary causes or results of market imperfections are monopolies, externalities, and the underprovision of public goods.[1] In the past several decades, the economics profession has come to recognize the problem of monopoly as more of a politically generated problem than a market defect. But the issues of externalities and public goods have blossomed.

Buchanan and Stubblebine (1962, 371) noted that "externality has been, and is, central to the neoclassical critique of market organization." It still is. Externalities are generally defined as costs that one party imposes on another without the latter's consent (Dahlman 1979). Positive externalities are asserted to be a problem when a provider of a service cannot capture enough of the benefits to make it worthwhile to produce as much of the service as would occur if such limitations did not exist. The involuntary exploitation of one party by another, a negative externality, is often alleged to require corrective public action.

Legislative action has two presumed benefits: 1) it reduces the inequity caused by unjust exploitation, and, of more importance to economists, 2) it enhances efficiency by requiring parties to pay compensation for the economic value of resources consumed that were not bargained for. If there is a positive externality, resulting in "underprovision" of a good, then again there is justification for intervention to ensure that more of a beneficial thing comes into being.

As Dahlman (1979, 141) noted in his review of externality, "The increasing complexity of modern technology and society seems to create yet additional unwanted side effects that require classification on a lengthening list of externalities." The general conclusion is that "some government action is automatically necessitated" or that changes in markets can be forced so that "economic agents can be made to take into account the side effects they generate" (Dahlman 1979, 141). That is, the government should regulate private activities to limit bads and should produce more public goods because the market oversupplies the former and undersupplies the latter.

Is it not odd that modern technology is presumed to engender increasing negative externalities? Does this presumption mean that increased wealth means increasing misery? Efficiency improves, more wealth is generated, yet more and more costs are imposed upon more unwilling victims. From a Walrasian-Paretian perspective, the problem is that many wealth-enhancing transactions create externalities; costs are imposed on others that could be eliminated by regulations that force parties to account for all costs. Environmental problems are usually cited as the prime example of the externality problem. The private sector does not produce enough environmental amenities (because much of the gain cannot be captured) and private transactions may impose environmental costs on those who are not a part of the transaction (air and water treated as zero-price goods). That, in a nutshell, is the economic justification for government involvement in environmental matters, a major class of externalities.

Existence Value

This chapter concerns one extension of the externality concept. The notion of existence value has come into play in the economics and legal literature, and in the law itself, in recent years. We use the term *existence value* to include various aspects of the "nonuse" value of natural resources; the "use value" of resources being market values based on what humans value in exchange. Market prices may not include "intrinsic values." Markets might ignore the fact that "natural resources may have value independent of humans, based on their status as natural creatures or objects" (Cross 1989, 281).[2] Existence (or nonuse) value includes "option value," the value of saving resources not now being used for possible future use, such as a trip to the Costa Rican rain forest; "vicarious value," the pleasure we get from thinking about something, such as the fact that the rain forest exists; and "intertemporal value," the value from leaving unexploited resources to future generations, so they can enjoy the rain forest. Proponents of these values know they are inherent in at least some natural resources but argue that they are not consistently sufficiently valued due to market limitations.

Existence value, like externality, is a fact. It refers to the pleasure we take from merely knowing that certain things exist. Individually we each have little influence over this existence. We suffer a loss if these things cease to exist, yet can do little to prevent the loss from occurring. Most of us obtain what economists call utility—psychic satisfaction— from the existence of our grandmothers and suffer a real loss from their deaths. That is, grandma has existence value for us, but there is not much of a market for grandmothers that allows us to transact for grand-motherly services.

More specific to our discussion here is the notion of the existence value of environmental amenities. Neither of us has visited the Costa Rican rain forest but we know it exists, we get pleasure from thinking about it, and we would like to visit it some day. We get benefits—a positive externality—from something we know to exist, even though we never contributed to help maintain the place. We would suffer a utility loss if we learned that a developer bought the place, chopped down all the trees, and left a moonscape.

What should be done about existence value? Some economists, prob-ably beginning with Krutilla (1967), assert that existence-value situa-tions pose another example of externality that must be dealt with by some sort of public intervention. That is, to preserve the rain forest, the existence value that many of us have for it should be exploited to allow the proper amount of resources to be commanded for that purpose. Next we consider the difficult problem of trying to do this.

Giving People What They Want?

Economists have long puzzled over the problem of getting people to reveal their true valuation for goods that are not revealed through the usual market interaction of suppliers and demanders. While the problem of demand revelation for public goods is not new, the issue has rearisen in the form of contingent valuation. Contingent valuation is an effort to get people to reveal their true monetary values for something (for exam-ple, environmental amenities). As a proponent of contingent valuation notes, "maintaining populations of native fish in an estuary, or protect-ing visibility at national parks are not themselves goods that are bought and sold in a market. Yet, placing a monetary value on them can be essential for sound policy" (Hanemann 1994, 19). Public officials can make better judgments about environmental amenities citizens want, and therefore should be produced, if citizens can reveal preferences to officials that cannot be expressed through the market.

We say that we value the Costa Rican rain forest, but talk is cheap; let's find out what happens when we must put our money where our mouths are. Genuine economic value requires that people expressing values be required to bear the wealth consequences of their expressions. A key problem with contingent valuation—namely, asking people *hypothetical* questions about their valuations—is getting people to be truthful.

The best contingent-valuation surveys appear to be ones where the sample of citizens is large enough (about 1,000) to meet statistical accuracy problems, are done face-to-face, provide certain background information and alternatives, and questions are skillfully worded to eliminate answers that are systematically too low or too high (NOAA 1993 and 1994). Are problems in such surveys too serious to make it sensible to use contingent valuation as a technique for public policy determination?

Supporters say, in short, that such surveys are the best we can do, so let's go with them. "In the presence of externalities, market transactions do not fully capture preferences. Collective choice is the more relevant paradigm" (Hanemann 1994, 19). Whether it is national defense or rain forest preservation, we should determine what citizens really want, otherwise we suffer the consequences of underprovision (the Commies get us and the rain forest disappears). Alternatively, we can undemocratically leave it up to the experts in government to divine some level of provision for us. "How the experts know the value that the public places on an uninjured environment, without resort to measurement involving some sort of survey, is unclear. When that public valuation is the object of measurement, a well-designed contingent valuation survey *is* one way of consulting the relevant experts—the public itself" (Hanemann 1994, 38).

Some scholars are not pleased with the quality of contingent valuation methods but because it is mandated by law in some instances, we must deal with it as best we can. "Whether the economics profession likes it or not, it seems inevitable to me that contingent valuation methods are going to play a role in public policy formulation. Both regulatory agencies and governmental offices responsible for natural resource damage assessment are making increasing use of it in their work" (Portney 1994, 16). The first major use of contingent valuation was in the suit by the state of Alaska against Exxon for the *Exxon Valdez* oil spill. The valuation placed the national value of the lost existence values from that incident at $3 billion. The Oil Pollution Act and Superfund both allow for contingent valuation of possible lost existence values. Critics assert "that the evidence supports the conclusion that to date, contingent valuation surveys do not measure the preferences they attempt to measure" (Diamond and Hausmann 1994, 46). This literature is substantive and complex. In short, talk is cheap; there is a difference between putting your money on the line and saying that you would be willing to put your money on the line. Numerous studies indicate that people consistently overstate how much they would really put on the line. When discussing the same environmental issue, asserted willingness-to-pay to help varied substantially depending on how much information the respondents were given, the sequence in which questions were asked, or whether the issue at hand stood alone or was combined with other environmental projects. For example, as Diamond and Hausmann (1994, 56) note, expressed willingness-to-pay to minimize the risk of oil spills off the Alaska coast ranged from a mean of $85 to 29 cents depending on how the issue was raised. Given the dubious value of the numbers generated by contingent-valuation surveys, an expert opinion about environmental matters may be more reliable than the survey numbers.

It's More Than a Measurement Problem

While critics of contingent valuation convincingly argue that available methods are too imperfect to generate trustworthy numbers, our thesis is that even if the numbers generated by surveys did not suffer from survey measurement problems they would be largely irrelevant. The application of contingency valuation to existence value is illegitimate as a method for "internalizing" alleged externalities. While our discussion here focuses on environmental examples, the principles are the same regardless of the kind of good involved.

Some ideas in economics come and go; they may be in fashion for a while as they are pondered, but the weak fall by the side. Wrongheaded notions matter little unless they escape the world of theory and infect public policy; then real damage may be done. Doctors once theorized that using leeches to bleed patients would drain patients of whatever caused their diseases. Of course, this alleged remedy did much more damage than good. Contingent valuation would matter little if it never left academic journals. But as Portney (1994) notes, contingent valuation has infected public policy decision making. Those who have certain special-interest agendas will naturally glom onto any pseudoscientific notion that appears to lend substance to what otherwise would be recognized as naked self-interested exploitation of fellow citizens.

In the case of contingent valuation, valuable resources are being allocated by a notion that cannot be justified by practical experience or by theory. Even if the practical problems of contingent-valuation surveys could be corrected, the concept would still be economically invalid. By reviewing below some first principles of economic valuation, we begin our case against the theoretical legitimacy of existence value.

Proper Economic Valuation Need Not Be Direct

To value something—to act in ways that promote the construction or preservation of that something for a particular use—rarely requires direct or conscious valuation by all persons who benefit from its existence. The incentive structure called "the market" weaves uncountable numbers of decentralized individual exchange relationships into an extensive web. Explicit valuations occur only at each of the countless nodes of this web—that is, at each "place" where an actual voluntary exchange happens. The results of these myriad direct valuations are communicated throughout the market, across space and time, as signals to market participants at other bargaining nodes. These signals serve as inputs into the decisions made by market participants who may be far removed from the source of each signal. Market participants receiving such signals make choices—personal valuations—based in part on these signals. Vast numbers of market participants are connected to each other by this web of direct and indirect feedback loops.

Market values are the unintended and undesigned results of this decentralized market activity. Each person has preferences and wealth and confronts the market prices of items that he is potentially interested in producing and consuming. When a person "values" a good, he does not intentionally determine the market price of that good. Instead, that person, as a supplier or a buyer, chooses how much of that good he will supply or purchase given the prices he reasonably expects to fetch or pay. Determination of the market price of a good is never exclusively in any single party's hands and is typically spread over such a large number of persons that no one person has more than negligible input into determining market values.

So while each individual at each node of exchange intentionally chooses his offer or acceptance price (in light of knowledge transmitted from elsewhere in the market [Hayek 1948b]), it is incorrect to suggest that market values are consciously chosen. Each price results from the interaction of numerous buyers and sellers, no one of whom controls market outcomes. Consumers determine the market values neither of final goods nor of the multitude of inputs whose production is necessary to the creation of final goods.

Only by connecting many people in a decentralized process of valuation does useful valuation become intellectually doable. Valuation becomes doable *because* no one person is responsible for determining the market value of any good, service, or amenity on the market. If economic efficiency required consumers consciously to value not only (say) automobiles for sale at dealerships, but, in addition, each of the millions of inputs used to produce automobiles, it would be impossible for consumers to render economically appropriate values for these items. How could any consumer know enough to value a steel-production facility, an extra acre of land for a test track, or a robot designed to weld various parts of a chassis?[3] All each consumer knows (and reveals) is how much he values a particular automobile relative to the other things he might purchase. Fortunately, that is all he needs to know. Appropriate valuations of the inputs necessary to produce cars is performed by upstream producers' actions.

Consumers rely upon suppliers because of the great wealth-creating advantages of the division of labor. But rather than emphasize Adam Smith's point about division of labor, we emphasize F. A. Hayek's point about the division of knowledge: "Through [the competitive market order] not only a division of labor but also a coordinated utilization of resources based on an equally divided knowledge has become possible" (Hayek 1948b, 88). Each supplier at each stage of production specializes not only in performing certain physical tasks but also in knowing certain unique bits of information. The steel-mill owner is well positioned, and has strong incentives, to learn all he can about the market for steel and about the various inputs available for producing steel. Upstream from the steel mill owner, the owner of a mining firm specializes in learning about the most profitable markets in which to sell ore, and about the various inputs available for mining ore. Each participant is a "valuation specialist" in learning about opportunities downstream and upstream from his own particular node in the market. The efficient operation of markets critically depends upon these independent valuation specialists—each of whom enjoys unique access to "knowledge of the particular circumstances of time and place" (Hayek 1948b, 84). The ongoing multitudinous adjustments made in light of each person's unique knowledge and skills are indispensable for the operation of an economy marked by a division of labor. The market prices that economists identify as propelling markets toward efficient outcomes cannot be derived by a process other than competition in decentralized and competitive markets. Values or prices arrived at by any other means are not comparable to, nor conformable with, the pattern of prices generated by market processes.

Of course, decentralized market processes generate appropriate values only for resources that are privately owned and whose owners can exclude others from enjoying the resources' fruits. With private owners able to appropriate sufficient revenue from the use or preservation of a resource, there is no reason to presume that a resource will be under- or overused.

Consider the existence of the *Mona Lisa*. There can be little doubt that many people value the existence of this painting and would willingly contribute at least modest sums to save it from destruction. But there is no need to ask everyone on earth whether and how much they value the existence of the *Mona Lisa*; nor is there a need to have every person who values its existence to contribute directly toward its preservation. Even if the painting happened to be owned by someone who is disgusted at the sight of it, the painting is safe because the owner can profit from its public display. By this process, the values of many people from around the world regarding the *Mona Lisa* are transmitted through the market to the *Mona Lisa*'s owner. The painting is exploited by the market, which means it is preserved.

But what about goods whose values are not appropriated by private owners—for example, the continued existence of an endangered species? As discussed in this volume by Anderson (1998) and by Epstein (1998), this problem may not be as intractable as often presumed and, as Ostrom (1990) has explained, people are very inventive at creating nonpolitical solutions when we look beyond our immediate experience. Nevertheless, let us assume that some endangered species or other environmental amenity may not be protected by the market. We contend that appropriate market-value surrogates cannot be derived through nonmarket means. While at first blush it is laudable to search for economic values to be used as bases for directing the political allocation of resources, a more careful study shows that the effort is futile and, potentially, perilous. There is no substitute for prices set decentrally in the process of voluntary exchange.

Verbally Declared Prices Are Not Good Surrogates for Market Prices

A fundamental error committed by those who argue that survey methods can provide reasonably accurate values to serve as surrogates for market prices is the belief that people have *a* value for each environmental amenity. However, people's economic values are not fixed and singular points but are, instead, schedules of different dollar figures dependent upon a nearly infinite variety of variables. Even to approach accurate valuations, survey methods must discover each respondent's schedule of valuations not only for environmental amenities but for *all* potentially produced goods and services *and* allow prices calculated from these valuations to change. These schedules of evaluations must each be *rich* and *marginalized*. By "rich" we mean that different valuation schedules for *each* amenity must be calculated, one schedule for each of a wide variety of variables that may affect a respondent's valuation of that amenity. By "marginalized" we mean that the questions asked must take account of the fact that economic valuation is not an all-or-nothing proposition but, instead, is a question of "more" or "less"—in space, intensity, and in time.

There are yet other problems with attempts to calculate prices independently of market exchange. Because answering survey questions does not bind respondents, answers are likely to be either ill thought out or excessive; either way, answers are almost surely unreliable. More importantly, even accurate answers to valuation questions will yield only maximum-demand prices, not appropriate economic prices. We review each of these problems in turn.

Surveys Must Discover Different Schedules of Values

Suppose a survey respondent is asked "How much do you value preservation of the snail darter?" Assume that this respondent answers honestly by reporting "$100." What meaning can we legitimately attach to this answer? Not much. One reason for the almost useless information conveyed by this answer is that an implicit addendum to the question is "all other prices, outputs, and your income unchanged." Indeed, the only possible way for the respondent to answer this question honestly is for the respondent to make, and accurately assess the consequences of, such assumptions. It would be illegitimate to use the answers generated by this question to construct a surrogate market price that is then used to determine whether or not to preserve the snail darter.

If answers to this question are used to determine whether or not to preserve the darter, a bias is introduced if the existence of even one additional such amenity is economically justified. This bias is a consequence of the inevitable seriatim nature of contingent-valuation surveys: a person is first asked how much he would pay to preserve the darter; he is then asked how much he would pay to preserve the Alaskan tundra; he is then asked how much he would pay to preserve a species of endangered trout living only in central Montana . . . and on and on. The nonsimultaneous nature of the surveys is fundamentally different from the market's simultaneous and continuous method of revealing values. In particular, this seriatim survey method yields existence-value measurements that are higher than the appropriate market prices for such existence.

Suppose, for example, that a large number of truthful people are each first asked "How much would you willingly pay to preserve the snail darter?" Each respondent can answer this question honestly and sensibly only by taking as given the prices for all other goods and services on which he spends, or might spend, his money. Of course, among the myriad other prices taken as given by each survey respondent are the prices each expects to pay to preserve the existence of other environmental amenities. Ceteris paribus, the greater the prices that each respondent expects to pay to preserve other environmental amenities, including amenities not yet known, the lower the amount each respondent is willing to pay to preserve the darter. If a respondent truthfully reports his valuation but does so on the assumption that the darter is the only environmental amenity he will be asked to help pay for, then the existence value he reports for the darter will be higher than it would be if he were to calculate simultaneously (and expect to pay) his existence values for all possible-to-preserve environmental amenities.

To solve the problem created by the seriatim nature of surveys, each respondent must simultaneously evaluate all potentially preserved amenities. But simultaneous evaluation is practically impossible. Because no respondent would at the time he answers the survey know the precise set of prices that are to exist for other "existence" amenities, the best that each respondent could do is to report a schedule of values for each preservation option. A respondent's schedule of values for one environmental amenity would relate the maximum amount he would pay to preserve that amenity given the many possible prices this respondent might conceivably have to pay to preserve umpteen other environmental amenities. A similar schedule of values would be required for each of the other umpteen environmental amenities *and* would include how much each respondent expects to pay for housing, food, clothing, and the other existing and future goods and services already under consideration.

Once aware that any plausible method of discovering economically appropriate prices for existence values requires that survey respondents offer schedules of different contingent valuations, proponents of existence valuation must devise practical means of determining from these reported schedules the appropriate set of prices and quantities for environmental amenities. For any one person, the system of simultaneous equations would be unimaginably vast. Practically, there is little hope that these could be solved in timely enough fashion to yield the correct set of equilibrium prices—not only because feeding such survey responses into a supercomputer would take time, but, more importantly, because valuations are not static. Valuations and the technical conditions of production constantly change. Hayek was surely correct when, in criticizing the schemes of the so-called "market socialists," he pointed out that

> Whether and how far anything approaching the desirable equilibrium is ever reached depends entirely on the speed with which the adjustments can be made. The practical problem is not whether a particular method [of calculating equilibrium prices] would eventually lead to a hypothetical equilibrium, but which method will secure the more rapid and complete adjustment to the daily changing conditions in different places and different industries. (Hayek 1948a, 188)

The fact that subjective valuations change is vital. One of the most crucial tasks performed by markets is to encourage people "on the spot," who possess special factual knowledge, to adjust their activities in light of the constantly changing data that emerge in markets. Adjustments are coordinated by changing prices communicated across the market. Much more so than static economic models reveal, the economic problem consists largely of ensuring adequate and prompt adjustments by millions of people, each of whom possesses unique bits of knowledge (Hayek 1948b, 90–91). Even if the correct solution to a set of simultaneous equations is calculated, implementing plans based on that solution would "solve" the economic problem only as long as preferences, technologies, resource availabilities, and available trading opportunities remain unchanged.

The essence of a market economy is its entrepreneurial dynamism and creativity (Schumpeter 1942). Market prices are not "correct" so much because they clear markets at any given moment but, rather, because they are condensed signals to market participants of trading and production opportunities. Unless prices quickly change to reflect changed facts and new opportunities as these arise—and unless resource owners are permitted to vary in response to these changed prices the ways in which they employ their resources—markets no longer clear and (more significantly) people who would make adjustments to better conform their actions with the changed economic circumstances never do so. The economy grows further and further out of kilter. Without some means to permit existence valuations to change as fluidly and as rapidly as other prices in the market, existence valuations are not acceptable surrogates for market prices.

Existence Valuations Must Be Marginal

To yield economically accurate prices, existence-value surveys must ask about marginal increments rather than lump-sum totals. It is more legitimate to ask about valuations of "more" or "less"—in space, intensity, and in time—than to ask about the existence value of an arbitrarily chosen lump of existence. For example, it is more appropriate to ask a survey respondent "How much do you value protecting for one additional year the unspoiled existence of one acre of the Costa Rican rain forest?" rather than "How much do you value protecting the existence of the Costa Rican rain forest?" The former question has a time element (one additional year), an intensity element (unspoiled), and a space element (one acre). None of these elements exist in the latter question; it specifies neither space, time, nor intensity of protection.

There are always different intensities of protection of the existence of environmental amenities. The most intense form of protection of the rain forest's existence requires that *all* effects of humanity be excluded from the rain forest—for example, airplanes would be prevented from flying at even high altitudes above the rain forest. Less intense protection would, for example, be consistent with allowing a handful of tourists into the rain forest. If a few ecologically sensitive tourists are allowed in on foot, this would be a more intense form of protection than if tourists are allowed in on tour buses. The range of different intensities of protection of the rain forest's existence is vast. An uncountable number of degrees of development separate a pure primeval rain forest from a nuclear waste dump.

To ignore marginal valuations by asking, instead, about alleged "total" valuations is to ignore the single most critical advance in economic science during the past century and a half: the marginal revolution. Ignorance of the margin is ignorance of the resolution of the diamond-water paradox. Suppose survey respondents are asked "How much do you value the continued availability of drinkable water?" The question implies that the alternative to the availability of drinkable water is no drinkable water. If the choice were "water or no water," then the value of water would be immense. Economists long ago recognized "the homely fact that commodities are esteemed not in accordance with their significance in general, but with that of any small unit of the available supply" (Knight 1935, 151). That is, economists saw that humans rarely confront such aggregated choices as "water or no water." Because water is extremely fungible and amply available in tiny marginal units, the total economic value of the world's stock of drinkable water, as calculated from the prices that consumers pay for their marginal units of water, is a minute fraction of what the value of this same stock of water would be if people were required to choose between the existence or nonexistence of water.

As with water, so too with environmental amenities. Even honestly and accurately answered survey questions about existence valuation will yield wildly different figures depending on how sensitive questions are to marginal units. Consider again a question about preserving the Costa Rican rain forest. If a respondent believes that the only alternative to complete, high-intensity preservation is complete destruction of the rain forest, then he is likely to express a monetary value higher than if he understands that the question is asking only about some additional increment of protection—say, to protect the rain forest for an extra year, or to prevent hiking in certain regions, or to have one additional acre protected. The upshot is that questions insensitive to marginalization generally yield valuation answers that are much higher than the valuations that would be revealed in competitive markets, were it not for the supposedly prohibitive transaction costs of overcoming collective-action problems.

Problems with Hypotheticals

The fact that surveys ask hypothetical questions unleashes the possibility of unintentionally misleading answers. If someone is asked how much he values a particular automobile, his answer will differ if he knows that he must actually pay the amount of his value declaration as compared to if he does not expect actually to pay the value declared. A person's valuation of any good varies depending on his probability estimate that he will actually be required to pay a declared value.

Consider an ordinary demand curve. Economists normally take for granted that the prices listed along the vertical axis are 100 percent probability prices. That is, if a buyer's offer to pay $6 per pound for ten pounds of beef is accepted, it is presumed he will with certainty pay $60 in exchange for the beef. But suppose that a buyer believes there is only a 50 percent chance that he will be required to pay the price that he offers for the beef he receives. If the buyer and the seller are risk-neutral, the buyer will offer to pay $120 for the beef (and the seller will accept). That is, the values reported vary depending upon the probability that the respondent will be required to pay any sum. The lower the respondent's estimate of the probability of his having to pay any of the monetary sums reported in his valuation schedule, the higher will be these sums.

Suppose now that someone is asked to express the dollar value that he attaches to the continued existence of the Costa Rican rain forest. The answer depends upon his estimate of the probability that he will have to pay the amount he declares. If the respondent is certain that his answer will not affect the amount (if any) he must pay toward maintaining the existence of the Costa Rican rain forest, he will express a higher valuation than if he expects with some probability that his answer will determine the amount he is asked to pay.

Alternatively stated, the lower the probability of any expressed valuation translating dollar-for-dollar into a requirement that the person expressing the valuation must actually pay the amount expressed, the farther down that person is on his demand curve for environmental amenities (even though the monetary figure he expresses is quite high). Existence valuations derived from such indecisive surveys—that is, surveys in which each respondent knows that his answer will have only imperceptible influence on how much, if anything, will be paid by taxpayers to preserve the existence of some environmental amenity—will inevitably be excessive.

The problem with hypotheticals does not end with the individual indecisiveness of each survey response. Answering hypothetical questions about consumer valuations is inherently different, and, we believe, more difficult than expressing genuine and decisive evaluative actions in the market. Survey respondents face "no cost to being wrong, and therefore [have] no incentive to undertake the mental effort to be accurate" (Freeman 1979, 916). This fact is especially important given that the complexity of problems increases with the hypothetical nature of the issues relevant to solving the problem.

If asked to pay $2 for a McDonald's hamburger, a consumer can reliably enough calculate whether buying that hamburger is for him at that moment a good deal. It is much more difficult for anyone to write down his demand functions even for as few as a dozen ordinary grocery items. How many of us can say with any confidence how much more ice cream we will purchase over the course of a year if the price of ice cream falls by 20 percent while the prices of all other goods and services in our consumption bundle remain unchanged? The fact that economists for heuristic reasons assume well-ordered and detailed consumer demand functions does not mean that these demand functions actually exist at any moment in well-ordered and detailed form over a wide range of prices, quantities, and qualities. And it certainly does not mean that each consumer can accurately report his own detailed demand function for even a single good. If Jones is asked how much more ice cream he will buy if ice cream prices fall by 20 percent, Jones can guess, but it is likely that his guess, no matter how honest and well-considered, will prove inaccurate if he actually confronts a 20 percent lower relative price of ice cream. Asking Jones to reckon his demand curves for *all* goods, services, and amenities under a welter of different conditions is to ask the impossible—even though, as we argue above, proper calculation of existence values cannot occur unless the calculating authority is given a full array of such valuation schedules from all citizens.

Consumers and producers in markets react to actual prices, and market prices are determined by actual, nonhypothetical choices. The market is a forum for making real, nonhypothetical exchanges, through time, at real, nonhypothetical prices. This is the only workable way for humans to make reliable economic decisions. A key virtue of competitive decentralized markets is that no one is required to perform Herculean intellectual feats. Market prices at any moment inform producers and consumers of relative resource and product availabilities. Each person makes market choices based upon his preferences that are relevant only within the range of the existing array of market prices. In turn, private property owners whose wealth is affected by these market decisions respond to the changes in market prices brought about by consumer choices (Hayek 1948b). The resulting array of prices reflects genuine, nonhypothetical valuations. The fact that economists can write down a system of simultaneous equations to be used for calculating different general-equilibrium prices for different assumed preferences and production techniques does not mean that individuals in real world markets know at any time what they would do at different prices. And the further are hypothetical prices from actual prevailing prices, the more speculative and hazardous become any such guesses ventured by consumers or producers.

The Relevance of Existence Value

People get pleasure merely from knowing that certain things exist. This fact does not by itself justify government rearrangement of property rights to reflect exchange values for existence amenities. Just because something gives pleasure to someone is insufficient reason to recognize a legal right in that something. Likewise, just because something gives displeasure to someone does not justify government efforts to halt that something.

Consider an obvious example: the real distress suffered by a business owner when a new rival enters his market. Should the government attempt to calculate this business owner's distress and weigh it against the subjective delight enjoyed by consumers and the new rival before deciding whether or not to permit the rival to operate? Clearly not. While it cannot be denied in principle that the agony suffered by business people who lose their livelihoods often exceeds the pleasure consumers enjoy as a consequence of more intense competition, it would clearly be foolish for government to police against competition on such grounds. The politics of this situation are quite different than the economics, as we know from the continuous efforts to invoke public intervention to limit efficiency-enhancing competition.

Most economists would agree with the above conclusion, and most would justify this conclusion by relying upon the Kaldor-Hicks welfare criterion.[4] However, we here offer a slightly different justification for preventing government from policing against competition on such utility grounds: namely, there is no hope that government could do so correctly. Sound government policy cannot be grounded upon allegations of subjective utility and disutility.

While everyone surely experiences subjective utility gains and losses that do not correspond to market money values, the fact of existence in humans of subjective utility does not justify government policy geared to that dimension. Of course, government policy and the law, if they are to serve useful social functions, must be geared to measures of human welfare. But because subjective utility is inherently unmeasurable, government cannot prudently be charged with the task of maximizing utility. Maximizing utility is an unavoidably personal chore. The appropriate role of the law is to foster rules and rights that maximize individuals' abilities to boost their own utilities as best they can. Reasonable people disagree over the precise contents of the appropriate set of rules and rights, but no one can reasonably assert that government can be trusted to act directly in the utility dimension. It is impossible for government officials to gauge subjective utilities and, hence, to weigh changes in one party's utility against changes in the utilities of other parties. A government empowered to maximize utility *directly* could not avoid acting chaotically. Such a government, even if operated by saints, by its nature could not govern according to rules; in practice it would be a ghastly tyrant.

To remove government from the business of directly maximizing utilities requires recognition and respect for private spheres of action, and private spheres of action require at least *some* quantum of private property rights. Hayek (1973, 107) expressed this truth as follows:

> The understanding that "good fences make good neighbors," that is, that men can use their own knowledge in pursuit of their own ends without colliding with each other only if clear boundaries can be drawn between their respective domains of free action, is the basis on which all known civilization has grown. Property, in the wide sense in which it is used to include not only material things, but (as John Locke defined it) the "life, liberty and estates" of every individual, is the only solution men have yet

discovered to the problem of reconciling individual freedom with an absence of conflict. Law, liberty, and property are an inseparable trinity. There can be no law in the sense of universal rules of conduct which does not determine boundaries of the domains of freedom by laying down rules that enable each to ascertain where he is free to act.

Thus, private property rights in this Lockean sense protect not only rights to use properties for commercial and industrial purposes, but the rights of every person to decide for himself on a wide variety of personal and aesthetic questions. Friedman (1962), like Hayek, points out that the absence of economic freedom inevitably strips people of political and personal freedoms.

An Infinite Regress

Proponents of existence valuation for environmental amenities should reflect seriously upon the full implications of their policy proposals. If government is given power to prohibit commercial development based on the existence value of Oregon forests and of quaint New England villages, there is no reason this power should not be used to protect existence values of other sorts. Nothing more objective than the balance of raw political muscle would determine the particular existence values protected at any moment by government.

There is no principled difference between an environmentalist who claims to suffer great utility loss with every acre of land commercially developed and, say, a fundamentalist Christian who claims to suffer great utility loss at the very *thought* that people are permitted to use pornography. There is no principled difference between an environmentalist who claims that just *knowing* of the existence of a species of trout raises substantially his utility and a bishop who claims that just *knowing* that people are forced to attend church on Sunday substantially raises his utility.

Talk is cheap. With government ready to regulate whenever a politically influential party vocally asserts a potential utility loss, law is supplanted by politics. Under such a system of governance there can be no predictability or principled policies. There can be no objective standard—beyond simply the vote count in the most recent election—for judging the propriety of government policy. Every person's action or nonaction, no matter how seemingly innocuous, is potentially an object of government regulation. Property owners might well fear for their legal right to use their lands as they choose. But so, too, would *all* citizens in *all* capacities fear for their legal right to live as they deem best. For every developer prevented from paving over forest land there will be an artist prevented from painting a picture or singing a song.

Can there be much doubt that a government empowered to protect subjective environmental sensitivities will also be a threat to protect the subjective sensitivities of those whose utility functions differ in content from that of the typical environmental advocate? Buchanan (1986, 339) points out that "[i]f I can resort to politics to impose my own preferences on the behavior of others . . . then it would seem that other persons, in working democratic process, can do the same to me. I may find that the political process is double-edged." As Wagner (1998) explains in this volume, once this path is taken, and property rights are up for political grabs, constitutional protections become meaningless.

Lest those on the political Left remain confident that government power to protect existence values will be used exclusively to promote their preferred goals, notice Robert Bork's justification of legislative efforts to outlaw homosexual sodomy:

> Physical danger does not exhaust the categories of harms society may seek to prevent by legislation, and no activity that society thinks immoral is victimless. Knowledge that an activity is taking place is a harm to those who find it profoundly immoral. . . . Moral outrage is a sufficient ground for prohibitory legislation. (Bork 1990, 123–24)

Although he does not use the term *existence value*, the rationale behind Bork's remarks is identical to that which motivates existence-value advocates. The list is potentially endless. In a later book, Bork (1996) endorses government censorship and other efforts to do what in his view would improve the moral tone of the nation. That motivation reduces to the following: if enough voters feel offended by the behavior of others, such feelings are sufficient to justify government coercion to prevent the offending behavior.

If it is appropriate for government to attempt directly to maximize utilities, and *if* a sufficient number of heterosexuals persuade the government that they suffer monumental utility losses just knowing that homosexual activity occurs, then on what principle can government refuse not to outlaw homosexual sodomy by consenting adults? None that we can see. Of course, homosexuals might successfully persuade the government that the utility they would lose from their sexual practices being outlawed exceeds the utility antihomosexuals stand to gain if homosexual sodomy is illegal. But there is no objective means of distinguishing these conflicting claims. And lack of any objective measure unleashes government by raw political power.

It is grossly imprudent to endorse government activity driven by raw political power, for such power easily devours the hands—and heads—of its feeders (Buchanan 1986). Make no mistake: to advocate existence valuation protection at the expense of private property and contract rights is to advocate government by raw political power. If the notion becomes widely accepted that government's appropriate task is to maximize utility rather than to foster a set of administrable rules that best promotes individuals' efforts to maximize their utilities, no principled grounds remain upon which government can be restrained from the worst excesses.

Government cannot maximize people's utilities directly. More importantly, a government that directly attempts to maximize people's utilities necessarily abandons the role of protecting spheres of individual domain within which each person freely chooses how best to maximize his utility. People each given some domain in which they are protected from political interference are much better able to enhance their utilities than are people whose most trifling actions are subject to override by government command.

Why Shouldn't People Have Property Rights in Existence Value?

Many who support active government protection of existence values argue that property rights in existence values are just as legitimate as are more traditional property rights over physical objects (Sunstein 1993). The argument, in brief, is this. All property rights arrangements are human artifacts. Being conventional, there is nothing naturally good or bad about one arrangement compared to any other arrangement. A right to develop land is not naturally or universally a superior form of property right than are all citizens' rights to unlimited access to land, or government's right to prevent development in order to protect existence values. Having chosen in the past to enforce what we today recognize as the traditional set of common-law private property rights, humans can today choose, if they wish, to alter these rights in order to recognize other interests.

Numerous misconceptions undergird this legal-positivist view of law. Law, of course, is ultimately justified by how well it serves citizens' interests. No rule should be maintained just because it is centuries old. Nevertheless, because law serves citizens' interests mainly by allowing them to form trustworthy expectations about the behavior of others (as well as of public authorities)—and to act on these expectations in ways that conform with the expectations of others—sound law generally is not "chosen" in any conscious way through collective-choice procedures but, rather, grows up organically from the everyday actions and conflicts of people (Cooter 1994; Morriss 1997).

Leoni (1961) argues that sound legal rules are no more capable than are correct market prices of being consciously chosen and enforced by a central authority. In neither case can authorities divine from abstract principles just what the law or the set of prices should be. Sound legal rules, no less than correct market prices, are discoverable only through a decentralized, competitive, and evolutionary process. Sound law, to steal a favorite phrase from Hayek (1967, 96), is "the result of human action but not of human design."

Sunstein commits the common error of supposing that because human institutions are the result of human action, the institutions are also the result of human design or choice—or that, if not the result of human design, are necessarily inferior to institutions consciously crafted and implemented. In fact, as Smith (1998) explains in this volume, any indispensable institutions were not and could not have been consciously designed. Examples include language, the worldwide division of labor, and most of the daily law that governs human interaction.

As Brubaker (1998) demonstrates in this volume, under the traditional common law of private property, property owners enjoyed legal protections of a certain set of expectations about how they could use their properties. For example, traditional common law protected each landowner's expectation that he could develop his land as he chose, as long as he did not physically damage adjoining lands. What is protected under traditional common law, then, are a certain set of expectations. Other expectations are necessarily not protected by common law. For example, a citizen's expectation that landowner Jones will not develop his land is not protected.

Because no legal system can protect all expectations, the practical issue then becomes which set of expectations the law should protect. Following Hayek, we insist that law cannot succeed if it protects as a legal right any expectation of "a particular concrete state of things" (Hayek 1973, 106) such as, for example, the expectation to a certain dollar amount of income, or the expectation that land and resources will be used only in certain particular ways. We can do no better than to quote Hayek at length.

[The best the law can do is to determine] only an abstract order which enables its members to derive from the particulars known to them expectations that have a good chance of being correct. This is all that can be achieved in a world where some of the facts change in an unpredictable manner and where order is achieved by the individuals adjusting themselves to new facts whenever they become aware of them. *What can re-*

main constant in such an overall order which continually adjusts itself to external changes, and provides the basis of predictions, can only be a system of abstract relationships and not its particular elements. This means that every change must disappoint some expectations, but that this very change which disappoints some expectations creates a situation in which again the chance to form concrete expectations is as great as possible.

Such a condition can evidently be achieved only by protecting some and not all expectations, and the central problem is which expectations must be assured in order to maximize the possibility of expectations in general being fulfilled. This implies a distinction between such 'legitimate' expectations which the law must protect and others which it must allow to be disappointed. And the only method yet discovered of defining a range of expectations which will be thus protected, and thereby reducing the mutual interference of people's actions with each other's intentions, is to demarcate for every individual a range of permitted actions by designating . . . ranges of objects over which only particular individuals are allowed to dispose and from the control of which all others are excluded. (Hayek 1973, 106–7, emphasis added)

Traditional common-law property rights "demarcate for every individual a range of permitted actions" and, hence, protect owners' legitimate expectations regarding this range of permitted actions. Humans thus interact in complex ways to promote their and their fellows' well-being. Experience has proven not only the workability of traditional common-law rules of property, contract, and tort, but their general superiority to centrally designed law.

It cannot be denied that a landowner who turns a forest into a shopping mall might disappoint the expectations of people who hoped to see the land remain undeveloped. But because it is impossible for the law to prevent *all* expectations from being disappointed, the mere fact of disappointed expectations proves nothing. Such government interference is justified only if it can be shown that attempts to legally recognize and protect existence values will promote greater coordination of mutually advantageous human activities. As we argue above, the theoretical and practical problems that unavoidably mar any attempt to turn existence values into legally protected property rights are immense. The immensity of these problems argues against unsettling rules of property developed over centuries that have proven their ability to promote peaceful cooperation and prosperity. Legal protection of existence value as some sort of generalized property right cannot work.

A Practical Way Out?

Proponents of government action guided by existence valuations might respond to the above arguments by alleging that we are too demanding in what we require of existence valuation surveys and legal efforts to protect existence values. The champion of existence valuation might concede that existence valuation surveys cannot generate general equilibrium prices but nevertheless insist that the existence valuations generated by well-sculpted survey questions provide accurate enough figures for guiding government efforts to protect existence values. We disagree.

The problems plaguing existence valuation surveys are emphatically not minor or secondary. Any derivation of prices or values from surveys and other such means not reliant upon data generated from actual market exchanges cannot legitimately be claimed to discover market values. *If* the government is in the business of protecting existence values, perhaps requiring such surveys will curb the arbitrary power of politicians or bureaucrats who would otherwise have an unchecked hand in deciding which alleged existence amenities deserve government protection. But this fact (if it be a fact) does not turn a sow's ear into a silk purse. It does not turn the arbitrary, untrustworthy, and noneconomic values derived from existence value surveys into close-enough approximations of genuine market values. In fact, pretending that existence value surveys provide economically meaningful data might well help to clear the way for economically unjustified political efforts to preserve alleged existence values. If existence value surveys unjustifiably enjoy the imprimatur of scientific economics, voters may well be less skeptical than otherwise of expanded political control over private property rights.

Hence, the most appropriate means of protecting the environment is abandonment of the existing command-and-control statutory structure and a return to adjudication of common-law rights. The decentralized common law will not always give exactly the right set of incentives to people to act in ways that maximize some plausible measure of social welfare. But when compared to even the best attainable system of command-and-control, a common-law regime is over the long run the most desirable one (Brubaker 1998; Yandle 1997).

First and foremost, because much of costs of litigating a dispute are borne by the parties involved, the common law is more sensitive than are legislatures to the administrative costs (broadly defined) of legal rules. Common-law courts have long been skeptical of claims for damages that are neither observable nor attributable directly to well-defined wrongs committed by the defendant (McCormick 1935, 53–56, 319–22). The reason for this skepticism is not so much that courts do not believe that people suffer pure utility losses. Rather, the reason for this skepticism is that courts are aware that properly administering any rule allowing damage payments for pure utility losses is impossible. Whatever utility gains are achieved by allowing recovery for pure utility losses are sure to be swamped by a combination of extremely high administration costs and utility losses engendered by erroneous findings for plaintiffs.

Second, the common-law-protected ability to purchase properties and to use these properties largely as owners choose itself provides a mechanism for protecting a good many, if not all, existence values. If land is alienable, and if people are permitted to pool their funds to purchase land, then people who value the existence of the Alaskan tundra are free to purchase all or part of the tundra and to prevent it from being developed. While it is true that free-rider problems may frustrate efforts of nondevelopers to raise enough money to purchase the land, such an outcome is not certain. Today, environmental groups and foundations concerned about the environment have on hand billions of dollars. The very fact that these groups have this money indicates that when it comes to raising funds for environmental purposes free-rider problems are not insurmountable, as Anderson (1998) explains. And these monies, of course, can be used by these groups to purchase lands in order to protect certain existence values. To the extent that people who value existence can pool their funds and bid for lands, existence values are not externalities. This is so whether a particular piece of land with high existence value is purchased by a conservation group or by a developer.

Suppose that some tract of a pristine forest in northern California is for sale. Environmental groups bid up to $5 million for the tract, while a lumber company bids $5.1 million. The tract is sold to the lumber company for logging. While it is true that some people would prefer that the trees on this tract of forest land remain standing, in this example no externality is present even in the face of logging. The reason is that the $5 million value bid by conservationists, which reflects the maximum monetary value conservationists were willing to pay for this tract of forest, is internalized on the lumber company. By having to bid against the conservationists for the land, the value to conservationists of preserving this land is internalized on the lumber company— regardless of who wins the bidding. As Yandle (1998) discusses in this volume, the lesson is that alienability of land and other resources goes a long way toward internalizing externalities.

Existence-value proponents will claim that the ability of people who value existence to free-ride on the financial contributions of others prevents appropriate amounts from being bid in competition with commercial buyers. Commercial buyers will thus not have internalized on them the full existence values of the lands they develop. Too much development thus occurs.

This free-rider problem may be real, despite the billions of dollars spent on environmental protection. But, on the other side, collectivizing land-use decisions necessarily creates a slew of free-rider problems that do not exist under common law property and contract rules. Huge free-rider problems plague any system in which people are asked to express in a voting booth or in a survey their existence values for this or that environmental amenity. As we argue above, because each individual's decision in a voting booth or in a survey questionnaire is costless to each individual, voting booths and existence value surveys permit each voter or respondent to express values without any need to consider costs—to him or to others. There is no good reason to suppose that free-rider problems that render imperfect traditional common law property and contract rules are any worse than those that infect collective decision-making procedures.

Existence Value as an Externality

The law allows parties to express their existence values by voluntary exchanges, such as conservation easements or land purchases obtained by environmental groups. The law also allows parties to use political influence to have the state take private land for environmental protection and compensate its owner. Implementing new rules allowing parties to assert existence values that they are unwilling to reveal through existing private and public legal mechanisms means that existing property rights will be less secure.

When property rights are insecure, "gains that would otherwise be available from exchange instead will be dissipated by searches for and defenses of takeable assets, and resources available for investment will be diverted toward less takeable uses" (Haddock, McChesney, and Spiegel 1990, 17). That is, in practice, if existence value becomes legally recognized, new incentives are unleashed for parties to attempt to grab resources. Resources will be devoted to litigation and other legal processes that would not have been so allocated (Anderson and Hill 1990; Haddock 1986). In the face of such a scramble for property, there is no assurance, even for those who think the world will be better if existence value were a legally protected right, that it will turn out the way they hoped. The result could be more work for lawyers and economists squabbling over how the new state of affairs would work out in practice, not greater environmental protection.

Did Bad Economics Drive Bad Law?

Commentators have discussed the use of economic tools and concepts, such as contingent valuation, that can be used to enhance the valuation of environmental amenities. Articles in leading law reviews make use of the notion (Farber 1996; Revesz 1996; Robinson 1996; Sunstein 1996). A notion first discussed in the economics literature in 1967 (Krutilla) eventually spawned more formal analysis that gives economic credence to legal commentators seeking to expand the legal status of environmental amenities. Far better to cite economic reasoning as a justification than just to assert that such protections should exist because the author likes the idea.

While economists may be flattered to think that economic analysis drives legal rules, in fact the notion of existence value has only scant support in sound economic theory. Nevertheless, the concept of existence value is now embedded in statutes. Some environmental statutes contain vague statements that may have political appeal but may not have been intended by most members of Congress to have substantive consequences at law, or at least the consequences that actually emerged. This does not mean that members of Congress necessarily regret sloppy draftsmanship of legislation; as McChesney (1997) has explained, political entrepreneurs can exploit any side of a problem, even if the problem is political in origin.

Legal Standing for Existence Value?

Those who wish to achieve particular objectives, such as nonexploitation of certain resources, can achieve that goal by adoption of a rule that allows them to intercede to prohibit resource use. A problem they face is that the law does not presume we have the right to intercede in matters that happen to have existence value to us. A leading case on standing in environment matters, *Sierra Club v. Morton*,[5] outlined the issues well. The Forest Service approved plans for commercial exploitation of resources on land the agency controlled. The Sierra Club sued to block the development, claiming standing to intervene based on its "special interest in the conservation and the sound maintenance of the national parks, game refuges and forests of the country."[6] The Supreme Court rejected the claim that "a mere 'interest in a problem' "[7] was sufficient to establish legal standing. Standing requires a more immediate interest, such as would be had by neighboring property owners affected by the proposed development.

Dissenters in this case argued for broad notions of legal standing. Justice Douglas was concerned that "the voice of the existing beneficiaries of these environmental wonders . . . be heard"[8] and that "those people who . . . know its values and wonders [should] be able to speak for the entire ecological community."[9] Similarly, Justice Blackmun, in dissent, argued for an "imaginative expansion of our traditional concepts of standing" so as to allow a group such as the Sierra Club that has "pertinent, bona fide, and well recognized attributes and purposes in the area of the environment"[10] to be able to litigate such matters. This issue has arisen in Supreme Court cases since then and, while the Court has never expressed sentiments as farfetched as those in the *Sierra Club* case, the Court has members who find merit in an expansive standing notion.[11]

The importance of standing is that, without it, the Sierra Club or any other distant party cannot get into court to reveal the existence value it places on certain environmental amenities. Even parties with standing must demonstrate market (use) value affected by the activities in question. Assertions about existence value matter little in most cases. Contingent valuation provides a tool for parties to put market values on claims that are given legal standing. The Supreme Court has not commented on the possible role of contingent valuation but recognizes a right in existence value created by the Endangered Species Act.

While it took almost two decades for the implications to emerge with full force in the spotted owl case,[12] in 1978 the Supreme Court recognized something close to the notion of existence value in the snail darter case.[13] The Court found that completion of the Tellico Dam by the Tennessee Valley Authority threatened the existence of the endangered snail darter fish in violation of the Endangered Species Act of 1973. The Court noted that the act did not attempt to balance costs and benefits; that tens of million of dollars had already been devoted to the project was irrelevant. As the Report of the House Committee on Merchant Marine and Fisheries had stated prior to passage of the act, "The value of . . . genetic heritage is, quite literally, incalculable."[14] The majority opinion also cited a commentator that:

> The dominant theme pervading all Congressional discussion of the proposed [act] was the overriding need to devote whatever effort and resources were necessary to avoid further diminution of national and worldwide wildlife resources. . . . Senators and Congressmen uniformly deplored the irreplaceable loss to aesthetics, science, ecology, and the national heritage should more species disappear.[15]

Individual species or their habitat, which obviously concerns existence value, may have nearly unlimited existence right or value at law, which need not be remotely related to contingent valuation which asserts to reveal existence values as determined by humans. While it was never clear that the Tellico Dam, snail darter aside, had greater benefits than costs, it is clear that providing protection for a portion of the habitat of the spotted owl, as required by the Endangered Species Act, has cost at least $10 billion (Nelson 1993, 3). There is no reason to think such a sum is related to the existence value that the public might place on such habitat.

Existence Value Codified

Existence value, as revealed by contingent valuation, is gradually being codified in parts of environmental law. The Comprehensive Environmental Response, Compensation, and Liability Act (CERCLA or Superfund)[16] and the Oil Pollution Act of 1990[17] authorize federal and state officials to seek natural resource damages that may include existence value.[18] Under both statutes, the relevant federal agency has issued natural resource damage assessment rules (NRDAs) that go beyond traditional concepts of damage remediation and compensation.

CERCLA allows the government to act as trustee to sue a wide host of responsible parties, for joint and several liability, for injury to natural resources from releases of hazardous substances. Natural resources include all aspects of the environment. The Department of the Interior (DOI) is required to issue NRDAs that "take into consideration factors including, but not limited to, replacement value, use value, and ability of the ecosystem or resource to recover."[19] Recovered damages must be "retained by the trustee[s], without further appropriation, for use only to restore, replace, or acquire the equivalent of" damaged resources.[20] This definition of damages is much broader than the traditional common law damage measure.

If pollution has ruined a parcel of land, so that no one would want to live on it, or has polluted a well so that it can no longer be used, what is the lost economic value of the polluted land or water supply? In most cases, lost use value, the traditional damage measure, is much less than the cost of restoration or replacement. As the Court of Appeals for the District of Columbia Circuit noted, "the market value of a natural resource is almost always less than the cost of restoring it."[21] The CERCLA damage rule may be applied to mean, in effect, that future generations have a right to the slice of the environment in question to be as it was in its natural state; we are not just to compensate the current generation for the use value of the slice of the environment in question. Of course, a high damage measure discourages future violations of CERCLA more than would a lost-use measure of damages, but since most Superfund sites came to be in violation of CERCLA after the fact, the effect has been to force society to devote significantly more resources to environmental restoration than would have been the case under traditional rules. The damage regulations published by DOI in 1986 were held too lenient; the agency was required to favor restoration over lost-use value.[22]

Restoration need not be remotely the same as contingent valuation, but both are likely to be much higher than lost-use values. The restoration option, which was first enacted as part of the Clean Water Act,[23] may mean little in case of extinction of a species that has no particular market value. The concern of environmentalists is that property owners may destroy species that have no clear market value, even though its nonuse value, as determined by contingent valuation, may be high to people concerned about such matters (Cross 1989, 307). The assumption is that without contingent valuation there will be more environmental degradation than with it in place as a deterrent mechanism.

Contingent valuation is expressly built into National Oceanic and Atmospheric Administration (NOAA) regulations for the Oil Pollution Act. NOAA hired Nobel Laureates Kenneth Arrow and Robert Solow to chair a panel of experts to determine if contingent valuation was a reliable enough method to be used in NRDAs. The panel concluded "that CV [contingent valuation] can produce estimates reliable enough to be the starting point of a judicial process of damage assessment, including lost passive-use values" (Portney 1994, 8).

The NOAA regulations allow every imaginable economic value to be added to damage measures. "A valuation approach may be implemented with separate calculations of losses and gains. A variety of valuation procedures is available for this purpose, including the travel cost method, factor income approach, hedonic price models, models of market supply and demand, contingent valuation, and conjoint analysis" (NOAA 1996, 452). DOI regulations are less formal, at this writing, but there is reason to suspect they may be headed toward the NOAA standards. DOI rules state that "at the discretion of the authorized official" damages will include lost "compensable value," which includes the use of contingent valuation for nonuse values when "no use values can be determined."[24] Some commentators criticize the DOI standard as too lenient and are pushing for a standard more like that adopted by NOAA, or tougher, so that contingent valuation could become standard procedure (Robinson 1996).

Conclusion

Scholars concerned with environmental quality have come to understand that the environment is unlikely to receive much protection when it is in the commons. If legal standing is given to rights such as existence value, it is easy to predict an increase in resources devoted to wrangling for the right to control of property subjected to claims based on existence value. When market-revealed values are rejected in favor of less meaningful measures, the results of the legal process must grow increasingly uncertain as agencies and courts attempt to resolve conflicting claims under a hodgepodge of assertions. Environmental quality is reduced, not enhanced, by such uncertainty.

Statutes such as the Endangered Species Act change common-law rights to property by granting statutory rights to certain species (effected by human agents) with respect to habitat protection. Under congressional supervision, to help enforce various statutes, agencies are adopting standards, such as existence value, that change the method of damage valuation away from the common-law standard of market value. While such moves are lauded and abetted by environmentalists who hope that such measures will enhance the quality of the environment, there is no reason to presume that will be the result. The common law and the market process give strong incentives to individuals to maximize the value of property over time, taking into account the current or future values of other parties. The fact that the existing regime does not yield perfection is asserted to be evidence of externalities that need corrective action.

The recognition of existence value, which may be operationalized by methods such as contingent valuation, disrupts the values that evolved in the market under the traditional rule of law. When the value of private property is threatened because it may be assigned to species for habitat or to other citizens who assert a higher value for property, an externality is created because ownership is less certain than before. Property formerly protected by clear rules of law may be subject to a variety of new rules that may or may not be enforced. Such property is effectively returned to the commons and is up for grabs. When ownership is uncertain because distant parties asserting existence value may be able to effect a limited claim, there is little incentive to invest in protecting property for habitat or for future generations.

Notes

1. Bator was not the only one to make this point, but for years most graduate economics students read his article as part of standard microeconomics.

2. Of course if natural resources do "have value independent of human beings," humans must acknowledge that value if there is to be any recognition of such value in either market or nonmarket settings.

3. Hayek took Schumpeter to task for falling into the trap of arguing that

because consumers directly value final outputs, and because the market values of final outputs are imputed back to determine the values of inputs, consumers ipso facto value inputs. As Hayek (1948b, 90–91) pointed out:

It is evident, however, that the values of the factors of production do not depend solely on the valuation of the consumers' goods but also on the conditions of supply of the various factors of production. Only to a mind to which all these facts were simultaneously known would the answer necessarily follow from the facts given to it. The practical problem, however, arises precisely because these facts are never given to a single mind, and because, in consequence, it is necessary that in the solution of the problem knowledge should be used that is dispersed among many people. . . . [W]e must show how a solution is produced by the interactions of people each of whom possesses only partial knowledge.

4. For a change to satisfy the Kaldor-Hicks criterion (and, hence, to be economically justified), it must be possible for those who gain from the change to pay enough money to those who lose in order to leave these losers no worse off in utility terms than they were before the change. If the winners can thus compensate the losers and still be better off with the change, then the change is justified according to this criterion.

5. *Sierra Club v. Morton*, 405 U.S. 727 (1972).

6. 405 U.S. 727, 730 (1972).

7. 405 U.S. 727, 739 (1972).

8. 405 U.S. 727, 750 (1972).

9. 405 U.S. 727, 752 (1972).

10. 405 U.S. 727, 757 (1972).

11. For a discussion of other cases and of this issue in more detail, see Farber (1996). The *Morton* case is no longer considered the leading word on standing; a more recent expression is found in *Lujan v. Defenders of Wildlife,* 112 S.Ct. 2130 (1992). In *Lujan,* the court affirmed the more traditional basis for standing.

12. *Babbitt v. Sweet Home Chapter of Communities for a Greater Oregon,* 515 U.S. 687, 115 S.Ct. 2407 (1995).

13. *Tennessee Valley Authority v. Hill,* 437 U.S. 153 (1978).

14. 437 U.S. 153, 178 (1978).

15. 437 U.S. 153, 177 (1978), quoting Coggins (1975, 321).

16. The Comprehensive Environmental Response, Compensation, and Liability Act, 42 U.S.C. §§ 9601–9657 (1988).

17. The Oil Pollution Act of 1990, 33 U.S.C. §§ 2701–2761.

18. A comprehensive discussion of these issues is found in Williams (1995). Note that CERCLA standards may be used in certain Clean Water Act violation cases. See *Kennecott Utah Copper Corp. v. Dept. of Interior,* 88 F.3d 1191 (D.C. Cir., 1996).

19. 42 U.S.C. § 9651(c)(2) (1988).

20. 42 U.S.C. § 9607(f)(1) (1988).

21. *Kennecott Utah Copper v. Dept. of Interior,* 88 F.3d 1191 (1996).

22. 51 Fed. Reg. 27, 674 (1986). These regulations were amended after pas-

sage of amendments to CERCLA in 1986 (SARA). The new regulations, 53 Fed. Reg. 5166 (1988), were challenged with the original regulations by various parties. The appeals court held that the statute required preference to be given to the restoration option, rather than allowing defendants to pay the lesser of restoration or lost use value. See *Ohio v. Dept. of Interior,* 880 F.2d 432 (D.C. Cir., 1989).

    23. 33 U.S.C. § 1321(f)(4–5) (1994).

    24. 43 C.F.R. §§ 11.80(b); 11.83(c)(1–2) (1994).

References

Anderson, Terry L. 1998. Viewing Wildlife through Coase-Colored Glasses, this volume.

Anderson, Terry L., and Peter J. Hill. 1990. The Race for Property Rights. *Journal of Law and Economics* 33(April): 177–97.

Bator, Francis M. 1958. The Anatomy of Market Failure. *Quarterly Journal of Economics* 72: 351–74.

Bork, Robert H. 1990. *The Tempting of America.* New York: Free Press.

———. 1996. *Slouching toward Gomorrah: Modern Liberalism and American Decline.* New York: HarperCollins.

Brubaker, Elizabeth. 1998. The Common Law and the Environment: The Canadian Experience, this volume.

Buchanan, James M. 1986. Politics and Meddlesome Preferences. In *Smoking and Society*, ed. Robert D. Tollison. Lexington, MA: Lexington, 335–42.

Buchanan, James M., and William Craig Stubblebine. 1962. Externality. *Economica* 29(November): 371–84.

Coggins, George Cameron. 1975. Conserving Wildlife Resources. *North Dakota Law Review* 51: 321.

Cooter, Robert D. 1994. Structural Adjudication and the New Law Merchant: A Model of Decentralized Law. *International Review of Law and Economics* 14: 215–28.

Cross, Frank B. 1989. Natural Resource Damage Valuation. *Vanderbilt Law Review* 42: 269–341.

Dahlman, Carl J. 1979. The Problem of Externality. *Journal of Law and Economics* 22(1): 141–62.

Diamond, Peter A., and Jerry A. Hausmann. 1994. Contingent Valuation: Is Some Number Better Than No Number? *Journal of Economic Perspectives* 8(4): 45–64.

Epstein, Richard A. 1998. Habitat Preservation: A Property Rights Perspective, this volume.

Farber, Daniel A. 1996. Stretching the Margins: The Geographical Nexus in Environmental Law, *Stanford Law Review* 48: 1247–78.

Freeman, A. Myrick. 1979. Approaches to Measuring Public Goods Demands. *American Journal of Agricultural Economics* 61: 915–40.

Friedman, Milton. 1962. *Capitalism and Freedom.* Chicago: University of Chicago Press.

Haddock, David D. 1986. First Possession Versus Optimal Timing: Limiting the Dissipation of Economic Values. *Washington University Law Quarterly* 64: 775–814.

Haddock, David D., Fred S. McChesney, and Menaham Spiegel. 1990. An Ordinary Economic Rationale for Extraordinary Legal Sanctions. *California Law Review* 78: 1–51.

Hanemann, W. Michael. 1994. Valuing the Environment through Contingent Valuation. *Journal of Economic Perspectives* 8(4): 19–44.

Hayek, F. A. 1948a. Socialist Calculation III: The Competitive "Solution." Reprinted in *Individualism and Economic Order*, ed. F. A. Hayek. Chicago: University of Chicago Press, 181–208.

———.1948b. The Use of Knowledge in Society. Reprinted in *Individualism and Economic Order*, ed. F. A. Hayek. Chicago: University of Chicago Press, 77–91.

———. 1967. The Results of Human Action but Not of Human Design. In *Studies in Philosophy, Politics and Economics*, ed. F. A. Hayek. London: Routledge and Kegan Paul, 96–105.

———. 1973. *Law, Legislation, and Liberty: Rules and Order.* Chicago: University of Chicago Press.

Knight, Frank H. 1935. Marginal Utility Economics. In *The Ethics of Competition and Other Essays*, ed. Frank H. Knight. New York: Macmillan, 148–60.

Krutilla, John. 1967. Conservation Reconsidered. *American Economic Review* 57: 777–86.

Leoni, Bruno. 1961. *Freedom and the Law.* Los Angeles: Nash.

McChesney, Fred S. 1997. *Money for Nothing: Politicians, Rent Extraction, and Political Extortion.* Cambridge: Harvard University Press.

McCormick, Charles T. 1935. *Damages.* St. Paul: West.

Morriss, Andrew P. 1997. Private Actors and Structural Balance: Militia and the Free Rider Problem in Private Provision of Law. *Montana Law Review* 58: 115–66.

National Oceanic and Atmospheric Administration (NOAA). 1993. Natural Resource Damage Assessments under the Oil Pollution Act of 1990: Proposed Rules. *Federal Register* 58: 4601.

———. 1994. Natural Resource Damage Assessments: Proposed Rules. *Federal Register* 59: 1062.

———. 1996. Natural Resource Damage Assessments. *Federal Register* 61: 440.

Nelson, Robert H. 1993. How Much Is Enough? An Overview of the Benefits and Costs of Environmental Protection. In *Taking the Environment Seriously*, ed. Roger E. Meiners and Bruce Yandle. Lanham, MD: Rowman & Littlefield, 1–23.

Ostrom, Elinor. 1990. *Governing the Commons: The Evolution of Institutions for Collective Action.* New York: Cambridge University Press.

Portney, Paul R. 1994. The Contingent Valuation Debate: Why Economists Should Care. *Journal of Economic Perspectives* 8(4): 3–18.

Revesz, Richard L. 1996. Federalism and Interstate Environmental Externalities. *University of Pennsylvania Law Review* 144: 2341–416.

Robinson, Judith. 1996. The Role of Nonuse Values in Natural Resource Damages: Past, Present and Future. *Texas Law Review* 75: 189–412.

Schumpeter, Joseph A. 1942. *Capitalism, Socialism, and Democracy.* New York: Harper.

Smith, Vernon L. 1998. Property Rights as a Natural Order: Reciprocity, Evolutionary and Experimental Considerations, this volume.

Sunstein, Cass R. 1993. Endogenous Preferences, Environmental Law. *Journal of Legal Studies* 22(2): 217–54.

———. 1996. Social Norms and Social Roles. *Columbia Law Review* 96: 903–68.

Wagner, Richard E. 1998. The Constitutional Protection of Private Property, this volume.

Williams, Douglas R. 1995. Valuing Natural Environments: Compensation, Market Norms, and the Idea of Public Goods. *Connecticut Law Review* 27: 365–491.

Yandle, Bruce. 1997. *Common Sense and Common Law for the Environment: Creating Wealth in Hummingbird Economies.* Lanham, MD: Rowman & Littlefield.

———. 1998. Coase, Pigou, and Environmental Rights, this volume.

Chapter 7

From Stakeholders to Stockholders: A View from Organizational Theory

William J. Carney

The public lands have been administered under congressional mandate to facilitate multiple uses of the land.[1] Because of this, the United States has operated the public lands as an odd kind of commons, where users lack the right to exclude others in many cases, and where users frequently pay far less than market value for access to these resources.[2] Ironically, at least one of the cornerstones of public land laws, the Taylor Grazing Act,[3] was enacted to solve the problem of the commons by limiting access for grazing through a permit system, but it failed entirely, as the BLM emphasized ranchers' desires for additional grazing rights (Coggins 1983, 2). Accordingly, we have witnessed competition to appropriate some portion of the commons by multiple interest groups. Not unexpectedly, resources have been dissipated in the competition, which is a continuing race as rights are renewed and reassigned (Anderson and Hill 1990; Gordon 1954). As a result of these costs and the costs of complying with bureaucratic regulations, some studies suggest the marginal value of grazing rights to southwestern ranchers is approaching zero (LaFrance and Watts 1995, 6). A related problem is the uncertainty surrounding grazing permit renewal, which attenuates property rights and creates further incentives for short-term exploitation by permittees (LaFrance and Watts 1995, 6). And because the prices

I thank George Benston, William Buzbee, P. J. Hill, Fred McChesney, Janusz Mrozek, and George Shepherd as well as participants at the Emory Law and Economics Workshop and the Political Economy Forum for their helpful comments on earlier drafts of this paper. The errors that remain are mine. Copyright © 1998 by William J. Carney.

charged are generally below market prices, the resources themselves have been dissipated through overuse and misuse. In short, government has encouraged interest groups to behave as destructively as interest group theory suggests they will.

Even by its own admission, the United States government has been a poor steward of our natural resources and environment. This is generally a story of fees that are set too low and resulting overuse of fragile resources. A 1988 study by the General Accounting Office (GAO) reported that 90 percent of federal streamside lands in Colorado managed by the government have been degraded, with poorly managed livestock grazing being the major cause (Weidenbaum, Douglas, and Orlando 1997, 12 n. 11). It also found that 60 percent of the BLM's grazing allotments were in less than satisfactory condition and that the agency was taking almost no action to reduce overgrazing (Oesterle 1996, 527 n. 29). Water quality and the recreation that depends on it are adversely affected. Overgrazing can cause serious erosion and can crowd out valuable game animals.[4] At the same time, while grazing on public lands costs the government $4.60 per animal unit month (AUM), the government collected grazing fees of only $1.35 per AUM in 1996 (Weidenbaum, Douglas, and Orlando 1997, 12; Cody 1996).[5] This was well below the costs of administering the programs.[6] In contrast, the average return to private landowners from grazing leases was $8.70 per AUM in 1991 (Wilkinson 1992, 81). While in some cases differences between public and private grazing leases may reflect the additional costs to ranchers of dealing with the federal government, in others underpricing and lack of property rights that discourage long-term investments by ranchers in the range result in the classic overgrazing pattern associated with a commons and a reduced value for the resource.

In addition to creating a new tragedy of the commons with the concomitant overuse of fragile resources such as grazing lands, government management, even of single use resources, often results in underpricing and overuse. Mining inevitably causes some environmental damage, but the government continues to subsidize it. Under the General Mining Law of 1872, mining claims can be maintained for $100 per year, and a patent costs $5 per acre—the value of western lands in 1872, with the government receiving no royalties, as is customary in the private sector (Weidenbaum, Douglas, and Orlando 1997, 13).[7] The damage from open-pit mining leaves scars that will last forever, while the tailings leach into streams for centuries; yet it continues to be subsidized by low government fees. The Forest Service sells timber for prices well below cost, with annual deficits estimated between $112 million and $1 billion (Weidenbaum, Douglas, and Orlando 1997, 14; Oesterle 1996, 528). Destruction of timber resources in the arid West tends to be very long term, and not only reduces resources available to wild animals but destroys the beauty of some areas for generations. The Forest Service leases out public lands for various recreational uses, from ski areas to marinas to sites for private homes, for far less than fair market value (General Accounting Office 1996). In short, the public lands are underpriced and overused, to the long-term detriment of the environment.

The problem extends to the national parks, which are not subject to the same multiple use mandates but are subject to similar tensions under statutes that are ambiguous about the choice between preservation and tourism (Jeffrey 1996, 98–104; Herman 1992, 5–8, 17–19). Many national parks have the same problems as crowded urban areas, including traffic jams and garbage disposal problems because of overuse, caused in part by underpricing of admission and overuse of park facilities (Herman 1992). National parks suffer from underpricing of use permits given to franchisees that operate hotels, restaurants, and other commercial facilities.[8] User fees are also well below market value and do not begin to cover operating costs.[9]

Overuse and underpricing are not new problems. A recent General Accounting Office study points out that it has issued numerous critical studies of the pricing issue.[10] The study further points out that the Forest Service is entitled to charge application fees to recover processing costs, but that it has not done so and cannot do so, because it has no cost accounting system (General Accounting Office 1996, 10–11). The inability of government even to calculate its costs, much less to recover them, suggests some fundamental and intractable problems in government management of its property. With government controlling 29 percent of the nation's land, these are serious problems worth addressing (Oesterle 1996, 522). How do we get government to behave as a rational owner of resources? What systemic factors prevent it from doing so, despite repeated calls for reform?

There are at least two problems. First, given the ambiguity of statutory goals and consequent bureaucratic discretion, government officials are responsive to multiple special interests when it comes to leasing or selling government resources.[11] The least powerful of these groups comprises taxpayers, so we see systematic underpricing. Underpricing means that the public lands operate as a modified form of commons, with all of the problems of overuse that entails (Hardin 1968). And because it is government that is giving away these resources, we see all of the costs associated with rent-seeking. Second, even when we recognize the problem and call for change, very little happens. Our agents at the BLM, the National Park Service, and the Forest Service perform very imperfectly for their presumably real principals.

One suggested approach to this problem of poor government performance in environmental areas is granting "stakeholders" a greater voice. Claims are made that some interests are disenfranchised in the government decision-making process and should be given a voice that is heard in a meaningful way. According to this argument, forcing the decision maker to consider all interests forces them to make defensible decisions (Poindexter 1995, 63). Panels of stakeholders have been employed in various settings—setting environmental policy for various industries,[12] including the manufacture of volatile organic compounds (Collins and Barkdull 1995, 242). The governor of Washington has convened forums of stakeholders to consider the future of the Bonneville Power Administration (Hemmingway 1996, 673). Hundreds of Canadian communities have developed round tables of stakeholders to resolve environmental issues (Downes 1995, 371). All of this suggests that giving voice to all groups will solve our environmental problems. One writer makes glowing claims for the accomplishments of Canadian round tables designed to produce sustainable economies:

> First, members of local round tables develop a vision of their community as a sustainable entity, leading to the development of locally based principles for sustainability. The whole community then reviews, debates, and revises these principles. Second, a round table provides information, teaches skills, encourages efforts in sustainable living, and heightens the public's understanding of sustainability. Third, round tables review government policies and programs, making recommendations in specific areas of sustainability. Fourth, round tables focus attention on specific issues of concern. Fifth, round tables monitor the state of local sustainability. Sixth, round tables help resolve conflicts over land and resource use. Seventh, round tables enhance community self-sufficiency through networking. Finally, round tables organize and undertake sustainable projects. (Fiorino 1996, 470)

These alleged accomplishments boggle the mind. When do these citizens find time to undertake the normal business of daily life? How do they assemble the infinite bits of information, "the knowledge of the particular circumstances of time and place," employed by all participants in markets in making their personal decisions about resource allocation, savings, investment and the like (Hayek 1945, 521)? Only two writers, to my knowledge, have asked cogent questions about the marvels of stakeholder involvement in difficult decisions about the environment:

> Obviously, there are important questions to address with regard to this proposal. First, why is there likely to be greater consensus among the affected individuals using a stakeholder panel mechanism than under the

current system of government lobbying? Second, who should sit on the panel? Third, will the panels simply become another arena of politics, thus replicating the current political problem of ignoring the ethical chorus in favor of environmental protection? Fourth, will the losers in this process refuse to abide by the decisions of the panels and appeal to politicians and judges for reversals? Fifth, do we have the luxury of time for these panels to resolve major outstanding environmental issues? (Collins and Barkdull 1995, 243)

Kenneth Arrow has provided a powerful analysis of how panels behave in his work on the voter's paradox. Arrow has shown that where there are multiple voters with different lexical ordering of their preferences and multiple choices, there will be no stability of outcomes in such a decision-making process. Further, Arrow's work demonstrates that outcomes under these conditions can be determined by agenda manipulation, hardly an example of rational policy making (Arrow 1963, 3).[13] Worse yet, the same phenomenon operates within each stakeholder group that has more than two members. Over time, new interests and values can develop, so the process of including all stakeholders may be endless. As one example, it is now claimed by some environmentalists that various aspects of the environment have importance not because of their instrumental value to citizens, but because of their own intrinsic values (Wales 1996). Thus governmental decision makers will be unable to determine the preferences of all stakeholder groups in any rational and orderly fashion.

Notwithstanding these difficulties, there are settings in which stakeholder interests can be mediated successfully. While suggestions of privatization are hardly new in this area, I suggest a manner of privatization that utilizes the corporate form, and utilizes it in a way that will maximize returns to citizens and avoid charges of a giveaway of valuable resources to special interests.[14] This form will conserve these valuable resources more effectively than government ownership has. As Dale Oesterle has written, the "government's land disposal record is as bad as its land management record," citing "fraud, frequent concessions to organized political groups at the expense of the public interest, and ubiquitous poor judgment," although he suggests that the Resolution Trust Corporation performed more adequately than prior government sellers (Oesterle 1996, 531).

Oesterle has provided an example of the problems government faces in sale decisions. Thirty percent of the coal produced in the United States comes from federal reserves (Oesterle 1996, 524). A decision to lease more coal for production in any year could affect coal prices. As a result, planning decisions about coal leasing "present tailor-made opportunities for titanic struggles between clashing interest groups. As a result, planning decisions for the past twenty-five years have resulted in swirl of controversy, litigation, and gridlock" (Oesterle 1996, 535). Thus even government decisions to sell assets run straight into the political thicket of interest group politics. Government attempts to create competitive auctions of these resources have been blocked by interest groups, both industry and environmental (Oesterle 1996, 535). Rather than hold a massive auction to sell off these resources, the government should place them in a number of new corporations and distribute shares to all citizens. In many respects this approach resembles the privatization of state industries in Eastern Europe.

The corporate approach addresses one of the issues raised by an important critic of free market environmentalism, James Krier, who has lamented the explanation of Anderson and Leal (1991) that solutions to environmental problems in a free market would occur because of the appearance of "environmental entrepreneurs," which he characterizes as a Panglossian solution. In response, Krier (1992, 345–46) argues that it would be valuable to study how successes were achieved in the management of environmental resources—how nongovernmental groups and institutions have overcome collective action problems as they sought the production of public or collective goods, like environmental quality. I offer the success of the corporate form in mediating between interest groups with claims on some of the rents created by firm activity as a more generalized model of how corporate management of environmental resources would operate. At the same time, I demonstrate that many of the goods about which Krier and others express concern are not always public goods, and that terms such as collective goods and existence values add nothing to our analysis.

Solving the Agency Problem

The first problem is how to get agents to pursue the interests of their nominal principals vigorously. Government officials have been anything but aggressive in this area. User fees have been below market value for a long time. How do we get government officials to act aggressively to represent the real owners of the public lands, rather than certain users of them?

These problems disappear if government were simply to "run its affairs like a business." But of course that is what numerous critics, from the GAO to environmental groups, have been demanding for many years. How do we achieve it? It's not enough to tell government officials they should be primarily loyal to the treasury, and that they should maximize revenues to the government. There are few rewards for the officials involved, since most revenues generated by their activities are general funds available to the treasury.[15]

In the private sector the answers are relatively straightforward. Corporate managers are held accountable by shareholders and market forces. These are powerful forces, and they all focus on the interests of shareholders as the residual claimants in the firm. They force managers to obtain inputs for production at the lowest possible cost, to operate firms efficiently, and to sell the output for the highest prices obtainable. In the context of the public lands, we could be sure that a firm owning these lands would have effective cost controls, would calculate the choices of cutting timber now versus holding it for future harvesting on the basis of discounted present value calculations, would know its cost of goods sold, and would attempt to minimize this cost and to maximize the net present value of expected profits.

Running the administration of the public lands like a business will only happen if these lands are owned by an actual business. This business could be owned by the taxpayers, but not by the government. In short, one way to arrange this is the very kind of privatization that has worked so well in Eastern Europe—the simple creation of a business corporation to own state assets, and the distribution of its shares to the public. Private ordering has produced a form of governance and resource allocation that is far more efficient than government can ever be in allocating resources to maximize welfare. To whom the shares are distributed is not very important; what is important is that they be privately held and traded in stock markets.[16]

The corporation represents a natural experiment in how to organize production activities where there are multiple factors of production, with owners of each claiming benefits from the joint production activities. Firms are constructed to solve agency problems in ways government could never duplicate. As a formal matter, corporations are created as separate legal entities by the state, with the right to sue and be sued in their own names and to hold title to property. The corporate form solves most collective action problems of shareholders by providing for shareholder election of centralized management, the board of directors. These directors are charged with the duty to manage the business of the corporation, and in that capacity they must monitor the activities of the corporation's officers and employees. Courts treat directors as owing fiduciary duties to the corporation; that is, they must act with the same care a reasonable person would employ under similar circumstances, and they must act with total loyalty to corporate (and shareholder) interests.

Agency costs have long been regarded as the central problem of organizing firms.[17] As a result, firms provide a variety of arrangements for monitoring and motivating agents, in the form of rigorous accounting standards audited by outsiders, the appointment of outside directors to corporate boards, annual election of directors, removal of directors, incentive compensation for managers, and requirements that managers invest heavily in the firm's stock (Jensen and Meckling 1976). While these are generally effective constraints on managers, they are not perfect. In these cases there are fallback constraints to deal with more egregious cases of managerial slacking. The traditional analysis of why this happens focuses on the operation of three markets—the market for products, the market for managers, and the market for corporate control.

Before discussing how these markets constrain managers we should note the primary role played by capital markets in measuring the performance of managers. Shares of corporations are freely transferable absent contractual arrangements to the contrary. When shares of large companies are widely held and traded in public stock markets, these markets are generally described as efficient. This means that these markets rapidly impound all new information about the value of the company's shares in its stock price, which is calculated on the discounted present value of the entire future stream of expected cash flows to shareholders (Fama 1970; Friend 1972; Grossman 1976; Kornhauser and Gordon 1986). Efficient capital markets are characterized by large numbers of knowledgeable professional traders and analysts who closely follow the performance of managers of various companies, and who buy or sell on the basis of any good or bad news about a company's performance. In essence, stock prices become the ultimate evaluators of the performance of management (Carney 1989).

First, there are product markets. Firms sell their products in competitive markets. With some minor exceptions, this will also be true for firms owning formerly public lands. The way to maximize profits is through maximizing the prices customers will pay, subject to the constraints of the slope of the demand curve for the firm's products. It is clear that government officials have failed to do this. They can, of course, sell all the resources available at below-market prices and point proudly to the volume of sales and the social utility of these sales. But managers of private corporations would not be satisfied with this, because it has not been the profit-maximizing strategy. Savvy managers of formerly public lands would unbundle their resources to the maximum extent possible, in order to maximize the number of bidders and the price paid for each part of this bundle of rights. For example, rather than giving grazing leases on large portions of national forest lands that include valuable recreational resources such as trout streams that can be degraded by bank erosion caused by cattle, grazing rights and stream access rights might be disposed of separately. Recreational users could then bid for rights to the banks of streams in competition with ranchers. Thus this profit-maximizing approach has the happy property of solving the conflicts among interest groups and pricing negative externalities. At the same time, managers of private firms would have a budget constraint never imposed on government managers—a cost constraint based on the need to maximize net profits, not just revenues. Where government officials may be rewarded for building bureaucratic empires, there are few such rewards in the private sector.[18]

Second, managers are constrained by the market for their own services, which forces incumbent managers to operate as efficiently as possible (Fama 1980). The market for managers controls management behavior because upper-level management positions are scarce and lucrative and create real demand for those positions. Not only are there managers outside the firm eager to replace existing managers if they falter, but there are also managers within the firm ready to step forward. These managers may even have incentives to point out the failings of their superiors to the board of directors, both to avoid blame for their superiors' failings and to encourage dismissals or demotions that will create openings for them. Civil service has never been able to devise such mechanisms.

Third, the market for corporate control operates to control abuses of managers' discretion. Stock prices for widely traded companies contain an implicit assessment of management quality, as well as assessments about future prices of the goods to be sold, and the cost of future raw materials. If public resources were owned by one or more corporations, stock prices would reflect these same factors. When firms are managed in a way that fails to maximize the discounted present value of future cash flows, stock prices fall, sending signals to both investors and competing management teams that something is wrong. Investors can then react through internal governance devices such as the proxy machinery to change management, if they can organize themselves. But even if they cannot, if mismanagement is severe enough, depressed stock prices create opportunities for other management teams to assemble the capital to make a takeover bid, acquire control of the company, and reform its management practices (Manne 1965).[19]

These systems are far from perfect in their operation. Like Churchill's description of democracy, they describe an imperfect system, but the best one we know. We should avoid the Nirvana Fallacy, of comparing the good with an idealized notion of perfection (Demsetz 1969).

If all public lands were divested into one corporation, it would have an enormous market value. That value might be so huge that a hostile takeover would become unthinkable, because of the enormous amount

of capital required for such an effort. Thus it would be better if resources were divested into a larger number of corporations, of a size
where they would be subjected to the pressures of the market for corporate control. Creating a series of such corporations could also avoid
anticompetitive results of divestiture.

The mechanisms of firms operating in private markets would thus
provide considerable assurance that managers will operate with a single-minded devotion to the interests of shareholders and will bargain at
arms length with all other groups—creditors, suppliers, and customers—to maximize profits for shareholders. Even those who are reluctant
to privatize the public lands would probably agree with most of these
claims. Their objections, I suspect, come on other margins, which are
briefly reviewed later in this chapter.

Solving the Interest Group Problem

Even if government officials were efficiently monitored and agency
costs were minimized, the problems of overuse and undercharging
would not disappear. Agency costs are only part of the problem. An
efficient agent has to know whom he or she represents, and what the
principal's goals are. Congress has been extraordinarily evasive about
the goals of management of public resources, so government officials
often lack a clear mandate. This is understandable in a political process,
where coalition-building requires political compromise, and in some
cases seems to require fuzzy goals. One of the major achievements of
the corporate form is to clarify goals for agents.

First, let's examine the goals specified in current laws about government resource management. In some cases there are legal mandates that
the public lands be managed for multiple uses,[20] which builds in the
problem of competition among interest groups for access to resources.
Congress has defined "multiple use" in a way that provides no discipline or accountability for resource managers in their allocation decisions. The definition deliberately rejects profit maximization for the
resource owner, stating that the goal is "not necessarily the combination
of uses that will give the greatest dollar return or the greatest unit output."[21] Indeed, the congressional mandate seems deliberately to preserve a huge domain for administrative discretion that cannot be
checked, because there is no measure of performance.[22] As a result,
responsible officials are under constant pressure from interest groups
not to raise fees for existing users or to provide more access for one
group or another.

The efforts of these interest groups involve lobbying and negotiations with the responsible government officials, litigation, and lobbying Congress, often all in the same matter. Members of these interest groups are the people with whom field officers of the BLM and Forest Service work on a daily basis, and with whom they develop relationships. In that sense, regulatory capture theory may partially explain what is occurring.[23] Decision costs for government officials are high, because managers of these assets are not subject to a single guiding rule. Worse, the results may be unstable, if various decision makers have different preferences (Arrow 1963). Lobbying for economic rents by various user groups under conditions of constant cycling of preferences is likely to consume a significant portion of the rents produced by these lands.

Private corporations face some of the same pressures. There is a common pool of firm revenues, on which various groups make claims. The firm's relations to these groups, representing both inputs in production and customers, are analogous to the multiple constituencies that make claims on the use of the commons represented by the public lands. The CEO of a major corporation is expected to treat suppliers fairly, to monitor them for fair labor practices if they operate in certain parts of the world, to provide fair wages and good working conditions for employees, to provide honest products to consumers at the lowest possible prices, to act as a good corporate citizen in supporting community arts and charities, and to protect the environment at the same time. Directors of corporations have to make decisions about the terms of exchange with each factor of production and with customers in the face of these demands, just as government managers have to allocate the scarce resources of the public lands.

If firms have any market power, then directors and the managers they hire have the ability to direct rents created by the firm's activities to the owners of any of the inputs or to other interest groups that claim to be stakeholders in the firm.[24] One classic view of the corporation takes the view that most corporations have some market power and generate some rents that can be distributed to these stakeholders (Nader, Green, and Seligman 1976).[25] If directors owed duties to all of these groups, you can imagine how decision costs within firms would multiply, as various groups fought for board control, engaged in log rolling with others to strike deals to share these rents, and engaged in strategic behavior such as agenda setting to control outcomes (Carney 1990, 419–20). Managers and directors would have no way to calculate whether they were maximizing aggregate welfare, because there would be no market test of the relative strength of the preferences of various interest groups. Elsewhere I have described this as the problem of information without markets (Carney 1990, 419). It appears to represent precisely the problem faced in the administration of the public lands.

The standard model of corporate governance avoids this dilemma by taking the position that shareholders, the suppliers of risk capital to the firm, are the ultimate owners of the firm. This leads to the rule that only shareholders can elect and remove directors, and to the further rule that directors owe a single-minded duty of loyalty to shareholders alone.[26] The duty of directors in this model is simply to maximize the discounted present value of the future stream of earnings available to shareholders.[27] The courts have been remarkably consistent in enforcing this rule for the past century and more. Thus they repeatedly have held that if creditors such as bondholders fail to gain contractual protection against corporate actions that increase the risk of default or frustrate their ability to convert debt into shares, that's too bad for the creditors.[28] The directors owe them no duties of fairness or loyalty and are expected to do whatever seems likely to maximize shareholder wealth, even at the expense of creditors who have failed to write complete contracts.[29]

These rules apply to other constituencies of the corporation as well. Employees are typically employed at will; that is, the corporation may terminate them at any time and for any reason unless they have contracted for additional job protection (Carney 1990, 405). Even where suppliers or customers have invested in assets that are specific to transactions with the firm, they are entitled to no protection from opportunistic behavior that might appropriate quasi rents beyond rules that contracts will be enforced and liability imposed for breach (Klein, Crawford, and Alchian 1978). Critics of this rule generally make the usual market failure arguments—asymmetric information, collective action problems, market power, and the like.[30] But thus far the courts have been remarkably unresponsive to these arguments, and market forces have constrained the ability of legislatures to write special benefits into corporate law for most interest groups.[31]

The rule that managers owe duties only to shareholders to maximize their wealth is expressed in the doctrine of waste: managers and directors simply lack authority to give away corporate assets to other stakeholders or constituencies unless the gift is reasonably calculated to bring an equivalent benefit to the firm.[32] The doctrine is so strict that not even a majority of the shareholders can ratify such a gift; it takes the consent of all shareholders to authorize it. The Delaware Supreme Court has even held that directors may not make gifts to former shareholders who had exchanged their shares for bonds, unless it benefitted present shareholders.[33] Further, when managers are tempted to serve themselves rather than the shareholders, as in defending against hostile takeovers, the Delaware courts have taken the lead in scrutinizing their actions carefully, rather than giving these decisions the usual deference granted under the "business judgment rule."[34]

This rule of exclusive loyalty to a single claimant on the corporate assets has the effect of eliminating much rent-seeking by interest groups within firms, and it limits challenges in the courts by these groups to breach of contract claims, rather than amorphous claims of unfairness that are costly to resolve. This rule of singular loyalty also has the benefit of limiting corporate managers to measurably efficient actions.[35] Owners of other factors of production are not to be paid more than the market rate for their inputs. Products will be sold for their full market prices. All excess returns belong to shareholders, who are the principal risk bearers in most firms. Allocating any available rents to shareholders has the effect of raising a firm's stock price in markets, making it cheaper, from the perspective of existing shareholders, to attract more capital. And rising earnings may signal that a firm has opportunities for the productive use of more capital, serving the goal of allocational efficiency.

This rule also has the effect of reducing decision costs within the firm (Committee on Corporate Laws 1990, 2270; Clark 1986, 20). Managers and directors need not weigh the costs and benefits of their actions for any group other than shareholders, and shareholder interests are measured simply by calculating the discounted present value of expected future cash flows from decisions. This by itself is a difficult enough task, where managers frequently err, but it is far simpler than learning the wealth effects on other stakeholders in the firm, much less their respective indifference curves for various kinds of benefits, all without the benefit of price signals. Finally, holding management accountable only to shareholders and measuring this on a discounted present value basis holds managers as strictly accountable as we know how to do, with management's performance measured through stock prices in efficient markets. If managers were to consider the welfare of other stakeholders in the firm, the clarity of this accountability would disappear, and managers would become accountable to no one (Carney 1990, 420–21; Committee on Corporate Laws 1990, 2270).

If the public lands were simply transferred to private corporations, and shares in these enterprises were issued to shareholders who would hold managers accountable in the normal way that shareholders do this, the problems of unclear goals and of political lobbying for rent creation would quickly be terminated. Who owns the shares initially is not terribly important, so long as it is not the government. As in Western Europe, where formerly government-owned industries are being divested, shares could be sold in initial public offerings (IPOs). Successful IPOs for steel companies and telephone companies make it clear that this is a manageable enterprise. This would provide revenues for the government. Or, following the Eastern European model, shares could simply be distributed without charge to all citizens.[36] I leave for the moment the difficult political problems of getting interest group support for such a project; various payoffs to interest groups might be required to move forward.

Beginning in the 1980s, we observed a disturbing trend in American corporate law. As corporate takeovers increased in frequency, corporate managers felt more threatened by the risk of displacement. Over the last five years of the 1980s about half the states adopted statutes that gave corporate boards permission to consider the welfare of constituencies other than shareholders, especially when considering the sale or merger of the company (Carney 1990, 386 n. 6 and authorities cited). In short, these were management-sponsored statutes, adopted by accommodating legislatures eager to please hometown management that provided political support and to protect them from outsiders who had no political influence (Romano 1987; Butler 1988, 374). These statutes essentially give management the power to be unaccountable to anyone. It is worth noting that the most competitive state, Delaware, did not adopt such a law. The initial charter for any corporation designed to own formerly public lands should specify that none of these provisions will apply to the corporation, and a state of incorporation should be selected where these provisions are not mandatory.

Finally, note how the privatization approach solves the transaction cost problem of negotiating with multiple users of a resource who value different properties of that resource. While government has to mediate politically to come up with a single solution, it does so without the benefit of prices that allow these users to express the intensity of their preferences. A corporation focusing on maximizing value for shareholders, simply by unbundling all of these attributes for sale, allows smaller interest groups with more discrete demands to bid effectively for that small fraction of the entire bundle of rights they value most highly, without being forced to acquire parts of the bundle of no value to them. Markets might even develop intermediaries that would speculate in these rights by buying a larger bundle than they require and attempting to unbundle them for resale at a profit.

Time Horizon and Monopoly Problems

There are serious objections to proposals to privatize the public lands, whatever the form of privatization. The use of corporations as the vehicle for privatization can answer many of the objections. The first objection is that the public lands should be managed to protect the interests of future generations as well as the present. The second objection may be that no one acting today can know the true long-term value of all resources presently owned by the government, and privatization today would lead to disposition at inadequate prices for some resources. Third, today's decision makers cannot possibly have enough knowledge of the value of all resources owned by government to obtain full value in a sale. Fourth, exploitation of fragile resources may create negative externalities for other private owners, such as stream pollution. Fifth, a private owner of the public lands would have monopoly power to restrict sales and raise prices for some resources. Sixth, there are some values in the public lands that cannot be captured in prices, much less allocated and preserved by them. I am not familiar with much of the literature in the environmental and property rights area, and I may have missed some of the major objections, and I may certainly miss some important responses.[37] But I can provide the perspective of organization theory and finance on these topics.

Protecting Future Generations

Some critics think of the public lands as a "bank" of resources to be preserved for future generations. This, of course, would require present generations to bear the costs of maintenance and foregone income for the benefit of future generations. We become, in this model, trustees for the welfare of the unborn. While this is an elevating thought, it is also a troubling one, because it proves too much. If this logic applies to the public lands, why not to all other resources, whether held privately or publicly? Does this mean we cannot consume any resources that are exhaustible? If not our generation, which generation can consume them? Over what time frame should they be exhausted?

Similar choices face corporate managers. Should firm revenues be distributed to shareholders, or reinvested in research and development to produce larger profits at some indefinite time in the future? Should landowners accelerate the extraction of oil and gas or other minerals? Managers get their guidance from markets in answering these questions. Investors discount the entire expected future stream of a firm's earnings to present value in setting stock prices. Whether managers consume resources now or hold them for future consumption is determined by expected present and future prices and costs of production, discounted to present value. When today's best projects will yield more profits than projects at some later stage, on a discounted present value basis, managers will choose to exploit a resource now rather than later. The relatively lower expected future prices tell managers that either additional resources will be found or that substitutes for particular resources will emerge.

On this basis, a management that exploits too early is forfeiting future profits that investors would value more highly. It doesn't even matter if some managers are myopic and choose to exploit too early, because, as Michael Jensen has said, managers may behave myopically, but markets do not (Jensen 1988, 26). A shortsighted management team will be punished through declining stock prices, as impersonal market forces adjust stock prices to reflect the present value of the entire stream of expected future earnings of a firm.

The wonderful thing about discount rates is that they are impersonal and do not depend on the time horizons of today's decision makers. All investors, regardless of their age, know that when they dispose of capital assets such as shares, new investors will buy them not only on the basis of the cash flows they can expect, but also on the expected proceeds of selling these assets to a third owner, and so forth. In that way future generations have an influence on today's investment decisions. While it may not be perfect, it is essentially the same mechanism that is used by government in calculating the costs and benefits of projects such as dams, although government calculations are unlikely to be as realistic, since there are no stock prices to decline if government makes a negative net present value decision.

One horror story that is told about the use of resources involves the takeover of Pacific Lumber in California in the 1980s. Pacific Lumber owned huge reserves of first-growth redwood trees, and after a takeover new management accelerated the rate of harvest to increase the total value of the firm.[38] As a wood resource, this appears to be a perfectly rational decision, because second growth redwood recovers pretty rapidly, so the company is unlikely to run out of redwood to harvest. Of course, some magnificent old growth trees will be eliminated in these holdings, and many conservationists have pointed to this as a tragic example of resource use in the private sector. The problem with this objection is that it only tells half of the story. Pacific Lumber didn't own all of the redwoods in California, by any means. The federal government remains a very large owner and makes much of its holdings available as a recreational resource. If Pacific Lumber were to preserve some old growth forests and attempt to charge admission to see them, it would be underpriced by the government, which charges nothing. Thus its return on park-like activities would be zero. If Pacific Lumber had owned all of these redwoods, it presumably would have recognized the recreational value of these trees and preserved a sufficient number to satisfy the present and expected future recreational demand.[39]

The real comparison should be between privately owned forests and publicly owned forests. While I have engaged in no empirical research on this subject, it is clear that private owners are not in the habit of harvesting timber at a loss, as the Forest Service apparently is. This can only mean that it is the Forest Service that is shortsighted in its timber management practices, not private owners.

The Risk of Overuse and Exhaustion

One of the major objections to private ownership is "short-termism." The argument is that managers of firms take short-term views of wealth and welfare and emphasize short-term payouts at the expense of the future. This is not only an objection of environmentalists but also of a significant number of academics who specialize in studying corporations. The standard argument states that stock prices are set by money managers, who are judged by quarterly results. These managers are said to judge corporate results on the basis of quarterly earnings, rather than expected long-term results.[40] This contradicts both theory and evidence. Theory argues that markets consider all expected earnings, no matter how distant. Discounting, of course, results in attaching greater value to near-term earnings than to long-term earnings, but this is a perfectly rational result of considering opportunity costs.

The evidence supports this theory. There is evidence that markets do indeed value research and development (R&D) projects, which forego short-term results in exchange for greater long-term expected payoffs.[41] This evidence shows that R&D activity is positively correlated with institutional ownership, suggesting that managers are able to communicate the expected value of long-term projects to institutional investors. A recent study indicates that markets can evaluate the expected impact of R&D on profits, at least in terms of the competitive setting of the firm announcing new R&D activity (Sunaram, John, and John 1996). In short, there is little reason to believe that there is a serious problem of short-termism in the United States.

Even if discount rates were imperfect protectors of future generations, we engage in a Nirvana Fallacy if we compare the results of this calculation with some notion of perfection. Moreover, the same problems apply to government in a more extreme form. However inadequately, government attempts to employ the same discount rates in weighing decisions about when to exploit resources. When government officials engage in cost-benefit calculations for public works, they necessarily use a discount rate. But if government officials do not know the costs of production, they can't even begin to calculate the profits or losses from an activity. If these costs are disregarded, it seems likely that government will exploit at a more rapid rate than the private sector.[42]

Finally, the worst case is that government officials do no present value calculations at all. Elected officials have very short time hori-

zons—no longer than the next election—and tend to make their calculations on that basis. They may well put pressures on appointed officials
to respond to political time horizons, rather than those of markets. In
the area of the public lands, public officials may be most responsive to
current lobbying and political pressures, which rarely have anything to
do with rational present value calculations. A prospective user of the
public lands with no property rights in those lands is the ultimate short-
term calculator; politics are uncertain and carry a very high discount
rate, so that whatever benefits can be gained today far outweigh whatever may be left for tomorrow.

A final concern deals with property dispositions. To the extent that
privatization leads to the sell-off of smaller parcels by corporations to
disparate owners, the possibility for the creation of new negative externalities exists. While existing environmental protection and nuisance
laws provide some background level of assurance that these externalities will not be extremely costly, there is still the risk of some loss of
aggregate value through disaggregation of ownership. But any rational
seller selling off a single parcel must recognize that some uses could
depreciate the value of neighboring lands the seller retains and would
take steps to restrict the use of the sold parcel to protect against such
losses. In short, this is simply planned development, and the seller intends to maximize the aggregate value of its entire holdings.

The Limits of Present Information

If government were to auction off all the public lands tomorrow, there
would be a risk of windfall losses for government and windfall gains
for some lucky but ignorant buyers. Lands sold for their timber or grazing rights might contain valuable minerals. Sales of mineral rights
would inevitably involve both underestimates and overestimates of mineral deposits. But it is equally true that if government does not create
incentives to engage in research and discovery by selling off these resources, these hidden assets may remain hidden and unused indefinitely.
One who engages in such research without property rights only creates
a public good, which is typically underproduced. One purpose of the
mining laws is to provide such incentives, although it does so on terms
much more generous than those provided in the private sector. But other
assets are likely to remain hidden if they are not sold.

A profit-maximizing natural resource corporation probably would not
engage in an auction to sell off all of its assets immediately. That certainly is not the behavior we observe in the private sector. Some resources might be leased, as minerals are today. The mineral lease, with
royalty payments, is one market solution to unknown values. When

firms buy other firms, uncertainties about the real value of the acquired business frequently lead to "earn-out" provisions, in which sellers will receive more consideration if certain profit targets are met. Uncertainty may lead to leases for terms rather than sales, with rents set at some percentage of the output from the resource, as in the case of shopping center leases.[43] In other cases uncertainty may lead to accepting stock in the buying corporation as consideration for the asset, to assure participation in any unexpected gains. Most of these solutions appear to have been ignored by the government.

Externalities

There is little doubt that managers may make decisions that create negative externalities for others not in privity of contract with them, and which thus are not currently priced. But this objection is so general that it clearly applies to government managers as well as managers in the private sector. Clear-cutting of timber may lead to soil erosion and runoff that pollutes streams. Leasing full access to stream banks to ranchers for grazing permits may degrade the water quality in these streams. Subsidized mining leases that do not require control of runoff from mine tailings may have the same impact. Environmental impact studies are no assurance that these externalities will be avoided; either the studies can be influenced by the preferred choice of agency managers,[44] or an adverse statement can be dealt with by claiming that the preferred use is cost effective—that the benefits to society outweigh the negative externalities, a claim that is never put to a market test by fully pricing the use to compensate for the externality.[45] Government is also a major polluter and seems to take the longest to clean up its act, whether it involves nuclear waste from defense establishments, effluent from municipal sewage plants, or other sources.[46]

Part of this problem can be solved by unbundling property rights so all users, no matter how specialized, can bid against other users without having to pay for more than they want (see Anderson and Leal 1991). Grazing rights, for example, would not by themselves exclude recreational users from being on the range, unless the rancher bought these rights as well, in which case he would be bidding against recreational users only for the specific use. Similarly, grazing rights need not include access to all stream banks unless purchased separately, in competition with fishing interests or downstream municipalities that prefer cleaner water for domestic use. Development rights, in terms of construction of structures, might be separated from the fee simple interest in scenic lands in order to give recreational users the ability to bid against developers. Rights to divert and use government-owned water rights might be separated from the right to warm the water or pollute it, once again giving recreational users the ability to bid only for those rights they really value. Mineral rights might exclude the right to pollute streams with various chemicals used in mining processes, which could be auctioned separately. There are probably many other examples of how rights could be unbundled to fully price the negative externalities. This unbundling would substitute for present multiple use rules that lead to interest group competition that dissipates resources.

A major objection to this solution to the externality problem involves the collective action problems that might be faced by various users, such as recreational users, who are numerous, widely dispersed, and often sporadic users of these resources. While all of these are problems, recreation is an industry, and I would be surprised if entrepreneurs did not appear to take advantage of an opportunity to own and market various recreational rights. Private parks are evidence of the exploitation of market opportunities in recreation.[47] Thus all of the trout fishermen of the world need not organize to buy property rights in the continued clean flow of the Yellowstone River at levels sufficient to sustain a healthy trout population; it is enough that some entrepreneur raise the capital to do so, in order to sell fishing rights to recreational users. It might even make sense for the corporate owner of former public lands to sell these rights at retail to those interested in fishing the stream, although I would expect that a more specialized manager would attach greater value to this resource. Salmon and trout streams in Europe have operated under private ownership for a long time and have survived even though population pressures are far more intense than here. I have fished a premier eastern trout stream where the farmer limits the access of his cattle to the stream in order to protect the stream banks and water quality so he can maximize revenues from fishing. Even his row crops are separated from the stream by grass to reduce siltation.

The Problem of Monopoly

One objection to privatization through corporations would properly be the problem of monopoly; another is the problem of monopsony.

Monopoly Power

In many parts of the West the government owns the vast majority of the land. If all of this land were given to a single corporation, it would have a geographic monopoly that it could exploit through high prices. Related to this is a problem of appropriation of quasi rents. Many ranches have been built on a specific relationship to the public lands that assumes the ability to graze animals on these lands. Specific capital has been invested on the fee lands, in the form of irrigation systems to provide meadows to produce the hay needed for winter for large numbers of animals that graze the public lands in the summer. A single owner of the high meadows has the ability to appropriate the quasi rents associated with these investments.[48]

From the public's point of view, this is hardly an objection at all. As a taxpayer, I might argue that government has failed to exploit its geographic market power for generations and has thus failed to maximize revenues to the treasury, for the benefit of all citizens. But the reciprocal of that argument is that exercise of that monopoly power would restrict output from the public lands and raise prices to markets generally. Accordingly, I would prefer that government, or successor corporations owning these lands, charge a market-clearing price that would prevail if there were no monopoly.

To focus on local geographic monopolies is to use a microscope when a wide-range lens is more appropriate. These lands only have value for the goods and services they can produce for wider markets. These markets, whether for beef, wool, minerals, or recreation, are competitive. Increases in rents charged for the use of these lands will reduce demand for them, and where competitive product markets exist for the output of these lands, there will be a competitive equilibrium that constrains the price government or corporations can charge. The problem of monopoly is readily solved by using multiple corporations to own fractions of those resources where government presently has market power.

The problem of appropriation of existing quasi rents is a real one. Indeed, it exists with government ownership as well as with private ownership. Many private landowners have paid prices for ranches that include the discounted present value of grazing rights at below-market rates. Any rate increase appropriates some of these quasi rents, whether by government or a private owner. With private ownership, we might expect a once-and-for-all solution through the sale of fee interests in lands that have such relationships.[49]

Monopsony Power

There is also a conflicting objection to privatization: that there is a monopsony problem. The pattern of private land ownership in the West is one of private ownership of river valleys and public ownership of more arid lands. Those staking claims under Homestead and Desert Land acts quite naturally selected the lands that provided the required base for more extensive operations: those with ready access to water, that could be irrigated to support more intensive agricultural activities, whether crop cultivation or simply irrigated hay meadows. As a result, private landowners may control access to large amounts of the public lands. This is particularly true where access depends on travel through the valleys of tributary streams that flow into the major rivers that are surrounded by privately owned lands.

Where a monopolist government faces a monopsonist landowner, we have a bilateral monopoly. The seller, whether government or a private corporation, should have a relatively long time horizon about getting the appropriate return from its resources. Accordingly, the seller should be able to withstand a long stalemate. Because it holds a much larger portfolio of lands than any private lessee or prospective buyer, it should be able to hold out for the market-clearing price for what it has to offer. If the bilateral monopoly problem is intractable, the once and for all solution is a sale to the monopsonist buyer.[50]

Protecting the Noncommercial Use

I have tried to demonstrate that where recreational uses are valuable, corporations will respond by marketing recreational opportunities, often in coordination with other uses of the resource, through unbundling of rights. But there are some uses that are not commercially valuable as recreation that are valued by some citizens.[51] The spotted owl and the snail darter are two of the more prominent examples. Others refer to "existence values"—the value of resources, such as vistas, that a person may know he or she will never see (Rose 1994, 1030–31).

Uses such as this are sometimes argued to have values that cannot be captured in prices. Some environmentalists have described them as "priceless."[52] This is a standard ploy of those who fear relying on markets for resource allocations. More recently, apparently in response to economic analyses of property rights issues in environmental regulation, the existence value advocates have attempted to attach hypothetical monetary values to these amenities, apparently always at levels high enough to trump any conventional cost-benefit analysis (Boudreaux and Meiners 1998).[53] Those using these techniques seem not to claim these goods are public goods, probably because exclusion of users is so often feasible. Yosemite National Park's principal features lie in a narrow valley with only one entrance; Yellowstone National Park, like many others, has only a few roads that enter it through rugged terrain. The existence of private parks, scenic easements, and controlled development by single owners of large parcels are evidence of attempts to preserve values that are not always readily priced. These solutions demonstrate that prices are indeed available to solve many of these problems.

Nothing prevents corporate owners of formerly public lands from marketing rights designed to protect these species, to the extent that endangered species laws don't already do this in a more general way.[54] Some conservation organizations already operate in this manner, purchasing property rights to protect species and other environmental values.[55] Philanthropists have a history of donating park and forest land, as the Rockefellers did in both Grand Teton National Park and Acadia National Park, and as George Vanderbilt did with land constituting Pisgah National Forest. Private game preserves protect selected species, and in the process provide habitat for nongame species as well. Nothing would prevent the federal government from also purchasing such rights, although it should do so in competition with other buyers, rather than through the use of the coercive power of eminent domain. By outspending other buyers for such resources the government would identify the true opportunity cost of preserving various species and provide a means for voters to judge whether preservation was really worth the price. This approach would eliminate the ability to argue that some resource was "priceless" and should be protected no matter how great the cost. At present the full opportunity costs of such preservation decisions are unknown; requiring their purchase would reveal the cost and improve the quality of debate and decision making in these choices.[56]

A related argument is that private ownership would lead to the homogenization of environmental resources, as theme parks dominated natural views (Menell 1992, 494). This argument misses the reality that markets are far more responsive to the preferences of small groups than government; that entrepreneurs have stronger incentives to identify these preferences and to create market niches to satisfy them, where government too often adopts a one-size-fits-all approach.[57]

The Public as Stakeholders

It is sometimes argued that the general public has an interest in the environment beyond that of particular interest groups. I am not certain whether this is another form of the existence value argument, or an argument that everyone has property rights in all aspects of the environment, wherever they occur. If it is the latter, it is merely the destruction of all private property rights, and thus my suggestions, which are based on increasing the quantity of private property, are flawed by their assumption of rules of private property. In other words, an assertion of a public interest in all aspects of private property trumps all attempts at an efficiency analysis, and responding to it is beyond the scope of this chapter. Government has historically dealt with issues of negative externalities either through common law remedies of trespass and nuisance or more direct taxation and regulation. These approaches would remain applicable to newly privatized public lands.

Enforcement Costs

A major criticism of free market environmentalism is that enforcement of property rights is not free (Brunet 1992; Krier 1992, 332ff). While this is true, it is hardly a serious indictment of private property rights. If government is incompetent at the most basic functions, such as protecting private property rights, why should it be left with the far more complex task of allocating resources (Hayek 1945)? But a private owner of resources is not simply relegated to the use of a costly and uncertain legal system. Private alternatives to adjudication have been developing at a rapid rate to displace costly, cumbersome, and uncertain judicial systems of dispute resolution. Further, there are private contracting solutions to problems of opportunistic breaches of contract. In a world of private dispute resolution, parties may be able to contract in advance about liquidated damages or other remedies in a more effective way. Bonds to secure performance can be required, and leases could be terminated on short notice for serious breaches. In short, if government dispute resolution is sufficiently inefficient, it will be (and is being) replaced by private resolution.[58]

Conclusion

There can be little argument that government has served as a poor steward of the public lands. Resources have been underpriced and overused, creating precisely the tragedy of the commons that ownership is thought to prevent. But when the ownership is the government, the competition for use of the commons is transferred from the resource itself to the halls of Congress and the offices of the responsible agencies, where substantial resources are dissipated. Privatization through transfer to a publicly owned corporation solves the immediate risk of a government giveaway to private interests by giving the indirect ownership of the lands to all the people, and it solves the long-term problems of management that have plagued Congress and the responsible agencies. Decisions about present versus future use will be made in a disciplined way that considers both the interest of today's and tomorrow's citizens, as owners of the corporations. In recognizing the benefits of corporate ownership of valuable resources we are well behind the enlightened nations of Eastern Europe that have already privatized government property. It is time we catch up.

Notes

1. Forest Service: 16 U.S.C. § 528 (1996); Bureau of Land Management (BLM): 43 U.S.C. § 1732(a) (1996).

2. One recommendation of the Public Land Law Review Commission called for sale of some public lands chiefly valuable for grazing, which would have eliminated the commons problem on some lands (Public Land Law Review Commission 1970, 115).

3. Before 1934, the public range lands were a commons that was overgrazed. The Taylor Grazing Act of 1934, 43 U.S.C. §§ 315–315o-1 (1996), was intended to address the problem, but failed; by 1976 most acres under BLM administration under the act were producing less than half of estimated historic levels of useful forage.

4. "Livestock grazing has radically altered vegetation over tens of millions of acres, destroyed riparian areas, polluted streams, created massive soil erosion, displaced wildlife, desecrated archeological sites, and spoiled prime recreational areas" (Feller 1995, 705).

5. While the Clinton administration proposed to increase these fees in 1993, the House reacted to ranchers' pressures with a bill to block proposed rulemaking to accomplish this. A similar rule-making proposal was made in 1994, but the final regulations abandoned the grazing fee increase (Feller 1995, 709–12; Cody 1996, 3–4).

6. Agency estimates of the cost of grazing programs range from $2.40 to $3.24 per AUM for the Forest Service and from $2.18 to $3.21 for the BLM (Cody 1997, 8). Weidenbaum's estimate of $4.60 per AUM is derived from yet another government document (Congressional Budget Office 1995, 229). The variance in these estimates in government publications may simply be further testimony to the lack of effective cost accounting for administration of the public lands. One study estimates the 1994 direct deficit in grazing programs at $76 million and suggests total deficits, including indirect government costs, approached $200 million (Hess and Holechek 1995, 3).

7. Under the Mining Act of 1872, a claim may be maintained by performing $100 worth of work each year (30 U.S.C.A. § 28). Once a claim has been proven to possess commercial quantities of minerals, the claimant is entitled to a patent at a cost of $5 per acre (30 U.S.C.A. § 29).

8. One commentator describes the difference between concession fees received by the National Park Service and the revenues earned by concessionaires from their activities as "astonishing." In 1989, total concession fees were $31.79 million, while concession revenues were over $1.5 billion (Jeffrey 1996, 134).

9. The fee for an automobile and five passengers in 1916, the first year of the National Park Service, was $7.50. By the 1990s the fee had increased to $10.00 (Jeffrey 1996, 132).

10. General Accounting Office (1996, 13), states that the GAO has been criticizing recreational user fees at least since 1982, and that others have also made this criticism.

11. This blurring of priorities is evidenced in the Federal Land Policy and Management Act of 1976 (FLPMA), 43 U.S.C. §§ 1701–82 (1996), which one authority criticizes because "Congress failed to confront or resolve the historic tensions and conflicts in public rangeland management" (Coggins 1983, 9).

12. Carol Browner, administrator of the Environmental Protection Agency, announced in 1994 a "Common Sense Initiative," in which panels of stakeholders were convened for six industries to identify environmental problems and solutions. These panels represented companies, trade associations, environmentalists, state and local officials, and "environmental justice advocates" (Fiorino 1996, 470).

13. The example offered by Arrow (1963, 3) is as follows:

Let A, B, and C be the three alternatives, and 1, 2, and 3 the three individuals. Suppose individual 1 prefers A to B and B to C (and therefore A to C), individual 2 prefers B to C and C to A (and therefore B to A), and individual 3 prefers C to A and A to B (and therefore C to B). Then a majority prefer A to B, and a majority prefer B to C. If the community is to be regarded as behaving rationally, we're forced to say that A is preferred to C. But in fact a majority of the community prefer C to A.

14. This proposal does not address distributional issues that are separate from efficiency issues. Distributional issues are already addressed by a host of other laws, beginning with the progressive income tax. If further distributional adjustments are deemed politically desirable, many means are available, including criteria for distribution of shares of new corporations owning privatized public resources.

15. Fifty percent of grazing fees are returned to the agencies to be used for range improvement, while the balance is allocated to the states and the U.S. Treasury (Cody 1996, 2). Range improvement funds provide only indirect benefits for bureaucrats, by enlarging agency budgets and command over resources.

16. Broad distribution to the public has democratic appeal that could overcome the pleadings of current users for preferences. On the other hand, public stock offerings by government, of the kind used to privatize state monopolies in Western Europe, could provide funds to repurchase lands where political support for government ownership was strong enough once the opportunity cost of government ownership was revealed through market transactions. Thus government could repurchase national parks, in whole or in part, with these funds.

17. "The directors of such companies, however, being the managers rather of other people's money than of their own, it cannot be well expected that they should watch over it with the same anxious vigilance with which the partners in a copartnery frequently watch over their own. . . . Negligence and profusion, therefore, must always prevail, more or less, in the management of the affairs of such a company" (Smith [1776] 1937, 700).

18. Where a robust theory argues that government bureaucrats desire to maximize budgets (see generally Niskanen 1971), the only arguments that similar behavior drives corporate officers occur at the margin, where firms have monopoly power and free cash flow (Williamson 1963). These arguments were devel-

oped before the full flowering of the market for corporate control. For an illuminating account of how hostile takeovers and leveraged buyouts were the engines for change in firms where management had lost sight of the goal of maximizing shareholder returns and sought to mediate among stakeholders, see Stern, Bennett, and Chew (1995).

19. Stock price declines have another positive effect; in today's world, much of managers' wealth is tied to the value of a company's stock, either because managers are expected to invest a large share of their savings in it through stock option plans, or because compensation, in the form of bonuses, is tied directly to stock prices.

20. 16 U.S.C. § 528 (1996); 43 U.S.C. § 1732(a)(1996).

21. 16 U.S.C. § 531(a) defines "multiple use" to mean "The management of all the various renewable surface resources of the national forests so that they are utilized in the combination that will best meet the needs of the American people; making the most judicious use of the land for some or all of these resources . . . and harmonious and coordinated management of the various resources, each with the other, without impairment of the productivity of the land, with consideration being given to the relative values of the various resources, and not necessarily the combination of uses that will give the greatest dollar return or the greatest unit output." How an owner of multiple resources can consider the relative values of resources in the allocation process without taking into consideration profit maximization is not addressed.

22. See, for example, Blumm (1994).

23. See, generally, McCraw (1975), Levine and Florence (1990), and Stewart (1975). The suggestion of capture with respect to grazing permits is found in Coggins and Lindeberg-Johnson (1982, 50–51).

24. I have argued that in competitive markets the amount of discretion available to managers to allocate resource among stakeholders is minimal (Carney 1990).

25. This argument is based on the premise of managerial discretion stemming from market power first outlined in Berle and Means (1933).

26. The classic statement of the rule is *Dodge v. Ford Motor Co.*, 170 N.W. 668 (Mich. 1919); for a more modern statement, see *Revlon, Inc., v. MacAndrews & Forbes Holdings, Inc.*, 506 A.2d 173 (Del. 1986) holding that while "a board may have regard for various constituencies in discharging its responsibilities," that concern could not interfere with stockholder interests when selling the corporation. See Macey (1991).

27. Courts have shown reluctance to phrase the duty in strictly financial terms, refusing to recognize that stock prices could properly reflect all publicly available information about future revenues, as the Efficient Capital Market Hypothesis suggests. The closest the Delaware Supreme Court has come is the following: Directors have a broad statutory mandate to manage the business of the corporation, which "includes a conferred authority to set a corporate course of action, including time frame, designed to enhance corporate profitability. Thus, the question of 'long-term' versus 'short term' values is largely irrelevant because directors, generally, are obliged to charter a course for a corporation

which is in its best interest without regard to a fixed investment horizon" (*Paramount Communications, Inc. v. Time, Inc.*, 571 A.2d 1140, 1150 [Del. 1990]).

28. These cases hold that bondholders' rights are solely a creature of contract, and that bondholders are not owed fiduciary duties. The classic statement is *Parkinson v. West End St. Ry.*, 53 N. E. 891, 892 (Mass. 1899) (Holmes, J.); for more modern statements see *Simons v. Cogan*, 549 A.2d 300, 302–03 (Del. 1988) and *Metropolitan Life Ins. Co. v. RJR Nabisco, Inc.*, 716 F. Supp. 1504, 1524 (S.D.N.Y. 1989).

29. There are limits to such behavior, of course; corporations, like individuals, may not convey their assets for less than full value in order to frustrate creditors. But that is a general rule of law that prohibits a certain type of fraud, not a special rule that grants creditors any special status within the firm.

30. Metropolitan Life Insurance Company sought to avoid the consequences of a lack of covenants in RJR Nabisco's bonds preventing a leveraged buyout that dramatically increased leverage and reduced the value of outstanding bonds by making arguments that the bond market was not competitive, that bond issuers were selling as effective monopolists, and that the terms offered were unconscionable. These arguments were summarily rejected by the court (*Metropolitan Life Ins. Co. v. RJR Nabisco, Inc.*, 716 F. Supp. 1504 [S.D.N.Y. 1989]). For an argument that bondholders are naive investors, see Coffee (1986, 68–69).

31. There are a few exceptions in the United States: antitakeover legislation may benefit managers at the expense of shareholders for example, but even here competitive forces have induced leading states to go slow in changing corporate laws. There are far more exceptions in Europe, where competition among jurisdictions is virtually precluded, and one finds significant protections for labor, management, and creditors written into European company laws (Carney 1997).

32. For a discussion of the erosion of this doctrine in the context of charitable giving, see Carney (1993). The doctrine remains firm outside this area.

33. *Revlon, Inc. v. MacAndrews & Forbes Holdings, Inc.*, 506 A.2d 173 (Del. 1986).

34. In *Unocal v. Mesa Petroleum Co.*, 493 A.2d 946 (Del. 1985), the Delaware Supreme Court noted the "specter" of self-interest in director decisions to resist takeover bids and held that the burden was on directors to show a reasonable belief in a threat to corporate or shareholder welfare, and that the defensive tactics were reasonably related to the threat.

35. For large firms with shares traded in public markets, the expected efficiency of managerial decisions is measured rapidly in terms of stock price adjustments. There may, of course, be times when asymmetric information prevents markets from understanding the value of managements' choices immediately, but this is a special problem limited to innovations not previously observed in markets or the availability of private information to management. In the latter case, managers can sometimes signal such private information through their own stock purchases or corporate stock repurchases, subject to the constraints of insider trading rules.

36. If one is concerned that poor citizens will lack bargaining power to purchase the share of resources on the public lands they prefer, one could address

distributional issues by distributing these shares in a regressive manner. No initial distribution of shares should have a significant effect on the ultimate allocation of the resources, if shareholders pursue rational profit-maximizing strategies (Coase 1960).

37. Writing outside one's own specialty creates the risk of failing to give credit to those who first made important arguments. I apologize to all those unknown (at least to me) authors. I am certain that I am reinventing many wheels in this discussion.

38. Before the takeover, Pacific Lumber was described as operating "as if the Sierra Club were in charge," while after the takeover the rate of cutting old-growth forest doubled (*National Law Journal* 1988, 24).

39. As a private owner, Pacific Lumber might face a public goods problem, because public highways run through redwood forests, so it would be difficult for Pacific Lumber to exclude those unwilling to pay to view these trees. In short, it might be necessary to privatize the road as well. Another solution would be to clear-cut lands near public highways, and charge admission to reach a scenic and remote old-growth area.

40. For an example of this attitude in corporate law, see Lowenstein (1983, 300).

41. An SEC study shows: 1) that R&D has increased as a percentage of firm revenues as institutional ownership has increased; 2) that firms with low R&D expenditures were more likely to be targets of takeover bids; and (3) that firms announcing new R&D expenditures showed an increase in stock prices at the time of the announcement (Securities Exchange Commission 1985). See also Chan, Martin, and Kensinger (1990); but see Doukas and Switzer (1992) (finding insignificant stock price effects).

42. An additional reason for excessively rapid exploitation involves an agency cost—the tendency of bureaucrats to favor projects that increase current budgets (Anderson and Leal 1991, 52–54).

43. The difficulty with term leases may be assuring that the asset, such as rangeland, is returned in as good a condition as when it was leased. Private owners of resources such as shopping centers assure that their property is not abused through careful monitoring.

44. One critic claims that "BLM and Forest Service land use plans and their accompanying environmental impact statements (EISs) do not contain the economic and environmental information necessary to determine the harms and benefits of grazing in particular areas" (Feller 1995, 707–8). He also asserts that citizens who urge these agencies to assess the appropriateness of grazing on particular parcels "find themselves engaged in a bureaucratic shell game in which the agencies avoid the issue by sliding it back and forth between their land use planning processes and their decision-making processes for individual grazing allotments" (Feller 1995, 708).

45. See, e.g., *Nat'l Wildlife Fed'n v. BLM*, No. UT-06-91-01 (U.S. Dept. of the Interior, Office of Hearings & Appeals, Hearings Div., Dec. 20, 1993) *petition for stay denied*; 128 IBLA 231 (Mar. 1, 1994), *petitioner's motion to dismiss intervenors' appeal for lack of standing granted in part, denied in part;*

216   William J. Carney

129 IBLA 124 (April 13, 1994), ruling that the BLM failed to make a "reasoned and informed decision that the benefits of grazing the [Utah desert] canyons outweigh[ed] the costs," including damage to vegetation, riparian areas, archeological sites, and scenic and recreational values.

46. The city of Atlanta has been in violation of water quality standards with respect to its sewage for many years, and currently pays fines of over $7 million per year, which downstream users argue are inadequate to persuade the city to clean up its effluent to meet legal maximums (Yandle 1998, 145).

47. Timber companies have responded to market demands for recreation by improving game habitat and using controlled burns to stimulate forage growth and by protecting riparian zones that preserve cover and food. In the case of International Paper Co., recreation provides approximately 25 percent of operating profits in the mid-South region (Anderson and Leal 1992, 302–3).

48. See, generally, Klein, Crawford, and Alchian (1978).

49. Klein, Crawford, and Alchian (1978) argue that vertical integration is often explained by the presence of appropriable quasi rents and the inability to create agreements that solve the problem.

50. This assumes that the monopolist owner of former public lands would avoid ownership of operating businesses such as farms and ranches, because the agency costs would be excessive.

51. Some conservation uses may free ride on other uses with greater commercial value, however. When promoters of fisheries purchase water to assure minimum stream flows or purchase pollution rights to protect game fish, they may incidentally protect some nongame species. Thus the snail darter may benefit from protection of coldwater fisheries that hold trout, for example.

52. For example: "[B]efore these priceless bits of Americana (such as a valley, an alpine meadow, a river, or a lake) are forever lost or are so transformed as to be reduced to the eventual rubble of our urban environment, the voice of the existing beneficiaries of these environmental wonders should be heard" (Houck 1994, 498); congressional failure to specify priorities among multiple uses "and the Act as a whole dictate that the goods and services to be produced will be predominantly those not susceptible to precise dollar measurement" (Coggins 1983, 51); "most environmental resources are incapable of being accurately priced" (Blumm 1992, 372). Others avoid the issue by describing property rights in public lands as "a natural heritage and national asset that belong to all of us" and thus inalienable without the consent of all? (Public Land Law Review Commission 1970, 33).

53. Costanza et al. (1997) undertake a valuation of the total value of the world's ecosystem by estimating the consumer surplus and net economic rents from each segment of this system, although it is not clear how they derive supply and demand curves in this exercise.

54. *Endangered Species Act of 1973*, P. L. No. 93-205, §§ 2–15, 17, 87 Stat. 884 (1973) (codified as various sections of 16 U.S.C. (1996).

55. Both the Nature Conservancy and the Environmental Defense Fund have been purchasers of property rights for environmental purposes (Huffman 1992, 350 n. 8).

56. For a criticism of cost-benefit analysis in the absence of market prices, see Farber (1993, 1282–85). Farber notes that prices in this setting are arbitrarily determined and often vary wildly from one agency of government to another.

57. Menell (1992, 494–95) argues that preferences for unspoiled natural settings such as Yosemite Valley might be "inchoate" and thus not fully priced in markets. This argument proves too much, since it can be made about any preference for which an author has a personal preference that he fears is not shared by a sufficient number of consumers to support the supply of the good he or she personally prefers without paying for it directly.

58. This is a partial answer, at least in the context of the public lands, to Krier's (1992, 342) critique of Anderson and Leal's arguments, "Why won't markets in environmental resources be tainted by the very evils of government about which Anderson and Leal complain?"

References

Anderson, Terry L., and Peter J. Hill. 1990. The Race for Property Rights. *Journal of Law and Economics* 33(April): 177–97.

Anderson, Terry L., and Donald R. Leal. 1991. *Free Market Environmentalism.* San Francisco: Pacific Research Institute for Public Policy and Westview Press.

———. 1992. Free Market Versus Political Environmentalism. *Harvard Journal of Law and Public Policy* 15(2): 297–310.

Arrow, Kenneth. 1963. *Social Choice and Individual Values*, 2d ed. New Haven: Yale University Press.

Berle, Adolph A., and Gardiner Means. 1933. *Private Property and the Modern Corporation.* New York: Macmillan.

Blumm, Michael C. 1992. The Fallacies of Free Market Environmentalism. *Harvard Journal of Law and Public Policy* 15: 371–89.

———. 1994. Public Choice Theory and the Public Lands: Why 'Multiple Use' Failed. *Harvard Environmental Law Review* 18: 405–32.

Boudreaux, Donald J., and Roger Meiners. 1998. Existence Value and Other of Life's Ills, this volume.

Brunet, Edward. 1992. Debunking Wholesale Private Enforcement of Environmental Rights. *Harvard Journal of Law and Public Policy* 15: 311–24.

Butler, Henry. 1988. Corporation-Specific Anti-Takeover Statutes and the Market for Corporate Charters. *Wisconsin Law Review* 1988: 365–83.

Carney, William. 1989. The Limits of the Fraud on the Market Doctrine. *Business Lawyer* 44: 1259–92.

———. 1990. Does Defining Constituencies Matter? *University of Cincinnati Law Review* 59: 385–424.

———. 1993. The ALI's Corporate Governance Project: The Death of Property Rights? *George Washington Law Review* 61: 898–953.

————. 1997. The Political Economy of Competition for Corporate Charters. *Journal of Legal Studies* 26: 303–29.

Chan, Su Han, John Martin, and John Kensinger. 1990. Corporate Research and Development Expenditures and Share Value. *Journal of Financial Economics* 26: 255–76.

Clark, Robert C. 1986. *Corporate Law*. Boston: Little Brown & Co.

Coase, Ronald H. 1960. The Problem of Social Cost. *Journal of Law and Economics* 3(1): 1–44.

Cody, Betsy A. 1996. *Grazing Fees: An Overview*. 96-450 ENR. Washington, D.C.: Congressional Research Service, Environment and Natural Resources Policy Division.

————. 1997. 96006: Grazing Fees and Rangeland Management. *Issue Brief* 8. Washington, D.C.: Congressional Research Service.

Coffee, John. 1986. Shareholders Versus Managers: The Strain in the Corporate Web. *Michigan Law Review* 85: 1–108.

Coggins, George Cameron. 1983. The Law of Public Rangeland Management IV: FLPMA, PRIA, and the Multiple Use Mandate. *Environmental Law Journal* 14: 1–131.

Coggins, George Cameron, and Margaret Lindeberg-Johnson. 1982. The Law of Public Rangeland Management II: The Commons and the Taylor Act. *Environmental Law Journal* 13: 1–101.

Collins, Denis, and John Barkdull. 1995. Capitalism, Environmentalism, and Mediating Structures: From Adam Smith to Stakeholder Panels. *Environmental Ethics* 17: 226–44.

Committee on Corporate Laws, Section of Business Law, American Bar Association. 1990. Other Constituencies Statutes: Potential for Confusion. *Business Lawyer* 45: 2253–71.

Congressional Budget Office. 1995. *Reducing the Deficit: Spending and Revenue Options*. Washington, D.C.: U.S. Government Printing Office, February.

Costanza, Robert, Ralph d'Arge, Rudolf de Groot, Stephen Farber, Monica Grasso, Bruce Hannon, Karin Limburg, Shahid Naeem, Robert V. O'Neill, Jose Paruelo, Robert G. Raskin, Paul Sutton, and Marjan van den Belt. 1997. The Value of the World's Ecosystem Services and Natural Capital. *Nature* 387: 253–60.

Demsetz, Harold. 1969. Information and Efficiency: Another Viewpoint. *Journal of Law and Economics* 12(April): 1–22.

Doukas, John, and Lorne Switzer. 1992. The Stock Market's Valuation of R&D Spending and Market Concentration. *Journal of Economics and Business* 44: 95–114.

Downes, Bryan T. 1995. Toward Sustainable Communities: Lessons from the Canadian Experience. *Willamette Law Review* 31: 359–401.

Fama, Eugene. 1970. Efficient Capital Markets: A Review of Theory and Empirical Work. *Journal of Finance* 25: 383–417.

————. 1980. Agency Problems and the Theory of the Firm. *Journal of Political Economy* 88: 288–307.

Farber, Daniel A. 1993. Revitalizing Regulation. *Michigan Law Review* 91: 1278–96.

Feller, Joseph M. 1995. 'Til the Cows Come Home: The Fatal Flaw in the Clinton Administration's Public Lands Grazing Policy. *Environmental Law Journal* 25: 703–14.

Fiorino, Daniel J. 1996. Toward a New System of Environmental Regulation: The Case for an Industry Sector Approach. *Environmental Law* 26: 457–87.

Friend, Irwin. 1972. The Economic Consequences of the Stock Market. *American Economic Review* 62: 212–19.

General Accounting Office. 1996. *U.S. Forest Service Fees for Recreation Special-Use Permits Do Not Reflect Fair Market Value.* GAO/RCED-97-16. Washington, D.C.: U.S. Government Printing Office.

Gordon, H. Scott. 1954. The Economic Theory of a Common-Property Resource: The Fishery. *Journal of Political Economy* 62(April): 124–42.

Grossman, Sanford T. 1976. On the Efficiency of Competitive Stock Markets Where Traders Have Diverse Information. *Journal of Finance* 31: 573–85.

Hardin, Garrett. 1968. The Tragedy of the Commons. *Science* 162: 1243–48.

Hayek, Friedrich A. 1945. The Use of Knowledge in Society. *American Economic Review* 35(September): 519–30.

Hemmingway, Roy. 1996. The Second Annual "Who Runs the River?" Colloquium: Restructuring the Northwest Power System. *Environmental Law* 26: 669–74.

Herman, Dennis J. 1992. Loving Them to Death: Legal Controls on the Type and Scale of Development in the National Parks. *Stanford Environmental Law Journal* 11: 3–67.

Hess, Karl, Jr., and Jerry L. Holechek. 1995. Beyond the Grazing Fee: An Agenda for Rangeland Reform. *Policy Analysis* 234. Washington, D.C.: Cato Institute.

Houck, Oliver A. 1994. The Secret Opinions of the United States Supreme Court on Leading Cases in Environmental Law, Never Before Published! *University of Colorado Law Review* 65: 459–516.

Huffman, James L. 1992. Protecting the Environment from Orthodox Environmentalism. *Harvard Journal of Law and Public Policy* 15: 349–70.

Jeffrey, Michael I. 1996. Public Lands Reform: A Reluctant Leap into the Abyss. *Virginia Environmental Law Journal* 16: 79–143.

Jensen, Michael C. 1988. Takeovers: Their Causes and Consequences. *Journal of Economic Perspectives* 2: 21–48.

Jensen, Michael C., and William Meckling. 1976. Theory of the Firm: Managerial Behavior, Agency Costs and Ownership Structure. *Journal of Financial Economics* 3: 305–59.

Klein, Benjamin, Robert G. Crawford, and Armen A. Alchian. 1978. Vertical Integration, Appropriable Rents, and the Competitive Contracting Process. *Journal of Law and Economics* 21: 297–326.

Kornhauser, Lewis, and Jeffrey Gordon. 1986. Efficient Markets, Costly Information, and Securities Research. *New York University Law Review* 60: 761–849.

Krier, James. 1992. The Tragedy of the Commons, Part Two. *Harvard Journal of Law and Public Policy* 15: 325–47.

LaFrance, Jeffrey T., and Myles J. Watts. 1995. Public Grazing in the West and "Rangeland Reform '94." *American Journal of Agricultural Economics* 77: 447–61.

Leal, Donald R. 1995. Turning a Profit on Public Forests. *PERC Policy Series* PS-4. Bozeman, MT: Political Economy Research Center.

Levine, Michael, and Jennifer L. Florence. 1990. Regulatory Capture, Public Interest, and the Public Agenda: Toward a Synthesis. *Journal of Law, Economics and Organization* 6(special issue): 167–98.

Lowenstein, Louis. 1983. Pruning Deadwood in Hostile Takeovers: A Proposal for Legislation. *Columbia Law Review* 83: 249–334.

Macey, Jonathan R. 1991. An Economic Analysis of the Various Rationales for Making Shareholders the Exclusive Beneficiaries of Corporate Fiduciary Duties. *Stetson Law Review* 21: 23–44.

Manne, Henry G. 1965. Mergers and the Market for Corporate Control. *Journal of Political Economy* 73: 110–20.

McCraw, Thomas K. 1975. Regulation in America: A Review Article. *Business History Review* 49: 159–83.

Menell, Peter S. 1992. Institutional Fantasylands: From Scientific Management to Free Market Environmentalism. *Harvard Journal of Law and Public Policy* 15: 489–510.

Nader, Ralph, Mark Green, and Joel Seligman. 1976. *Taming the Giant Corporation*. New York: W. W. Norton.

National Law Journal. 1988. Tall Timber Tension: The Redwoods Meet the Law. February 1, 1–24.

Niskanen, William. 1971. *Bureaucracy and Representative Government.* Chicago: Aldine, Atherton.

Oesterle, Dale A. 1996. Public Land: How Much Is Enough? *Ecology Law Quarterly* 23: 521–75.

Poindexter, Georgette C. 1995. Addressing Morality in Urban Brownfield Redevelopment: Using Stakeholder Theory to Craft Legal Process. *Virginia Environmental Law Journal* 15: 37–70.

Public Land Law Review Commission. 1970. *One Third of the Nation's Land.* Washington, D.C.: U.S. Government Printing Office.

Romano, Roberta. 1987. The Political Economy of Takeover Statutes. *Virginia Law Review* 73: 111–98.

Rose, Carol M. 1994. Environmental Lessons. *Loyola of Los Angeles Law Review* 27: 1023–47.

Securities Exchange Commission, Office of Chief Economist. 1985. Institutional Ownership, Tender Offers, and Long-Term Investments. Washington, D.C., April 19.

Smith, Adam. [1776] 1937. *The Wealth of Nations*, ed. Edwin Canaan. New York: Modern Library.

Stern, Joel M., G. Bennett Stewart III, and Donald H. Chew Jr. 1995. The EVA Financial Management System. *Journal of Applied Corporate Finance* 8(2): 32–46.

Stewart, Richard. 1975. The Reformation of Administrative Law. *Harvard Law Review* 88: 1669–813.

Sunaram, Anant K., Teresa A. John, and Kose John. 1996. An Empirical Analysis of Strategic Competition and Firm Values: The Case of R&D Competition. *Journal of Financial Economics* 40: 459–86.

Wales, Leonard J. 1996. Environmental Claims and Citizen Rights. *Environmental Ethics* 18: 133–48.

Weidenbaum, Murray, Christopher Douglas, and Michael Orlando. 1997. Toward a Healthier Environment and a Stronger Economy: How to Achieve Common Ground. *Policy Study* 137. St. Louis: Center for the Study of American Business, Washington University.

Wilkinson, Charles F. 1992. *Crossing the Next Meridian: Land, Water, and the Future of the West.* Washington, D.C.: Island Press.

Williamson, Oliver E. 1963. Managerial Discretion and Business Behavior. *American Economic Review* 53: 1032–57.

Yandle, Bruce. 1998. Coase, Pigou, and Environmental Rights, this volume.

Chapter 8

Habitat Preservation: A Property Rights Perspective

Richard A. Epstein

The recent decision of the United States Supreme Court in the much-anticipated case of *Babbitt v. Sweet Home Chapter of Communities for a Great Oregon*[1] was a disappointment on many levels. For the record, some of my disappointment was personal, for I penned an amicus curiae brief[2] whose arguments seemed to be entirely ignored by each of the three justices of the Supreme Court who wrote in the case: Justice Stevens for the Court,[3] Justice O'Connor in concurrence,[4] and Justice Scalia (joined by Chief Justice Rehnquist and Justice Thomas) in dissent.[5] But the concerns go deeper than rejection and neglect, to address some very fundamental questions about the reasoning and outcome in the case itself. The substantive issue in *Sweet Home* is of central importance for the understanding of property rights: does the loss of habitat of an endangered species constitute a form of species harm that should be treated akin to some tort or wrong, or does the owner of the land have full rights to use or sell the habitat as he sees fit, subject only to the eminent domain power of the state? Yet this set of largely mechanical opinions, in large measure by design, did not reach the profound economic and constitutional issues raised by the broad issue of habitat

I should like to thank Frank Michelman and Stephen Williams for their instructive comments on an earlier draft of this paper, and Todd Molz for his valuable research assistance on an earlier version of this article. A longer version of this chapter appeared as "*Babbitt v. Sweet Home Chapters of Oregon*: The Law and Economics of Habitat Preservation," *Supreme Court Economic Review*, vol. 5 (1997). Reprinted by permission of the author and the University of Chicago Press.

protection. For the justices, the key feature of this case was one of legal pedigree: Did the secretary of the interior act pursuant to his statutory authority in putting forward the challenged regulation under the Endangered Species Act?[6] The dominant focus of the judicial inquiry sought to square the regulation with the ESA and gave the government the benefit of the doubt along the way.

Whatever one might think about the proper techniques of statutory construction, it is (or at least should be) clear that a court in construing a statute should have fewer degrees of freedom than the legislature that wrote it. It may well be that some naive form of plain meaning will not do the job in many cases, but, if so, the effort must be made to set the disputed provision within the larger context of the appropriate statute, with due consideration for the purposes for which the statute was passed. There are few general principles that prove substitutes for the best rule of statutory construction, which is a close reading of full provisions, and not an isolated examination of what is meant by a single word, whether it be *discrimination* in a civil rights statute, or *harm* in an environmental statute such as the ESA.

But statutes can be amended and repealed and even clarified. *Sweet Home* would never have reached the Supreme Court as an exercise in statutory construction if the ESA had contained a single additional clause that said: "Provided: Habitat modification or destruction shall not be regarded as the 'taking' of an endangered species within the meaning of Section 9 of the Act." This observation about the clarity of language is meant to be substantively neutral. Thus this case would have been dispatched every bit as quickly, albeit in the opposite direction, if the ESA had stated: "Provided, that the FWS shall have full power to treat the destruction or modification of habitat as the taking of an endangered species under this Act." At some point therefore, disputes over meaning and interpretation, properly so-called, become both arid and pointless. Everyone knows what the statute means. The critical dispute is over policy and choice.

This chapter takes up just this question of principle. Exactly what proviso should be engrafted on the ESA by amendment? Once that question is put forward in a forthright fashion, it is easy to draft language that avoids a judicial reprise of the *Sweet Home* dispute. The question is, what language? In attacking this question, I argue that the better social outcomes are achieved if the revised and refurbished ESA follows the common law rules on property rights. The full regime contains three parts. First, changes in habitat can be made at will by owners unless and until they constitute a nuisance to the property of others. Second, private parties and government agencies may purchase habitat in voluntary transactions. Third, government agencies may also exercise their takings power, conditioned on their willingness to pay just compensation. The reason for accepting this tripartite regime is purely functional. All relevant parties will operate under superior incentives if the government is required to pay compensation when it takes land for habitat preservation or restricts its ordinary use for the same purpose. The power to initiate changes must be offset by the willingness to bear the financial dislocations they induce.

Facing these questions of principle is ever more vital today. The ESA has had a rocky history. Since its adoption in 1973 it has attracted avid supporters who regard the ESA as the centerpiece of a sound environmental program. It has also been scorned by equally fierce detractors who regard its operation, if not its conception, as one unmitigated disaster that should be stopped, if necessary, by prompt and wholesale repeal. The battle that began over a facial challenge to the regulation has spilled over into the halls of Congress, which until April 1996 limited the appropriations necessary for listing new species for protection under the act.[7] Over the long haul, it is uncertain whether ESA will survive in its current form and, if not, what approach will be adopted in its stead. The *Sweet Home* decision is one chapter in an ongoing debate. It closes the book only on the narrow question of administrative law before it.

Questions of policy are rarely divorced from questions of constitutional law, and those constitutional queries form the subject of the third section of this essay. The discussion here is in part a continuation of the normative analysis conducted in section 2. Indeed it could hardly be otherwise. The standard policy analysis worries about the creation of incentives on the various private and public actors, about the relative efficiency of public and private choice, and the impacts that decisions by one person have on the actions and welfare of others. The analysis is often couched in the language of social welfare, which itself appeals to the well-known compensation criteria of economics: did the loser receive compensation for the changes made, so that everyone was at least as well off after the change as before? Could the winners have paid the losers enough to bring them back to their previous level of welfare and still have remained better off themselves? With tests like this in operation, it is easy to see the close connection between policy and constitutional analysis. The change in legal regime constitutes the taking; and the offsetting benefits, if any, may constitute the required compensation for the associated losses. The courts have already faced, and rebuffed, various forms of takings challenges in the environmental area generally, and with endangered species in particular.[8] The question is whether they are right to have done so.

Economic Analysis

The Endangered Species Act (ESA) fit in well with the dominant environmental mood of the 1970s. The act had as its objective the implementation of a comprehensive scheme of regulation to protect endangered species from extinction. That task required at a minimum prohibitions against actions that killed or captured those protected species. But that task also extended to the regulation of the environment in which those animals and plants lived and reproduced. The basic purposes of the ESA are set out in section 1 of the act, which stresses the risks that economic growth poses to the survival of endangered species. In order to prevent their extinction, the act then spells out the penal and administrative steps to counteract it.

The major question of statutory interpretation in *Sweet Home*—and to the Supreme Court justices who decided it, the case only involved issues of statutory construction—was whether the secretary of the interior had acted within, or had exceeded, his delegated powers by treating habitat modification and habitat destruction as "taking" under the ESA. The term *taking* is a term of art that receives a special definition under the ESA. The basic framework of which it is a part has at its heart section 9 of the ESA, which makes it unlawful "for any persons subject to the jurisdiction of the United States to . . . (B) take any species within the United States or in the territorial sea of the United States."[9]

The definition section of the ESA in turn defines *take* to mean: "to harass, harm, pursue, hunt, shoot, wound, kill, trap, capture, or collect, or to attempt to engage in any such conduct."[10]

The contested regulation then interprets this definition provision as follows:

> *Harm* in the definition of "take" in the act means an act which actually kills or injures wildlife. Such act may include significant habitat modification or degradation where it actually kills or injures wildlife by significantly impairing essential behavioral patterns, including breeding, feeding, or sheltering.[11]

Having noted the statutory framework here, I shall ignore the interpretative questions that I have discussed at length elsewhere (Epstein 1997). In this context my task is to consider, free from the embarrassments of statutory construction, whether the policy articulated in the FWS regulations should be incorporated into the ESA as a matter of sound national policy. Answering that question drives us to assess the economic and social consequences of the various institutional arrangements.

To facilitate this discussion, I have divided the analysis into seven sections. 1) Is it right to treat the destruction or modification of habitat as "equivalent" to the destruction of the listed species? 2) What are the uses and limitations of the common law of nuisance? 3) How might private agreements expand environmental protections? 4) What are the timing consequences of choosing coercion (regulation) over purchase to the individual landowner? 5) How do the different rules of coercion and purchase play out in multiperiod, multiparty games? 6) Should the special problems of environmental valuation—as they relate to the recognition of second order preferences and the willingness to pay and willingness to accept—influence any initial assignment of rights? 7) What is the role of the condemnation alternative in habitat acquisition?

False Doctrine of Equivalents

Treating habitat destruction as though it were just the same as the killing of animals often rests on an assertion of the following equivalence. Loss or modification of habitat should be treated just as if it were the loss or destruction of individual animals because the end results are the same in the two cases. Let the habitat be destroyed and the protected species is destroyed, just as though it was hunted or trapped. The equivalence of results is said therefore to justify an equivalence of treatment between the two cases, not only as a matter of ordinary language, but also as a matter of first, and highest, principle. Thus if killing an animal is wrong, so to is taking its habitat. Indeed the wrong is if anything far greater since radical and substantial changes in habitat are ordinarily thought to be a major source of species deprivation.

The oversimplification of this purported equivalence takes on several levels. The only indisputable point established by the extreme examples is that if the earth is destroyed all species are destroyed with it—at which point the interpretation of the ESA will not bulk large in the grand scheme of things. The harder questions, however, are directed to cases involving partial modifications of habitat or partial destruction of species. Thus suppose we were to test the proposition of equivalence by asking whether we should react the same to the destruction of all members of a given species or all present habitat for that species. In the case of the former, any regeneration is precluded by the destruction, but the same result does not necessarily follow with total habitat destruction. Animals and plants have strong survival instincts, and their ability to migrate to different locations, and even thrive, is not inconsiderable, even if it is not complete. The loss of present habitat is not the same as the loss of *potential* habitat, some of which may be colonized only when necessity calls. The process is familiar in nature, which has its fair share of fires, tornadoes, earthquakes, storms, infestations, and plagues, all of which can disrupt or destroy habitat and send local species on forced marches to new terrain. The wide variations in finches is in large measure a response to changes in conditions (from wet to dry, for example) that no legal regime can control (Wiener 1994). No one wants to make light of the loss or transformation of given habitat, but the debate over the survival of any particular species cannot start and end with the assumption that these porcelain creatures are utterly unable to take any adaptive measures of their own. The destruction of all present habitat does not lead to the destruction of the species. It opens up a set of empirical questions as to which new territories and lands can become the home for displaced members of a species. Sometimes the loss in question will be great. But in other cases it will be less so.

The calculations become still more complicated when one speaks about the partial killing of a species or the partial destruction of its present habitat. Thus conduct a simple thought experiment that asks whether it is more dangerous to kill 10 percent of a given species or to take 10 percent of its habitat. Once again the problem does not admit any unidirectional answer. One obvious scenario is that the partial destruction of habitat could well result in a migration of its residents into other portions of the same territory, thereby leading to overcrowding and greater species destruction. Alternatively (and to hazard a guess, more probably), a nomadic species that wanders the full range of some larger territory could preserve more than 90 percent of its original population on a smaller habitat base.

There is little question that uncertainties of this sort strengthen the claim for some form of government control. After all, if the loss of habitat could bring in its wake more or less destruction than a comparable percentage loss of species members, then by all means let the government experts decide whether the risks in question require bold steps to counteract them. The mere fact that a 10 percent reduction in habitat could result, alternatively, in no loss of species or a 50 percent loss in species breaks any necessary link between habitat destruction and species destruction. But it leaves open the claim that the difficulty in making these judgments fairly calls for the acceptance of a high degree of government discretion in this area.

The matter is still far from resolved, for the difference between habitat destruction and species destruction bulks still larger when one looks at the other side of the equation. Thus even if we assume that habitat destruction and species destruction amounted in some approximate sense to the same thing from the point of view of the endangered species, it hardly follows that identical interests are sacrificed to the same end. Thus the major consequence of not killing a particular species is that it will continue to multiply. There might well be some collateral consequences in terms of its interaction with other species, but these will be limited by the degrees of freedom that property owners preserve over their own land. But the private sacrifice from a prohibition on habitat modification cuts far more deeply, precluding as it does any alteration of current land uses, and, perhaps, the continuation of present uses in light of their consequences. It is just for that reason that the resistance on this front is so great, which offers good reason to doubt the total social equivalence of the two practices. But to repeat this hardly means that habitat protection is unimportant: for many species it may be the only road to secure survival. But a consideration of all relevant issues does suggest that the stakes are high on both sides of the line.

The Use and Limits of Nuisance

The subject of species preservation seems to offer clear scope for government action of some sort. The question, however, immediately arises, what rules should guide the use of government discretion and why? Here it is important to note that ordinary actions for trespass and nuisance do play an important part in any overall strategy and indeed lie at the core of the section 9 prohibition. But common law actions for trespass and nuisance are forlorn in the context of habitat preservation, because so much of the modification and destruction of habitat targeted by the ESA typically comes from ordinary husbandry of land: the clearing of trees, the cutting of grasses, the construction of houses, the diversion of waters for drink and irrigation (subject to its own distinctive rules), and the like. It would take a stunning reversal of hundreds of years of legal history if these activities, generally productive, were now, for the first time, castigated by the common law as generally harmful.[12] None of the controversial applications of government power, for example, come within a hundred miles of the Restatement definitions of nuisance.[13]

When applied to its traditional scope—to pollution, discharges, wastes of all sorts, kinds, and descriptions—the law of nuisance represents a good first rough and ready means to regulate by law relations *between neighbors*. The initial presumption is that activities on the land of A are predominantly A's concern, so that the presumption should be set against the neighbor who wishes to stop or alter them.[14] Only in the event that an invasion takes place does the balance of convenience shift, and even then the object of relief is not to stop the activity that generated the invasion, but to stop the invasion itself—a difference that allows activities on one's own land to continue subject to one distinct set of constraints. But the tort of trespass and nuisance is designed to mediate the conflicts between neighboring property owners, and the values that it protects are the values that both those owners share.[15] On this view those actions that have primarily local effect are those that self-interest alone will regulate: I do not have to be persuaded not to damage my own lands any more than I need to be persuaded not to step on my own foot.[16] The best cases for legal intervention are those where the individual's own property is an insufficient hostage for his own good conduct. At that point the force of the law is needed to counteract the situation where one person internalizes the gains from action while imposing a substantial fraction of its costs on others.

The environmental impulse behind the ESA, however, is not concerned with policing the interactions with neighbors. Its calling card is not that my actions have harmed the flora and fauna, endangered or not, that others own. It is that they have harmed the flora and fauna—period. Harm to this environment as such (measured by a very human standard of what is better and worse) becomes the touchstone for intervention. The boundary line between neighbors is displaced by the boundary line between human actions and their consequences to the physical or biological world. To give but one illustration of the common problem, Vermont's land use statute begins with a preamble that stresses the fundamental divide between the individual and the environment: "the unplanned, uncoordinated and uncontrolled use of the lands and the environment of the state of Vermont has resulted in usages of the lands and the environment which may be destructive to the environment and which are not suitable to the demands and needs of the people of the state of Vermont."[17] The rank order of relevant concerns is not inadvertent but suggestive: the harm to the environment comes first, and the unsuitability of development to the demands of the people within the state comes second.

Even so, that statute survived an as-applied takings challenge in *Southview Associates, Ltd. v. Bongartz*,[18] when the court sustained the Vermont Environmental Board's refusal to issue a permit for land development on the ground that the proposed project would destroy some portion of deeryard that sheltered deer during the winter. The doctrinal ground of the decision was that the use of the land by deer did not constitute a "permanent physical invasion" by other individuals of the sort that was held to require compensation in *Loretto v. Teleprompter Manhattan CATV Corp., Inc.*[19] The loss in use from the development restriction in the Vermont case had, of course, far greater impact, but in the end the state proved triumphant because of the lesser nature of the formal restriction. So long as the landowner retained the right to exclude trespassers from the land, "this 'invasion' is relatively minor, consisting of an occasional, seasonal, and limited habitation by no more than 20 deer."[20] It seems clear that the government has demonstrated a good public use for the land in question. But it is far less clear that its separation between natural and human uses of the land compels the result that it reached in the Vermont case. In principle, at least, the question remains: what devices, if any should be used to control against those excesses when measured by these widespread human desires?

Private Land Use Restrictions

Within the classical common law theory, the law of nuisance does not set the outer limit of sensible steps to protect environmental interests. The common law also facilitates coordinated private responses to environmental threats. Many planned unit developments contain restrictions that go far beyond those required by the law of nuisance, with regard to both aesthetics and environmental ambiance. The explanation is clear enough: it is in the interest of the developer as the original common owner of the property to impose these restrictions *universally* on all units before sale. His own objective function is simply to maximize the revenues from the project, wholly without regard to any high-minded ecological or environmental crusades. But in order to achieve that result he has to cater to the consumption preferences of his potential purchasers. Ordinary consumers buy a bundle of private and common elements. In general it would be odd for potential purchasers to place a very high value on the amenities found within their own units, and a very low value on those appurtenant to common areas located nearby. Indeed one reason why people, particularly people of means, buy in planned unit developments is to obtain the security that their neighborhood will not move in unwelcome directions without their consent, or at least the consent of their like-minded (and equally endowed) representatives.

To be sure, any set of restrictions, set-asides, and dedications imposes costs on the individuals who are subject to them. But each buyer at the time of purchase makes his calculations over the net position. If the restrictions imposed on others are worth more to a given buyer than the inconvenience that similar restrictions impose on him, then he will sign on to the plan. The original developer therefore has the right incentives to seek value maximization, and the buyers can sort themselves out among developments in Tiebout-like fashion, choosing whatever mix of environmental and social amenities are available (Tiebout 1956). In this market, the developer can in effect sell habitat preservation for those who care about it for aesthetic or moral reasons, without having to force others to pay for amenities they do not want. The routine use

of covenants shows in dramatic fashion that the law of nuisance is not
the last word in habitat protection. That honor goes to the mutual and
reciprocal covenants that are found in voluntary arrangements. Do we
need more?

Coerce or Purchase: The Timing Consequences

For good and sufficient reasons the United States government does
not act as the common owner of all land in the United States. But the
tactics that are available to private landowners and developers are surely
available to it. It can accept the narrow and sensible definitions of nuisance law and, when its power has been exhausted, seek to obtain the
rest of its habitat regime by other techniques: voluntary purchase and
condemnation, specifically authorized under the ESA, remain available.
The gist of the inquiry is how using these techniques compare to the
alternative of designation by regulation.

Purchase and condemnation should work together well relative to the
designation process that the law now adopts. Except in rare cases, I
believe that the government should be able to resort to either voluntary
purchase or compulsory purchase for habitat protection, and to choose
the mix between them. But the present preferred strategy of acquisition
by designation and regulation should be denied the government (which
has become all too accustomed to its use).

In order to see why this is the case it is useful to conduct a point by
point comparison of the two rival systems. That inquiry begins when
land is subject to private ownership but is not subject to habitat designation under the ESA. The critical behavioral questions go to the conduct
of both private and public parties under these two alternative regimes.
With respect to the current system of habitat designation, one important
point is that loss of habitat prior to designation carries with it no adverse
legal consequences. The anticipation effects in this market are therefore
enormous.[21] If there is any sense that private land will be subject to
controls, then the best strategy for the private owner is to destroy the
habitat before it becomes protected: "shoot, shovel, and shut up" becomes the war cry. It may not work in all cases. Sometimes the habitat
is too valuable to the owner; sometimes it is connected with the property rights of other individuals. And indeed there has already been an
official response in the form of a "safe harbor" promise that any large
property owner who undertakes habitat improvement will not have to
pay the price down the road in the form of future development restrictions.[22] But these covenants are not universal in scope and require con-
fidence that they will be respected over time when the remedies for
government breach are uncertain at best. Absent strong ownership

rights, the unmistakable incentive remains in all cases: destroy habitat now in order to preserve freedom of action later.

Anticipating designation can quickly become quite counterproductive. Suppose that land in its untouched state is worth 100 to its owner, but 200 to the government as habitat. Should the land be developed, it is worth 1,000 to the individual, but only worth 10 as habitat. What kinds of behavior can be expected given those valuations in a world in which habitat preservation proceeds by designation? The simple answer in these circumstances is that the private owner will destroy the habitat even if he does not begin the development, so long as he can detect the whiff of designation in political airs. The only way that he can perfect his development rights is to take steps before the government designation has its adverse consequences.

In this situation it is tempting to celebrate the outcome because the 900 units of value preserved clearly dominate the 190 in value that are lost. After all, a move from 300, predevelopment, to 1,010, postdevelopment, surely counts as some form of an overall social improvement. But that celebration would be hasty for at least two reasons. First, the designation system is a crude instrument that works (at least as a first approximation) as an all-or-nothing choice. Suppose someone could fashion a creative solution that allows development worth 950 to be combined with limited habitat protection that is worth 150, for a total of 1,100 instead of 1,010. Here there is a clear advantage of 90, which could be obtained by successful negotiation between potential adversaries, unless eroded by the corrosive effects of high transaction costs. Yet all that potential gain is lost because there is no negotiation to be had since the government is still in designation mode. Instead, the critical variable is one that has the private owners, or their property rights association, lobbying government to make sure that the designation does not take place, or at least does not take place quickly, or bypasses their lands. So designation systems have two substantial costs: one is destruction before designation, and the other is use of the political process to deny, delay, or deflect the designations that might come.

The point here is an old one. In a world of habitat designation by statute, property rights are not well defined.[23] The upshot is rent-seeking again. The social costs of running the present system include the revenues dissipated in seeking to firm up a favorable decision on the designation question. The enormous sums that are spent for acquiring and keeping broadcast licenses, for example, are only spent because the rights are held subject to the risk of nonrenewal. Although the context differs, the consequences are the same with respect to habitat designation: The legal void leads to mutually combative and socially wasteful behavior until the rights are established, if they are established at all.

The purchase system contains none of those disadvantages, so long as it is *not* paired with a designation system. To see why this is the case, assume that the government approaches an individual landowner bearing both carrots and sticks. The offer is to purchase the land at some price, but the threat is that if the purchase is not consummated designation will follow in its stead. Here the landowner finds it enormously dangerous to hold out for a higher price, since the time-delay in the transaction could be sufficient to allow the government, working on a separate track, to complete the designation process that would make the purchase superfluous. The private owner faced with these dual threats will surely be well-advised to guard against the risk that the purchase offer is a fig leaf to buy time for the designation to take hold. If, therefore, the first offer is not sufficient to cover the anticipated profits from development, then destruction of habitat becomes the first-best private solution. That risk of Armageddon does not arise when the habitat designation is kept off the table from the outset.

The costs of running the designation system, moreover, *increase* as the habitat value of land rises. Thus suppose that the previous example is modified such that the value of the land with development rights is still 1,000, but the value of the land as habitat is now 4,000. A legal designation that reduces the working value of the land to the owner to 10 still costs him 990 units of value. His private incentive therefore to strip the land before designation takes place is as great as it is before. It hardly matters that the social loss is far greater than before, or even that the payment to the landowner of any sum greater than 1,000 and less than 4,000 permits both government and private holders to be better off than before. To be sure, the government may try to move more quickly to designate the land as habitat, but that proposal could lead to the still earlier destruction of habitat if the landowner obtains wind of the situation. The basic instability is quite simply this: A public benefit remains a private burden so long as acquisition by designation is treated as a feasible government strategy. Habitat destruction is preferable to habitat preservation so long as that imbalance remains: "shoot, shovel, and shut up" becomes not only a bit of folklore, but also a dominant strategy to holders of sensitive land that lie in the path of future designations.

As should be evident, a system of voluntary purchase or condemnation radically changes the incentives for both sides in the predesignation period. In this new environment, it is always to the advantage of an owner to bring valuable habitat to the attention of the government and to take steps to preserve it in its ideal condition for sale. But those incentives may not work as well in the first example, where the habitat is worth at most 200 and the development rights are worth 1,000. In that case, the transaction costs could easily exceed the benefits preserved (just as they could exceed the costs of designation).

This example, however, does not establish the superiority of habitat designation, precisely because the level of habitat gain is small relative to the next best use. The important cases are those where the development rights, although substantial, still lag behind the habitat values, as when the former are worth 1,000 and the latter 4,000. In this case, the owner has no incentive to skimp on preservation because his best opportunities lie with sale, and not development. The hard task may well lie in getting the government to respond quickly enough when the offer comes its way. Yet even here that constraint should not loom large. The government may be the only party who can condemn land, but it is *not* the only party that can buy in a voluntary market. The Audubon Society, the Nature Conservancy, or any one of a thousand charitable or business organizations can come forward to make the purchase, just as environmental organizations can buy up pollution rights in the open market in order to retire them—while reserving the right to resell them if conditions change.[24] To the extent that they are not involved in lobbying or other political activity, their contributors could obtain charitable deductions, thereby alleviating any free-rider problem that might otherwise crop up.[25] The switch from the regulation mode to the purchase mode thus has the important advantage of widening the field. Buying land to protect habitat need not be any more (or less) difficult from other transactions associated with land.

And so too selling the land. Governments too often act like museums. Once the purchase is made, then resale is quite unlikely, especially on so sensitive an issue as conservation. The reason, of course, becomes clearer when we peel back the convenient label, "the government as owner," and find beneath it an elaborate mechanism that gives many different groups and persons a lever on the process of government decision making. No one single person has a firm hand on the tiller, and the internal institutional arrangements, unlike those of a corporation, freeze in place a political status quo and do not shift rapidly with market and technological developments. Nonprofits—an important category of institutions on conservation matters—also have conservative characteristics that put them in an intermediate position, with some resemblance to both government and private profit-making institutions. For these structural reasons a private charitable owner may also find it difficult to sell land, but on balance may have an easier time of it. The private charity will not face the broad-scale political pressures, and it is better able to reinvest the proceeds in habitat if that should prove necessary.

The most difficult question to ask about this analysis is why it has proved so spectacularly unpersuasive to committed environmentalists.

In part it is because they believe that they should not have to pay to acquire that which they think they already own. But I suspect that the reasons go deeper. In some cases, I think, they harbor genuine doubt that incentives matter to the degree that this analysis suggests that they do. The point here is not peculiar to environmental issues, for the same question comes up whenever there is a choice between market mechanisms and government fiats. It is always easier to impose the later when acting on the happy belief that the desired incentives to produce are not thereby altered. Yet even that explanation is not enough. I suspect that one portion of the argument is that the scope of the habitat designations are in some cases so large and pervasive, that there is no belief that the (unwashed) public would ever accede to them if these transactions were put on budget. So the private calculation of the firm environmentalist is to take the risk of interim dislocations in order to expand as vigorously as possible the scope of government action. If that is the case, then we have here, as in other cases such as rent control,[26] a preference for off-budget devices that conceal the true costs of government actions from the public at large. At this point we can identify a powerful convergence between the protection of private property and the strengthening of responsible democratic influences, one that is all too easy to overlook. The just compensation requirement forces the government and the public to make explicit trade-offs between different goods, in order to determine their value to the polity at large. Environmental groups may think that their preferred programs could not survive this scrutiny. But it hardly follows that they should therefore win out by covert means.

Coercion Versus Purchase: A Multiple Period, Multiperson Game

Voluntary purchase has yet another key advantage over coercion. It ensures stability of expectations at the conclusion of the transaction. This issue, like so many in environmental law, is not unique to this context. The basic point is clearly illustrated by the hardy question of why it is not cheaper to end conflict by buying out the aggressor instead of resisting him. In a single period game, with one victim and one assailant, it would be difficult to oppose this strategy of appeasement and compromise, at least on the artificial assumption that the agreement between the parties is capable of costless and perpetual enforcement. Both sides gain from the transaction, and there are no concerns with either interactions in future periods between the same parties or with third-party effects. The isolated transaction produces mutual gain, and if it is cheaper to surrender than to fight, so be it.

The restrictive nature of the condition, however, indicates the danger of an appeasement strategy. Agreements to abstain from the use of force are, to say the least, not self-enforcing. If force allows A to extract an advantage in period one, why should he not resort to the same tactic in period two? This appeasement solution may result in a mutual gain, even relative to the costs of defense, but only in the short-term. Once multiplied over countless episodes, this appeasement strategy is a dead loser. The immediate losses no longer buy future peace. Sooner or later, usually sooner, it becomes more cost effective to resist the aggression than to yield to it; resistance raises the costs to the other side and thus deters repetition of aggression instead of inviting it.

The dangers of appeasement are compounded when third persons wait in the wings. If one person can use the force to extract the benefit, others can play that game as well. So even if concessions in one transaction could be structured to neutralize the original aggressor, imitation of the original strategy by others could yield the same grim outcome: long-term destruction is the price of short-term appeasement. So it is that individuals learn that they must stand up for themselves. The law backs them up when they resist aggression, but not when they commit it. Stated otherwise, the baseline position *never* gives each person the right to attack every other person, and thus it does not encourage consensual corrections from that baseline that take the form of bribing others to refrain from the use of force. To sanction that baseline is to invite perpetual insecurity that no set of voluntary corrections could speedily and accurately correct, as one bribe is never enough so long as other potential aggressors wait in the wings. To keep aggression from becoming the routine armament of ordinary life, the law sets its face against it, not behind it. There are good reasons, independent of political whim or ancestral worship, to support an initial distribution of legal rights that respects the autonomy of each individual.[27]

The same logic carries over to property. Suppose the rule said that anyone could use the property of anyone else unless he were kept out by brute force. At this point, the hapless owner might seek to contract with his worst enemy to regain the use of his land. But any contract confined to a single assailant could not secure peace, because someone else could appear at the boundary line and demand either access or compensation. So too a third. Once again the transactional difficulties are enormous, and it hardly pays to require the owner to erect extensive fortifications to keep all comers off. So the law throws its weight on the side of the owner. If this or that outsider has special use for someone else's land, then a voluntary transaction that allows him in for one period can be concluded. Entry for subsequent periods or by other individuals is not part of the deal. The single owner is in a position to make both kinds of exchanges. The virtues of a right to exclude, like those of the right to personal autonomy, might not be apparent in a single-period two-person game. But it becomes dominant, if not decisive, once those two assumptions are relaxed.[28]

The issue of habitat preservation looms so important in environmental contexts because it presents a rerun of this basic protection of property rights in miniature. If the question before Congress was simply whether the government should be able to restrict use without compensation for a single owner in a single period, the best argument against the government is that it should never be allowed to exercise powers without responsibility, so that the compensation mechanism becomes the device that induces it to internalize gain against loss. But even here the argument is not decisive against a skeptical protest, which asks: Why assume that the rights of alteration and development were lodged in the landowner in the first place? Assignment of property rights over nature do not come from nature, but are social creations, so we might as well create them in favor of the public writ large if it looks like only distributional issues are at stake.

That invitation must be rejected once we relax the naive assumption of a single-period game. The government is always a player, and if it can designate its rights in the one case, then it can designate them in the next. In the first period it announces that this alteration of land is not permissible. The landowner protests and seeks protection by buying out the initial designation in exchange for "mitigating" the loss that development has imposed: some portion of the land is set aside for habitat, some tax is imposed, and its proceeds are used to purchase habitat similar to that which has been displaced. The owner has parted with real resources; the government has taken advantage of a single law from its inexhaustible supply. In the next period, the rules can be changed again so that further restrictions are imposed, requiring still further purchases by the landowner seeking relief. But once again real resources are expended only on one side. The exactions can continue until there is nothing left to surrender. The process leads to protracted and difficult negotiations, especially when the lands of several different owners fall within some local or regional Habitat Conservation Plan.[29]

A rule that requires voluntary purchase blocks any scenario that allows government to consume ordinary property rights by littles. Now the government has to put real resources on the table the first time round, and each successive time. In each case it now has to compare the gains and the losses of its action. In no case can it confiscate by littles. In this multiperiod, multiperson environment, the choice of the property rule matters and it is the common law rule that comes out best. This is so not because of some atavistic yearning or necessary, prepolitical truth, but because it is the only rule that promotes stable expectations between the parties. The law of property is often said to state the relationship of an owner to the world over time. "Property is nothing but a basis of expectation; the expectation of deriving certain advantages from a thing which we are said to possess, in consequence of the relation in which we stand towards it" (Bentham 1882, 111). There are good practical reasons why it should assume this form.

Environmental Evaluation

The conclusions reached above seem secure on the standard assumptions of scarcity and self-interest. But in an environmental setting, assumptions of a rational choice variety are questioned on the ground that any effort to attach numbers to the gains and losses of certain alternatives underestimates the complexity of the task. It is easy to posit that environmental gains are to some extent not commensurate with the economic dislocations that they create but are justified with reference to some "second order preference" that transcends the ledger-like examples that I gave.[30] The unmistakable bent of this point is to expand the scope of the environmental effort by putting it in a preferred place relative to other goods. It is therefore appropriate to examine the complications introduced by two important skeptical strands in modern economic theory: the place of second order preferences and the differential between willingness-to-pay (WTP) and willingness-to-accept (WTA).

Second Order Preferences

Conventional legal analysis assumes that preferences cover the domain of choices that are made by individual actors. Second order preferences assume that individuals have preferences about the preferences that they, and other individuals, hold about these first order preferences. For these purposes, one can assume that second order preferences do matter. Yet even so, it is hard to see why their invocation should alter the balance between coercion and purchase, even if it might increase the budget available for habitat acquisition. Private individuals and governments have knowledge of the tendencies that are said to give these environmental values their preferred status. I am doubtful about the entire enterprise of second order preferences and prefer to think of them as ways of attacking the usual set of prisoner dilemma issues that haunt the precincts of collective choice. My first order preference is to act noncooperatively within the rules of the game as structured. My second order preference is for a set of rules that blocks all defections from some cooperative solution, my own included. So understood, second order preferences are neither good or bad until we have some sense of their larger social context. My willingness to overfish the common pool can be corrected by social restrictions that honor my second order preferences for conservation, an outcome we should applaud. But if my first order preference is to compete with rivals in the same industry, why praise some second order preference to enforce cartel restrictions on output? The difference in external effects in the two cases—positive in the first, negative in the second—fully accounts for the differences in the social response to the two cases.

But let it be supposed that this reductionist account of second order preferences lacks subtlety and philosophical sophistication. It hardly matters for the purpose at hand, which is to determine the social strategy for implementing any collective preference for habitat preservation. The status of these preferences, be they of the first or second order, is neither enhanced nor reduced because money changes hands in order to buy the habitat in question. At most the second order preferences, assuming that these amount to more than some prisoner's dilemma or holdout problem, should give the government a greater spur to appropriate the dollars to purchase superior goods. The government, moreover, can never plead its own poverty as a reason to take without compensation. It always has available a taxing power to generate, after public deliberation and with legislative consent, the resources (taken from ordinary activities) that can then be redirected toward ends that have, by assumption, a higher value. The practical political choice therefore is not between different orders of goods: it is over the method of acquisition for those goods of a higher order. The prosaic difficulties that plague the designation system at issue in *Sweet Home*, chiefly the propensity for overclaiming, remain just as they would with any other restriction on land use that imposes large private losses for small public gains.

Willingness-to-Pay Versus Willingness-to-Accept

Nor is the case for habitat designation justified by pointing to the well-known gaps between the willingness-to-pay and the willingness-to-accept,[31] or as it is sometimes called, the offer/ask differential. The difference between these two numbers is often called the "endowment effect," so as to signal that the value of an asset depends on where it is located, or who is endowed with it. No matter what the terminology, the former of these two quantities represents the amount that individuals are willing to pay to acquire something that they do not possess. The latter represents the amount of money that they must be paid to get them to part voluntarily with something that they do possess. The naive assumption of many writers has been that the two figures will generally converge so that the differences between them can safely be ignored in dealing with public policy analysis (Willig 1976). Once that is done then the usual prescriptions of the Coase theorem will apply, and we can be confident that the resource in question will end up in its highest value use.[32]

The recent experimental literature seems to report a different picture. The WTP is systematically lower than the WTA. Thus in one recent study, jury instructions for personal injury actions were framed in two different ways (McCaffery, Kahneman, and Spitzer 1995). The first set of instructions asked the jury to decide how much money it would take to secure the ex ante consent of an individual for the injuries that had been inflicted upon him. That "selling price" approach asked in effect the jury to calculate the WTA. The alternative instructions stressed the amount of money that was necessary after the fact to make the victims whole. This "make whole" test was designed to elicit the WTP, the amount that the injured party would, as it were, pay to recover his health again. While the correspondence between the WTA and the selling approach as against the WTP and the make whole approach may not be perfect, the two sets of instructions evoked in an experimental setting very different responses from juries asked to deliberate on the matter. The make whole approach yielded a (logarithmic) mean of $151,448, and a median of $290,000, while the selling price approach yielded a mean of $331,042 and a median of $527,000, both differences too large to ignore.

A similar pattern has been observed in experimental work directed to environmental issues. Typical of these results is the instructive study by Boyce et al. (1992) of Norfolk Island pines—a small house tree that could be easily moved. That study showed that under a variety of conditions it took more money to get an individual to part with a tree than it did to acquire one. Boyce and her colleagues asked the question about WTP and WTA under two different scenarios. In the first, all that happened was that the experimental subject either acquired (WTP) or surrendered (WTA) the tree in question. In these two "no-kill" settings, the experimental subject owned the tree and demanded a mean price of $8.00 to give it up. Yet he would only pay $4.81 to purchase the same tree (so long as he thought it would not be killed by its present owner). But once the destruction of the tree was built into the experiment, both bids got higher: $18.43 for the WTA with the killing, to $7.81 for the WTP with the killing.

The combined results of this study suggest that three forces are operating. First, there is an evident bias in favor of the security of possession: persons want to keep what they have more than they want to acquire what they do not own. Perhaps it is a manifestation of the subjective value that comes from close association with a particular good, with the sense that you are personally "invested" in those things to which you have formed an attachment. For these purposes, the exact origins of the sentiment are less important than its evident hold on human psychology. Second, individuals have a detached concern with what happens to the tree, independent of who owns it. Once it was understood that the tree would be destroyed, then both the WTA and the WTP rose. Third, there is, as the authors suggest, a heightened responsibility for the destruction of the tree when a subject knows that he already has the power to protect it. So long as other persons could purchase the tree, the capacity for avoiding this harm (or the responsibility for its destruction) does not rest so clearly on the subject asked to make the choice. Perhaps that is why the ratio between WTA/WTP jumps from 1.77 ($8.00/$4.51) to 2.35 ($18.43/$7.81) as one moves from the no-kill to the kill scenarios—a suggestive, but not overpowering shift.

For these purposes, however, the critical inquiry is how this WTA/WTP differential plays out in the habitat preservation context. One obvious point is that the initial allocation seems to matter, but it does so in a way that strengthens the case for requiring the government or others to purchase needed habitat. The difference between WTA/WTP reflects the bias of the status quo, the common law world prior to the ESA, where the individual landowner owned the habitat on his property. As such he is not a purchaser, for whom the WTP becomes the operative number, but the owner, for whom the higher WTA controls. Indeed an owner's preferences should be more closely analogous to the WTA-kill figure. In this world, we should expect that these owners would be reluctant to part with, or voluntarily destroy, the habitat that remains on their land. In addition, the owners are not randomly selected, as are the students who populate the usual economic experiments. These owners are likely to have the greatest affinity to the environment and to preserving critical habitat located on it. Development requires a transformation in use.

Another question is, which side of the WTA/WTP spread should be used to evaluate these changes in proposed land use? Here we no longer have the sharp dichotomy between owner and buyer that is a constant feature of the experimental literature. Rather the lines are blurred. Do we treat the landowner as though he always owned the rights to develop the land, so that when these are stripped from him the appropriate measure of value is the WTA? Or do we think of the landowner as not yet possessing these potential development rights, so that they should be valued by some lower WTP figure? To the owner, the former figure looks appropriate precisely because one central purpose of property is to create stable expectations for future use of property, as Bentham

(1882, 111) had argued. That result seems especially plausible where an owner delayed development in early years in explicit reliance on the legal rule that preserved that development right for future years. If so, then the modern land use case law that postpones the time of "vesting" to the time that legal rules are actually used runs into clear conflict with the experimental literature.[33] The present owner's rights to future use are in common contemplation vested when the original owner takes first possession of the land. All this is not to say that some attenuation of the possessory sense might not be appropriate for the future use of present rights, so that some blended number, as yet untested in the experimental literature, should dominate the account. But even so, the invocation of the WTA/WTP split in this context calls, as several writers have already noted, for boosting the level of compensation in takings cases beyond the market value figure that represents the current law (Knetsch and Borcherding 1979; Ellickson 1989; Fischel 1995, 192).

Those discussions, however, have had limited import because they are directed to the question of how much compensation should be paid in physical dispossession cases, where the taking itself is admitted, and the only open question is how much compensation should be provided. Even if we put the constitutional question aside, the task here is to decide whether any compensation should be paid for a regulatory imposition on a given landowner who remains in possession. At this point, one could argue a fortiori that compensation for the loss of development and use rights should be paid, and that it should reflect some premium over market value. More concretely, the individual landowner has within his bundle of rights both the habitat preservation and the development option. Does he attach WTA valuations to both, and, if so, do both call for the same psychological premium? It is possible at least to assume that both sticks in the bundle of rights are subject to WTA valuations so that any rate of substitution between them should be unaffected by the WTA/WTP differential.

One consequence of this observation is that even if the government does nothing, its habitat preservation program has a certain measure of success because it can rely on the high WTA to protect the critical habitat from casual destruction. Yet the common complaint is that habitat is often destroyed prematurely to avoid regulation, which suggests that the regulation must have enormous negative impact, precisely because it has to overcome the strongest inclinations of present property holders, that is, situations with WTA-kill. Why then pursue remorselessly that confrontational course of action? Descriptively, part of the explanation lies in the contested nature of the ownership rights in question—an issue that is never put into relief in the experimental literature, which treats the property rights in objects such as the Norfolk pines as well defined. The environmental debates are not blessed with the same clarity in rights delineation. The public willingness to use force rests on a strong conception that the endangered species is not private property. The upshot is that the public, or at least the most vocal supporters of the ESA, attach a high WTA evaluation to the species and the habitat on which it depends. Yet here the collision course is virtually guaranteed because the individual landowners, including those who prize their local habitat, also think themselves owners of the land, resentful of outside interference with their classical prerogatives. They also attach, at a guess, WTA evaluations for the development rights normally associated with common law ownership, which they treat as a grounded social expectation about property rights. The environmentalists reject that conception on the ground that after successive generations of Supreme Court opinions, it has become clear that the protection of *existing* uses counts for far more than the protection of future uses, which is why, for example, amortization of *existing* land structures receives far greater constitutional respect than does a prohibition against a new use for a site that already has an existing use, as in all the landmark preservation cases.[34]

The differences are important as a matter of theory, for all the experiments on WTA/WTP differentials operate off a unitary conception of ownership that corresponds to the clearest case of compensation under the takings law, outright dispossession.[35] The literature has not developed any coherent means to deal with attitudes toward the gain or loss of the individual sticks in the proverbial bundle of rights. The upshot is regrettable. We have a case where each side thinks that it owns 75 percent or more of the bundle. The fights over the environment arise in part because both sides claim the higher WTA valuation for what one of them has to lose.

At this point the conflict shapes up quite differently from the choices typically posed in the experimental examples. No longer is it clear who is an owner and who is an outsider, given the different social conceptions of rights that both sides bring to the table. Each side thinks of itself as the owner (or at least environmental steward) of the disputed resource, and as such we have in law what has been found in nature: a replication of the gargantuan battles over turf. Two butterflies will fight hardest for use of a cone of light when each thinks that it is the sole and prior possessor of the space. And the same is doubtless true of territorial conflicts between land-based animals, of which humans are one sort. Both sides fight hardest to defend home turf; and now both sides think of themselves in the role of defender.

Little of course can be done to disabuse either side of its sociological conception of who is the owner of what, and indeed each side can look to its own allies to gain support for its own conception. But with all that said, the alternative strategy of voluntary purchase should be highly successful for this reason: the government in seeking to preserve the habitat simply reinforces that which individuals already have the greatest inclination to do. Habitat preservation is not trying to take and destroy the habitat against the will of the owner. It seeks to preserve it, something for which some owners at least are reasonably inclined to do without coercion: witness the enormous steps that builders take to prevent the destruction of an unendangered but beautiful tree.

As with all points in this area, there are still differences between them. The usual owner may be less concerned about the preservation of the original trees and more concerned about the maintenance of an appropriate place to live. The difference is often found not in the end position, but in how it is reached. The environmentalist is opposed to destruction and wishes to minimize the amount of dislocation in construction. The builder and owner care more about cost, and are more willing at the margin to adopt a strategy of level-replant-and-refurbish, which environmentalists tend to deplore. But this gap is not insurmountable. Take the mixed set of owner expectations, and the eager government buyer of habitat should find a ready market at a reasonably low price, so long as it does not neutralize the other productive values of the land. The voluntary purchase of wetlands can usually be completed at attractive prices. It is therefore possible to use the purchase system to reinforce whatever higher order preferences individuals have about habitat preservation issues, without having to invoke highly coercive means to achieve those ends. In sum, the consideration of the special features that might attach to environmental issues reinforces the case for sticking with the original common law system of property rights that requires the purchase of habitat rights. Further, it gives some reason to believe that offers for voluntary purchases will elicit strong responses, without all the endless hassles that now routinely mar the mitigation process associated with any Habitat Conservation Plan.

The Eminent Domain Option

Thus far I have argued that voluntary purchases are systematically superior to a system of habitat preservation by designation. But here, as in other areas, voluntary purchases may not be suitable for all occasions. It is generally acknowledged that preservation of contiguous tracks makes for better habitat than preservation of isolated bits of land. The habitat preservation project therefore opens up the state, or other potential purchasers, to the conventional hold-out objections. Enter condemnation. The threat to condemn the property at its market valuation effectively negates the holdout problem. In principle, the ideal standard for these condemnations is the price at which willing buyers and willing sellers, in possession of all relevant information, would exchange the property in a world in which there are no special public benefits that the private owner could seek to extract.

Unfortunately, the legal standards as they have developed with respect to admitted condemnations of real property often leave landowners in positions worse than those they would occupy after a voluntary exchange.[36] The first and most obvious point is that market value is below subjective value of land in those cases where the land is not on the market. Generally, land holdings are in equilibrium so that throwing off a seller that does not wish to part with property is quite a different matter from paying voluntary sellers who want to leave, and who thus announce that their current use value is below the exchange value they attach to the property. But subjective value is not the whole story.

Still another part of the difficulty has to do with the transaction costs attendant to sale. In a voluntary transaction, the seller asks whether the amount received *less transaction costs* is greater than the use value of the property in question. In condemnation situations, where valuation and appraisal are often in issue, the transactions costs are higher than they are in ordinary exchanges, but these costs are not compensable, so that the market price standard results in a double loss for the property owner.[37] The current legal rules compensate the landowner for the property taken by the government, but not for the consequential losses inflicted on the landowner. The unwanted dislocations from the process, while publicly generated, are privately borne. The compensation rules thus go overboard: they block the holdout problem, but only at the cost of leaving the original owner worse off than he would have been from a voluntary exchange in a competitive market. As such the condemnation alternative under current law looks like a hybrid: part designation and part compensation. Yet even so resistance is likely to be less to (partial) condemnation than to (pure) designation: the partial compensation reduces the gains from resistance, and thus the likelihood that resistance will occur. Since the government has to incur its own noncompensable expert fees to carry out the condemnation, it has some incentive, weaker than ideal, to reach a voluntary settlement—bargaining again in the shadow of the law.

Be that as it may, the problems so raised are not beyond repair. The Supreme Court could—and should—change its compensation rules so that they embrace the costs thrown on private parties in virtue of the condemnation initiative. To be sure, in some cases the additional price will deter the government action, but that change in behavior is exactly what a price system is supposed to achieve. Once the full costs of government action are brought home to its decision makers, then (to use an odd phrase) total government cost will equal true social costs, which should reproduce a general social improvement. At present it is highly unlikely that Congress will ever make a change of this sort on its own initiative. Current federal budgetary law requires that all increases in government revenues be offset elsewhere in the system. A change in the total practice of compensation therefore could not take place, even if it generated a social improvement, unless paired with some independent reform, which could be either good or bad in itself. The budget process is designed to constrain (after a fashion) spending, which is a far cry from responding to the question of overall social welfare.

The Supreme Court, however, is not wedded to any budgetary constraints when it announces the compensation rules for takings cases. It could make these much needed changes, which only restore the law to the position that Blackstone envisioned it would have,[38] without undermining the scope of the welfare state. At this point, the issue of habitat preservation loses some of its novelty but none of its importance. Setting up the right schedules for compensation makes the case comport more with the prices that would be paid in the voluntary market. Indeed, the relative cheapness of the voluntary transaction suggests that more cases would go that way than through condemnation. Nothing prevents the government from asking for bids on habitat and then taking those that promise the most gain for the lowest cost.

Constitutional Issues

These arguments clearly imply that the importance of habitat preservation as a social issue does not support the takeover-by-coercion regime now in effect. The common law system of property rights may not have been organized with the present range of environmental conflicts clearly in mind, but, suitably buttressed by the equally traditional system of eminent domain power, it comes out better than the regulatory alternative that received a free pass in the *Sweet Home* case. Yet if the above analysis is correct, then that decision, which assiduously avoided all constitutional takings questions, is infirm in two distinct ways. First, as a matter of statutory construction it mistakenly reads the "take" definition broadly in uneasy contradistinction to its rendering of "takings" under the Fifth Amendment. Second, if it can be shown that the dominant strategy in these habitat cases is purchase, whether by agreement or condemnation, then it appears that the government's proposed interpretation of the ESA suffers yet a larger defect: it is unconstitutional under the takings clause of the Constitution. That conclusion follows from the most traditional of legal analyses.[39] The bundle of property rights encompasses possession, use, and disposition. The use rights in question are only limited by the principles of nuisance law. The restrictions against habitat modification cut far deeper than the law of nuisance and thus can be initiated only with compensation.

I regard these conclusions as inescapable given that the text, structure, and function of the takings clause all point in the same direction. But the case law is quite different. Although I do not have the superhuman energy to wade through all the precedents in the area, it is important to indicate what I think to be the fundamental errors of the dominant modern synthesis. The problems arise with both halves of the takings analysis: the nature of the individual interest in private property and the permissible justifications for state regulation. On the first side, there is resistance to the traditional accounts of property that stress the exclusive use and control that a person may make over his own land. That reluctance is compounded by regarding exclusive possession as an end in itself, and not as a means to secure valuable use of the property so possessed. To be sure, the modern cases have held that regulation that strips land of all economic use could count as a taking even if the possession is left undisturbed. But sharp restrictions on the changes of use patterns are often regarded as mere uncompensable land use regulations. More importantly, on the other side, the control over environmental issues is placed at the core of the state police powers, without much regard over the form in which that control is exerted. The force of the one-two punch is often inexorable. The initial step is to call into question the status of the private interest seeking protection. The closing blow is to elevate the public justifications for these restrictions on private uses.

Here is how it works. The original premise of exclusive possession is designed to protect the landowners against the unwanted entrances of others. With the ESA and other forms of land use regulation the disputed entry is not by ordinary individuals, but by animals that have no private owner. Within the classical common law system, these animals were subject to capture by anyone, including the owner of the property where they were found. By the same token, no other person was responsible for the harms that these animals might have committed before they were reduced to private ownership. Trespasses by cattle and other animals become torts only when these have been reduced to ownership by another person.

One way to look at the ESA is as a regime that reduces members of certain designated species to public ownership without the usual necessity of capturing the animal first. But ownership is normally a dual-edged sword. The owner of the animal is entitled to damages in the event that it is hurt or killed by another (or indeed by the animal of another). Yet by the same token that owner can be liable in tort for the harms caused by animals within his control. In such a world the assertion of ownership is not an unmixed blessing given that the liabilities could easily exceed the benefits. But not for the peculiar form of government ownership under the ESA. Here the government abstains from making any formal declaration of ownership. But by the same token it imposes fines for the harm or destruction to animals that are only consistent with that claim. Yet by eschewing ownership claims, it seeks to insulate itself from liability for the harms that these animals could cause by their trespasses. Heads I win, tails you lose.

The modern law aggressively supports this position. The state has only assumed a trusteeship position over animals and has not reduced them to ownership. Indeed the rules of capture, which have so often been attacked on the ground that they encourage individual grabbing of animals, are now treated in exactly the opposite fashion, that is, as a logical imperative: "It is pure fantasy to talk of 'owning' wild fish, birds or animals. Neither the States nor the Federal Government . . . has title to these creatures until they are reduced to possession by skillful capture."[40] The upshot has been that the court could hold that the killing of marauding but protected grizzly bears in defense of property could be fined under the ESA in part because the government has not taken private property when it strips owners of their right to defend property from external threats.[41] The argument in effect is that all individuals have to bear some incidental loss in order to pursue some larger social good, that is, the preservation of endangered species whose continued existence is to the benefit of us all.

This argument is in strong tension with the standard account of social contract theory, which posits the protection of property (the Lockean "lives, liberties and estates") as the major function of government.[42] That social contract has two sides. First, individuals give up their right to self-help, which is surely done here. Second, the state supplies a substitute form of neutral protection that does not suffer from the sins of partiality that render the older system so unstable. In this context, self-help has been removed, and nothing has been supplied in its place. It might well make sense to deny property owners both self-help and neutral protection, so long as cash compensation is provided. But it is just the consequence that recent decisions have denied.

Yet surely this is exactly the kind of case for which compensation seems most appropriate. There is little question that the benefits of preserving endangered species are regarded as societal in the strongest sense of that term. No one posits that those persons who live and work in the vicinity of the endangered species benefit disproportionately from its preservation. Think of the various rationales that are put forward for species preservation: continuity with nature's past; the preservation of a reservoir of plants, animals, and chemicals that will provide new pharmaceuticals and new food sources; the psychological awareness that the world is a better place because humans have done their part to preserve biodiversity.[43] Let us accept all these rationales as completely valid. Not one of them bears any trace of localism; none of them posits some larger set of benefits to those persons whose land provides habitat for the protected species than for the public at large. But the burdens are surely disproportionate, given the loss of livestock and other valuable property are concentrated on those few members of society whose property is located in some critical habitat region. At this point, it becomes obligatory to invoke the famous rationale behind the takings clause. "It is axiomatic that the Fifth Amendment's just compensation provision is 'designed to bar Government from forcing some people alone to bear public burdens which, in all fairness and justice, should be borne by the public as a whole.' "[44]

Yet this proposition is hardly a showstopper, for the chaotic state of affairs of takings law is reflected in the melancholy truth that each general assertion has its equal and opposite proposition. So while the decisions in support of property rights quote the last sentence, the decisions against them invoke its qualification: "There is no set formula to determine where regulation ends and taking begins."[45] And it is clearly this member of the contentious pair that has won out in environmental litigation.

But why should this be the case? In part the appeal here is to history and tradition. There is a long list of impressive cases that have upheld various forms of fish and wildlife preservation statutes against a variety of constitutional challenges, including takings, due process, and equal protection.[46] But a closer look reveals the enormous gap that lies between the earlier and the modern cases in ways that tie in directly to the habitat preservation cases. For example, the modern court that upheld a fine for destroying a marauding grizzly bear also went out of its way to quote a 1917 New York decision, which contained these words:

> Wherever protection is accorded harm may be done to the individual. Deer or moose may browse on his crops; mink or skunks kill his chickens; robins eat his cherries. In certain cases the legislature may be mistaken in its belief that more good than harm is occasioned. But this is clearly a matter which is confided to its discretion. It exercises a governmental function for the benefit of the public at large and no one can complain of the incidental injuries that may result.[47]

The language looks powerful, but some unquoted portions of the opinion tells a more complicated story. Thus the New York court outlined the scheme that it upheld as follows:

No person shall molest or disturb any wild beaver or the dams, houses, homes or abiding places of same (Laws 1904, ch. 674, section 1). This is still the law, although in 1912 the forest, fish and game commission was authorized to permit protected animals which had become destructive to public or private property to be taken and disposed of. (Laws 1912, ch. 318)[48]

What are the components of the plan? First and foremost is that it allows the defense of property from the depredations of animals, which was of course the disputed point in the case involving marauding grizzlies. No one can be certain but it is likely that the New York court would have found a constitutional violation if the owners were not permitted to take and dispose of those wild animals that had become destructive to private property.

Second, the New York statutory scheme protected both the animals from direct destruction, as in section 9 of the ESA. It also offered some protection for beaver habitat, by the protection of the "dams, houses, homes or abiding places of same." It is doubtful that anyone would have bothered to attack the ESA if its definition of habitat had been so narrowly drawn. But on any reading, the New York statutory scheme offers only a pale shadow of the view of habitat protection found under the ESA. Thus under the old New York statute, the landowner could have killed the beaver that cut down his trees, and he certainly could have cut down the trees himself before the beaver got to them. It is therefore hardly clear that this New York court would have found the present section 9 regulation as consistent with its view of the Constitution. But the modern court that relied on the New York case made no attempt to point out the genuine differences in statutory schemes, let alone explain why the differences are irrelevant. For my part, I think that even the New York system is constitutionally suspect. The preservation of beaver is a systemwide virtue with concentrated adverse consequences. So why not compensate this landowner for the loss and destruction of his property, to the extent that state legislation deprived him of its means of defense?

The use of precedent in this case is not a unique event. Another illustration of the same practice is found in a pair of California cases. The more recent decision, *Sierra Club v. Department of Forestry and Fire Protection*,[49] upheld a challenge to two timber logging plans of the Pacific Lumber Company on private property, which had been approved by the state forestry department on the ground that it did not contain sufficient protection of certain rare species that were dependent on virgin, old-growth forests. Once again, the logic of the decision and the use of precedent are noteworthy. First, Pacific Lumber dutifully cited

Locke but was immediately chastised on the ground that Locke's "300-year-old-essay Concerning Human Understanding . . . has very little to say regarding California's system of THP's [timber harvest plan]."[50] The more telling point was that once the court looked beyond general political principles, it fastened on not only the marauding grizzly and beaver cases just discussed, but also on broad language from a 1935 case of its own:

> All private property within the state is held subject to the general police powers. It is conceivable that private property in every fish and game district in the state might suffer some damage through the restrictions of the Fish and Game Code generally, but this is a damage which the property owner must bear in the interest of the general welfare.[51]

Once again it looks as though the fundamental premise of the disproportionate impact test has long been displaced by the state interest in wildlife protection. But once again, a closer look at the case reveals a pattern that is quite at odds with the restrictions at issue in the recent case. In the 1935 case, the plaintiff attacked provisions of the California Fish and Game Code that authorized the state to establish different hunting seasons in different areas of the state. The new rules for the department in which her lands were located suspended the "open season" in order to preserve fish and game. But the statutory rule for her region provided that "any lawful occupant of privately owned lands, or an employee of such occupant, may take, hurt, or kill on such lands predatory or destructive birds or mammals."[52] The obvious balance struck by the general scheme was that protected animals could roam at will until they caused destruction to specific property. The ostensible vice of this statute was that it denied to others the like ability to kill and capture game such that "the protection afforded wild game by the statute might result in such an increase thereof that her garden might be injured by the invasion of predatory birds and wild animals."[53] It seemed evident that the plaintiff was complaining against an ostensible discrimination that cut in her favor, with respect to a set of injuries that had not yet occurred (which were accordingly described as "conceivable"). Yet unlike the scheme for protecting beavers in the New York case, the scheme here placed zero restrictions on habitat modification, and like the scheme in that case allowed the use of force in defense of property. It seems very hard to find in this scheme the sort of disparate impact that anyone should think worthy of constitutional protection. But the differences between this set of restrictions and those at issue under the ESA or its modern California analogues are palpable. At this point the basic question again arises: if the protection of endangered species is so important, why should not the public pay for it? It surely pays through general revenues for the inputs that the government buys to implement the scheme, including salaries and equipment. Why should it not pay for the animals that are consumed in its operation? The early cases under the police power protected against the destruction of animals by force, as does section 9 of the ESA. They provided some narrow protection of habitat drawn far more narrowly than those necessary for "breeding, feeding or sheltering." So why assume that the invocation of the police power in the earlier contexts resolves the issue today, especially in the absence of any nuisance-like showing by landowners?

So understood, the takings argument that was so studiously avoided in *Sweet Home* seems to resonate with all the great themes of that area. It shows clear restrictions on use, not to prevent ordinary private wrongs but to provide great public benefits, for which the government should be prepared to pay. But so long as the Supreme Court continues to treat the takings clause as though it protects only a small fraction of the sticks—chiefly the right to exclude other individuals, most of the time—found in the common law bundle of property rights, then the habitat modification issues raised in *Sweet Home* will be litigated as though they raise only questions of statutory interpretation and administrative law. The larger issues will be left to political processes under a set of legal rules that hardly induces Congress and the states to follow the promptings of their better nature.

Notes

1. 515 U.S. 687 (1995).
2. Richard A. Epstein, William H. Mellor III, Clint Bolick, and Scott G. Bullock, Institute for Justice, Amicus Brief for respondents in *Babbitt v. Sweet Home Chapter of Communities for a Great Oregon.*
3. 515 U.S. 687, 690.
4. 515 U.S. 687, 708.
5. 515 U.S. 687, 714. It should take no imagination to see that the typical lineup from liberal to conservative is preserved intact in this case. Beginning on the left with the four core liberals (Stevens, Souter, Ginsburg, and Breyer), we usually find Kennedy and O'Connor in the middle, and Rehnquist, Scalia, and Thomas on the right. There are not enough links in the chain to cover the full spectrum of political views, but no matter what the issue today, the progression of the liberal four, Kennedy, O'Connor, Rehnquist, Scalia, and Thomas seems strong on almost all contentious issues. The break points may differ from case to case, but it is hard to find any case of reversed ordering.

6. The Endangered Species Act of 1973, 81 Stat. 884, 16 U.S.C. § 1531 (1994), hereinafter the ESA or act.

7. Done in April 1995, see Emergency Supplemental Appropriations and Rescissions for the Department of Defense to Preserve and Enhance Military Readiness Act, Public Law 104–6, 109 Stat. 73, 86, 104th Congress, 1st Session (April 10, 1995).

8. See, for example, *Christy v. Hodel*, 857 F.2d 1324 (9th Cir. 1988) (upholding ESA even when it prevented a landowner from shooting marauding grizzly bears attacking his sheep); *Sierra Club v. Department of Forestry and Fire Protection*, 26 Cal. Rptr. 2d. 338 (Cal. App. 1993) (striking down timber harvesting plan approved by state agency).

9. 16 U.S.C. § 1538(a)(1)(B).

10. 16 U.S.C. § 1532 (19).

11. 50 C.F.R. § 17.3.

12. Historically, the definition of nuisance has been quite stable. See, for example, Brenner (1974). Some claim it is infinitely variable. For instance, Keeton et al. (1984, 616) say: "There is perhaps no more impenetrable jungle in the entire law than that which surrounds the word 'nuisance.' It has meant all things to all people, and has been applied indiscriminately to everything from an alarming advertisement to a cockroach baked into a pie." However, these are more representative of the weirdness of the marginal case, and not of the mainstream application of doctrine.

13. *Restatement (Second) of Torts* Ch. 40, §§ 822–31 (ALI, 1965).

14. For my discussion of some of these issues, see Epstein (1979 and 1995a, 384–88, 399–405).

15. For the development of the model, see Ellickson (1993).

16. For discussion, see Epstein (1995b).

17. 1969 Vt. Laws No. 250 § 1 (original findings); 10 Vt. Stat. Ann. Pt. 5, Ch. 151 (1993) (history).

18. *Southview Associates, Ltd. v. Bongartz*, 980 F.2d 84 (2d Cir. 1992).

19. 458 U.S. 419 (1982) (installation of small cable company box pursuant to government regulation required payment of compensation to the affected property owner).

20. 980 F.2d at 95 (footnote omitted). The use of the scare-quotes around "invasion" marks the attenuation of the original doctrine.

21. For discussion of the point, see Thompson (1996).

22. See Kenworthy (1995) cited in Percival et al. (1996, 1238).

23. See Coase (1959, 14) where, speaking of the rise of the FCC, he said: "Professor Siepmann seems to ascribe the confusion which existed before government regulation to a failure of private enterprise and the competitive system. But the real cause of the trouble was that no property rights were created in these scarce frequencies."

24. Ironically, the retirement option makes no sense if the government could simply issue new permits to take up the slack. So the permit system cannot work if the government-created property rights are infinitely malleable.

25. For my defense of this mode of support for the public activities under-

taken by private groups, as opposed to government coercion or government grants, see Epstein (1993, 306–12), criticizing government funding of the arts through the National Endowment of the Arts.

26. See, for example, Justice Scalia's dissent in *Pennell v. City of San Jose*, 485 U.S. 1, 15, 21–24 (1988), which attacks the off-budget nature of rent control subsidies as a way to avoid the scrutiny of the political process.

27. For an elaboration, see Epstein (1995c, 53–70).

28. One possible exception to the basic rule concerns the tension between rules of fencing-in and fencing-out as applied to cattle trespass. A rule that required a cattle owner to fence in his animals gives others the right of exclusion, without the need of having to erect an expensive fence to enforce it. The rule of fencing-out requires that fence be built for the exclusive rights to be obtained. Note that even this rule does not give the outsider the right to rip down the fence once built, which would be the situation if everyone had the right to use everyone else's land. The interesting question is to identify the circumstances in which the fencing-out rule might be efficient. Note that cattle habitually wander, and fences are expensive to erect and maintain. If private holdings are large, and all the owners raise cattle, grazing and branding may well do better than fencing animals in. But once the land uses become mixed or more intensive, even this qualified limitation of the right to exclude loses its advantages. See Ellickson (1991) for a more extensive discussion of the relevant determinants.

29. For discussion, see Thompson (1996, 12–17). In its rear guard effort to blunt criticisms of its position, the Clinton administration has proposed exempting some small plots from the overall set of habitat restrictions and for expediting the process in ways that reduce the cost, uncertainty, and delay for small owners. See U.S. Department of the Interior (1995).

30. For development of this argument, see Sunstein (1993, 222–23).

31. For summaries of the literature, see Hoffman and Spitzer (1993); Sunstein (1993, 225–30).

32. For discussion see, for example, Kahneman, Knetsch, and Thaler (1990); Hovenkamp (1991).

33. *Avco Community Developers, Inc. v. South Coast Regional Commission*, 553 P2d 546 (Cal. 1976).

34. See, for example, *Penn Central Transportation Co. v. City of New York*, 438 U.S. 104 (1978).

35. See, for example, *Kaiser-Aetna v. United States*, 444 U.S. 164 (1979).

36. For a discussion, see Epstein (1985, 51–56). *Monongahela Navigation Co. v. United States*, 148 U.S. 312 (1893), limited the compensation award to the value of the "property taken," which excludes all forms of consequential loss suffered by the owner for which there is no offsetting gain to the government. Land appraisals, for example, are not covered by the just compensation clause. See *United States v. Bodcaw*, 440 U.S. 202 (1979). For a striking demonstration of how goodwill and other intangible assets can disappear under the takings ax, see Kanner (1969).

37. *United States v. Bodcaw*, 440 U.S. 202 (1979).

38. Speaking of the need to acquire land for roads, Blackstone (1979, 1:135) writes: "In this, and similar cases the legislature alone can, and indeed frequently does interpose and compel the individual to acquiesce. But how does it interpose and compel? Not by absolutely stripping the subject of his property in an arbitrary manner; but by giving him full indemnification and equivalent for *the injury thereby sustained.*"

39. On which, see Epstein (1985).

40. *Douglas v. Seacoast Products, Inc.*, 431 U.S. 265, 284 (1977).

41. See *Christy v. Hodel*, 857 F.2d 1324 (9th Cir. 1988).

42. See Locke ([1689] 1980, ch. 9 and 11).

43. The arguments for biodiversity in all its fullness have been articulated with considerable force. See Wilson (1984).

44. *First English Evangelical Lutheran Church v. County of Los Angeles*, 482 U.S. 304 (1987), quoting *Armstrong v. United States*, 364 U.S. 40, 49 (1964).

45. *Goldblatt v. Town of Hempstead*, 369 U.S., 590, 594 (1962) (finding police power justification for preventing extraction of gravel). The words "set formula" were picked up in *Penn Cent. Transp. Co. v. City of New York*, 438 U.S. 104, 123–24 (1978) (parallel citations omitted):

> "While this Court has recognized that the "Fifth Amendment's guarantee . . . [is] designed to bar Government from forcing some people alone to bear public burdens which, in all fairness and justice, should be borne by the public as a whole," *Armstrong v. United States*, 364 U.S. 40, 49 (1960), this Court, quite simply, has been unable to develop any "set formula" for determining when "justice and fairness" require that economic injuries caused by public action be compensated by the government, rather than remain disproportionately concentrated on a few persons. See *Goldblatt v. Hempstead*, 369 U.S. 590, 594 (1962). Indeed, we have frequently observed that whether a particular restriction will be rendered invalid by the government's failure to pay for any losses proximately caused by it depends largely "upon the particular circumstances [in that] case." (*United States v. Central Eureka Mining Co.*, 357 U.S. 155, 168 [1958])

46. See, for example, *Christy v. Hodel*, 857 F2d, 1324, 1334 (9th Cir. 1988), citing *Mountain States Legal Foundation v. Hodel*, 799 F.2d 1423, 1428–29 (10th Cir. 1986); *Sierra Club v. Department of Forestry & Fire Protection*, 26 Cal. Rptr. 2d 338 (Cal. App. 1993).

47. *Barrett v. State*, 116 N.E. 99, 100 (NY 1917), quoted in *Christy v. Hodel*, 857 F.2d 1324, 1335 (9th Cir. 1988).

48. 116 N.E. at 99.

49. 26 Cal. Rptr. 2d 338 (1993).

50. 26 Cal. Rptr. 2d at 344 n.2, quoting *Platt v. Philbrick*, 47 P2d 302, 304 (Cal. App. 1935) (citation omitted).

51. 26 Cal. Rptr. 2d at 303.

52. 26 Cal. Rptr. 2d at 303.

53. 26 Cal. Rptr. 2d at 303.

References

Bentham, Jeremy. 1882. *Theory of Legislation*, 4th ed. London: Trubner.

Blackstone, William. [1765] 1979. *Commentaries on the Law of England*, ed. Stanley N. Katz. Chicago: University of Chicago Press.

Boyce, Rebecca, et al. 1992. An Experimental Examination of Intrinsic Values as a Source of the WTA-WTP Disparity. *American Economic Review* 82(5): 1366–73.

Brenner, Joel Franklin. 1974. Nuisance Law and the Industrial Revolution. *Journal of Legal Studies* 3(2): 403–33.

Coase, Ronald H. 1959. The Federal Communications Commission. *Journal of Law and Economics* 2(1): 1–40.

Ellickson, Robert C. 1989. Bringing Culture and Human Frailty to Rational Actors: A Critique of Classical Law-and-Economics. *Chicago-Kent Law Review* 65(1): 23–55.

———. 1991. *Law Without Order: How Neighbors Settle Disputes.* Cambridge: Harvard University Press.

———. 1993. Property in Land. *Yale Law Journal* 102(6): 1315–1400.

Epstein, Richard A. 1979. Nuisance Law: Corrective Justice and Its Utilitarian Constraints. *Journal of Legal Studies* 8(1): 49–102.

———. 1985. *Takings: Private Property and the Power of Eminent Domain.* Cambridge: Harvard University Press.

———. 1993. *Bargaining with the State.* Princeton: Princeton University Press.

———. 1995a. The Harm Principle—And How it Grew. *University of Toronto Law Journal* 45(4): 369–417.

———. 1995b. The Permit Power Meets the Constitution. *Iowa Law Review* 81(2): 407–32.

———. 1995c. *Simple Rules for a Complex World.* Cambridge: Harvard University Press.

———. 1997. *Babbitt v. Sweet Home Chapters of Oregon*: The Law and Economics of Habitat Preservation. *Supreme Court Economic Review* 5: 1–57.

Fischel, William A. 1995. The Offer/Ask Disparity and Just Compensation for Takings: A Constitutional Choice Perspective. *International Review of Law and Economics* 15(2): 187–203.

Hoffman, Elizabeth, and Matthew L. Spitzer. 1993. The Divergence between Willingness-to-Pay and Willingness-to-Accept Measures of Value. *Washington University Law Quarterly* 71(1): 59–114.

Hovenkamp, Herbert. 1991. Legal Policy and the Endowment Effect. *Journal of Legal Studies* 20(2): 225–47.

Kahneman, Daniel, Jack L. Knetsch, and Richard H. Thaler. 1990. Experimental Tests of the Endowment Effect and the Coase Theorem. *Journal of Political Economy* 98(6): 1325–48.

Kanner, Gideon. 1969. When Is "Property" Not "Property Itself": A Critical Examination of the Bases of Denial of Compensation for Loss of Goodwill in Eminent Domain. *California Western Law Review* 6(1): 57–88.

Keeton, W. Page, Dan B. Dobbs, Robert E. Keeton, and David G. Owen, eds. 1984. *Prosser & Keeton on Torts*, 5th ed. St. Paul: West Publishing Co.

Kenworthy, Tom. 1995. Deal Gives Woodpeckers Golf Habitat. *Washington Post*, March 2, A19.

Knetsch, Jack L., and Thomas E. Borcherding. 1979. Expropriation of Private Property and the Basis for Compensation. *University of Toronto Law Journal* 29(3): 237–52.

Locke, John. [1689] 1980. *The Second Treatise of Government*, ed. C. B. Macpherson. Indianapolis: Hackett Publishing Co.

McCaffery, Edward J., Daniel J. Kahneman, and Matthew L. Spitzer. 1995. Framing the Jury: Cognitive Perspectives on Pain and Suffering Awards. *Virginia Law Review* 81(5): 1341–420.

Percival, Robert V., Alan S. Miller, Christopher H. Schroeder, and James P. Leape. 1996. *Environmental Regulation: Law, Science & Policy*, 2d ed. Boston: Little, Brown.

Sunstein, Cass R. 1993. Endogenous Preferences, Environmental Law. *Journal of Legal Studies* 22(2): 217–54.

Thompson, Barton H. 1996. The Endangered Species Act: A Case Study in Takings and Incentives. *Stanford Law Review* 49(2): 305–80.

Tiebout, Charles. 1956. A Pure Theory of Local Expenditures. *Journal of Political Economy* 64(5): 416–24.

U.S. Department of the Interior. 1995. Protecting America's Living Heritage: A Fair, Cooperative and Scientifically Sound Approach to Improving the Endangered Species Act. Washington, D.C., March 6.

Wiener, Jonathan. 1994. *The Beak of the Finch: A Story of Evolution in Our Time*. New York: Knopf.

Willig, Robert D. 1976. Consumer Surplus Without Apology. *American Economic Review* 66(4): 589–97.

Wilson, Edward O. 1984. *Biophilia*. Cambridge: Harvard University Press.

Chapter 9

Viewing Wildlife through Coase-Colored Glasses

Terry L. Anderson

By definition wildlife presents a unique problem for students of property rights because it lives in "a natural undomesticated state." Being in this state implies a lack of human interference and control. Moreover, removing wildlife from its natural undomesticated state is costly. Hence wildlife is typically an open access resource and potentially subject to overexploitation.

Of course, if wildlife is not scarce either because of abundance on the supply side or because it has no value to humans on the demand side, leaving wildlife as an open access resource will not matter. Under these conditions, economic overexploitation cannot occur.

As the value of wildlife rises, ownership will matter. In the common pool, wildlife is subject to the rule of capture where the only good animal is a dead animal. This was the case with bison in late-nineteenth-century America. In the buffalo commons there was no incentive to leave animals for future reproduction; if you did, someone would kill them before you reaped the gain from your conservation. Not surprisingly, open access wildlife are subject to extinction, a subject that has received significant attention in the economics literature.

Of concern in this chapter, however, are the problems created by unowned wildlife when those wildlife conflict with other assets such as

I am indebted to P. J. Hill, Andy Hanssen, and David Buschena for their comments and to Donald Leal for allowing me to use examples from our coauthored book, *Enviro-Capitalists: Doing Good While Doing Well* (Anderson and Leal 1997). The essay was completed while I was a John M. Olin Visiting Fellow at the Cornell Law School.

land or domesticated livestock. In this case, conflicts will arise over who is responsible to whom for damages caused. Is the owner of the assets affected by the wildlife obligated to accept the consequences of the wildlife? Again, if the wildlife is not valuable to others, the owner of other assets can simply eliminate the wildlife without imposing costs on others. Controlling mosquitoes provides an obvious example (assuming there are no external costs from spraying). But if the wildlife are valuable, are the people who value them obligated to compensate the asset owner for damages? For example, do elephant lovers in the United States have an obligation to rural Africans who lose crops or lives to rogue elephants? More generally, the question is: Who will capture the value of wildlife and who will bear the cost of providing habitat?

With rising wildlife values either for consumptive use or existence values and with conflicts over wildlife damage, property rights theory suggests that people will put effort into defining and enforcing rights to wildlife. How successful they are will depend on two types of transaction costs, those related to the technology of defining and enforcing property rights and those dependent on the costs of contracting with other resource owners.

Traditionally the costs of defining and enforcing property rights depend on the costs of fencing, but in a more modern context they could include radio tracking or satellite monitoring (see Anderson and Leal 1991). Obviously, constraining or monitoring the movement of wildlife reduces their natural undomesticated state and changes the nature of the good, but it also allows owners to capture the value of the wildlife and hence provides the incentive to conserve species and enhance habitat.

Contracting costs are the costs of negotiating, measuring, and monitoring agreements among owners of assets combined in the production process. These will depend on many variables, including the number of people involved, the ease with which wildlife impacts can be identified, and the informal and formal rules that govern human interaction. These rules can be particularly important to the extent that the state claims ownership of wildlife as it usually does in the United States.

This chapter focuses on these contracting costs and on the ability of individuals to contract with one another to determine who owns the wildlife. It is based on the insights of Ronald Coase, who won the Nobel Prize for his writing on the reciprocal nature of costs that arise when the use of assets conflict with one another. Few economists have analyzed the ownership of wildlife in terms of Coase's ideas. Two exceptions are Amacher, Tollison, and Willett (1995) and Lueck (1995). Amacher et al. consider the problem of eagle protection in a Coasean context. As they note, "the problem of devising a scheme to protect the eagle is parallel to some extent to that of the pollution example. That is, for the eagle problem, transaction costs and other costs of internalizing the relevant externalities . . . are significant and warrant the investigation of alternative liability assignment schemes" (Amacher, Tollison, and Willett 1995, 45). Lueck focuses on the transaction costs of wildlife management determined mainly by the wildlife territory relative to the optimal size of land holdings in other uses (especially agriculture). From the transaction cost paradigm, Lueck concludes that the property rights and regulations over wildlife "exist because they economically mitigate the wealth dissipation that results from incomplete ownership" (Lueck 1995, 21).

Coase's (1960) insights into the reciprocal nature of costs are used here to consider how transaction costs vary with alternative property rights and liability regimes and how contracting and vertical integration allow owners of wildlife and wildlife habitat to cope with positive transaction costs. The next section applies the Coasean framework to different combinations of single and multiple owners of habitat and single and multiple owners of species, asking how alternative property rights and liability regimes affect transaction costs. Integration of wildlife ownership and habitat ownership provides an alternative to contracting that is the subject of the third section of the chapter. The fourth section contains case studies of contracting and vertical integration that suggest ways in which private parties are able to reduce the transaction costs associated with preserving wildlife and wildlife habitat. The chapter concludes with a discussion of the difficulty of contracting when wildlife and habitat are owned by the state.

The Reciprocal Nature of Wildlife Cost

Wildlife and wildlife habitat will be underproduced through market processes if the contracting costs between the owners of wildlife and the owners of habitat prohibit exchange. As Coase pointed out, this is because, without contracting, reciprocal costs from individual A's actions can impact individual B's production costs. For example, in the case of a domestic cow owned by individual A wandering onto the property of individual B, the property rights can specify that the owner of the cow has the right to let his cow wander or that the owner of the land has a right to be free from wandering cows. Coase taught us that the assignment of rights is immaterial to the efficiency of the outcome if transaction costs are zero. In other words, either A bears the costs if he must pay for damage caused by his wandering cows, or B bears the costs if he must pay A to keep the cows out. Coase's point was that either way, the costs are borne by someone. Of course, the distribution of wealth will vary dramatically with alternative rights assignments.

When transaction costs are positive, however, not only will alternative property rights and liability rules change the distribution of wealth, they will alter the allocation of resources by altering the ability of owners to contract with one another over the costs. Positive transaction costs arise because it is difficult to identify who is causing what costs or because it is difficult to exclude free riders. In the case of wildlife, the extent of these two problems will depend on the number of habitat owners and species owners and on the difficulty of identifying and assigning reciprocal costs.

There are seven combinations of habitat ownership and wildlife ownership determined by single or multiple ownership of species and single and multiple ownership of habitat and by the separability of costs. In the case of multiple ownership of either habitat or species, there is the possibility that the reciprocal costs are separable, meaning that they can be assigned to a given landowner or species owner, or that they are nonseparable, meaning that they cannot be easily determined and assigned. Therefore, multiple ownership raises the possibility of the free rider problem or the holdout problem. We consider here the transaction costs associated with the seven different combinations and the implications for private contracting for wildlife habitat.

Single Species and a Single Habitat Owner

Begin with the simplest combination of one habitat owner and one species owner. Like Coase's and later Ellickson's (1986) wandering cattle or like Cheung's (1973) orchard owners and beekeepers, the allocation problem is a matter of two owners contracting with transaction costs, a function of measuring and monitoring the contractual terms. Assuming that the measurement and monitoring costs are low, the assignment of rights or liability makes little difference. For example, if there is a single owner of lions and those lions prey on livestock, either the single lion owner will have to pay the single livestock owner or vice versa; either way there will be no external costs and the optimal number of lions and livestock will be determined by private contracting. Under these conditions we would expect contracting between owners to handle reciprocal costs.

Single Species and Multiple Habitat Owners

Transaction costs rise with increasing numbers of habitat owners and species owners[1] and with the costs of measuring and monitoring reciprocal costs associated with the interaction between habitat owners and species owners. First, suppose that there are multiple habitat owners with a single migrating species owned by one party and that the impact of migrating species on alternative land uses are measurable or separable. In the case of marauding lions this means there are now many livestock owners, but there is still only one owner of lions. In the Coasean context the habitat owners can either pay the species owner to mitigate losses from predation or the species owner can compensate the habitat (livestock) owners for their losses.

In this case, as with Coase's train emitting sparks and burning crops, making habitat (livestock) owners liable introduces the potential for a free rider problem. With a train passing many landowners, if one owner pays the train owner to reduce sparks, the rest can free ride. Hence, the transaction costs of collective action among landowners can negate the possibility of a contractual solution. Similarly, if one livestock owner pays the lion owner to reduce the number of lions, other livestock owners benefit without paying. Even if the impact of the species on each habitat owner is easily identifiable, the greater the number of habitat owners, the greater the costs of collective contracting. Hence, where the species migrate among multiple properties, assignment of liability to the species owner reduces transaction costs by eliminating the potential free rider problem among habitat owners.

The case of multiple habitat owners and a single species owner is complicated further if the species depends on all the habitat but the contribution of each property is not separable. For example, suppose a herd of elk spends the winter feeding on one property, the spring calving on another property, and the summer and fall feeding on another. If each property is necessary to survival of the species, it will be difficult to separate the contribution of each habitat owner. Joint production without separability implies that each habitat owner contributes to the overall production of the species, but contributions are not easily measurable. This is similar to joint inputs in any production process wherein separating contributions of individual inputs is costly or where withholding the services of a specialized input reduces the rents from production. In this situation, the owner of a nonseparable input can engage in postcontractual opportunism and hold out for a higher share of any rents from production (see Klein, Crawford, and Alchian 1978). In this case the holdout problem makes contracting between multiple parties more difficult and makes the potential gains from integration higher, a point discussed below.

Multiple Species Owners and a Single Habitat Owner

Now switch the example to multiple species[2] and a single unit of habitat utilized by all the species but owned by one individual. Assuming species cannot be restricted from the habitat, the free rider problem flips to the species owners. If any single species owner contracts with the habitat owner for provision of habitat, other species owners can enjoy the fruits of the contract without paying. In the Coasean context, this is equivalent to open range with multiple cattle owners. One cattle owner paying a crop owner to allow access for cattle that cannot be excluded allows the other owners to free ride. However, making the crop owner bear the cost of grazing or paying each cattle owner to keep out his cattle still internalizes the reciprocal cost and reduces transaction costs associated with the free-rider problem. In this case, rules that hold the landowner liable encourage the landowner to contract with each individual species owner to obtain the optimal number of species.

Suppose, however, that the costs to the single habitat owner of hosting multiple species are nonseparable, meaning that it is not possible to discern the impact of an individual species on the output of land. Postcontractual opportunism raises its ugly head on the side of the species owners, each of whom can hold out for a larger share of any production rents, if the habitat owner is required to pay species owners to keep them off his property. Again under these circumstances, integration of input ownership into a single firm may provide a lower-cost way of eliminating the holdout problem.

Multiple Species and Multiple Habitat Owners

The highest transaction costs occur when there are multiple owners on both sides of the transaction. Even if costs are separable, multiple owners of species and multiple owners of habitat all have an incentive to free ride. But if costs are nonseparable, multiple owners of species and multiple owners of habitat also have an incentive to act opportunistically and hold out for a larger share of the rents. Again an integrated firm offers a private contractual solution to this transaction cost problem.

The Wildlife Firm

As Coase (1937) noted in his much earlier paper on "The Nature of the Firm," when contracting costs for individual owners of property are high enough to prevent contracting, transaction costs can be reduced by integration with all inputs owned by a single residual claimant. This integration makes the owner of the firm the residual claimant and hence gives him the incentive to take account of reciprocal costs. There is still the problem of measuring and monitoring input performance, but the residual claimant gains from accurately accessing the marginal benefits and marginal costs associated with measurement and monitoring.

In the case of wildlife, where multiple owners of either habitat or species or both create the free rider problem and/or the holdout problem, integration provides a possible solution to private contracting. If a single firm owns both the habitat and the species, reciprocal costs are internal to the single-owner decision maker. As with any type of joint production, the owner of wildlife and wildlife habitat may still face problems of assessing the nature of costs in joint production, but correctly doing so improves profits. Lions and leopards both may kill livestock and the damage contribution of each may be costly to discern, but the owner benefits from finding the optimal mix.

As Cheung (1983) points out, the most extreme form of vertical integration is the state where all inputs and outputs are owned by the sovereign government. This would mean that the state would own both the wildlife and wildlife habitat. Unfortunately, vertical integration via the political sector raises the prospect of three other types of transaction costs, especially when there are multiple agencies for both species and habitat.

1. Legal constraints make it difficult if not impossible for different agencies to contract with one another. For example, the Endangered Species Act essentially assigns species ownership to the U.S. Fish and Wildlife Service, but state fish and wildlife agencies also claim some authority over species. The habitat, on the other hand, is controlled by the Forest Service, the Bureau of Land Management, the National Park Service, and state land agencies, to mention a few. Like private parties, the agencies can act as free riders or holdouts. Moreover, these agencies are often restricted from contracting with one another to reduce species. Witness the problem of reducing the number of bison migrating out of Yellowstone National Park into Montana or the difficulty of reintroducing species such as wolves or grizzly bears onto public lands.

2. Agency personnel are not residual claimants with a clear objective function such as profit maximization. This makes it difficult to hold agencies accountable and to reward them for producing the optimal mix of wildlife and habitat.

3. The principal-agent problem is exacerbated in the political sector where it is difficult to know whether the agency is producing what the citizen/principals desire. Because of the difficulty of the state acting as an agent for the citizens, state ownership is a form of multiple ownership with all its attendant problems.

Though vertical integration in the form of state ownership can overcome the free rider problem and holdout problem, these other three
transaction costs reduce the likely success of state ownership.

Of Coase and Wildlife

The various combinations outlined above can be illustrated with case
studies of how private contracting can solve wildlife habitat problems,
even in a world of positive transaction costs, and of how public laws
can raise transaction costs, making private contracting difficult.[3] The
examples of private contracting show how transaction costs have been
overcome to assign rights and liability, engage in contracts, and measure and monitor contract performance. In some cases, as Coase suggested, private contracting between separate parties can resolve the
reciprocal nature of costs, in others integration works better, and in
others political ownership is tried with mixed results.

Private Contracting

A perfect example of private contracting to solve the problem of
wildlife damage comes from the unlikely case of a predator, the wolf.[4]
Realizing that wolf reintroduction into the northern Rockies was so controversial because it would require livestock to bear some costs from
predation, Hank Fischer, northern Rockies representative for Defenders
of Wildlife, took an innovative tack. He and his group claimed liability
for the potential predator. In 1987, Fischer raised a fund of approximately $100,000 by selling prints by a well-known Montana artist de-
picting wolves howling around the geysers of Yellowstone National
Park. There may still be some free riders among people who value
knowing wolves are roaming the mountains of Montana, but voluntary
contributions tied to a poster were sufficient to put a compensation fund
in place.

Fischer announced that his group would use these funds to compensate livestock owners for losses due to wolf predation. Since the incep-
tion of the compensation program, the fund has paid out approximately
$45,000, a small amount compared to the corpus of the compensation
fund.

Of course, some controversy arises over the burden of proof that predation on livestock is due to wolves. Defenders of Wildlife defers to
the Montana Department of Livestock's predator control officer whose
responsibility it is to investigate livestock kills. If he says it is a wolf,
the fund pays; if he is not sure, it does not. For livestock owners who

experience losses and who are convinced wolves are the culprit but cannot prove it, there is a perceived flaw in the system. But any system of liability requires proof, and so some will bear uncompensated losses because the burden of proof is not met. The important part of this story is that it shows how assignment, or in this case acceptance, of liability for the species "owner" provides a Coasean solution to the single species, multiple habitat owner problem.[5]

Elk provide another example of private contracting where contracting costs are higher because the contribution of each habitat owner is non-separable. Elk migrate among properties—spending spring on one property where they raise their young, summer and fall on another property where they graze on lush grass, and winter on another where they struggle to survive until the spring thaw. Separating and measuring the contribution of each parcel is impossible because each is crucial to species survival.

Ted and John Flynn, third-generation ranchers who live on their family cattle ranch near Townsend, Montana, overcame the multiple habitat owner problem in 1987 by organizing hunters into a group called Greyson Creek Meadows Recreation, Inc. Through this organization recreation members pay a fee that is used to contract with several landowners for access to hunting. In the "good old days," hunters could range for miles in any direction without seeing other people and without worry of trespass. But things began changing in the 1980s. With only a few hunters seeking access, landowners could be neighborly and provide a "free lunch," but population and hunting pressure were increasing the cost to the landowner of providing that lunch.

Facing more restrictions on access, the Flynns and their friends had to adjust if they wanted to preserve habitat and access. Land ownership around the Flynn ranch is fragmented, ranging from small cabin sites to thousands of acres, and these smaller units cannot provide the diversity the elk need. Obtaining access to the land in fragmented ownership required that the Flynns organize Greyson Creek Meadows Recreation, Inc., to collect fees and exclude nonpayers. The land involved elk range for all seasons. According to the organization's rules, Greyson Creek members pay a fee for access and in some cases an additional fee if animals are harvested on a specific piece of property. The group also posts and patrols the land against trespass, carries liability insurance, and agrees to abide by several other rules including only driving on the properties to retrieve game or get to cabin sites. For the landowner, this arrangement removes most of the hassles of managing hunters and provides additional income. In 1996, members of Greyson Creek paid an annual fee of $450 for individuals and $500 for families for combined fees of approximately $15,000 for approximately 30,000 acres of private land.

While not as productive as large, contiguous holdings, the Greyson Creek properties have abundant numbers of elk and deer and increasing populations of black bears, mountain lions, coyotes, and eagles. With vehicular access restricted, both game and nongame species are being found in areas where previously there was too much human pressure. Members are encouraged to harvest the more mature elk and deer so as to improve the quality of the herds. The Flynns are cutting some timber on their property, but they are doing so selectively to balance timber profits, cattle grazing, and wildlife habitat. Though there are no annual game censuses, Greyson Creek members agree that the restricted access and more systematic management of the properties have increased the number of species they see and improved the quality of the recreation experience.

Migrating waterfowl also provide an example of private contracting with multiple landowners. Ducks and geese migrate over vast territories, nesting in Canada, flying across the United States, and wintering in Mexico. While all the habitat contributes to the survival of waterfowl, the nesting habitat is critical. Between the 1950s and the 1990s, North American duck migrations fell from more than a hundred million to less than fifty million because nesting habitat was lost in the upper midwestern United States and in southern Canada.

Recognizing this problem, Charles Potter, then director of the Delta Waterfowl Foundation, essentially claimed "liability" for the ducks while they are nesting. Potter recognized that farmers in the region known as the prairie pothole region were draining potholes to create additional farmland. This was creating a classic reciprocal cost Coasean problem; draining the potholes was impacting waterfowl, but keeping the habitat meant less productive farmland.

The Delta Waterfowl Foundation, supported entirely from private contributions from individuals, companies, conservation organizations, and private foundations, contracts with farmers to produce waterfowl by protecting the nesting habitat around prairie potholes on their land. Delta Waterfowl believes that the Adopt-A-Pothole program can make a significant impact because 95 percent of the ducks raised on the prairies of the upper Midwest and southern Canada are produced on private farmlands. Prior to the program, the landowner had little or no economic incentive to maintain or restore pothole habitat and may have even faced a disincentive from government farm programs that subsidized draining potholes.[6] As a result, over the last fifty years hundreds of thousands of acres of potential duck factories have been lost.

The Adopt-A-Pothole program created a way of raising capital from hundreds of individual contributors in the United States and Canada by giving them a sense of ownership in a pothole. Each contributor receives an aerial photograph of his or her adopted pothole, a quarterly report on its status, and an annual estimate of duck production. Adopt-A-Pothole achieves its goal through innovative contractual arrangements consisting of multiyear land leases and production contracts. The land leases pay farmers approximately $7 per acre to maintain pothole habitat and $30 per acre to restore pothole habitat. Production contracts, on the other hand, pay directly for duck production, thus giving the farmer an incentive to invest in improving nesting habitat.

The program has been overwhelmingly successful both in terms of raising capital and in terms of duck production. Contributions totaled nearly $1 million after only two years of operation, and the list of supporters grew from 250 to more than 1,000 individuals and organizations. By 1994, some 18,000 pothole sites had been enrolled from farms in Manitoba, Minnesota, and North Dakota, providing nesting habitat for mallards, canvasbacks, shovelers, blue-winged teal, green-winged teal, gadwalls, lesser scaup, redheads, and pintails. These adopted potholes are fast becoming North America's duck factories. For instance, nest density is twice as great for adopted sites compared to unadopted sites, and nesting success averages 51 percent for adopted sites compared to 10–15 percent for unadopted ones. Moreover, for those adopted potholes using a special Delta Waterfowl Foundation nesting device affording greater protection from predators, nesting success was an astounding 90 percent (Delta Waterfowl 1993). Such early accomplishments have earned the program accolades from the conservation community. On June 8, 1994, the U.S. Wildlife Service named the Adopt-A-Pothole program the winner of its National Wetlands Conservation Award for the prairie pothole region.

Because South African laws allow private landowners who game fence their property to claim ownership of any wildlife contained therein, innovative approaches to contracting for wildlife and their habitat are evolving in that country. Dave Varty and Allan Bernstein, cofounders of Conservation Corporation (Conscorp for short), make no apologies for the fact that Conscorp is trying to turn a profit from wildlife. To the contrary, they, along with many other conservationists in southern Africa, believe that having profits as the driving force is the key to ensuring that wildlife and wildlife habitat will be around in the future.

Varty and Bernstein created one of the first large-scale businesses to invest in wildlife conservation. Prior to forming Conscorp, Varty owned Landolozi Reserve, one of South Africa's most successful commercial private wildlife ranches, and Bernstein was managing director of a company that raised money for investment in sub-Saharan Africa. As of 1995, the partners had raised $40 million[7] and had plans for a $20 million expansion project. In addition to Landolozi, Conscorp opened Phinda Reserve comprising 17,000 hectares of private land; negotiated an innovative contract with Kruger National Park that incorporates the 14,000-hectare Ngala private reserve on the western boundary into the park but gives Conscorp exclusive operating rights; and established Singita Reserve with 15,000 hectares where the Big Five (elephant, rhinoceros, cape buffalo, lion, and leopard) can be seen. The corporation is also diversifying beyond its initial four game lodges in South Africa by planning a new, 49,000-hectare game reserve near Victoria Falls in Zimbabwe.

Though wildlife ranching is not new to South Africa, the innovative contracting that Conscorp uses to make wildlife pay is. The corporation generally owns only small land parcels, enough to accommodate its lodges. For the rest, Conscorp contracts with surrounding landowners for conservation services. Rather than having to tie up capital in vast tracts, Conscorp has contracted for access to private lands for game viewing and hunting.

Consider the articles of association that Conscorp developed to contract with private landowners to form the Mun-Ya-Wana Game Reserve[8] in South Africa's northern Transvaal province. Mun-Ya-Wana encompasses 30,000 hectares. Among others purposes, the articles state that the purposes of the reserve are "to promote and conserve endemic wildlife and habitat within the confines of the area. . . ; to establish the Reserve as a sanctuary in perpetuity for endemic wildlife and habitat so as to enable sustainable resource utilisation . . . ; to endeavour to increase the area of the Reserve . . . ;" and "to maximise the long term economic and ecological value of the properties." Above all, the company tries to minimize congestion because "large numbers of persons on the Reserve are undesirable."

Because Conscorp is catering to tourists who want to enjoy game in the natural African bush, the company strives to keep all development on the reserve "congruent with the principle of minimal environmental impact and minimal aesthetic impact." Road use is strictly limited to those specified in the Articles of Association. Game drives must avoid residential areas and are coordinated through a radio network, with each member responsible for erecting and maintaining a base station. The number of game drive vehicles and boats is controlled by the company to avoid congestion problems. The architecture of all the structures erected on the reserve must be "ecologically and aesthetically sympathetic," and "the siting of structures and services on and to the reserve are placed in unobtrusive places so as not to have an adverse affect on the surroundings." To promote wildlife and maintain a natural setting, landowners agree not to keep domestic animals, even including dogs and cats. They can build structures on their property but only with written consent from the company and only after submitting detailed drawings and artist's impressions. To maintain the integrity of the reserve, landowners cannot subdivide their properties, and cannot undertake other commercial activities such as prospecting or establishing tent villages or caravan parks without agreement from the company.

Why would landowners be willing to agree to all of these restrictions by including their lands in the reserve? In a word, profits. Conscorp estimates that dry land cattle ranching earns approximately $21 per hectare per year and cropping earns $68. This compares to nearly $200 to $300 per hectare per year in Conscorp reserves. Conscorp director, Howard Geach, says, "We are demonstrating a form of land use involving wildlife as a sort of cash crop" (quoted in Koch 1995).

The perimeters of Conscorp properties are fenced with an eight-foot high game fence made of twelve strands of high-tensile smooth wire, and game within cannot be "tethered or enclosed in any cage or fence" and "irrespective of that game's ownership, will be entitled to graze, browse or feed anywhere on a reserve." To guarantee that animals cannot leave the reserve, each landowner is responsible for erecting a perimeter fence to company standards for the land under his control, but maintenance of the fence is the responsibility of the company. By the same token, to ensure the most natural setting and to guarantee free range for the animals, the landowner must "lift and remove the fences which surround or traverse his land, save where the fence in question is a perimeter fence . . . or a protection fence immediately adjacent to a dwelling." The company erects gates and garrisons guards at the gates to control access.

Because game is free to move anywhere on the reserve, Conscorp has written a very detailed contract specifying the rules for culling, hunting, and capturing. Prior to admission into the company, a census is conducted of the number and species of game for each landowner. If this census shows that the landowner's game populations are insufficient to contribute to the overall purposes, "then the prospective member shall be obliged to supplement the species, in kind or in cash as may be agreed with the Company." Each year another census is conducted to determine net changes in game populations, and the company allocates "proportionally to each land controller the overall increase or decrease in game numbers." Any disagreements over numbers are arbitrated by the state wildlife agency known as the parks board, and decisions are final and binding on all parties. Members are not allowed to introduce any new species to the reserve without prior written consent of the

company, but consent may only be withheld if the species is not indigenous to the region. The company can also introduce species with those
introduced becoming the property of the company. The agreement
allows landowners to "cull, hunt, or capture game" provided the activities follow the laws, regulations, and rules of the wildlife authorities
and provided the landowner obtains a permit from the company specifying the number of game to be taken. Any member who did not contribute any of a particular species to the collective herd is not entitled
"to hunt, cull or claim ownership or benefit from the proceeds of any
sale of that specie except where a separate agreement is in place." The
hunt, cull, or capture must take place within the landowner's boundaries. If an injured animal escapes to land controlled by another, "only
the leader of the hunt and one tracker may follow the specie of game in
question onto the land of another member in accordance with the rules
laid down from time to time."

Special provisions are made for the introduction of a species, such as
the rhinoceros, for trophy hunting. Again the animal cannot be prevented from ranging over the reserve, but when it wanders onto land
controlled by another, "the landowners will be obliged to agree on a
method of resolving this problem and allowing the owner of the introduced animal to hunt the animal on the property where it has moved to.
In the event that the parties cannot agree, it will fall upon the disciplinary committee of the directors or, failing that, the Directors to rule as a
matter of urgency in this matter to achieve a speedy solution." Conscorp has effectively used private contracting to overcome the transaction
costs that could preclude a Coasean solution.

Input Integration

Where transaction costs associated with private contracting between
separate owners are high, input integration where wildlife and habitat
are owned by a single firm provides an alternative. The first example
comes from the White Mountain Apache Indian Reservation in eastern
Arizona where the tribe effectively owns the land and the wildlife. The
reservation boasts a herd of 7,500 free-ranging elk on 750,000 acres of
diverse habitat ranging from oak chaparral at lower elevations to mixed
conifer forests at higher elevations.

Hunting records over two decades give some idea of the success elk
hunters enjoy on the Fort Apache Reservation. From 1977 to 1995,
nontribal hunters have taken ninety bull elk that have made either
Boone and Crockett or Safari Club record books. One of these, in the
"nontypical" category, scored 445 points and ranked second in the
world in 1996. By comparison, this is about the same number of record

elk that have been taken from the entire state of Montana since record keeping began in 1932. Since 1980, nontribal hunters have enjoyed a 90 to 95 percent success rate on guided trophy elk hunts, with an average Boone and Crockett score hovering around 366.[9]

Let there be no misunderstanding; the trophy elk population on Fort Apache is not solely the work of mother nature. The resource base is large, the habitat is prime, and, according to reservation biologists, the genetics of the herd are ideal for producing trophy elk. But management has also played a pivotal role in producing trophy elk on the reservation.

Prior to 1977, elk hunting on the reservation provided good hunting in relation to nearby national forest lands. Still, it was nowhere near the quality it is today. Then the Arizona Game and Fish Department maintained responsibility for wildlife management on the reservation. It used its personnel to patrol the reservation during hunting season. Typical of state game policies, the state agency maximized the number of hunter opportunities by issuing 700 nontribal hunting licenses priced at $150 each for any size antler elk. The revenues from license sales went to the state. Left out of the management equation were the residents of the reservation, the White Mountain Apache tribe.

Though the Arizona Game and Fish Department might have maximized hunter numbers, it did not maximize hunting quality. From 1970 to 1976, only three record-book elk were harvested on the reservation. Moreover, the situation was likely to get worse considering the evidence from other states such as Montana, Idaho, and Washington where large numbers of hunters resulted in overharvesting of immature bulls, the seed crop for future trophy bulls (see Wenders 1995).

Fortunately for both the tribe and the reservation's elk, tribal leaders recognized that they could do a better job and earn significant returns for the tribe by integrating their ownership of the habitat with ownership of the elk. To capture these potential benefits, the tribe assumed control of hunting on the reservation and implemented its own management philosophy.

In 1977, with the backing of Tribal Chairman Ronnie Lupe and the eleven-member Tribal Council, Phillip Stago, director of the Fort Apache recreation department, informed the state that the tribe was assuming complete control of all hunting and fishing on the reservation. Eventually, the state acquiesced, removing state wardens from the reservation for the 1977 hunting season.

The tribe's first step toward quality management was the reduction of hunting pressure on immature bulls. It accomplished this by ending the general (any antler) state-sanctioned elk hunt and replacing it with the trophy elk hunt. Elk hunting permits declined dramatically from 700 under state management in 1977 to thirty under tribal control in

1979. At the same time, the tribe increased the price of a permit tenfold from $150, the price charged by the state, to $1,500 in 1979. Even though total short-term revenues declined, those that were collected from the sale of permits were retained by the tribe. Moreover, the reduction in harvest led to a significant increase in long-term revenues.

It took the tribe several years and a U.S. Supreme Court case to get the state completely out of wildlife management, but by 1981 the tribe finally had complete control. Under tribal ownership of the species and the land, the quality of hunting blossomed. Mature bulls as a percentage of all bulls observed on the reservation increased dramatically and now stand at 73 percent, a sign of a quality herd. Not only did the number of mature bulls increase significantly, the number of record-book elk increased from just three during the final six years of state management to an average of eight per season under tribal management.

On the other side of the globe, Black Africans are using communal ownership of elephants and lands to solve wildlife and habitat conflicts.[10] As the following story suggests, the conflicts can be significant when they involve elephants.

Darkness comes quickly to the East Caprivi, being so close to the Equator. Bevan Munyali, a village game scout, appointed by his community who live in this region of Namibia, helps light the fires.

Together with the other men, they will spend the night in this farmer's corn field, trying to protect their food crops from the elephants. Usually it is the lone bulls that come, as they have each night this week, trampling the crops and eating hundreds of pounds of corn as they pass through the area. Bevan is worried. He must balance the farmer's concerns regarding the elephant with his own task, which is to help his community to conserve their natural resources and the wildlife in the area.

Hours slip past. Bevan and the farmer doze beside the glowing embers. But then the crack of dry branches wakes them, indicating that something big is moving in their direction. Two fully grown bull elephants crash into the field. The farmer shouts to wake the others, and in unison they start banging steel pots together. The elephants turn to face the noise, their sensitive ears flapping in aggravation. Then they charge. Three tons of muscle standing eighteen feet high at the shoulder, the bulls rush forward, sending the farmer and his family running for safety.

Realising the danger, Bevan fires two blasts from his shotgun into the air, in the hope that the elephants will retreat. Instead, one of the bulls wheels around and heads straight towards him. Defenseless, Bevan retreats from the field. The elephants continue on their way, eating and trampling the ripe corn underfoot. No doubt, the farmer and his family will be short of food for the remainder of the year. (Hylton n.d., 5)

This account of a peasant farmer's struggle against wild animals is rarely portrayed in Hollywood versions of African wildlife, but it shows the potential costs to Africans trying to sustain a living off their land. Wildlife management problems result because indigenous people trying to live off the land often have to compete with wildlife; in other words, wildlife is a liability rather than an asset. These people generally resent the fact that land is being set aside for animals rather than for people. Moreover, out of the parks and reserves come lions, leopards, elephants, and hippopotamuses that range onto communal lands where they destroy crops and livestock and occasionally people.

Inspired by wildlife experts and environmental groups such as the World Wildlife Fund, the Zimbabwe government has tried to change the incentives by allowing vertical integration of land and wildlife ownership. The government's innovative wildlife management program is known as CAMPFIRE (Communal Area Management Plan for Indigenous Resources). This "entrepreneurial approach to rural development" (Environmental Consultants [Pvt] Ltd. 1990, 3) is based on the principle that the benefits from wildlife must go to those who pay the financial and social costs of coexisting with wild animals.

The Nyaminyami District Council with a human population of 35,000 and communal lands totaling 363,000 hectares offers a prime example of how CAMPFIRE can work. In 1989, its inaugural year, Nyaminyami's CAMPFIRE project generated Z$272,000 from safari hunting and another Z$47,000 from culling to keep local wildlife populations under control. With the major capital costs of Z$201,933 covered by funds donated by conservation groups, the district had Z$16,000 to distribute among the twelve separate communities after paying operating and administrative costs and allocating 12 percent for capital investment and reserves (Thresher 1993, 45).[11]

Another early CAMPFIRE success came in the Beitbridge District.[12] However, unlike Nyaminyami, the Beitbridge project was financed completely by the returns from wildlife. Recognizing that different communities within the district make more sacrifices to provide wildlife habitat, the Beitbridge Council distributed wildlife profits unequally to communities within the district, giving more to those communities that produced more, higher-valued animals. In 1990, the Beitbridge District CAMPFIRE project generated Z$50,235 from hunting. Of that amount, the community of Chikwarakwara received Z$43,930 or 87 percent of the total because it was the top wildlife producer. Two other neighboring communities received much smaller amounts because of lower animal numbers. National parks also paid the Beitbridge District Council Z$46,000 for revenues accrued from past safari hunting, from which Chikwarakwara received another Z$20,000. Free to determine how their proceeds would be used, the people of Chikwarakwara decided to pay each of the 149 households in the community Z$200 as a wildlife dividend. The remainder of the earnings went toward building a school and purchasing a corn grinding mill. Though the Z$200 dividend may not seem like a lot to wealthy westerners, it represented nearly a doubling of average annual income for each family.

Changing attitudes toward wildlife are becoming apparent among the people involved with CAMPFIRE. "Now the people of Beitbridge are reported to be talking seriously about how to control poaching. They are considering the possibility of reducing a household's cash payment by the value of any animal poached by any of its members, e.g., Z$75 for an impala" (Thresher 1993, 50).

CAMPFIRE projects in other districts have taken their cue from these early successes. The Binga District project capitalizes on its long shoreline at the western end of Lake Kariba and the adjacent Chizaria National Park that forms a repository for wildlife that roam onto communal lands. The project includes a lease with a private hunting safari operator and joint ventures with two photographic safari operators. Plans are also underway for a commercial fishing venture. The Hwange District is developing the "scenic attractions and natural resources" near the Zambezi River and Victoria Falls by forming joint ventures with two photographic safari operators who are building tourist camps in the areas (Environmental Consultants [Pvt] Ltd. 1990, 23). Bulalima Mangwe District has set aside a marshy area west of the Natal River for an elephant herd that forms the basis for safari hunting agreements between the district council and private operators.

Another example from South Africa illustrates how integration of land and wildlife ownership can solve the Coasean problem. In South Africa, landowners who fence their land according to governmental requirements own the wildlife species within the fences, even if the wildlife had been free ranging prior to the fences. Under these rules the single landowner can integrate to become the owner of multiple species as well. This integrated owner then usually contracts with professional hunters who are carrying out management practices and providing paying customers.

Angus Brown and his partner Clive Perkins are professional hunters who have contracted with Piet Lamprecht, the owner of approximately 20,000 acres in the northern Transvaal province of South Africa. According to their contract, Angus Brown Safaris provides the accommodations and guide services while Piet provides the habitat. In this case the accommodations include beautiful African huts with walls woven from reeds and roofs thatched from grass. Horns from animals indigenous to the area adorn the walls and skins cover the floors. Food in the camp is typical South African fare highlighted by the wild meat killed by the hunters. Natural pans and developed water holes (bore holes as they are called there) provide water for the animals in this arid land on the edge of the Kalahari Desert. At these water points, archery hunters sit in tree stands or ground blinds for hours waiting for animals such as the zebra to come for their daily drink. Of course, all of these capital improvements are possible only because hunters are willing to pay a fee for the services.

Perhaps more important, however, is the impact that hunting revenues have on land management. As a landowner, Piet Lamprecht gets a share of the daily hunting fees paid by the customers. He also gets nearly two-thirds of the trophy fees paid for each animal. These trophy fees are crucial to the incentives faced by Angus, Clive, and Piet, for unlike most hunting in North America where hunting fees generally go to state or federal agencies, trophy fees in South Africa go to the people who have the largest stake in good wildlife management. Like a menu at a restaurant, the hunter faces a price list for the animals available:[13] tsessebe, $1,500; zebra, $750; kudu, $700; wildebeest, $700; blesbok, $250; warthog, $100; impala, $80; and the list goes on. Angus, Clive, and Piet mutually agree on these prices that reflect the relative scarcity of the species. With warthogs and impala abundant, their prices are low; with tsessebe and waterbuck scarce in the region, their prices are high.

What impact do these fees have? On the demand side for the hunter facing a budget constraint, the trophy fees force a careful weighing of preferences against price. Hunters might think a tsessebe would make a nice addition to the trophy room, but the price of $1,500 translates into two or three of the less scarce big animals such as zebra or kudu. Indeed, though not available on Piet's property, Angus Brown Safaris can arrange hunting for elephant or rhino, the two most scarce of the hunted species, at a price of $12,000 and $28,000, respectively. Needless to say, this reduces the quantity demanded by pricing most hunters out of the market.

The supply-side impacts of these incentives are important because they compensate the landowner for providing a home for the wildlife. Piet's ranch used to be mainly a cattle operation with some cultivated fields of peanuts and cotton, but the potential for hunting profits has changed this. All but a handful of cattle have been removed from the land. Interior fences necessary for cattle management are being removed to give wildlife a freer range, and water points are being converted from troughs to more natural water holes. Because of hunting revenues, instead of carrying several hundred brahma cattle, the land supports approximately 500 impala, 150 kudu, 100 wildebeest, 150 gemsbuck, 50 tsessebe, 50 waterbuck and numerous other species. Angus, Clive, and Piet begin each hunting season with an estimate of the number of harvestable animals and agree on prices for each species.

They consider ways to improve the habitat and whether it would be profitable to invest in importing other species, such as cape buffalo, indigenous to the region but now largely absent. Without the profits from hunting, less habitat would be available for the indigenous species of the Kalahari and fewer animals would survive.[14]

Well-known safari writer Peter Hathaway Capstick captures the important nexus between hunting and habitat management in South Africa.

> The interesting thing is that untold hundreds of thousands of hectares and *morgen* that even a few years ago were scrub grazing for a mix of game and cattle have now been entirely allocated to game. Why? Economics, as always. Game pays its own way, eats nearly anything, is more resistant to disease and predators and generally produces a higher and better use for the land. . . . Even the old enemies become assets to the farmer who switches from cattle to game. One friend of mine used to lose as many as thirty calves a season to leopards. . . . Now, those same leopards are worth a cool $1,000 to $1,500 [in 1995 the values would be $2,500 to $3,000] each to sport hunters, not a bad trade-off for animals that caused a liability of well over ten grand and had to be poisoned! Tell me, is that bad for leopards? . . . This sort of thinking is, then, the basis of the modern mechanics of the safari industry in Africa, whether in South Africa or Sudan. Once again, the elemental economic rules apply, whether to the garment district of New York City or the wait-a-bit thorn of the Luangwa Valley or the Okavango Swamp: What can justify its existence stays, what can't must go, whether a skirt-manufacturing plant or a herd of impala. Sorry, I don't make the rules. (Capstick 1983, 18–19)

Problems with State Ownership

Because the costs of contracting among private parties or the costs of integrating ownership are not trivial, the typical approach especially in the United States has been to establish state ownership of wildlife.[15] Given the high costs of defining and enforcing property rights to wildlife, this extreme form of input integration can make sense (see Lueck 1995). Regarding state ownership of wildlife, Lueck and Yoder (1997, 123) argue that "the structure of wildlife institutions generally complements the modern political philosophy of federalism." The national government controls species that migrate across international and state boundaries, and state governments control wild species that migrate within state boundaries.

But governmental ownership is certainly not without its problems for two reasons. First, state ownership of wildlife can thwart the establishment of private rights to wildlife ownership and the evolution of innovative contractual arrangements. Because state ownership puts wildlife in the category of a public trust, some scholars and practitioners contend that private landowners certainly should not be able to profit from allowing access to wildlife and perhaps should not even be able to exclude the public from access even if the wildlife are on private land. As a result, in Montana, for example, private landowners can charge access fees but they have no control over bag limits or seasons, and they cannot charge trophy fees associated with successfully bagging an animal. Even opening a game farm with "introduced" wildlife is nearly impossible in Montana, where the state wildlife ownership is the dominant legal doctrine.

The second problem with state ownership results from the difficulty of contracting between state agencies or between state agencies and private landowners. With state ownership there is no residual claimant to the benefits of improving wildlife or habitat management. Indeed for the most part, the governmental agencies responsible for wildlife management have no control over habitat. For example, suppose a state game agency wants to increase the number of elk on U.S. Forest Service land currently used for cattle grazing and that the value of the land for wildlife is clearly greater than for cattle. Although there are potential gains from trade, federal multiple use management laws would make it impossible for contracting to take place (see Hess and Holechek 1995).

The bison migration from Yellowstone National Park further illustrates the problem. Because the bison carry brucellosis, a bacteria potentially harmful to livestock and humans, the bison are not welcome by many outside the park. In effect the National Park Service owns the bison while they are in the park, but once they cross into Montana, they become the responsibility of the Montana Department of Fish, Wildlife, and Parks and the Montana Department of Livestock. When they cross, however, the bison are generally on U.S. Forest Service land. Combining the lack of clear bison ownership by any agency with the different responsibilities and the political pressures, it is small wonder that bison migration from Yellowstone Park is so controversial. If Yellowstone Park officials were liable for the potential damage from brucellosis and could contract with other agencies to mitigate the problem, contractual solutions might even evolve in the context of governmental ownership. However, with no clear liability, the problem will remain a political football.

Conclusion

Viewing wildlife through Coase-colored glasses teaches some important lessons. In resolving the locus of rights and hence liability, ownership of both habitat and wildlife should be put into the hands of residual claimants who have the ability to trade those rights. The contracting examples presented above occur because private actors have established a residual claim on the rents from wildlife and are able to contract for the relevant inputs to produce those rents. Hank Fischer's wolf compensation scheme, for example, works because he has to worry about repeat dealings with ranchers and because he and his group capture some of the benefits associated with the existence of wolves. South African wildlife are thriving because private landowners and wildlife owners (sometimes one and the same) are residual claimants who can contract over inputs.

State and federal laws and policies should do all they can to lower the transaction costs of defining and enforcing rights to wildlife and habitat and of trading those rights. Where transaction costs allow it, private ownership should be encouraged; where they are prohibitive due to the holdout and free rider problems, governmental ownership may be the only choice, but even here, liability must be clear and contracting with other agencies and private landowners should be allowed. Lueck and Yoder (1997, 123) conclude that "as the value of wildlife and wildlife habitat increase over time, we expect that the analogous institutions corresponding to wildlife will become more well defined. . . . [W]e might expect to see more private management units . . . with government regulations assigned only to those aspects of private contracting that are most contentious."

One of the most contentious private contracting problems is that the benefits associated with providing wildlife habitat cannot be measured or captured by a residual claimant. Though the free rider problem is no doubt real, the above cases suggest that private contracting is working despite positive transaction costs. Facilitating these solutions often requires getting legal restrictions on ownership of habitat and wildlife out of the way so contracting can take place. Perhaps there would still be underprovision of species preservation, but this is not a reason to throw the baby out with the bath water. Just because there might be a free rider problem, we need not forgo the potential benefits of private contractual solutions. As Coase noted, the view through Coase-colored glasses would be entirely rosy were it not for transaction costs. On the other hand, even with positive transaction costs, wearing Coase-colored glasses gives us a clearer view of how private contracting for wildlife could work.

Notes

1. In the case of species, there can either be multiple owners of a single species or multiple owners of different species. Either case raises the possibility of the free rider problem or the holdout problem.

2. It does not matter if there are different species owned by different owners or multiple numbers of the same species owned by different owners. It is the fact that there are multiple owners of species that increases the transaction costs. If there are different species, it is assumed that they use the same habitat as might be the case of elk and deer.

3. This subtitle is patterned after Ellickson (1986). The case studies in this section are drawn from Anderson and Leal (1997).

4. It should be noted that the term *owner* is used loosely here. In the first case that follows, clearly wolves are not owned in a legal sense. But responsibility for damages they cause has been accepted by Defenders of Wildlife, making the organization a de facto owner at least in terms of liability for damages.

5. Of course, this solution is not a true property rights solution because Fischer is not legally liable for all wolves. If the wolf population grows, there is some point at which economics would say there are enough wolves, but will Fischer be willing to bear the liability for this many wolves? And if he is, he might decide that some wolves should be shot, but the U.S. Fish and Wildlife Service may not let him. Hence there is no assurance that the optimal number will be obtained.

6. See Anderson and Leal (1991, 57) for further discussion of the impact of farm subsidies.

7. All dollar figures were computed assuming a ratio of 3.66 South African rand to the dollar.

8. All references to terms of agreement between Conscorp and the landowners come from the Certificate of Incorporation and Notarially Certified Copy of Memorandum and Articles of Association available from the Conservation Corporation, P.O. Box 1211, Sunninghill Park 2157, South Africa.

9. For details, see Anderson and Leal (1997, 150–53).

10. For further details see Hess (1997).

11. Conversions from Zimbabwe dollars were made assuming Z$1 is equivalent to approximately U.S. 40 cents.

12. For details, see Thresher (1993) and Anderson and Leal (1997, 153–56).

13. These are 1996 prices.

14. Data are from conversations between the author and Angus Brown. See Anderson and Leal (1997, 69–72).

15. For an excellent discussion of state wildlife ownership, see Huffman (1995).

References

Amacher, Ryan C., Robert D. Tollison, and Thomas D. Willett. 1995. The Economics of Fatal Mistakes: Fiscal Mechanisms for Preserving Endangered Predators. In *Wildlife in the Marketplace*, ed. Terry L. Anderson and Peter J. Hill. Lanham, MD: Rowman & Littlefield, 43–60.

Anderson, Terry L., and Donald R. Leal. 1991. *Free Market Environmentalism*. San Francisco: Pacific Research Institute for Public Policy and Westview Press.

————. 1997. *Enviro-Capitalists: Doing Good While Doing Well*. Lanham, MD: Rowman & Littlefield.

Capstick, Peter Hathaway. 1983. *Safari: The Last Adventure*. New York: St. Martin's Press.

Cheung, Steven N. S. 1973. The Fable of the Bees: An Economic Investigation. *Journal of Law and Economics* 16(1): 11–33.

————. 1983. The Contractual Nature of the Firm. *Journal of Law and Economics* 26(1): 1–21.

Coase, Ronald H. 1937. The Nature of the Firm. *Economica* 4(November): 386–405.

————. 1960. The Problem of Social Cost. *Journal of Law and Economics* 3(1): 1–44

Delta Waterfowl. 1993. *Delta Waterfowl: Adopt a Pothole Summary Report*. August.

Ellickson, Robert C. 1986. Of Coase and Cattle: Dispute Resolution among Neighbors in Shasta County. *Stanford Law Review* 38(February): 623–87.

Environmental Consultants (Pvt) Ltd. 1990. *People, Wildlife, and Natural Resources—The CAMPFIRE Approach to Rural Development in Zimbabwe*. Harare, Zimbabwe: Zimbabwe Trust.

Hess, Karl, Jr. 1997. Wild Success. *Reason* 29(5): 32–41.

Hess Karl, Jr., and Jerry L. Holechek. 1995. Beyond the Grazing Fee: An Agenda for Rangeland Reform. *Policy Analysis* 234. Washington, D.C.: Cato Institute.

Huffman, James L. 1995. In the Interests of Wildlife: Overcoming the Tradition of Public Rights. In *Wildlife in the Marketplace*, ed. Terry L. Anderson and Peter J. Hill. Lanham, MD: Rowman & Littlefield, 25–42.

Hylton, Victoria. n.d. *The Wild Harvest*. Southern Wild Productions, Johannesburg, South Africa.

Klein, Benjamin, Robert G. Crawford, and Armen A. Alchian. 1978. Vertical Integration, Appropriable Rents, and the Competitive Contracting Process. *Journal of Law and Economics* 21: 297–326.

Koch, Eddie. 1995. Hunting for Solutions. *Optima*, August.

Lueck, Dean L. 1995. The Economic Organization of Wildlife Institutions. In *Wildlife in the Marketplace*, ed. Terry L. Anderson and Peter J. Hill. Lanham, MD: Rowman & Littlefield, 1–24.

Lueck, Dean, and Jonathan Yoder. 1997. Federalism and Wildlife Conservation in the West. In *Environmental Federalism*, ed. Terry L. Anderson and Peter J. Hill. Lanham, MD: Rowman & Littlefield, 89–131.

Thresher, Valerie. 1993. Economic Reflections on Wildlife Utilization in Zimbabwe. Master's thesis, University of California, Davis.

Wenders, John T. 1995. The Economics of Elk Management. In *Wildlife in the Marketplace*, ed. Terry L. Anderson and Peter J. Hill. Lanham, MD: Rowman & Littlefield, 89–108.

Chapter 10

Cooperating on the Commons: Case Studies in Community Fisheries

Donald R. Leal

Avoiding the "tragedy of the commons" has entailed essentially two policy prescriptions, both grounded on the argument that user cooperation is not possible (Hardin 1968). The first calls for turning management of the commons over to the government with its "major coercive powers" (Ophuls 1973, 228). Unfortunately, this approach has a tendency to promote inefficient production and often fails to prevent resource depletion (see Anderson and Leal 1991, 51–60; Anderson and Leal 1993, 161–83; and Leal 1995). The second calls for privatizing the commons. Not surprisingly, this approach has been shown to lead to much lower production costs, much higher incomes, and greater conservation for relatively stationary resources such as oysters (see Agnello and Donnelly 1975 and 1979). However, privatization isn't feasible in every situation. It may be too costly or socially unacceptable.[1]

Often omitted from policy prescriptions is the possibility that, at least in some cases, a community of users can apply their own system for managing the commons. This chapter reviews examples of these as they are applied to fisheries. The fact that they exist goes against the prevailing assumption that, left on their own, users are always locked into a destructive pattern of competition.

A similar version of this chapter was published in *Taking Ownership: Property Rights and Fishery Management on the Atlantic Coast*, ed. Brian Lee Crowley. Halifax, NS, Canada: Atlantic Institute for Market Studies, 1996. Reprinted with permission.

Customs, Culture, and the Commons

Until recently, traditional economic analysis has given scant attention to the potential for societal norms as constraints on human behavior, on the grounds that human nature is inherently self-interested (see Ostrom 1990; Anderson and Simmons 1993). But real-world examples to the contrary have forced institutional economists to confront the prospects of customs and culture as constraints on human behavior. In the absence of either government control or individual ownership, not all resources held in common are subject to the tragedy of the commons (Ciriacy-Wantrup and Bishop 1975). In the Swiss alpine regions, for example, communally owned lands have remained productive for grazing and logging for centuries (Netting 1981). The rules governing access and use of these lands are devised by villagers. Similarly, indigenous populations around the world sustain resource production collectively without government control or private property rights (Rushkin 1986; McCay and Acheson 1987; Berkes 1989; Schlager and Ostrom 1992; and Anderson 1995).

In light of these examples, political economists have become increasingly interested in customs and culture as constraints on human action. In her analysis of the commons, Ostrom (1990, 35) considers the constraints of societal norms that she believes:

> reflect valuations that individuals place on actions or strategies in and of themselves, not as they are connected to immediate consequences. When an individual has strongly internalized a norm related to keeping promises, for example, the individual suffers shame and guilt when a personal promise is broken. If the norm is shared with others, the individual is also subject to considerable social censure for taking an action considered to be wrong by others.

Though the exact conditions under which societal norms arise are not yet well understood, several factors have come to characterize "long enduring" community management systems (Ostrom 1990, 90). These are systems that have survived anywhere from one hundred to a thousand years overcoming various social, political, and economic changes. As such, they are considered desirable design features for community management. A list of these factors follows.

1. Boundaries must be clearly defined so that individuals within a group know which resources they can harvest and how, and so that individuals outside the group know when they are trespassing.

This factor is viewed as a critical step in promoting collective action on the part of users sharing the commons. So long as boundaries are uncertain no one knows what is being managed and for whom. Moreover, local users face the threat that any benefits achieved through community management run the risk of being captured by outsiders. The presence of clearly defined boundaries is what distinguishes this form of common property from one that is subject to open access.

2. Group decisions require rules that determine how the group parcels out the value of the resource.

Simply defining the boundaries of a resource is not enough, however, because it is still possible for a limited number of appropriators to increase extraction rates so that they dissipate potential rents or totally destroy the resource itself. To avoid these outcomes, communities must develop rules of appropriation and users must adhere to these rules.

3. Customary rules must be linked to the time-and-place-specific resource constraints so that resulting rules are efficient. If they are not, there will be pressure to change them.

Tailoring rules to local conditions is another important contributor to robustness and longevity. Such rules take into account specific attributes of the resource being exploited, local economic and political conditions, and cultural views.

4. Because there is always the potential for self-gain, resources must be devoted to monitoring and enforcing the rules. That is, there either must be rewards for individuals who abide by rules or sanctions against those who violate norms.[2]

Ostrom (1990, 93–94) notes "that even in repeated settings where reputation is important and where individuals share the norm of keeping agreements, reputation and shared norms are insufficient by themselves to produce stable cooperative behavior over the long run." She goes on to note that there is indeed "substantial evidence" that participants in long enduring community management systems carry out effective monitoring and sanctioning activities to ensure rule compliance. Moreover, when appropriators design and enforce their own rules, they learn from personal experience which rules work and which do not, and which rules achieve the highest net benefits.

5. Where conflicting demands are likely to arise between group members, resolution mechanisms such as local arenas for bargaining are necessary (Ostrom, Walker, and Gardner 1993).

Even in smooth-functioning groups, disagreements are inevitable. A mechanism for settling such disagreements is critical to maintaining cooperation on the commons. In community systems where the likelihood of conflict is high, well-developed court mechanisms have been in place for centuries.

6. The rules must not be subject to change by higher levels of government.

According to Ostrom (1990, 101), when community management systems devise rules that lack legal authority to back them, they remain fragile at best. The danger is that outsiders may use the government to overturn the rules devised by a community.

For these factors to emerge and to be maintained on the commons, members perceive themselves as having strong group identity. A group that is relatively homogenous is said to have strong group identity. For such a group, "outcomes to other group members, or to the group as a whole, come to be perceived as one's own" (Brewer 1979, 322). Group identity reduces the efforts that people must devote to centralized authority or to definition and enforcement of private property rights, but it requires that members invest in maintaining societal norms and in keeping out people who do not share these norms. In the modern context, the controversy over restricting immigration illustrates how costly this can be.

If group identity is to be preserved, resources must be invested in limiting entry to individuals willing to accept the group's standards of conduct and to produce and maintain customs and culture. Tests for initial acceptance include such mechanisms as knowledge of the group's history, language requirements, and residency requirements. Rituals, ceremonies, and formal and informal education (apprenticeship programs, for example), also provide ways of inculcating customs and culture.

Ultimately, however, limiting entry requires the ability to threaten credible force to exclude individuals not sharing the groups' perspective. This requires collective action by the members that may be as simple as excluding an individual from some collective activity with significant economies of scale or as complex as mustering arms and threatening war. The modern nation state is the main mechanism for the latter role, but informal groups such as producer associations and social clubs play a role in excluding nonmembers and enforcing societal norms.[3] However, these informal organizations may lack the legal authority to exclude would-be entrants.

Outsiders wishing to enter the commons have two choices; they can negotiate with the group for permission to use the resource, or they can force their way in.[4] In either case, customary constraints are tenuous at best. With trade, formal, transferable property rights will be necessary, and, once traded, the users may not all share the group's perspective. Preventing trade with outsiders or requiring strict standards of acceptance for entry are two methods communities use to ensure integrity of the group. Such restrictions may be discomforting to some in the sense that those who value the resource may not be able to trade freely for it. On the other hand, such restrictions must be weighed against the net benefits generated by the community in sustaining use of the commons.

If access to the commons is opened to outsiders through conquest, the question is how, if at all, entry will be limited. Codifying and formalizing property rights is one solution. This substitution diminishes the role of customs and culture, but two possibilities for dissipating the value of the resource remain. First, codifying and formalizing rights begs the question of who gets those rights. Hence it pays to invest in the political process that allocates rights. Second, if the rights are not truly exclusive, chances for the tragedy of the commons are greatly enhanced.

Though both could have easily been avoided following customary Indian fishing rights, both of these value-dissipating options typified the Euro-American development of the Northwest Pacific coast salmon fishery.

Lessons from the Past

The coastal Tlingit and Haida Indians of pre-white Alaska had strong incentives to avoid the tragedy of the commons for sockeye salmon. Sockeyes are different from chinook, chum, and other salmon because they arrive early in spawning streams, remain there the longest, and show the lowest variation in numbers returning from one year to the next. Duration and stability, coupled with high nutritional value, explain why sockeyes were an important food source for the Indians. They are not found everywhere, however. Sockeyes migrate only in stream systems that include a freshwater lake. Their relative scarcity encouraged Indians to establish clear boundaries specifying who had access to the limited number of stream systems where sockeyes congregated on their journey to spawning beds. Access to these locations was limited to the clan or house group, the social organization that could be supported by the resource. The optimal size of organization was determined mainly by the scale economies associated with fishing. Thus, because five to eight men were required to deploy most traps and weirs, the house group generally possessed customary fishing rights at the mouth of a stream. However, in one case where a particularly large trap could be used, the village was the unit of ownership (De Laguna 1972, 387). Very small creeks could be "the special preserves of individuals" (Olson 1967, 12).

Langdon (1989, 308) notes that in addition to property rights "to the all-important salmon streams, natural resource territories included bear- and goat-hunting areas, berry and root patches, hot springs, sea otter grounds, seal and sea lion rocks, shellfish beds, cedar stands and trade routes." These management units could exclude other clans or houses from their fishing territories, thus localizing management decisions and restricting the potential for capturing the value of the resource to members of the clan or house. When territories were infringed upon, the trespasser was required to indemnify the owning group or potentially face violent consequences (see Oberg 1973 and De Laguna 1972).

Consistent with economic theory (see Demsetz 1967 and Anderson and Hill 1975), Northwest coastal Indians did not define and enforce property rights to resources that were not scarce. The Tlingit did not establish territorial claims to streams where species such as the pink or dog salmon were abundant (Olson 1967, 12). They also treated the open ocean as a commons because their technology did not allow overexploitation when salmon were in this environment. However, some bands did claim ownership of bottom fishing grounds for two important food sources, halibut and cod.

Management decisions were linked to the time-and-place-specific resource constraints through the eldest clan male or the *yitsati*. This person generally possessed superior knowledge about salmon runs, escapement, and fishing technology and therefore was in the best position to be the "custodian or trustee of the hunting and fishing territories" (De Laguna 1972, 464). The yitsati or "keeper of the house" had the power to make and enforce rules regarding harvest levels, escapement, fishing seasons, and harvest methods. Though there is debate over just how powerful the yitsati was (see Olson 1967), it is clear that salmon runs were sustained over long periods by local collective-choice rules that parceled out the rents from the resource and that these rules took into account time-and-place-specific knowledge. According to De Laguna (1972, 464), the yitsati "had the power of life and death in enforcing these regulations," thus guaranteeing that self-interest not constrained by societal norms could be sanctioned by collective force. The yitsati also assisted in parceling out goods produced collectively to members of the clan (Oberg 1973, 92–93).

To minimize enforcement and transaction costs within the proprietary groups, rights initially could not be transferred to those outside the clan. According to Oberg (1973, 63), "the exchange of clan property is against all principles of clan unity and never occurred in the old days." This allowed those with a proprietary interest in a fishing location to exclude people who might not abide by customary norms limiting self-interest.

Such limits on transfer conflicted with European notions of property in a heterogeneous society. The Russians were the first to confront Indian fishing rights. Acting as a monopolist, the Russian American Company denied individuals the right to fish, thereby making itself the sole negotiator with the Indians. The company then had the choice of using force to take fishing rights from the Indians or trading with them. It used both depending on relative military strengths, transaction costs, and the value of the salmon fishery in question. According to Goldschmidt and Haas (1946, 109), "The Russians . . . recognized the native ownership of this bay by giving the owner food and clothing." Langdon (1989, 314) concludes that "the introduction of the practice of leasing fishing rights was a fundamental departure from previous Tlingit practice and appears to be the Russians' major influence on the principles of property and management of salmon resources used by the Tlingit."

When the United States purchased Alaska from the Russians in 1867, leasing gave way to military conquest. "The major purpose of the military in retrospect was to protect U.S. citizens in their encroachment on Tlingit resources and impose U.S. legal concepts. This period has been termed the era of *flagrant neglect* in Alaskan history" (Langdon 1989, 314). Indeed by neglecting the authority of Tlingit to establish fishing rights and substituting the public trust doctrine from English common law, the U.S. government created the tragedy of the commons. "[B]y 1900 American common property principles were in force throughout southeast Alaska, at least insofar as the Tlingit and Haida were unable to keep Euro-Americans from fishing where they wanted to commercially" (Langdon 1989, 318). By allowing anyone to place traps and weirs at the mouths of rivers, there was little incentive to worry about escapement; a fish left to spawn was a fish potentially caught by someone else.

Washington

Not surprisingly, the result of ignoring native fishing rights was the same "legally induced technical regress" Higgs (1982) described for the Washington salmon fishery. Indians along the Columbia River had rights similar to those of the Tlingit. The Indians had private rights to fishing sites along the river and had intertribal agreements to allow sufficient upstream migration to ensure salmon recruitment. Unfortunately, once again state and federal governments allowed newcomers to circumvent these rights by placing nets across the mouth of the Columbia, ultimately decimating salmon populations and leading to state regulation. As Scott (1988, 19) notes, such political action runs counter to a long history of recognizing private rights in coastal fisheries "when we consider that there were already, in 1200 AD, in tidal waters, territorial fishing rights in England and a form of territorial salmon rights throughout the world in the 19th century, the legislative process can only be said to have reduced the characteristics of individual fishing rights."

Instead of recognizing the well-defined and enforced fishing rights, the U.S. legal system encouraged a race to catch fish where they gathered to spawn. Because this quickly depleted salmon runs, traps and weirs were banned only to be replaced by purse seine boats powered by internal combustion engines. The race to catch salmon moved to open waters. Ironically, from the country where private property was considered bedrock law came a socialistic legal system driven by political and military power.

Contemporary Community Fisheries

There are many contemporary examples of community managed fisheries. Most are spontaneously developed, informally organized arrangements that exist or existed without government recognition.

Maine's Matinicus Island

Francis and Margaret Bowles provide an example of a contemporary communal management system for lobster and herring fisheries off Matinicus Island, Maine. For the island's local lobster fishery, fishers claim a well-defined area of approximately 200 square kilometers around the island and actively defend it through extralegal means.

> They customarily signal a territory violation by opening the door and tying a half-hitch around the buoy of an outsider's trap. If this signal is ignored, an island lobsterman may haul up the outsider's traps and dump them together so that the buoys and warps become tangled. Actual trap cutting ensues only if these measures fail to convey the wisdom of removing the offending gear from the disputed area. (Bowles and Bowles 1989, 243)

The island's lobster fishery has operated successfully for over a century without official state recognition, despite expansion into regional markets and dramatic improvements in boat style, fishing technology, and navigational equipment. And while the number of fishers in the fishery has deviated little from the original number of thirty-six, movement in and out of the fishery does take place. Over the 1970–82 period, for example, Bowles and Bowles (1989, 239) observe that twenty-one men entered or left the fishery.

To ensure group conformity, island fishers strictly control who is accepted into their fishery. For instance, either one must live on the island and have island kinship ties or one can purchase property from a local fisher who then becomes an informal sponsor. The latter approach is akin to an apprenticeship program. In addition, one must demonstrate a willingness to cooperate with other fishermen and respect their fishing rights and equipment. A newcomer must also make the necessary investment of wharf access, boat, and traps. In the 1980s, this investment totaled roughly $125,000 (Bowles and Bowles 1989, 236).

On well-defended waters like those off Matinicus Island lobster fishers have instituted their own conservation efforts, benefitting both lobsters and fishers. "On Matinicus and Green Island, fishermen have agreed among themselves to limit the number of traps used," notes Acheson (1993, 73). In addition, in comparison to more open lobstering areas off Maine, well-defended areas like Matinicus have higher lobster density and higher fisher incomes. One measure of lobster density is catch-per-unit-of-effort. On Matinicus, catch-per-unit-of-effort is a little over twice that of more open areas (Acheson 1993, 74). In addition, incomes are almost 40 percent higher (Acheson 1993, 74).

Since the early 1900s, the island's herring fishery has provided an important supplement to lobstering. Two fishing techniques are used in the herring fishery. One is stop seining, which is the blocking of coves with nets after herring have entered them. The other is purse seining, which is netting herring in open water. While herring distribution and abundance are less predictable than lobster, the fixed nature of stop seining has encouraged the development of "purchasable and transferable" rights to use specific island coves to net herring (Bowles and Bowles 1989, 233). These rights are recognized and respected by local fishers. Sanctions for violating these rights are similar to the lobster fishery, including property destruction. In contrast, purse seining for herring lacks a limited entry system. Bowles and Bowles (1989, 255) conclude that excluding other purse seiners from a specific location is just not worth the "logistical costs" because of the variable distribution and abundance of herring in open water. As one might suspect, purse seining for herring in open water is highly competitive.

Lobstering and herring stop seining have benefitted because island fishers have been able to limit entry and introduce their own conservation measures for over a century. Still, Acheson (1993, 80) states that "[t]he of state of Maine could also annihilate the entire territorial system if it so chose by vigorously enforcing laws concerning trap cutting. It chooses not to do so. But the point should not be lost that the territorial system (i.e., communal ownership rights) exists only because of the benign neglect of the state." If the state should decide to intervene and deny the community's ability to prevent outsiders from accessing these local fisheries, boundaries would no longer exist and the incentive to maintain the community's management system would fall by the wayside.

Valensa, Brazil

Past success is no guarantee that a locally managed system will survive when the appropriation rules in place lack legal authority. The fishery in Valensa, Brazil, is a case in point (Cordell 1972). Initially, Valensa fishers encountered serious conflicts over the use of different fishing gear in a nearby estuary. Violence would erupt when different gear was placed too close together and became entangled. In addition, fishers would compete over the best fishing spots. Over time, local fishers came up with two approaches to resolve these problems. First, they divided the estuary into different fishing zones, each zone being assigned only one allowable gear. Second, they assigned fishing spots by drawing lots to determine the order in which a particular fishing spot could be used by each fisher. For decades, local fishers had been relieved of the problem of excluding outsiders because no one else was interested in fishing the estuary.

Unfortunately, the Brazilian government ignored local management success when it decided to "modernize" the Valensa fishery. The government made new nylon nets available to anyone who qualified for a bank loan arranged by the government through the *Banco de Brazil*. But local fishers did not qualify for the loan and did not have enough capital to purchase the nets on their own. A few wealthy individuals around Valensa qualified for the loans and purchased the nylon nets. They hired men who had never fished the estuary before to fish it using the nylon nets. The local fishers' management system crumbled as old and new fishers fought over fishing spots. Eventually the fishery was overharvested and abandoned.

Nova Scotia's Port Lameron Harbor

In devising fisheries policy, higher levels of governments often fail to take into account the use and effectiveness of locally managed systems. There are numerous fishing villages along the east coast of Canada where fishing has been the main source of income for generations. Fishers in many villages have developed a system of rules governing access and use of nearby fisheries. Davis (1984) describes one such system developed by the ninety-nine fishers of Port Lameron Harbor, Nova Scotia. Port Lameron fishers use a diversity of gear to catch cod, halibut, herring, mackerel, and lobster in nearby coastal waters. As one fisher explains, there are strong traditional ties among local fishers. "I've fished here all my life. So did my father and his father. Men in my family have been fish'n here for a long time. If anyone's got a right to fish here it's me and I'm no different than most of the fellas fish'n here" (Davis 1984, 145). Local fishers see themselves as having exclusive rights to their territory, which extends seaward 25 kilometers and along the coast 20 kilometers, and actively defend it against outsiders.

> For example, a Port Lameron Harbour fisherman, after setting his longline gear, watched a fisherman from a neighbouring harbour set his gear close to and, on occasion, across his line. Subsequently, the Port Lameron Harbour fisherman contacted the "transgressor" on the citizen band radio to complain about this behaviour. Other Port Lameron Harbour fishermen who were "listenin' in" on the exchange demonstrated support for their compatriot by adding approving remarks once the original conservation had ended. The weight of this support, coupled with the implied threat of action, i.e., "cutten' off" the offenders gear, compelled the erring fisherman to offer his apologies. (Davis 1984, 147)

In addition, local fishers have developed their own management strategy to avoid conflicts between fishers using different gear. Fishers divide their territory into different sectors, each sector distinguished by the particular fishing gear allowed.

Federal fishery authorities failed to recognize territorial boundaries and local management strategies in devising fisheries policy. Instead of providing legal backing, their initial efforts in the late 1970s were confined to requiring licenses for all fishing vessels and gear up and down the east coast of Canada. While such a requirement seems to pose little threat to local fishers, Port Lameron fishers did not enjoy a good experience during implementation. Local fishers failed to get gill net licenses for herring when they were first issued and were later denied access to these licenses when the government decided to freeze the total number available. The fishers vehemently protested and the government eventually allowed them to obtain the licenses. Still, the whole experience left Port Lameron fishers doubting whether the government would ever take their local strategies into account in future policy action. In the words of one fisher, "What do they know about what we do? Fisheries Officers are only around here now and then. How do they know what's best for us? We've fished here for a long time and we know what's best for the fishing ground. We know what it can take" (Davis 1984, 156). In contrast to federal fisheries policy, Martin (1979) notes that when provincial authorities controlled fishery policy years earlier, they had essentially supported locally managed fisheries. For example, in keeping with one of the conditions for successful community management, provincial authorities would provide arenas for local fishers to meet regularly and work out any conflicts over territories and gear.

Alanya, Turkey

In addition to intrusion and nonrecognition by government, sometimes it is the failure of local fishers to limit access themselves that places a local management system at risk. Berkes (1986) notes that unconstrained competition for the best fishing spots among the approximately one hundred local fishermen at Alanya, Turkey, was leading to conflict and, at times, violence in their fishery. A local fishing cooperative then designed a system that minimized the incentive to compete. Before each season, a list of eligible Alanya fishers is prepared along with a list of fishing locations on the commons. Selection of the latter is based on the most recent input from fishers and endorsed by them. In addition, care is taken in spacing fishing sites so that a fisher working in one site cannot effectively block the passage of fish to another nearby site occupied by another fisher. Fishers draw lots for their initial assignment of fishing sites on opening day of the season. Each day thereafter, each fisher then moves east to the next site until the end of January. After January, each fisher reverses course and moves west to the next site. This gives everyone about the same opportunities at the stocks of fish whose migration pattern goes from east to west between September and January and then from west to east from January to May. The local management scheme has apparently eliminated the need to fight over prime fishing sites, as evidenced by the fact that there were no signs of overcapitalization (Berkes 1986, 73–74). Still, the rules devised by the local cooperative do not include a rule for limiting access to local fishers. If fishers from outside the community ever decided to enter the fishery, the problem of competition could rematerialize.

Special Cases: Limiting the Catch

For the most part, community management in fisheries focuses on limiting entry and determining how fishing will be conducted to reduce wasteful conflicts among fishers. There are times, however, when a community of fishers has an opportunity "to control prices" (Christy 1996). In these incidences, fishers focus on limiting the size of the catch.

Yokohama City Fisheries Cooperative in Japan is one example. "Triggered by a sudden decrease in the value of the mantis shrimp following a bumper catch during the latter half of the 1970s, this cooperative started to limit the total catch by allocating individual quotas to each boat in 1977 in order to restrict the supply to market" (Hasegawa 1993). Similarly, during the 1950s, a local fishing cooperative in Raritan Bay, New Jersey, set individual quotas in the porgy and menhaden fisheries (McCay 1989). And in the 1970s, a similar quota system was developed by local fishers in the region's whiting fishery (McCay 1980).

The activities of Gulf Coast shrimpers during the 1930s through the 1950s fall into this category as well. Johnson and Libecap (1982, 1007) observed that shrimp fishermen unions and trade associations emerged along the Mississippi coast "to limit entry and negotiate price agreements with wholesalers and canneries." Their policies appear to have enhanced member incomes. But such efforts fell victim to the courts, which refused to exempt the collective actions of these groups from antitrust prosecution.

> A cooperative association of boat owners is not freed from the restrictive provisions of the Sherman Antitrust Act . . . because it professes, in the interest of the conservation of important food fish, to regulate the price and the manner of taking fish unauthorized by legislation and uncontrolled by proper authority.[5]

Nevertheless, by negotiating minimum price floors for smaller shrimp with local wholesalers that exceeded prices in distant locales, these organizations were successful in reducing the quantity of smaller, lower-valued shrimp demanded from Mississippi waters. A review of the transcript of the case and interviews "indicate that price fixing had the objective of increasing the value of the total catch by directing effort toward larger, more valuable shrimp" (Johnson and Libecap 1982, 1008). The unions' strategy to ensure a steady stream of large shrimp from the fishery seems to have worked. Louisiana shrimpers soon entered Mississippi waters in search of higher-valued, larger shrimp and that situation led the unions to take action to deny entry (Johnson and Libecap 1982, 1009). Ironically, the unions' effort to conserve the fishery by protecting small shrimp is now being carried out by every Gulf Coast state in the form of state-instituted, minimum-size rules for harvesting shrimp.[6]

The fact that these spontaneously developed management systems exist or existed leads one to reject the argument that competitive users are always incapable of supplying their own management systems for the commons. Unfortunately, because these approaches have not been recognized by government, and may in fact be declared illegal, they are always at risk of being dismantled.

In some instances, the government has supported community management systems. This support has been beneficial, since government recognition gives stability.

Scotland's Private Salmon Fisheries

In Scotland, privately held, transferable salmon fishing rights have existed for centuries. These rights exist for both territorial waters out to 12 miles and inland waters, and they pertain to commercial and recreational fishing. They were originally vested with the Crown, "but, as with land, the fishing rights have, over the centuries, been granted away to various persons" (Williamson 1993, 2). Today, individuals, companies, associations, conservation trusts, and fishing clubs own salmon fishing rights in Scotland. The Crown still holds the rights to some of the salmon fisheries, and these are managed by the Crown Estate Commissioners and may be leased to private parties.

The right to fish for salmon carries with it the right of the holder to exclude other fishermen from a well-defined area of water. Parliament has strengthened this right by making it a criminal offense to fish for salmon without written permission from the owner of the fishing right. Deed titles clarify the extent of this right, referring to sections of land that serve as reference points for boundaries. For example, a title might specify "the exclusive right of fishing for salmon in sea ex adverso the lands" (quoted in Williamson 1993, 2). The courts have supplied further clarification of this right when fishing changed from primarily near-shore areas to open-water areas using boats and nets by ruling that "the private right of property in the fishery does indeed extend to fishing from boats in the open sea" out to the twelve-mile territorial limit (Williamson 1993, 3). Definition was further refined when, along with other members of the European Community, Scotland prohibited fishing for salmon in waters beyond its territorial limit out to its 200-mile Exclusive Economic Zone (EEZ). In Scotland, salmon fishing rights stand on their own merit, reflected by the fact that salmon fishing rights do not require ownership of riparian land. The Scottish approach even contrasts with England where salmon and trout fishing rights are privately owned for inland waters but where the open ocean is a commons.

Communities of owners of salmon fishing rights were created by an act of Parliament designating 101 salmon fishery districts. Each district consists of the catchment area of a river or group of rivers and the adjacent sea. Owners in each district form a District Salmon Fishery Board to protect and develop the fishery. Boards appoint "water bailiffs" with powers to police the fisheries for poaching activities. They also invest in and operate hatcheries for restocking rivers. Each board is self-financed by levies on owners in the district. These boards exemplify how owners can implement internal rules, restrict entry into their territories, and coordinate funding for otherwise public goods.

Scotland's private salmon fisheries provide an opportunity for modern review of how a predominantly self-regulating system can work. Within Scotland's 200-mile limit, the government restricts salmon fishing to not more than 12 kilometers seaward. It also sets fishing dates and prevents the use of certain gear and the taking of immature salmon. But within these bounds, each owner is free to determine his own level of fishing effort. For example, there is no licensing of fishermen or fishing gear, and there is no restriction on the amount of fishing gear or on the amount of fish that can be taken. In essence, there is far less regulation than is typical of other salmon fisheries that are politically managed.[7]

Despite the absence of extensive government controls, Scottish salmon stocks have not been overfished by commercial fishermen. Indeed, the fisheries are healthy enough to support a lucrative inland salmon sport fishery on famous salmon rivers such as the lower Tay, Tweed, and the Spey. These rivers are managed for profit by those who own salmon fishing rights.

For the most part, the fishing effort for salmon is controlled by private owners of fishing rights. A commercial salmon fisherman, because he has an exclusive right to fish, determines fishing effort without worry of competition from interlopers. The decision to catch fish becomes a function of salmon abundance, the costs of fishing, and the benefit of allowing escapement. Moreover, to the extent that anglers located upstream and commercial fishers are able to carry out trades to catch fewer fish at sea, commercial owners will be able to realize additional benefits by investing in conservation.

Scotland was the first major salmon fishing country to prohibit the use of drift nets, the technology that has typically led to overexploitation in other fisheries. Unlike the Pacific Northwest where open water fishers usurped the Indian rights, the open ocean commons has been closed. Not coincidently, the ban, instituted in 1962, was supported by Scottish fishermen who could see harm to their long-term interest in salmon as a result of indiscriminant netting at sea. In contrast, in England, where the right to fish for salmon is a public right, drift netting continued until very recently when the government began a slow phase-out on the country's northeast coast.

Because salmon fisheries can be bought and sold in Scotland, salmon fishers are able to acquire fishing rights to a large enough area to operate efficiently. For example, management of salmon fishing in the estuary of the River Tay was consolidated near the turn of the century, when a single company purchased the fishing rights. The company decreased fishing effort, causing an increase in the annual return from the net fisheries in the estuary and in the annual return from the sport fishery upstream.

The Scottish system also seems to respond well to changing market conditions. It is now accommodating the growing demand for Atlantic salmon angling. The Atlantic Salmon Conservation Trust (Scotland) Ltd. recently purchased coastal salmon-netting rights from commercial netters for the purpose of *not* operating them, in order to increase salmon returns for the upstream sport fishery (Williamson 1993, 6).

Norway's Lofoten Fishery

Norway's Lofoten fishery has been described as the largest commercial cod fishery in the world both in terms of number of participants and the size of harvests (Jentoft and Kristoffersen 1989, 355). There have never been quota regulations in the fishery,[8] nor has there ever been a special licensing system. For nearly a century, fishers have successfully implemented their own fishing regulations, a responsibility delegated to them by the Norwegian government.

Over the last one hundred years, the fishery off the Lofoten Islands has been of considerable importance to Norway's fishing industry. During the 1980s, the number of fishers varied annually from 4,000 to 5,000, and the annual catch averaged approximately 110 million pounds (50,000 tonnes). In 1983, the export value of cod taken from the Lofoten fishery amounted to $140 million. About one-fifth of all Norwegian fishers get a substantial part of their income from the Lofoten fishery. Even though participants are considered local fishers from Norway's coastal communities, the group as a whole must also be considered heterogenous because of the variety of fishing gear they employ. Boats, for example, vary from 20 to 100 feet in length, with the largest made of steel and the smallest made of wood, and allowable gear includes hand line, long line, gill net, and Danish seine.

The impetus for self-regulation came from the enormous crowding problems and frequent gear conflicts experienced in the fishery during the latter half of the nineteenth century. Near the end of the century, Lofoten fishers decided they needed regulation to overcome crowding and gear problems, but they wanted to carry it out themselves because they believed "practical and local knowledge of the fishery" was necessary (Jentoft and Kristoffersen 1989). In 1897, the Norwegian government enacted the "Lofoten Law," which gave responsibility for regulating the fishery to them. The law presented the principles for organizing fishers democratically so they could decide the rules of the fishery and resolve conflicts.

The management system consists of fifteen control districts, each with separate, well-defined territories and responsible for developing and implementing regulations, enforcing these regulations, and resolving disputes among fishers within it. Enforcement includes fisher inspectors elected from each gear group and a public control force that includes control officers and inspection vessels. Judgments for regulation violations are rendered by the local magistrate. Both regulation and dispute resolution are carried out by each district's regulatory committee, made up of representatives from each gear group. The regulatory duties carried out by the committee include dividing the district's territory into separate fishing grounds, determining the size of each ground, and reserving each for a particular gear type. To participate in the fishery for a season, fishers must register with and obey the rules of the waters for the district in which they will fish.

Even though there is no direct rule to limit the number of fishers, fishing effort is controlled indirectly because the committee decides how big each space for a given gear type will be. For example, Danish seining, which represents the upper scale of fishing power among the allowable gear groups, has the least space available in the fishery. As a consequence, only about 15 percent of the participants in the Lofoten fishery use Danish seines. With some exceptions, fishers have determined which gear is allowed into their fishery; big, factory-owned trawlers and purse-seiners have never been allowed access to the Lofoten fishery.

Japan's Fishing Cooperatives

The large network of fishing cooperative associations (FCAs) governing much of Japan's near-shore fisheries provides a different look at a government-sanctioned system. By law, FCAs own the fishing rights to specific territories extending as much as 10 kilometers seaward (Jentoft 1989, 142). They manage the fishery resources in the best interest of their membership, subject to guidelines and conditions set down by national and prefectural governments. "They started as organizations to administer regulations, but gradually expanded into other areas, such as marketing, processing, leasing out fishing equipment, purchasing supplies, education and the like" (Jentoft 1989, 142). To fish a specific area under the jurisdiction of a cooperative, a fisher must be a member and comply with its rules or risk being expelled from the organization and its fishing area. Today, there are around five thousand associations scattered around Japan's coast.

Historically, these cooperatives have their roots in both community customary law and formal laws of Japan's feudal era—from 1603 to 1867. By feudal times, the increasing number of fishers on the limited coastal areas created many disputes within and among coastal villages. To help resolve these disputes, the feudal lords granted territorial fishery rights to village guilds and encouraged them to work out solutions among themselves. This system has undergone further refinements since then. In 1884, the government enacted "Working Rules for Fishermen's Associations" in which fishery management was transferred from the village guild to a "fishery association" made up of local heads of families who were fishers (Herrington 1972, 421). In 1941, the fishery association became known as the fishing cooperative. Sweeping reforms shortly after World War II enabled all fishers from a local community—not just heads of families—to be eligible for membership in a local cooperative.

How well do the cooperatives work? Cordell (1989, 334) observes that the overall benefits of these organizations can be seen in "the stability of coastal catches" and fisher incomes that are "equal to or above the national average." Herrington (1972, 438) noted years earlier that the cooperatives "have provided an effective and sensitive means" of limiting but not eliminating overfishing and of addressing the complexities of local administration "without requiring a massive government bureaucracy."

Although the rules have legal backing, adherence to them within a Japanese cooperative still depends very much on the cohesiveness of the local community. Ruddle and Akimichi (1989, 365) conclude that "[c]ommunity norms are flouted at one's peril and threat of social banishment (*murachibu*) is real and horrifying. On the other hand the anonymous regulations established by the prefecture [regional government]—and even more so those imposed by some faceless bureaucrat in remote Tokyo—are, in general, perceived as being far less binding." Short (1989, 380) confirms the importance of community cohesiveness:

Befu (1980) has documented examples of cutthroat competition and frequent conflict among fishermen of the Inland Sea region. What, then, prevents similar conditions from occurring in Shukutsu? The answer, I believe, lies in the social and cultural forces that bind the fishermen into a relatively tight-knit, cohesive group in which individuals are willing to compromise their interests for the sake of their group.

Short (1989, 384) also addresses conservation in light of community cohesion. In the case of the sea-urchin fishery, for example, the responsible FCA has imposed its own strict size limit, and members enforce it with the power of their own sanctions:

> When the sea urchin fishermen return to harbor, they dump their catches onto a plastic sheet for a sight check. No one really bothers to inspect closely, but a fisherman who takes undersized urchins can not expect to go undetected for long. Peer pressure is a strong motive for conforming to the regulations, but the threat of sanctions, such as gossip or even withdrawal of the accustomed mutual aid and assistance, must also be an important factor. (Short 1989, 383)

Short (1989, 383–84) notes that when an entire stock can be controlled by an individual FCA, members perceive themselves as ultimate beneficiaries of conservation. Unfortunately, when a fish stock spends only part of its time in an FCA's territory the benefits of conservation are weakened. For example, Otaru gill-netters in one FCA do not restrain their harvests on mobile flat-fish species, because they feel that any effort to do so would primarily benefit the trawlers who harvest them in waters that lie beyond the FCA's boundaries. Such a situation points to one notable weakness in the Japanese system: Well-defined community property rights do not extend out far enough to provide adequate coverage for certain mobile fish. If they did, then conceivably a near-shore FCA could resolve a coverage shortfall in a stock it shares with an outer fishery simply by purchasing a certain number of harvest rights (as in Scotland) from fishers in that fishery. It could also enter into a partnership with the outer fishery to determine how they would share the catch.

Fisher Management Based on Quota

Two governments have recently experimented with devolving fishery management to fisher organizations by allocating them quota and letting them manage it. The results have been mixed so far. In Canada, the Atlantic Herring Fishermen's Marketing Cooperative was given such authority in the mid-1970s for the Bay of Fundy herring fishery (Peacock and MacFarlane 1986). The federal Department of Fisheries and Oceans allocated exclusive quota to the cooperative and it, in turn, assigned individual quotas among its members. The cooperative was also responsible for policing vessel quotas, distributing surplus quota among the fleet, and collecting statistical information for the government. The government improved the cooperative's bargaining power with local processors by allowing its members to make "over the side" sales to foreign vessels. This provided an extra incentive for fishers to join the cooperative. In its first three years, the cooperative "so enhanced the earnings of fishermen, the quality of fish caught, and the ability to manage the fishery that many people began to see the Bay of Fundy herring fishery as a panacea and as a model for other fisheries" (Rettig 1986, 18). Unfortunately the cohesion in the cooperative soon disappeared. A group of fourteen fishers split away from the cooperative in a conflict over gear. Overfishing resumed, fish quality declined, and fisher earnings fell. The final blow for the cooperative came when the government withdrew the authorization for the cooperative's members to make over-the-side sales to foreign vessels. Members were left with little incentive to stay in the cooperative, and the cooperative unraveled. While the collapse of the fishery was due to excess capacity and the government's failure to deal with it at the outset of the cooperative program (Peacock and MacFarlane 1986), there were also problems with the cooperative itself. Unlike Norway's Lofoten fishery, there was no mechanism in place to resolve disputes among different gear users within the cooperative. And while the cooperative supposedly had a self-policing function, there were no real sanctions in place to support this function. The fact that the cooperative did not have the power to exclude from the fishery any fishers who decided to leave the cooperative was another indication that its power to regulate was highly suspect.

In the United Kingdom, the government has tried a similar experiment with better results so far. The experiment is highly unusual in that it is being tried with offshore fisheries. In the early 1970s, when the United Kingdom joined the European Economic Community, producer organizations were set up around the country. Their function was to organize raw-fish sales from the offshore fisheries' catch and to administer the community's price-support scheme. Initially, regulations on the fisheries were carried out by the government and quota was allocated to individual fishers. In 1984, the British government decided to allocate quota to each producer organization and let it distribute that quota among its members. Each organization also became responsible for regulating fisheries in their sector and enforcing the quota allocations among its members (Jentoft 1989, 142–43).

So far, the system has worked well although producer organizations see room for improvement. John Goodlad, chief executive of the Shetland Fish Producers' Organization Limited, thinks it has been a successful demonstration of devolution of management responsibility from the British government to fishers (Goodlad 1986). Chief executives in the

Scottish fish producers' organizations concur. Producer executives also believe that, because they carry out a marketing function, the regulations they devise will not disrupt the supply of fish greatly, and so fish prices have held fairly stable. In addition, there is more flexibility than there was under the old system. Thus, if, during the course of the year, it becomes clear that a producer organization will fall under its quota, the difference is added to next year's allocation. If, on the other hand, a producer organization overshoots its quota, the difference is subtracted from next year's total. Neither was the case under the old system. One problem voiced by many producers was that they did not completely control quotas. According to producer executives this deflates an organization's ability to maintain cohesiveness among members and weakens its power to regulate.

The final two community solutions are to be found in recreational fisheries. These examples provide additional insights into possible community approaches for fish that spend part of their time at sea and part in inland waters. Either of these could some day constitute a carefully controlled commercial Atlantic salmon fishery in addition to the present recreational fishery.

Environment Resources Management Association (ERMA)

The final necessity for the recovery of Atlantic Salmon—after the years of reducing river pollution and the temporary halting of the netting of Atlantic salmon on the high seas—will come, Les Dominy of the Atlantic Salmon Federation believes, from local Canadian communities and sportsmen. In Dominy's view, because "governments are simply running out of money," it is necessary "to unleash community energy, enabling local people to become stewards of their watersheds and fisheries" (quoted in Robinson 1994, 22). Moreover, the devolution of authority enables locals who tend to resist top-down regulations to use their time-and-place-specific knowledge, their knowledge of the idiosyncracies of each salmon river. Local responsibility along with the right economic incentives can foster strong local stewardship of amenities. According to the Atlantic Salmon Federation's Dr. John Anderson, "When communities and sportsmen have a vested interest in their local river, they begin to think of it as 'ours'; they want to do what they can to take care of it and increase production" (quoted in Robinson 1994, 22).

The Exploits River near Grand Falls, Newfoundland, provides a recent example of what can happen with community management of an Atlantic salmon fishery. Initially using public funding, the community constructed a fish elevator that allows salmon to climb past the 150-

foot waterfall on the river. Whereas the waterfall prevented fish from migrating any farther than nine miles upstream for spawning, construction of the fishway opened two hundred additional miles of river for salmon to spawn. The increase in salmon production has been astounding. Before the fish elevator opened in 1989, no more than 2,000 salmon migrated up the Exploits River to spawn under ideal conditions. But in just four years after the elevator became fully operational, returning spawning salmon numbered 20,000 to 22,000 fish per year. Looking down the road, the prospects are even brighter, as local managers foresee 100,000 returning fish in the next decade (Robinson 1994, 24).

The fish elevator project was spearheaded by the Environment Resources Management Association (ERMA), a private, nonprofit community organization. Conceived in 1983 and operational in 1985, it is an offshoot of early efforts by the Grand Falls Chamber of Commerce to enhance salmon-fishing prospects on the Exploits River and thus bring in more sport fishers—and their money—to the community. To launch its elevator project, ERMA submitted a proposal to various government agencies for financial support. Funded with federal dollars, ERMA employs fifty people to operate the elevator project and also an ultramodern hatchery and interpretation center.

The economic impact in the community is felt as more salmon have attracted more fishers to the community. ERMA manager Fred Parsons recalls when there were only 1,500 fishers on the Exploits per season. Now ten times that number of fishers flock to the river. According to Parsons, the Exploits River even competes effectively with salmon fishing on the Gander River, a world-famous salmon fishery in central Newfoundland. Parsons estimates, conservatively, that the Exploits' salmon fishery is bringing roughly C$3 million into the community.[9] The interpretation center, which gets 40,000 visitors per year, brings in additional tourist dollars.

Because salmon sport fishing is so important to the community's economy, ERMA has its own volunteer antipoaching patrol. Capitalizing on the immense popularity of the river among local fishers, ERMA trains some of these fishers to spot poaching activities. Volunteers are provided with a crest and a cap to let other fishers know that the river is under constant surveillance.

While public funding launched this community effort, Parsons and fellow ERMA workers are working to establish a fee fishing system to fund ERMA's operating costs for the fishway, the hatchery, the interpretation center, and future projects. "This will be tricky at first," says Parsons, because local fishers want their "turf" for fishing and fear that big dollars from visiting fishers will push them off the river. But Parsons believes that a well-planned fee fishing program can relieve these

anxieties. For example, ERMA is entertaining the idea of creating different fishing sections along the river to provide more options for fishers: Some sections will be more exclusive and therefore command
higher fees; others will be open to all at lower fees.[10]

Another potential revenue source may come from commercial harvesting of excess salmon. Says Parsons, "We foresee the day when a
limited commercial fishery can be permitted here without hurting the
river's salmon resource."[11] Parsons's strategy for commercial harvesting is like the management of early native salmon fisheries, when a
system of territorial fishing rights were in place along Pacific Northwest
salmon rivers prior to European settlement. Once the Exploits River
reaches optimum production numbers, a predetermined number of returning salmon would be allowed to pass through the fishway and continue upriver, guaranteeing an adequate number of fish for spawning
and for sport fishing. Then the fishway could serve as a trap, allowing
a local commercial fishermen's cooperative to harvest salmon. Parsons
feels that would help offset losses incurred by commercial fishermen
who have been hurt by the ban on netting salmon at sea.

A realist, Parsons thinks that the government can no longer afford to
undertake conservation efforts, so private conservationists and communities must devise and support efforts to produce natural amenities. In
Parsons's words, "The day of barking at the government is long gone.
We want to be part of the solution."[12]

Quebec's Community-Run Systems

Next door, in the province of Quebec, cooperation among an eclectic
collection of local groups has become an integral part of the community
solution. The provincial government tried for years to limit salmon gill-
netting by the Micmac Indians at the mouth of the Cascapedia River,
but the efforts were to no avail. Then, in 1992, a different tack was
tried. The government agreed to allow a local board to take over management of the fishery and to allow this board to be financed by Cascapedia user fees. The composition of the board lent itself to
cooperation because half of the board members were Micmacs while
the other half were local sportsmen and other community members.

Within two years, a new spirit of cooperation prevailed in the Cascapedia River salmon fishery. Gill-netting was greatly reduced by the
Micmacs, and in return, Micmacs were trained as river guides and river
guardians. More than one hundred Micmacs are employed as guides,
private wardens, and in other activities related to support of the salmon
sport fishery on the Cascapedia River. The income generated for the
tribe and the local economy from these services has more than compen-

sated for the reduced gill-netting. Salmon are worth about $30 when caught commercially, but $400 when caught by a sport fisher (Robinson 1994, 25). Harmony, conservation, and a lucrative sport-fishery are the byproducts of this locally managed fishery.

The Cascapedia River story is not the only success story in Quebec, largely because of the province's system of ZECs, or zones of controlled exploitation for hunting and fishing. In these zones, sportsmen pay various fees to local management organizations to hunt or fish species such as moose, bear, salmon, brook char, walleye, and lake trout.

To appreciate the impact of ZECs, it helps to know their history. Beginning in the 1880s, the provincial government began leasing huge areas of Crown land to private hunting and fishing clubs—in the early 1960s, they were leasing 60,000 square miles. These leases generated revenue for the government, provided jobs for people living in small remote communities, and provided the government with private guardians of game in remote regions where policing costs would otherwise be high.[13]

Because leases were neither long term nor transferable, the government was able to reverse its policy on private leasing in the mid-1960s. This reversal was prompted by the fact that people living in the population centers—especially Montreal, Quebec City, and other cities along the St. Lawrence River—were enjoying greater prosperity and more leisure time and, as a consequence, demanded more recreational opportunities. New road construction made remote areas more accessible. The areas under lease to private hunting and fishing clubs were especially attractive because, after years of private protection, fish and wildlife resources remained abundant.

Mounting public demand prompted the government to cancel many leases between 1965 and 1978. By the end of this period, half of the leases, which were attached to some 2,200 pieces of Crown land encompassing 29,923 square miles were canceled, and the government began turning some areas into government-run wildlife reserves for public use.

As more leases were canceled and as more government-run reserves were established, the costs of managing wildlife and recreation and of enforcing wildlife regulations exacted a heavy toll on government resources. Because the government eventually lacked sufficient funds and manpower to manage its reserve system, in 1978 it established hunting and fishing ZECs as a new user-fee-based concept for managing Crown lands. Two years later, the government established salmon-river ZECs, to capitalize on the growing popularity of inland salmon sport fishing and to incorporate local knowledge into the river management system. These salmon ZECs provided access to rivers containing Atlantic salmon, anadromous brook char, and landlocked brook char. And in 1987, the government expanded the use of ZECs to include waterfowl management. As of October 1994, eighty-two ZECs had been established throughout Quebec: sixty-three were general fish and game ZECs, eighteen were salmon fishing ZECs, and one was a waterfowl ZEC.

For each ZEC, a nonprofit corporation with a managing board of directors contracts with the government to develop recreation through user fees, to assist in monitoring fish and wildlife populations, and, in conjunction with government guidelines, to set and enforce seasonal harvest regulations. The government has provided subsidies for ZEC start-up costs and, until 1995, for operating costs where user fees were insufficient. This led critics to charge that ZECs often underprice recreational activities, encouraging overuse of resources and budget shortfalls. Also, some ZECs seem to lack important functional support, such as policing. In 1995, however, all ZECs were required to rely on their own income for support. The requirement for ZECs to be self-supporting should provide stronger incentive for them to price their recreational goods more realistically.

According to Yannick Routhier of the Ministère de l'Environnement et de la Faune, the management concept for ZECs is best characterized as a kind of "cooperative" whereby users have, through elected representatives on the managing board of directors, a voice in managing recreational use and controlling wildlife resources.[14] Routhier notes that many ZEC boards have broadened their composition to include other local business interests, such as chambers of commerce, and tribal interests, who want to promote economic opportunities from ZEC amenities. For example, the Corporation de Restauration de la Jacques-Cartier has responsibility for managing the Rivere Jacques Cartier, an Atlantic salmon sport fishery located approximately 100 miles northeast of Quebec City. Its board of directors has eighteen members, nine of whom are elected by recreational users and nine of whom come from municipalities within the river basin. The Rivere des Escoumins, another salmon fishery located 150 miles northeast of Quebec City, has a managing board of which one-third is recreational users, one-third local municipalities, and one-third Montagnais Indians (Ministère de l'Environnement 1994, 7).

In comparison to national forests in the United States, where hunting and fishing access and road use are priced at zero, fees are charged for ZEC membership (C$20) and road use (C$5.50 per day or C$40 per year). Fees for hunting and fishing vary. The average daily fishing fee for species other than Atlantic salmon ranges from C$12 to $15. The daily rate for fishing in a salmon ZEC, the crème de la crème of sport fishing, runs as high as C$75. Fees also vary with exclusivity of use. In the Ste. Marguerite salmon ZEC, for example, a ZEC member pays a daily salmon-fishing fee of C$32 on sections where the number of rods is unlimited, but C$59 where the number of rods is limited.[15] Nonmembers enjoy the same access privileges but at slightly higher user fees. Gross income from fees on the Ste. Marguerite was about C$140,000 in 1994, about equal to expenses for maintaining roads, providing private wardens, monitoring wildlife numbers, and carrying out conservation projects.

In addition to steady financial progress, ZECs are showing positive conservation results because of curtailed poaching activities and improved local management. Jean-François Davignon of the Atlantic Salmon Federation notes widespread improvements in protecting, monitoring, and conserving salmon fisheries (Davignon n.d.). Overall, he points out that ZEC managing corporations hire a combined force of 116 auxiliary wardens from local communities to assist the government in protecting wildlife and fisheries. For salmon rivers on the Gaspé Peninsula, salmon-spawning runs are much improved under local management. For example, "In 1984, Gaspé Peninsula rivers were only at 30 percent of required salmon spawners. Today, they are averaging between 80 percent and 100 percent" (Davignon n.d., 2). Among other benefits, a well-run ZEC can help bring much-needed income to a local area. For example, Nelson Bryant writes in the *New York Times* that salmon fishing in the Ste. Marguerite salmon ZEC resulted in US$1.5 million income to the local area (Bryant 1989).

Conclusion

The study of community management systems presents fertile ground for research if for no other reason than it challenges the notion that, without state control or pure privatization, users will always be locked into the tragedy of the commons. Certain conditions, such as clearly defined boundaries and strong internal sanctions, apparently allow these systems to withstand the test of time. It remains a fertile area for future research as to what situational variables are necessary, in addition to group homogeneity, for users to adopt institutional changes on their own for managing the commons.

Notes

1. For example, it would not make sense to divide up a fishing grounds and assign private property rights to the partitions if fish were highly mobile and

their concentrations unpredictable. Also, privatization can arouse intense opposition if it is seen as creating a "monopoly" to a natural resource.

2. Anderson and Hill (1983) provide a discussion of how residual claimancy enhances the prospects of individuals abiding by locally established rules.

3. Many activities of young people require that parents and children participate in fund-raising activities even though it might be more efficient for them to work at other independent jobs to raise money. A possible explanation for requiring participation is that it excludes those less interested in the activity and inculcates values that help overcome the free-rider problem.

4. Anderson and McChesney (1994) explain this choice.

5. *Gulf Coast Shrimpers and Oystermens Association v. United States*, 236 F. 2nd 658 (1956).

6. In general, the possibility of a local fisher group monopolizing fish prices is even more remote today because better transportation and storage systems for fresh fish ensure an even greater number of potential suppliers. Instead of monopoly concerns, the real concern today is the severe overfishing caused by the lack of an effective management system—i.e., a system that limits entry and controls fishing enough to ensure a steady supply of fish over time.

7. According to fishery analyst Herman Savikko of the Alaska Department of Fish and Game, the cost of administering controls as a percentage of total returns amounts to 2 percent in Alaska but 50 percent in the state of Washington.

8. Resource biologists contend that there is no observable relationship between the catch in Lofoten and the size of the spawning stock returning to Lofoten from the Barents Sea four to five years later. They argue the main threat for the sustainability of the cod stock is the government-regulated Barents Sea trawler fishery, the main catch of which is immature cod.

9. Fred Parsons, manager, ERMA, telephone interview by author, 20 December 1995.

10. Parsons interview.

11. Parsons interview.

12. Parsons interview.

13. Yannik Routhier of the Ministère de l'Environnement, telephone interview by author, 14 September 1995.

14. Routhier interview.

15. Information received by fax from Yannick Routhier, dated 22 November 1995.

References

Acheson, James. 1993. Capturing the Commons: Legal and Illegal Strategies. In *The Political Economy of Customs and Culture: Informal Solutions to the Commons Problem*, ed. Terry L. Anderson and Randy T. Simmons. Lanham, MD: Rowman & Littlefield, 69–83.

Agnello, Richard J., and Lawrence P. Donnelly. 1975. Property Rights and Efficiency in the Oyster Industry. *Journal of Law and Economics* 18(2): 521–33.

———. 1979. Price and Property Rights in the Fisheries. *Southern Economic Journal* (October): 253–62.

Anderson, Terry L. 1995. *Sovereign Nations or Reservations? An Economic History of American Indians*. San Francisco: Pacific Research Institute.

Anderson, Terry L., and Peter J. Hill. 1975. The Evolution of Property Rights: A Study of the American West. *Journal of Law and Economics* 18(1): 163–79.

———. 1983. Privatizing the Commons: An Improvement? *Southern Economic Journal* 50(2): 438–50.

Anderson, Terry L., and Donald R. Leal. 1991. *Free Market Environmentalism*. San Francisco: Pacific Research Institute for Public Policy, and Boulder: Westview Press.

———. 1993. Fishing for Property Rights to Fish. In *Taking the Environment Seriously*, ed. Roger E. Meiners and Bruce Yandle. Lanham, MD: Rowman & Littlefield, 161–83.

Anderson, Terry L., and Fred McChesney. 1994. Raid or Trade: An Economic Model of Indian-White Relations. *Journal of Law and Economics* 37(April): 39–74.

Anderson, Terry L., and Randy T. Simmons, eds. 1993. *The Political Economy of Customs and Culture: Informal Solutions to the Commons Problem*. Lanham, MD: Rowman & Littlefield.

Befu, H. 1980. Political Ecology of Fishing in Japan: Techno-Environmental Impact of Industrialization in the Inland Sea. *Research in Economic Anthropology* 3: 323–92.

Berkes, F. 1986. Marine Inshore Fishery Management in Turkey. In *Proceedings of the Conference on Common Property Resource Management, National Research Council*. Washington, D.C.: National Academy Press, 63–83.

———. 1989. *Common Property Resources: Ecology and Community-Based Sustainable Development*. London: Belhaven Press.

Bowles, Francis P., and Margaret C. Bowles. 1989. Holding the Line: Property Rights in the Lobster and Herring Fisheries of Matinicus Island, Maine. In *A Sea of Small Boats*, ed. John Cordell. Cambridge, MA: Cultural Survival, Inc., 228–57.

Brewer, Marilyn B. 1979. Ingroup Bias in the Minimal Intergroup Situation: A Cognitive-Motivational Analysis. *Psychological Bulletin* 86: 307–24.

Bryant, Nelson. 1989. Quebec Zones Aid Fish and Anglers. *New York Times*, July 13.

Christy, Francis T. 1996. Paradigm Lost: The Death Rattle of Open Access and the Advent of Property Rights Regimes in Fisheries. Paper presented at the Eighth Biennial Conference of the Institute of Fisheries Economics and Trade, Marrakesh, Morocco, July 1–4.

Ciriacy-Wantrup, S. V., and Richard C. Bishop. 1975. Common Property as a Concept in Natural Resources Policy. *Natural Resources Journal* 15: 13–27.

Cordell, John C. 1972. The Developmental Ecology of an Estuarine Canoe Fishing System in Northeast Brazil. Ph.D. dissertation, Stanford University.

————, ed. 1989. *A Sea of Small Boats*. Cambridge, MA: Cultural Survival, Inc.

Davignon, Jean-François. n.d. *The Quebec ZEC Story*. Quebec: Atlantic Salmon Federation.

Davis, A. 1984. Property Rights and Access Management in the Small-Boat Fishery: A Case Study from Southwest Nova Scotia. In *Atlantic Fisheries and Coastal Communities: Fisheries Decision-Making Case Studies*, ed. C. Lamson and A. J. Hanson. Halifax: Dalhousie Ocean Studies Program, 133–64.

De Laguna, Frederica. 1972. *The Story of a Tlingit Community*. Bureau of American Ethnology Bulletin 172. Washington, D.C.: U.S. Government Printing Office.

Demsetz, Harold. 1967. Toward a Theory of Property Rights. *American Economic Review* 57(2): 347–59.

Goldschmidt, W., and T. H. Haas. 1946. Possessory Rights of the Natives of Southeastern Alaska. Report to the Commissioner of Indian Affairs. Juneau: U.S. Department of the Interior, Bureau of Indian Affairs.

Goodlad, John. 1986. Regional Fisheries Management: The Shetland Experience. Notes prepared for the Norwegian/Canadian Fisheries Workshop, Tromso, June 16–21.

Hardin, Garrett. 1968. The Tragedy of the Commons. *Science* 162: 1243–48.

Hasegawa, A. 1993. Activities of Japanese Fisheries Management Organizations Established by Initiatives of Fishermen's Groups. *FAO Fisheries Report*, no. 474, suppl. vols. 1 and 2. Rome: FAO.

Herrington, William C. 1972. Operation of the Japanese Management System. In *Alaska Fisheries Policy*, ed. Arlon R. Tussing, Thomas A. Morehouse, and James D. Babb Jr. Fairbanks, AK: Institute of Social, Economic and Government Research, 419–43.

Higgs, Robert. 1982. Legally Induced Technical Regress in the Washington Salmon Fishery. *Research in Economic History* 7: 82.

Jentoft, Svein. 1989. Fisheries Co-Management: Delegating Responsibility to Fishermen's Organizations. *Marine Policy* (April): 137–54.

Jentoft, Svein, and Trond Kristoffersen. 1989. Fishermen's Co-Management: The Case of the Lofoten Fishery. *Human Organization* 48(4): 355–65.

Johnson, Ronald N., and Gary D. Libecap. 1982. Contracting Problems and Regulation: The Case of the Fishery. *American Economic Review* 72(December): 1005–22.

Langdon, Steve. 1989. From Communal Property to Common Property of Limited Entry: Historical Ironies in the Management of Southeast Alaska Salmon. In *A Sea of Small Boats*, ed. John Cordell. Cambridge, MA: Cultural Survival, Inc., 304–32.

Leal, Donald R. 1995. Turning a Profit on Public Forests. *PERC Policy Series*, PS-4. Bozeman, MT: Political Economy Research Center.

Martin, K. O. 1979. Play the Rules or Don't Play at All: Space Division and Resource Allocation in a Rural Newfoundland Fishing Community. In *North Atlantic Maritime Cultures: Anthropological Essays on Changing Adaptations*, ed. R. Anderson and C. Wadel. The Hague: Mouton, 277–98.

McCay, Bonnie J. 1980. A Fishermen's Cooperative, Limited: Indigenous Resource Management in a Complex Society. *Anthropological Quarterly* 53: 29–38.

———. 1989. Sea Tenure and the Culture of the Commoners. In *A Sea of Small Boats*, ed. John Cordell. Cambridge, MA: Cultural Survival, Inc., 203–27.

McCay, Bonnie J., and J. M. Acheson, eds. 1987. *The Question of the Commons: The Culture and Ecology of Community Resources*. Tucson: University of Arizona Press.

Ministère de l'Environnement et de la Fauna. Direction Des Territoires Fauniques. 1994. *Controlled Zones (ZECs): Nature and Operations*. Service de la Gestion Déléguée, Quebec, May.

Netting, Robert. 1981. *Balancing on an Alp*. New York: Cambridge University Press.

Oberg, K. 1973. *The Social Economy of the Tlingit Indians*. American Ethnological Society Monograph 55. Seattle: University of Washington Press.

Olson, R. L. 1967. Social Structure and Social Life of the Tlingit in Alaska. *Anthropological Records*, vol. 26. Berkeley: University of California Press.

Ophuls, W. 1973. Leviathan or Oblivion. In *Toward a Steady State Economy*, ed. H. E. Daly. San Francisco: Freeman, 215–30.

Ostrom, Elinor. 1990. *Governing the Commons: The Evolution of Institutions for Collective Action*. New York: Cambridge University Press.

Ostrom, Elinor, James Walker, and Roy Gardner. 1993. Covenants With and Without a Sword: Self-Governance Is Possible. In *The Political Economy of Customs and Culture: Informal Solutions to the Commons Problem*, ed. Terry L. Anderson and Randy T. Simmons. Lanham, MD: Rowman & Littlefield, 127–56.

Peacock, F. Gregory, and Dougald A. MacFarlane. 1986. A Review of Quasi-Property Rights in the Herring Purse Seine Fishery of the Scotia-Fundy Region of Canada. In *Fishery Access Control Programs Worldwide*, ed. Nina Mollet. Fairbanks: Alaska Sea Grant College Program, University of Alaska, 215–30.

Rettig, R. Bruce. 1986. Overview. In *Fishery Access Control Programs Worldwide*, ed. Nina Mollet. Fairbanks: Alaska Sea Grant College Program, University of Alaska, 5–32.

Robinson, Jerome B. 1994. The Next Step for Atlantic Salmon. *Field & Stream*, September.

Ruddle, Kenneth, and Tomoya Akimichi. 1989. Sea Tenure in Japan and the Southwestern Ryukus. In *A Sea of Small Boats*, ed. John Cordell. Cambridge, MA: Cultural Survival, Inc., 337–70.

Rushkin, F. R., ed. 1986. *Proceedings of the Conference on Common Property Resource Management, National Research Council*. Washington, D.C.: National Academy Press.

Schlager, Edella, and Elinor Ostrom. 1992. Property Rights Regimes and Natural Resources: A Conceptual Analysis. *Land Economics* 68: 249–62.

Scott, Anthony. 1988. Market Solutions to Open-Access Commercial Fisheries Problems. Paper presented at the Association for Public Policy Analysis and

Management 10th Annual Research Conference, Seattle, WA, October 27–29.

Short, Kevin MacEwen. 1989. Self-Management of Fishing Rights by Japanese Cooperative Associations: A Case Study from Hokkaido. In *A Sea of Small Boats*, ed. John Cordell. Cambridge, MA: Cultural Survival, Inc., 371–87.

Williamson, Robert. 1993. Scottish Salmon Fishing Rights—A Transferable Property: The Consequences for Administration and Regulation. Paper presented at ICREI Colloquium, Paris, January 28.

Chapter 11

The Constitutional Protection of Private Property

Richard E. Wagner

Can private property be protected within the framework of democratic governance? More specifically, in the context of this volume, how likely is it that rights to resources and to environmental amenities can be made stable and relatively immune from government encroachment? Both theory and history present us with ambiguous responses. A nice summary of long-standing arguments that democratic governance is not sufficient for the task in the long run is presented by Alexander Tytler, an eighteenth-century Scots historian:

> A democracy cannot exist as a permanent form of government. It can only exist until the majority of voters discover that they can vote themselves largesse out of the public treasury. From that moment on, the majority always votes for the candidate who promises them the most benefits from the public treasury, with the result that democracy always collapses over a loose fiscal policy, always to be followed by a dictatorship and then a monarchy. (Quoted in Niskanen 1978, 159)

As Dan Usher (1992) explains with different language though to similar effect as Tytler, democratic governance based on voting does not mesh easily with private property. The contemporary literature on public choice, surveyed nicely in Mueller (1989) and Mitchell and Simmons (1994), seems largely, though not wholly, to reinforce the thrust of the type of thinking represented by Tytler.

I am grateful to P. J. Hill and Karen I. Vaughn for helpful suggestions on an earlier version of this essay.

In sharp contrast, Francis Fukuyama (1992), in his well-received *The End of History and the Last Man*, argues that liberal democracy stands at the end of history and so is to be followed by nothing else, simply because there is no alternative. Among other things, Fukuyama argues, only capitalism can deliver the goods and only democracy can satisfy man's need for recognition.[1] Fukuyama's claim about history will have to await the passing of time. His analytical argument, however, founders on its failure to make reasonable and meaningful distinctions and resembles an effort to tell us that a forest contains "trees and animals," without being any more specific or substantive. Any effort to derive some general relationship between property and democracy must confront the dependence of the substantive character of that relationship upon a variety of particular institutional details concerning types of property and forms of democracy. Without information regarding these details, it is impossible to identify any necessary relationship between property and democracy. Democracy may serve to secure liberty and property, but it may also serve to undermine them. Which happens depends on the particular details of the constitutive framework within which human relationships are governed.

In this chapter I seek to explain why this is so and to examine some of the particular institutional and constitutional principles and details that are necessary if democracy is to serve as a means for securing property and liberty. I start by exploring some important preliminaries concerning the relationship between normative and positive aspects of the problem of securing good governance, invoking analogies from classical moral education in the process. In short, good governance involves first of all a normative choice among contending principles to govern human relationships, with those principles in turn reinforced by a congruent institutional structure that provides compatible incentives to support those principles. From this point of departure, I point out that the relation between property and democracy cannot be explored at the level of abstract categories, because the meaningfulness of any such analytical exercise depends on some important substantive details concerning particular forms of property and democracy.

In particular regard to Fukuyama's claim, it is not liberal democracy, grounded in private property, but social democracy, grounded in common property managed by government, that is currently ascendant. Within contemporary socially democratic regimes, which have typically been misspecified as "mixed economies," there exists a clash between two systems of property and two systems of pricing. One is a system of market pricing organized under the rules of private property. The other is a system of political pricing organized under the rules of common property. The system of political pricing, moreover, is parasitical upon the system of market pricing, in the sense that common property and political pricing require the presence of private property and market pricing for their existence. This parasitical character of the political price system provides, perhaps, a kind of natural limit to the reach of social democracy. Whether it is possible to achieve an even stronger limit on the reach of government through constitutional design is considered in the closing sections.

The Didactic Relevance of Classical Moral Education

The ancient Greeks recognized that virtue was a matter of right knowledge reduced to habit through good practice. Conscious choice repeated often enough becomes habitual and unconscious. Right conduct is cultivated through the ability of right practice to create good habits. Conversely, wrong practice will cultivate bad habits and produce wrong conduct. This classical formulation has didactic value for thinking about the relationship between property and democracy.

To be sure, this classical concern was with the moral education of individuals. Nonetheless, the structure of the classical argument has relevance for the relationship between property and democracy. The ability of a system of democratic governance to secure property and liberty depends upon the habits of governance that are cultivated through democratic practice. In a setting of collective rather than individual choice, however, there is an additional step in this process, one that involves mediation among the participating individuals. Whether governance turns out for good or bad will depend importantly on those mediating relationships. Good habits still result from good practice, only the goodness or badness of the practice is a matter of collective and not individual choice. Desirable normative conduct is reduced to unconscious choice if the incentive features contained within a set of institutional arrangements reinforce that conduct. But if institutional arrangements do not reinforce such conduct through their weight of incentive, the desired normative conduct will diminish, just as, the classics recognized, virtue would diminish without its practice. What is necessary, then, is both knowledge about what constitutes good governance and the reduction of that knowledge to habit through good practice, with that practice mediated by an institutional framework that supports good practice over bad.

In *Federalist* 1, Alexander Hamilton asked "whether societies of men are really capable or not of establishing good government from reflection and choice, or whether they are forever destined to depend for their political constitutions on accident and force." Whether reflection and choice can triumph over accident and force is a matter of what might be called social agriculture. Agriculture attempts to improve upon what mother nature offers, by imposing reflection and choice upon what otherwise would be the products of fate. There are both normative and positive elements to social agriculture. Normatively, there must be some standard of desirability. Among other things, it must be possible to distinguish between desirable and undesirable forms of plant life. Vegetables may be put into the category of desired plant life while weeds are not, though even here the growth of knowledge may reveal useful properties of what were previously thought to be undesirable weeds.

All of the normative wishes in the world are useless, however, without some idea of how to achieve those wishes. People may prefer squash to ragweed, and squash in their stomachs to squash devoured by bugs. Without knowledge of how to restrain the bugs and weeds, however, the yield of squash for human consumption will be left to fate and fortune. It is the same for governance, as Hamilton noted in *Federalist* 1. We may recognize that people prefer to go through their lives free from fear of being preyed upon by others, whether in the form of local bandits or thugs, or in the form of invasions by foreign hordes. We may likewise recognize that people prefer to see their children grow up in prosperous, free, and peaceful environments, and not be plagued by poverty, enslavement, or war. Mere recognition of these preferences, however, does nothing to satisfy them. Mother nature may give us islands of peace and periods of prosperity, but to move beyond her offerings and limitations requires more than wishful thinking. It requires the application of intelligence concerning the social equivalents of the principles of soil chemistry and plant genetics, so as to allow the flowers and vegetables to flourish while restraining the weeds and bugs.

Good governance involves both normative and positive dimensions. There must be a normative vision of what good governance entails. In this respect, I presume that good governance entails human relationships based upon reciprocity and equality, and not based upon domination and supplication, even if perhaps moderated through some dose of noblesse oblige. For that normative vision to be reduced to institutionalized habit, however, the constitutional framework that mediates among participating individuals must channel collective practice in a manner that reinforces through its incentive-compatibility those normative foundations. The normative vision just stated takes seriously and substantively the affirmation in the Declaration of Independence that governments derive their just powers from the consent of the governed, but this vision can be reinforced or undermined, depending upon actual practice. Should that constitutional framework channel collective practice in a contrary direction, those normative foundations will erode through bad practice supported by bad institutionalized habits.

Property Forms and the Types of Democracy

While a rich vocabulary has developed to characterize the different forms of property relationships, for my analytical purposes it suffices to distinguish between private and common property as polar types. Property may be held individually or privately and be freely alienable, or it may be held in common and be inalienable. The problem of democratic governance differs, depending on the presumed property setting. To each form of property there corresponds a different type of democracy: private property is instantiated politically as liberal democracy; common property is instantiated politically as social democracy.

Liberal democracy reflects the normative orientation that people and their rights are prior to government, and that governments exist to secure those prior individual rights. This normative orientation is also consistent with the historical record that property rights arose prior to nation states, as noted by Vernon Smith (1998) in this volume. Government is a reflection of people's use of their rights. It most clearly is not a source of rights, because it is limited by those prior rights and the consent of the governed (e.g., McIlwain 1947). Liberal democracy entails the presumption that people can do as they choose without requiring state permission, provided only that they do not abridge the similar rights of other people in the process.

Social democracy represents the normative orientation that government should be the source of rights. Property is held in common, and government regulates access to the commons. What people may do individually resides ultimately within the domain of government. There can be no principled limit on the reach of government, because government is the source of rights. The only limit on the reach of government is the pragmatic one of the amount of political support that can be mustered. Under social democracy, collective judgments trump individual rights. To be sure, people will have spheres of autonomy under social democracy simply because, pragmatically speaking, governments cannot be involved in everything. Those spheres, however, are always subject to change as the dictates of political expediency change.

With respect to the environment, much of the present debate assumes the common property framework. Collective judgments about environmental issues are presumed to trump individual rights. If individual rights to resources exist, it is only because the government has chosen to tolerate such rights. With private property, an owner of land may choose whether to drain and fill some marshland or to leave it alone. If other people object to draining and filling, they can always make an offer for the land, and if their bid is accepted they can leave it as a marsh. With common property where the legislature is the arena where rights are determined and revised, the legislature may choose to remove from individual owners the right to drain and fill. Within a system of liberal democracy this would represent a clear taking of a component of property by government. Within a system of social democracy, however, there can be no taking because the legislature may grant and rescind rights as it chooses.

Whether they are made explicitly or left to the fortunes of history, we inescapably face a stream of constitutive choices concerning these two different principles by which human relationships are constituted and economic activities governed. We can face these choices directly with reflection and choice, or we can let them face us through accident and force. But face them we will in either case. A liberal democracy entails a commitment to the principles of property and contract as organizing principles that are suitable for a self-organized society whose individual members have their own purposes, and where the state itself has no purpose that does not derive from the consent of the governed. This constitutional commitment limits the activities of government to those that support rather than subvert the fundamental principles of property and contract that undergird a liberal order.

Without such a commitment, it is easy for accident and force to propel a change in constitutional regime without any conscious decision to this effect. The United States was founded on private property and liberal democracy, but much of the twentieth century has been witness to a continuing transformation into common property and social democracy. In his masterful little book, *Congress as Santa Claus*, the legal historian Charles Warren (1932) illustrated this type of change with respect to the constraints on federal legislation that are imposed by the Constitution's general welfare clause. Originally, the general welfare clause was a limitation on the ability of Congress to appropriate money, because appropriations could be only for the general benefit of all, as distinct from the particular benefit of some. Warren documented the transformation of this limitation over a century and a half into its opposite, whereby the general welfare clause ceased to be a limit on government because the general welfare came to mean whatever a congressional majority asserted it to mean. A government whose actions were limited by principles of private property was transformed into an unlimited government that managed the commons that had been created out of private property. A principle of limited government, liberal democracy, gave way to a principle of unlimited government, social democracy.

The treatment of endangered species provides a good environmental illustration of this transformation, as portrayed nicely by Richard Epstein (1998) in this volume. Endangered species will be protected within a framework of private property, with the extent of protection offered depending on the relationship between the value of the species and the cost of protection. As a species becomes less plentiful, its value rises and the incentives to offer protection through private protection strengthen. This is illustrated nicely for wildlife in South Africa, in the chapter by Terry Anderson (1998). A framework of private property is exceedingly flexible in accommodating a wide menu of approaches to the protection of endangered species. No doubt the simplest form is a direct real estate transaction, where people who want to protect a species buy the land on which a habitat resides. But private property can also accommodate numerous other, more complex arrangements. When the protection of endangered species is brought into the domain of collective choice, private property is transformed into common. When this happens, an owner of land can no longer do what he chooses to his land, for rather what he can do is subject to legislative approval and restriction.

The transformation from liberal democracy to social democracy takes place gradually, not by a single choice but as the product of numerous choices over the years. Suppose you found yourself playing football, and were pleased to do so. At various intervals over the ensuing years, changes were made in the rules of play. Would those changes in the rules maintain the integrity of the game or would they subvert it? One year's change might have made the ball rounder and heavier. Another year's change might have eliminated shoulder pads, while in yet another year the helmet was replaced by a soft cap. Still later the sizes of the teams were expanded and the time of a game lengthened by twenty minutes. With the further passing of time, the method of scoring was changed, though not in a way that seemed grossly to affect the aggregate score registered in games. Getting the ball into the end zone now counted only five points, while successful kicks could count either two or three points. Yet other changes in the rules led to an increase in the amount of lateraling and kicking, as well as to a change in the formations used at the line of scrimmage. Would you still describe yourself as playing football? Or might you recognize that you were now playing the quite different game of rugby instead?

Social Democracy as Tectonic Clash between Pricing Systems

Is it accurate to describe our present economy as a market economy? Was this description accurate a century ago? Do we still have the same economic system as we had a century ago, though with modified rules? Or do we have a different type of economic system, in which case if we had a market economy then we can't have one now? Just as some rules generate the pattern of interaction we call football while other rules generate the different pattern we call rugby, so would differences in social rules governing human interaction generate different forms of economic organization. A system of market pricing rests upon the principles or institutions of private property, freedom of contract, and personal liability (Eucken 1952). These principles comprise the framework of rules that constitute a market economy. Within the rules of a market economy, choices regarding the allocation of resources reflect a consensus among market participants.[2] Is Tulsa, Oklahoma, a suitable place to create a seaport? Within a regime of market pricing, the participants themselves reach an agreement as to the answer for such a question. There is no need for any resort to conflict and domination to reach a resolution over whether the conversion of Tulsa into a seaport would represent a more highly valued use of resources than any other use of those resources. People who think it would be a good idea to turn Tulsa into a seaport can compete openly with those who think the required resources would be more valuable in other uses. Those who are unwilling to bid sufficiently to assemble the required resources are, within the framework of rules provided by private property, freedom of contract, and personal liability, agreeing with those who secure command of resources, that the projects of the successful bidders are the most valuable anticipated uses of those resources.

Tulsa is a seaport today, and has been for around a generation now. The resources required to convert Tulsa into a seaport were not, however, assembled through a system of market pricing. Those resources were instead assembled through a different price system, a political price system whose constitutive rules are not the principles of property, contract, and liability. Whether economists speak of regulation or taxation, they typically construe the state as acting within the market economy to modify the terms of market exchange. Regardless of the extent to which the state might modify market prices, this perspective sees resources as allocated through a system of market pricing. Hence, there is but a single, unitary price system that governs the allocation of resources in society. Actually, there exist two distinct price systems in contemporary mixed economies. One is a system of market pricing, the other is a system of political pricing. Each has its own mode and principle of operation. Moreover, the political price system cannot exist on its own but can only exist parasitically upon the market price system.[3]

The market price system is equivalent to an all-comers track meet, whereas the political price system is equivalent to an invitation-only track meet. The parasitical character of political pricing means that, in this analogy, invitation-only meets are possible only because all-comers meets exist. The economic organization of milk, as the economic organization of agriculture generally, to pick but one among many possible illustrations, is most surely not governed by a system of open competition and market pricing. It is governed by a system of closed competition and political pricing. To be sure, there is a logic of economic relationships that is independent of the substantive forms those relationships might take. This logic is as applicable to contemporary mixed economies, regardless of the particular mix of collective and private participation in resource allocation, as it is to a pure market economy. The economic logic of markets can be used to analyze the market for milk when milk is produced under the closed market arrangements created by the contemporary system of marketing orders in the United States. It can likewise be used to analyze the production of milk under conditions of open competition.

The logic of pricing and allocation, however, is distinct from the historical or institutional conditions under which pricing and allocation occur. Only if milk were produced under open competition would it be substantively correct to say that the production of milk was organized through a system of market pricing. When production takes place under marketing orders, resources are allocated through a system of political pricing. Market pricing and political pricing are two distinct, though connected, sets of rules that guide the allocation of resources, and the boundary between the two systems of pricing forms a combat zone in society, as Webber and Wildavsky (1986) explain, particularly in their distinction between individualist-market and egalitarian-sectarian regimes. Politics, in other words, does not take place on a smooth, continuous surface, but on a tectonic landscape.[4]

In place of alienable and several ownership, a political price system invokes common ownership and management by committee. With private property the permission of no particular resource owner is required. Resources must be assembled with the agreements of owners, but there is no particular owner whose agreement is necessary. With common or state property, the permission of particular people is required, as with a zoning board or an Environmental Protection Agency. In place of contract, a political price system invokes duress and coercion. Command over resources can be secured through force and intimidation, and not just through agreement. In place of personal liability, a political price system invokes common liability. Losses that result because enterprises do not operate as initially anticipated or projected are not borne by the sponsors of those enterprises but are spread throughout the polity.

Governmental decisions concerning resource allocation, unlike those of organizations that participate within the market economy, are not constrained by the consensual requirements that a market economy imposes. Where market pricing reflects contractual relationships, political pricing reflects rapacious relationships. Government is thus able to generate a system of pricing that is different from what would emerge through market pricing. Indeed, it is the creation of such alternative prices that surely provides the reason why people seek to use government in the first place. If it were not for its ability to replace market prices with political prices, there would be no support for a system of political pricing. What is social reform, after all, but a change in prices?

Political pricing represents a different approach to making choices concerning resource allocation. It is an alternative price system whose operation is constituted by different rules than those that constrain the operation of a market price system. How different depends, perhaps, on constitutional and institutional matters. The Wicksellian approach or tradition in public finance seeks to have political pricing correspond to the same consensual principle that undergirds market pricing.[5] Other institutional formats diverge in various ways from the consensual principle.

I have no argument against the use of economic reasoning to examine the operation of markets under various governmental constraints. An economic logic is as capable of illuminating how it happened that Tulsa's becoming a seaport was an outcome of a system of political pricing, as it is of explaining why it would not have arisen within a system of market pricing. It is a mistake, however, to go from a general logic of pricing and allocation to characterize actual pricing and allocation as occurring under a system of market pricing, regardless of the rules governing human relationships and choices concerning resource allocation. Our knowledge of pricing and allocation is inadequate so long as we fail to recognize that we inhabitants of contemporary social democracies live in the presence of two distinct, though connected, regimes of pricing and allocation.

Parasitical Political Pricing as a Natural Limit on Government?

To note that market prices are self-generating and self-sustaining is not to assert that orderly and peaceful anarchy is a viable historical option. Rather it is to assert only that if people were to limit their activities to those governed by the principles of property and contract, an organized network of economic relationships will arise and these relationships will sustain themselves. We have authentic and coherent knowledge about the self-organizing features of a market economy. If people were to conduct themselves according to the principles that constitute a system of market pricing, an orderly and sustainable network of economic relationships would arise.

No such claim can be made about a collective economy. In the absence of private property, freedom of contract, and personal liability, market pricing will not arise. Resource allocation would require planning and allocation without markets. This is impossible, as recognized even by those faint-hearted proponents of communism who advocated the oxymoronic fiction of market socialism. It is conceivable that there could exist a market economy without a polity and political prices; it is inconceivable that there could exist a collective economy without a market and market prices.[6] Political prices are neither self- generating nor self-sustaining. The presence of a market economy and market pricing is necessary for a collective economy and political pricing to arise. Those enterprises that are organized through the state-regulated commons and its system of political pricing exist parasitically upon those enterprises that are organized through private property and genuine market pricing. A collective economy organized within a framework of common property can exist only in the presence of a host market economy that is organized within a framework of private property.

The constituency for political pricing and enterprises arises from the ability of those enterprises to provide advantageous pricing for at least some set of people. On the product side of the market, political prices must be lower than market prices for at least some buyers. On the factor side, political prices must be higher than market prices for at least some suppliers. The constituency for political pricing arises from these price advantages. There are two possible sources of price advantage for public enterprises. One is efficiency, as portrayed in the various models and claims of market failure. A public enterprise that was more efficient than the private substitutes would be able to secure price advantages for everyone. While efficiency cannot be ruled out analytically, its range of empirical applicability does seem tightly limited. The other source of price advantage is price discrimination. An inefficient public enterprise can still secure price advantages for some, so long as it can impose discriminatory pricing on everyone else.

It is common to model a firm as producing a single product and selling it at a uniform price. Aside from those exceptional cases where a public enterprise has superior efficiency, collective enterprises cannot sell at a uniform price. For if they were constrained to a single price, they could not generally compete with market-based enterprises. To be sure, it is sometimes claimed that political enterprises do not have to earn returns for equity holders, and thus have a lower cost of capital that can be passed along through lower prices. This claim is mistaken. Governments can generally borrow more cheaply than private enterprises not because they involve less risk and, hence, a lower cost of capital, but because they can shift risk from bondholders to taxpayers. Hence, what appears to be a lower cost of capital is really a byproduct of there being two prices at the factor supply level: one is a price to bondholders and the other is a tacit or implicit price to taxpayers. This latter component of cost is left out of the claim that the nonprofit status of government gives it a cost advantage over private firms.[7] A political enterprise may offer prices to some buyers that are lower than what market enterprises offer, but only because they also charge higher prices to other buyers—and have the ability to force consumption at those higher prices. If a market enterprise sells at a single price, the creation of a political enterprise will thus involve at least two prices, one below the market price and one above the market price. The higher price is necessary to make the lower price possible.

The organization of water supply provides numerous illustrations of the conflict between common and private property as frameworks for governing the organization of economic activity.[8] Irrigation, for instance, can be organized through either private property or common property, as illustrated by several of the essays in Anderson (1983). Suppose irrigation were organized collectively through common property, with a Bureau of Reclamation as the manager. The support for the collective irrigation enterprise will depend on the ability of the enterprise to offer lower water prices to its supporters. The collective enterprise cannot do this while charging a common price to all consumers. If it were to charge a common price, that price would be higher than what private enterprises could offer and the collective enterprise could not compete against enterprises organized within a framework of private property. The collective irrigation enterprise can establish a competitive position only if it charges lower prices to a group of sufficient size to secure the necessary political support. To accomplish this requires some form of price discrimination, with the higher prices charged to some people providing the means for awarding price reductions to supporters.

The central problem in maintaining a system of price discrimination, of course, resides in preventing the emergence of a secondary market in water. Should those who are offered low prices sell water to those who would otherwise be charged high prices, the discrimination scheme would disintegrate. Price discrimination requires the prevention of a secondary market, which in turn requires that transfers among buyers of rights to water be prohibited. A further obstacle to the maintenance of price discrimination to support a collective irrigation enterprise resides in the threat of alternative, privately organized sources of supply. The collective enterprise cannot exist as one competitor among many, at least so long as its revenues are derived from consumer payments. Some territorial monopoly in conjunction with prohibitions on transferability among customers are central imperatives for irrigation enterprises organized under common property.

Taxation offers yet another source of price discrimination that further strengthens the survival power of the collective enterprise. For one thing, the receipt of budgetary appropriations is a method of reducing the prices to customers by imposing charges on those who are not customers. Actually, there are two ways that taxation lowers the price to customers by imposing charges on those who are not customers. One operates directly through the appropriations process. The other operates through the cost of capital as the operation of the market for capital is repressed. Under private property the cost of capital to an irrigation enterprise would reflect investor expectations in an openly competitive market where enterprises have to compete for investors. With the collective enterprise, however, taxpayers become forced investors whose liability, moreover, is not limited by their investment. The collective irrigation enterprises organized within a Bureau of Reclamation do not compete for willing investors and do not have any direct cost of capital.

As the extent of collective enterprises organized within common property expands relative to the private enterprises organized under private property, an increasing number of market prices are suffocated or impaired and are replaced by political prices that are administrative and not grounded in preferences and technology. Although there is considerable controversy over the details of explanation, economists are agreed that a valuable feature of market pricing is the assistance it gives to economic calculation. Market prices serve as navigational aids to economic calculation. While prices are not sufficient information for effective economic conduct, they are necessary and powerful. They are navigational aids that improve the efficiency with which people get where they want to go, even if they cannot prevent people from wrecking or getting lost. Whatever the network of navigational aids that comprise a market economy might look like, the injection of political pricing disables some of those aids. Sometimes it does so completely, as equivalent to destroying a buoy. At other times it does so only partially, as in giving the buoy a loose and variable anchorage. In any case, a political price cannot compete directly against a market price, so the injection of political pricing into the economy must involve the degradation if not the destruction of market pricing in those areas most closely related to the price domain of the public enterprise.

Through the destruction or degradation of market prices, the growth of the political price system reduces the quality of the navigational aids that inhabit the economy. Contrary to Littlechild (1978), however, I offer no argument for any "fallacy" of the mixed economy. Rather what I offer is a line of argument suggesting that political pricing becomes more damaging as its scope expands. Even in a world of full market pricing, economic wreckage would arise, and in many ways. There would be all kinds of ways in which enterprises and projects will have been undertaken that do not turn out as planned. In some cases the actual outcome will have been less satisfactory than what was planned or anticipated, and the promoter as well as those who relied on him will suffer various kinds of capital losses. The opposite outcome is possible as well, of course, in which case the promoter finds himself with too small an enterprise. In any case there will exist unanticipated capital gains and losses in a purely market economy because the navigational aids that market prices represent can never be fully sufficient instruments for judgment and choice. The absolute value of capital gains and losses is an indicator of the extent to which plans have not been fulfilled.

As political pricing grows and market pricing weakens, the volume of economic wreckage will surely increase. Political prices attach themselves to particular market prices, extinguishing the market prices in the process. Due to the connectedness among market prices, there is little problem for political prices to substitute for market prices when their numbers are small. But as political prices proliferate and an increasing number of market prices have been extinguished, the informational value of market prices declines and economic calculation becomes increasingly difficult and mistaken. The economic wreckage that might be attributed to the degradation of the calculational aids represented by market prices are unlikely to be distributed uniformly throughout the economy. Their distribution would probably reflect the pattern of injection of political pricing into the economy. Economic wreckage would increase in those places where political prices had more fully degraded market prices. Environmental issues provide some prime examples of this economic wreckage because for numerous environmental amenities political prices have largely replaced market prices.

This has a number of potential empirical implications, or so it would seem. For one thing, the growth of political pricing would increase the volume of unanticipated capital gains and losses in the economy, relative to various economic aggregates. Growth in an economy characterized by a robust political price system would be distributed differently than growth in an economy dominated by market pricing. Provided only that political prices are not distributed uniformly throughout the economy, the variability of growth rates across the economy would expand along with the expansion in political pricing. More rapid growth would occur in those areas where the navigational aids offered by market prices had been less degraded by political pricing.

On the other hand, in those areas where political pricing was relatively strong and the reliability of navigational aids relatively weak, economic wreckage would loom larger. This greater riskiness would be accompanied by larger costs of capital to market participants who sail those waters due to the expansion of political pricing. Conversely, enterprises operating in areas where political pricing was relatively slight would have lower costs of capital.[9]

It is obvious that there is some limit to the extent to which the political price system can operate in a society, due simply to the parasitic nature of political pricing. Without a system of market pricing, political pricing cannot exist. This purely formal point sheds no insight into just where short of 100 percent that limit might reside. Whether it is possible to advance some numerical limit is dubious, because the limit could well depend on the particular location at which political pricing replaced or degraded market prices. In any case, contemporary social democracies do not possess a single system of market pricing whose operation is in various ways shaped and constrained through government. Rather they possess dual pricing systems, with political pricing bearing a parasitic relationship to market pricing. The economic organization of agriculture and broadcasting, for instance, takes place within a different system of property and pricing than does the economic organization of magazines and newspapers, just as surely as rugby and football entail different systems of rules for governing human relationships.

Ordnungstheorie and the Movement beyond Natural Limits

What I have characterized as the natural limit on the extent of common property and political pricing corresponds to the accident and force articulated by Hamilton in *Federalist* 1. It remains to be seen whether it is possible to limit further the reach of social democracy through constitutional craftsmanship. The Germanic tradition of *ordnungstheorie*, articulated nicely in Walter Eucken (1952), provides a nice vehicle for exploring the problem of limiting the reach of social democracy beyond that contained in the parasitical relationships between common and private property. Eucken invoked a fundamental distinction between the framework within which economic processes unfold and the specific operation of those processes. This formulation distinguishes two types of policy measures: those that shape the economic order and those that represent particular adjustments within the framework of that economic order.

The choice of frameworks is constitutional in character. This is a choice among different regimes and principles for governing human relationships. This is a choice that either we can make expressly or we can make by default, but make it we will in any case. Along one path lies the economic organization of a society where people relate to one another through reciprocity and equality, as provided by a framework of contract and private property. Along the other path lies the economic organization of a society where people relate to one another as grantors and supplicants, as provided by a framework of domination and common property. This alternative is the inexorable imperative of common property and social democracy, for those who are invited occupy a privileged position, and those who issue the invitations are grantors who can always count on having supplicants at their doorsteps.

It is easy, however, for piecemeal policy measures to generate incentives that ever more continually undermine the market economy, replacing liberty and responsibility with servility and dependence in the process. As a source of orientation for the conduct of economic policy for a liberal democracy, there is much merit to a requirement that state policy measures be congruent with the central operating features of a market economy, which entails the principles of property, contract, and liability. The point of such a constitutional orientation would be to give scope for government policy, only to do so in a way that such policy would tend to support the basic principles of a market economy, which are the principles of liberty, autonomy, and responsibility. The opposite principle is one that leads to differential ranks of overseers and underlings, to those who dispense noblesse oblige and those who are the recipients of that oblige.

The injection of nontransferability into water supply policy, for instance, would clearly be a nonconformable policy measure. States could still participate in the organization of water supply projects, but their modes of operation could not violate the principles of property and contract. Hence, states could not prevent the emergence of a secondary market for water. As an alternative illustration, a state could still be involved directly in the preservation of wetlands. Contracts with landowners to preserve marshes would conform to the principles of a market economy, whereas the direct imposition of prohibitions against draining marshes would violate the principle of conformability. A requirement that policy measures pass a test of market conformability is one that would seek to allow government to act consistently with the principles of private property while restraining it from transforming private property into common.

The distinction between conformable and nonconformable measures, if treated as a constitutional requirement for economic policy, might well serve as a kind of constitutional compass.[10] Starting from a normative affirmation of the central principles of a liberal society, such a compass would declare that a wide range of policy measures are open to the state, subject to the limitation that the particular content of those measures cannot violate the principles of private property, freedom of contract, and personal liability. In this manner, such a limitation on the possible domain of policy measures would perhaps restrict some of the problems of time inconsistency and path dependency that might otherwise operate to produce a degeneration of liberal democracy through liberal democratic processes. To be sure, questions of interpretation concerning the requirement that policy measures conform to the principles of property, contract, and liability would arise and would have to be confronted. Those interpretative questions would surely be no more difficult than those that surround First or Fifth Amendment interpretation these days.

At the same time, the problem of the elasticity of interpretation raises knotty issues. I would never want to depreciate the value of such scholarly efforts as those of Siegan (1980) and Epstein (1985), who show clearly how the Supreme Court has ceased its protection of private property in this century. At the same time, however, I think the task of restoring constitutional protection for property and liberty involves more than judicial criticism, if for no other reason than what is surely the reasonable presumption that the potential elasticity of interpretation surely varies directly with the amount of the stakes involved in any act of interpretation. While I do not think that any circle can be squared through sufficient interpretative creativity, I do think that there are a good number that can.

Hawaii Housing Authority v. Midkiff is a good illustration of the opportunities for interpretative creativity. Hawaii passed a statute that required landowners to sell their property to tenants. While the Ninth Circuit ruled unanimously against Hawaii, the Supreme Court reversed the Ninth Circuit, again unanimously. The reasons given made dubious references to an oligopolistic land market in Hawaii. Yet it would have been possible to craft a line of reasoning that actually had constitutional resonance. Article 4, Section 4 holds the federal government responsible for guaranteeing that the states maintain republican forms of government. There is a great deal of American republican tradition that holds that landownership rather than tenancy promotes the republican virtues. It would thus seem possible to craft a constitutionally resonant line of argument in support of Hawaii. While there are surely limits to the interpretative imagination, any approach to constitutional enforcement that seeks to protect private property must ultimately involve more than judicial procedures and interpretations.

Madison's Principle of Dual Security

Madison articulated an important principle of constitutional enforcement in *Federalist* 51, when he argued how governments would control both themselves and each other through the compound republic the constitution would establish:

> In the compound republic of America, the power surrendered by the people is first divided between distinct governments, and then the portion allotted to each subdivided among distinct and separate departments. Hence a double security arises to the rights of the people. *The different governments will control each other*, at the same time that each will be controlled by itself. (italics supplied)[11]

Among other things, there is a significant judicial asymmetry regarding the ability of the different governments to control each other, as noted in Niskanen (1978). Claims that a state legislature oversteps its bounds can be heard before federal forums. This is consistent with the proposition that no man should be a judge in his own cause. However, similar claims about the federal legislature can be heard only by federal officials. This places the federal government as a judge in its own cause. Madison's principle of dual security would seem to require that claims about federal constitutionality should be heard in state-convened forums, in one fashion or another, for otherwise the federal government is standing as a judge in its own cause.

This insulated position of the federal government was strengthened by the Sixteenth and Seventeenth Amendments. The former allowed Congress to levy taxes without regard to apportionment among the states, while the latter did away with the ability of states to select senators. Together, they elevated the federal government to a relatively monopolistic position within our federal system of government. Unlike the federal government, individual states exist in a relatively competitive environment where they must attract residents in an open economy. It is reasonable to treat states as if they operate under some Wicksellian principle of approximate unanimity. It is now different for the federal government. The Sixteenth and Seventeenth Amendments expanded the ability of the federal government both to place states in a prisoners' dilemma setting with respect to their acquiescence in federal programs and to participate in the organization of coalitions of interest groups that cut across state lines.

The prisoners' dilemma setting is well illustrated by federal grant programs, which are commonly used as a vehicle by which the federal government expands it reach, in environmental as well as in other areas. A state does not have to participate in a federal grant program. If it does not, however, its residents will pay the same federal taxes in any case. Individual states are placed in the position of paying and participating or paying and not participating. That nonparticipation will simply leave larger revenues to be spent among the states that do participate. All states may well prefer that none participate and that federal taxes be lowered instead. But they are never given this choice. A very different situation would be created if the federal government had to sell such programs to the states. A state that chose not to participate would at the same time be choosing lower federal tax payments for its residents.

In the private law of contract there is a concept of duress. What is the equivalence of duress in public law? It would surely represent collective action that was contrary to the will of a participant in that action. At present the "consent of the governed" articulated in the Declaration of Independence is treated only formally and not substantively. Hence it is said that we consent to governmental actions because we don't kill ourselves or emigrate or agitate for insurrection. What if the consent of the governed were taken to be a substantive promise? A consideration of this question is well beyond the scope of this essay. Madison's principle of dual security suggests we look in two places for an answer. One is to the division and fragmentation of authority within a unit of government. The other is to the ability of different levels of government to check each other, as envisioned in the principle of a competitive federalism.

We are witnessing a growing call supported by increased litigation for taking seriously and accurately the Fifth Amendment's strictures against the taking of private property. We are also witnessing a growing interest in bringing the Ninth and Tenth Amendments back into play as methods of protecting private property. I have no quarrel with any of these efforts. I do, however, think that the success of those efforts also requires more substantial institutional reformation along the lines of creating a federal system of government that is openly competitive, which in turn would take seriously Madison's recognition in *Federalist* 51 that the protection of private property against government requires that each level of government be able to police the other.[12]

Peroration

The environmental issues discussed in this volume are but an example of a much larger issue, namely, how can government be constrained within a modern democracy? Good governance requires both a clear normative map and constitutive arrangements that reinforce congruent practice. Augustine, in his *City of God*, tells the story of a pirate who was captured and brought before Alexander the Great. When Alexander castigated the pirate, the pirate responded: "I do my fighting on a tiny ship, and they call me a pirate; you do yours with a large fleet, and they call you Commander." Augustine, in noting that the pirate's response to Alexander was wholly accurate, asked: "In the absence of justice, what is sovereignty but organized brigandage?" Justice may exist when human relationships are governed by reciprocity and exchange, but it can never exist when they are governed by domination and supplication, and yet domination and supplication are natural outcomes of common property and social democracy.

Notes

1. Less sweeping in scope but to the same effect is Donald Wittman's (1995) claim that democracy is economically efficient, in sharp contrast to the predominant thrust of the contemporary literature on public choice.

2. See, for instance, De Angelo (1981) and Makowski (1983).

3. For a clear recognition of this dual system of pricing, and of the parasitical character of political pricing, see Maffeo Pantaleoni (1911). For amplification, see Wagner (n.d.).

4. On the tectonic character of politics, see Robert Young (1988).

5. Wicksell's (1896) formulation is described in terms of the contemporary literature on public choice in Wagner (1988).

6. See, for instance, the papers collected in Hayek (1935). In a related vein, Roberts (1971) shows that the Soviet Union did not replace market allocation with collective planning, but rather created a form of political price system that sought some anchorage in some semblance of market pricing.

7. Even Lott's (1990) model of predatory pricing by public enterprises derives some of its features by virtue of the public enterprise's being able to operate without regard to returns to stockholders-taxpayers, and hence to operate with a second source of financing outside that raised directly from prices.

8. For valuable treatises, see Hirshleifer, DeHaven, and Milliman (1960) and Ostrom (1953).

9. To be sure, the presence of political pricing is not the only reason for the cost of capital to vary among enterprises.

10. In this vein, see, for instance, Leipold (1990), Streit (1992), and Vanberg (1988).

11. For a crisp articulation of Madison and the federalist vision, see Vincent Ostrom (1987).

12. Competitive federalism is discussed in Wagner (1995).

References

Anderson, Terry L. 1998. Viewing Wildlife through Coase-Colored Glasses, this volume.

———, ed. 1983. *Water Rights: Scarce Resource Allocation, Bureaucracy, and the Environment*. San Francisco: Pacific Research Institute.

De Angelo, Harry. 1981. Competition and Unanimity. *American Economic Review* 71: 18–27.

Epstein, Richard A. 1985. *Takings: Private Property and the Power of Eminent Domain*. Cambridge: Harvard University Press.

———. 1998. Habitat Preservation: A Property Rights Perspective, this volume.

Eucken, Walter. 1952. *Grundsätze der Wirtschaftpolitik*. Tübingen: J. C. B. Mohr.

Fukuyama, Francis. 1992. *The End of History and the Last Man*. New York: Free Press.

Hayek, Friedrich, ed. 1935. *Collectivist Economic Planning*. London: George Routledge and Sons.

Hirshleifer, Jack, James C. DeHaven, and Jerome Milliman. 1960. *Water Supply: Economics, Technology, and Policy*. Chicago: University of Chicago Press.

Leipold, Helmut. 1990. Neoliberal Ordnungstheorie and Constitutional Economics. *Constitutional Political Economy* 1: 47–65.

Littlechild, Stephen C. 1978. *The Fallacy of the Mixed Economy*. London: Institute of Economic Affairs.

Lott, John R., Jr. 1990. Predation by Public Enterprises. *Journal of Public Economics* 43: 237–51.

Makowski, Louis. 1983. Competition and Unanimity Revisited. *American Economic Review* 73: 329–39.

McIlwain, Charles. 1947. *Constitutionalism: Ancient and Modern*, rev. ed. Ithaca, NY: Cornell University Press.

Mitchell, William C., and Randy T. Simmons. 1994. *Beyond Politics: Markets, Welfare, and the Failure of Bureaucracy*. Boulder, CO: Westview Press.

Mueller, Dennis C. 1989. *Public Choice II*. Cambridge: Cambridge University Press.

Niskanen, William A. 1978. The Prospect for Liberal Democracy. In *Fiscal Responsibility in Constitutional Democracy*, ed. James M. Buchanan and Richard E. Wagner. Leiden: Martinus Nijhoff, 157–74.

Ostrom, Vincent. 1953. *Water and Politics: A Study of Water Policies and Administration in the Development of Los Angeles*. Los Angeles: Haynes Foundation.

———. 1987. *The Political Theory of a Compound Republic*, 2d ed. Lincoln: University of Nebraska Press.

Pantaleoni, Maffeo. 1911. Considerazioni sulle proprieta di un sistema di prezzi politici. *Giornale degli Economisti* 42: 9–29 and 114–33.

Roberts, Paul Craig. 1971. *Alienation and the Soviet Economy*. Albuquerque: University of New Mexico Press.

Siegan, Bernard H. 1980. *Economic Liberties and the Constitution.* Chicago: University of Chicago Press.

Smith, Vernon L. 1998. Property Rights as a Natural Order: Reciprocity, Evolutionary and Experimental Considerations, this volume.

Streit, Manfred E. 1992. Economic Order, Private Law and Public Policy: The Freiberg School of Law and Economics in Perspective. *Journal of Institutional and Theoretical Economics* 148: 675–704.

Usher, Dan. 1992. *The Welfare Economics of Markets, Voting, and Predation.* Ann Arbor: University of Michigan Press.

Vanberg, Viktor. 1988. 'Ordnungstheorie' as Constitutional Economics—The German Conception of a 'Social Market Economy.' *ORDO* 39: 17–31.

Wagner, Richard E. 1988. *The Calculus of Consent*: A Wicksellian Retrospective. *Public Choice* 56: 153–66.

———. 1995. A Competitive Federalism for the New Century. *Madison Review* 1(Fall): 34–40.

———. N.d. Parasitical Political Pricing: A Natural Limit on the Size of Government? *Journal of Public Finance and Public Choice*, forthcoming.

Warren, Charles. 1932. *Congress as Santa Claus.* Charlottesville, VA: Michie Publishing Co.

Webber, Carolyn, and Aaron Wildavsky. 1986. *A History of Taxation and Expenditure in the Western World.* New York: Simon and Schuster.

Wicksell, Knut. 1896. *Finanztheoretische Untersuchungen nebst Darstellung und Kritik des Stuerwesens Schwedens.* Jena, Germany: Gustav Fischer.

Wittman, Donald. 1995. The Myth of Democratic Failure. Chicago: University of Chicago Press.

Young, Robert A. 1988. Tectonic Policies and Political Competition. In *The Competitive State*, ed. Albert Breton, Gianuligi Galeotti, Pierre Salmon, and Ronald Wintrobe. Dordrecht, The Netherlands: Kluwer Academic Publishers, 129–45.

Index

Acheson, James, 284, 291, 292
Agnello, Richard J., 283
Akimichi, Tomoya, 300
Alchian, Armen A., 3, 6, 23, 38, 198, 263
Alexander the Great, 334
Amacher, Ryan C., 260–61
Anderson, Terry L., 3, 4, 9, 16, 27, 38, 39, 74, 160, 175, 176, 187, 192, 205, 260, 283, 284, 288, 320, 321, 326, 340
Arizona Game and Fish Department, 273
Arrow, Kenneth, 45, 180, 191, 197, 212n13
Atlanta Constitution, 145
Atlantic Herring Fishermen's Marketing Cooperative, 301–2
Atlantic Salmon Federation, 303
Attorney-General v. Birmingham, 94
Audubon Sanctuary Program, 141–42
Audubon Society, 235
Augustine, 334

Babbitt v. Sweet Home Chapter of Communities for a Great Oregon, 223–24, 225, 226, 240, 247, 253, 253n5
Ballard v. Tomlinson, 89
Bamford v. Turnley, 93
Barkdull, John, 190–91
Baron-Cohen, Simon, 68

Barro, Robert J., 41, 44 (table 2.1), 46, 48, 49 (table 2.3)
Barzel, Yoram, 37, 38
Bate, Roger, 98
Bator, Francis M., 153
Beach, William W., 44
Beamish v. Glenn, 96
Benson, Bruce, 5, 7
Bentham, Jeremy, 129, 239, 242–43
Berkes, F., 284, 294
Bernor, R. L., 59
Bernstein, Allan, 269–70
Bishop, Richard C., 284
Blackstone, William, 89, 92, 93, 247
Block, Walter, 42–43, 44 (table 2.1), 46, 48
Boas, Franz, 59
Bolin, Bert, 45
Borcherding, Thomas E., 243
Bork, Robert H., 170
Boudreaux, Donald J., 3–4, 16, 19, 22, 23, 26, 78, 123, 208, 340
Bowles, Francis P., 290–92
Bowles, Margaret C., 290–91
Boyce, Rebecca, 241
Boyle v. Rogers, 91
Bracton, Henry of, 88–89
Braeutigam, Ronald, 109
Brannlund, Runar, 127
Brewer, Marilyn B., 286
British Cast Plate Manufacturers v. Meredith, 106

Brown, Angus, 276–78
Brubaker, Elizabeth, 3, 12, 138, 172, 174, 340
Brunet, Edward, 210
Bryant, Nelson, 308
Buchanan, James M., 3, 20–21, 22, 124, 153, 170, 171
Bureau of Land Management, U.S.: grazing rights and, 187–89, 215n44; habitat and, 265; interest groups and, 197; ownership of western lands by, 11; practices of, 16; water management by, 326, 327
Butler, Henry, 200
Buysse v. Town of Shelburne, 95

Camerer, Colin, 76
Campbell, Richard S., 98
Campbell Soup Company, 142
CAMPFIRE, 275–76
Canadian Environmental Law Research Foundation, 98
Canadian Pacific Ry. v. Roy, 104, 108
Canadian property rights: American influences on, 88, 100–101, 102–4, 105–6, 110, 111; English common law and, 88–89; erosion of, 104–12; injunctions v. damages in, 89–90; nuisance and, 92–97; restoration of, 87, 112–13; riparian rights and, 97–104; trespass and, 90–92
Capstick, Peter Hathaway, 278
Carney, William, 4, 22, 28, 39, 194, 197, 198, 199, 200, 340
Cheung, Steven N. S., 262, 265
Christy, Francis T., 295
Ciriacy-Wantrup, S. V., 284
Clark, Robert C., 199
Clean Water Act, 180
Coase, Ronald H.: bargaining model of, 74–75, 120, 132–39; common law rules and, 137–39; externalities and, 18, 120, 132–49; intellectual influence of, 121–22, 127; market forces and, 121–22,

132–34; rule of law and, 43, 121; social cost theory of, 2, 3, 17, 18, 22, 31n4, 37, 38, 40, 43, 50, 110, 120, 241; "The Nature of the Firm" of, 264; transaction costs and, 17–19, 38, 261–66. *See also* wildlife management
Cody, Betsy A., 188
Coggins, George Cameron, 187
Cohen, Mark A., 143
Collins, Denis, 190–91
Committee on Corporate Laws, 199
common law: Coase and, 137–39; erosion of, 106–8, 111–12; exclusive possession under, 248; existence value and, 174–76; injunction and, 89–90; nuisance under, 92–97, 114n7, 229–32, 248, 254n12; origins of, 88–89; riparian rights under, 97–100, 113n4, 138; trespass under, 90–92, 113n2, 229–32, 248. *See also* Canadian property rights, property rights
commons, tragedy of, 8, 188, 283, 287, 289, 308
commons management: impact of customs and culture on, 284–87; in Switzerland, 284. *See also* community fisheries management
Communal Area Management Plan for Indigenous Resources (CAMPFIRE), 275–76
community fisheries management: of Atlantic salmon, 303–5; based on quota, 301–3; in Brazil, 292; in Canada, 302, 303–5; catch limitations in, 28, 294–96; government involvement in, 28, 289, 290, 292–94, 295, 296–97, 299–300, 301–3, 304, 305, 306–8; by Gulf Coast shrimpers, 295–96; in Japan, 294–95, 299–301; by Maine lobster fishermen, 290–92; in New Jersey, 295; in New Zealand, 28; in Norway, 298–99; in Nova Scotia,

292–94; property rights and, 287, 288, 289–90, 293, 296–98, 299, 300, 301; in Quebec, 305–8; rules for, 284–86, 308; in Scotland, 296–98, 302–3; by Tlingit and Haida Indians, 287–89; in Turkey, 294; in United Kingdom, 297–98, 302–3; by Washington Indians, 289–90

Comprehensive Environmental Response, Compensation and Liability Act (Superfund), 157, 179

Congress, U.S.: compensation and, 247, 253; Endangered Species Act and, 225; private property and, 320–21; public lands and, 187, 196–97, 210, 212n11; Seventeenth Amendment and, 332; Sixteenth Amendment and, 332; takings and, 238

Conservation Corporation (Conscorp), 269–72

Constitution, Canadian, 87

Constitution, U.S.: Endangered Species Act and, 225, 247–53; Fifth Amendment of, 247–53, 331, 333; First Amendment of, 331; general welfare clause of, 320; Ninth Amendment of, 333; Seventeenth Amendment of, 332; Sixteenth Amendment of, 332; takings clause of, 247–53; Tenth Amendment of, 333

contingent valuation: codification of, 180; defined, 155–56; environmental amenities and, 160–63, 181; Exxon *Valdez* and, 156–57; irrelevance of, 157–67; in public policy, 157–58; Supreme Court and, 178; truthfulness and, 156. *See also* existence value, value

Cooter, Robert D., 172

Cordell, John C., 292, 300

Cosmides, Leda, 58

Costanza, Robert, 45

Council on Environmental Quality, 145

Coursey, Don, 37, 45, 146

Crawford, Robert G., 198

Cross, Frank B., 154, 180

Dahlman, Carl J., 153, 154

Dalton, George, 62

Dasgupta, Partha, 45

Davignon, Jean-François, 308

Davis, A., 293–94

Davis, Gareth, 44

Davis, Lance E., 9

Davis, Peter N., 138

De Alessi, Louis, 3, 4, 20, 21, 25, 27, 130, 148, 341

De Alessi, Michael, 3, 8, 9, 24, 28, 29

Declaration of Independence, 318, 333

Defenders of Wildlife, 266, 281

De Laguna, Frederica, 288–89

Delta Waterfowl Foundation, 268–69

Demsetz, Harold, 3, 8, 18, 38, 39, 195, 288

Department of Interior, U.S., 179–80

Desert Land Act, 207

De Vany, Arthur S., 11

de Waal, Frans, 57, 58–59

Dewees, D. N., 109

Diamond, Jared, 57

Diamond, Peter A., 157

Didow v. Alberta Power, 91

Donnelly, Lawrence P., 283

Douglas, Christopher, 188

Downes, Bryan T., 190

Drysdale v. C. A. Dugas, 97

economic growth: developing countries and, 49–50; empirical studies on, 40–41; environmental quality and, 45–51; neoclassical model of, 40; property rights and, 37–38, 43–51

efficiency, 153–54

Egenhofer, Christian, 127, 132

Eggertsson, Thráinn, 3, 38, 45

Ellickson, Robert C., 38, 39, 93, 109, 243, 262

Ellis v. Clemens, 98

Endangered Species Act of 1973: as
bad policy, 1–2, 181, 225, 247;
constitutionality of, 225, 247–53;
existence value and, 178–79; false
doctrine of equivalents and,
227–29; nuisance and trespass and,
229–32, 248; objective of, 226;
proposed common law amendment
of, 224–25; purchase under,
232–39; species ownership under,
265; *Sweet Home* decision and,
223–24, 225, 226, 253; takings
under, 224, 226, 247–53, 255n36
Endres, Alfred, 3
Entick v. Carrington, 90
Environment Resources Management
Association, 304–5
Environmental Consultants [Pvt.]
Ltd., 275, 276
Environmental Defense Fund, 141
environmental problems: causes of, 2;
central planning and, 3–4, 16–17;
in developing countries, 49–50;
government as cause of, 4,
144–45; government as solution
to, 21–27, 29–30, 104–12, 120,
126–32, 148–49, 153–54; market
as solution to, 4, 27–30, 120,
132–49; public-owned entities
and, 144–45; reciprocity of costs
and, 22; rent seeking and, 24–25;
rising incomes and, 146–47; technological innovation and, 29;
transaction costs and, 2, 3. *See also*
common law, economic growth,
externalities, property rights
Environmental Protection Agency,
140, 323
Epstein, Richard A., 1–2, 30, 160,
226, 320, 321, 331, 341
Estrin, David, 90
Eucken, Walter, 322, 329
European Council Regulation, 143
Everett v. Paschall, 93
existence value: codification of,
179–80; common law as alternative to, 174–76, 181; dangers of,
169–71, 173, 180–81; defined,
154–55; difficulty in determining,
161–67; as externality, 176; legal
standing for, 177–79, 180–81;
marginalization of, 164–65; markets and, 158–67; property rights
in, 171–73; public lands and, 208;
relevance of, 167–69; of wildlife,
260. *See also* contingent valuation,
value
externalities: defined, 153; government and, 21–27; legislative action
and, 153–54; markets and, 17–21,
27–29, 125, 153; public lands and,
205–6. *See also* Ronald N. Coase,
environmental problems, existence
value, A. C. Pigou

Fairview Farms v. Reynolds Metals,
92
Fama, Eugene, 194, 195
Farber, Daniel A., 177
Federalist 1, 317, 318, 324
Federalist 51, 333
Federal Register, 121, 122 (figure
5.1)
Federal Water Pollution Control Act
of 1972, 130
Feibel, C. S., 59
Fesseha, N., 59
Field, Barry C., 3, 8
Fiorino, Daniel J., 190
Fischel, William A., 243
Fischer, Hank, 266, 280
Fish and Wildlife Service, U.S., 224,
226, 265, 269
Flaherty, David H., 88
Flynn, Ted and John, 267–68
Foldvary, Fred, 20
Folke, Carl, 45
Ford Motor Company, 140
Forest Service, U.S.: habitat and, 265,
279; interest groups and, 197; *Si-
erra Club v. Morton* and, 177; tim-
ber sales by, 188–89, 214n44
Forsythe, Robert, 76, 78

Freeman, A. Myrick, 166
Freuchen, Peter, 61
Friedman, Milton, 169
Friend, Irwin, 194
Friesen v. Forest Protection, 91
Fukuyama, Francis, 316
Fuller, John L., 67

Gardner, Roy, 286
Gastil, Raymond, 41–42
Gauthier v. Naneff, 99, 102, 103
Gazzaniga, Michael, 67
General Accounting Office, 188, 189, 192
General Mining Law of 1872, 188, 211n7
Goldschmidt, W., 289
Golf Course Superintendents Association, 142
Goodland, John, 302
Gordon, H. Scott, 2, 3, 38, 187
Gordon, Jeffrey, 194
Grandin, Temple, 69
Green, Mark, 197
Greenfield, P. M., 63
Greyson Creek Meadows Inc., 267–68
Groat v. Edmonton, 93, 103–4
Grossman, Gene M., 45, 50, 146, 194
Gwartney, James, 42–43, 44 (table 2.1), 46, 48

Haas, T. H., 289
habitat protection: constitutional issues involving, 247–53; designation and, 232–36; eminent domain and, 245–47; false doctrine of equivalents and, 227–29; nuisance and trespass and, 229–32, 248; private land use restrictions and, 231–32; property rights and, 223, 233, 237–39, 243–44, 247–48; second order preferences and, 239–240; *Sweet Home* decision and, 223–24, 225, 226, 240, 247, 253, 253n5; takings and, 230–31, 240, 244–45, 247, 253; voluntary

purchase and, 232–45; willingness-to-pay vs. willingness-to-accept and, 240–45. *See also* wildlife management
Haddock, David D., 176
Hailsham, Lord, of St. Marylebone, 90, 91
Halewood, Michael, 109
Hamilton, Alexander, 317–18
Hammersmith and City Railway v. G. H. Brand, 107, 108
Hanemann, W. Michael, 156
Hardin, Garrett, 38, 39, 189, 283
Harris, J. W. K., 59
Harvard Business School, 141
Harvey, Christopher, 89, 98
Hasegawa, A., 295
Hausmann, Jerry A., 157
Hawaii Housing Authority v. Midkiff, 331
Hawkes, Kristin, 61
Hayek, Friedrich A., 4, 14, 120–21, 149n2, 158, 159, 163, 167, 168–69, 172–73, 181–82n3, 190, 210
Helton, Charmagne, 145
Hemmingway, Roy, 190
Heritage Foundation, 43, 44 (table 2.1), 46, 48
Herman, Dennis J., 189
Herrington, William C., 300
Hess, Karl Jr., 279
Higgs, Robert, 289–90
Hill, Kim, 61
Hill, Peter J., 3, 8, 9, 38, 39, 176, 187, 288, 341
Hitachi, 140
Hoffman, Elizabeth, 72, 74–76, 78–80
Holechek, Jerry L., 279
Holling, C. S., 45
Holmes, Kim R., 43
Home Depot, 140
Homestead Act, 207
Horovitz, Joel, 76,78
Horwitz, Morton J., 106, 109, 111
Humphrey, Nicholas, 66, 80

Hylton, Victoria, 274

Imperial Gas Light and Coke v. Samuel Broadbent, 89
International Country Risk Guide, 43, 44 (table 2.1), 48
International Organization for Standardization, 140

Jansson, Bengt-Owe, 45
Jeffrey, Michael I., 189
Jensen, Michael C., 194, 202
Jentoft, Svein, 298–300, 302
Johannes, R. E., 3, 8, 9
John, Kose, 203
John, Teresa A., 203
Johnson, Bryan T., 43
Johnson, Ronald N., 295
Joskow, Paul L., 13, 41

Kahneman, Daniel, 76, 241
Kaldor-Hicks welfare criterion, 168, 182n4
Kaplin, Hillary, 61
Keefer, Philip, 37, 41, 43, 44
Kerr v. Revelstoke Building Materials, 91
The King v. Edward Pease, 106
Kirkpatrick, Melanie, 43
Kirzner, Israel M., 4, 25
Klein, Benjamin, 198, 263
Klein, Richard G., 59, 62, 198
Knack, Stephen, 37, 41, 43, 44
Knetsch, Jack, 76, 243
Knight, Frank H., 51n1, 164
Knowlton, B., 59
Koch, Eddie, 271
Konar, Shameek, 143
Kormendi, Roger C., 40
Kornhauser, Lewis, 194
Krier, James, 192
Kristoffersen, Trond, 298–99
Krueger, Alan B., 45, 50, 146
Krutilla, John, 155, 177

LaFrance, Jeffrey T., 187
Lambrecht, Piet, 276–78

Landa, Janet T., 7
Langdon, Steve, 288, 289
Lauer, T. E., 89
Lawson, Robert, 42–43, 44 (table 2.1), 46, 48
Leal, Donald R., 4, 8, 27, 38, 192, 205, 260, 283, 341–42
Lee, Jong-Wha, 44 (table 2.1), 46, 48, 49 (table 2.3)
Lee, Richard, 62, 66
Leoni, Bruno, 172
Levin, Simon, 45
Libecap, Gary D., 3, 9, 11, 16, 38, 295
Littlechild, Stephen C., 328
Locke, John, 249, 252
Loretto v. Teleprompter Manhattan CATV Corp., Inc., 230
Lucas, Alastair R., 98
Lueck, Dean, 11, 260–61, 278, 280

Macaulay, Hugh H., 128
MacFarlane, Dougald A., 301, 302
Macklem, Patrick, 98
Madison, James, 332, 333
Mäler, Kärl-Gotsn, 45
Mangels, J., 59
Manne, Henry G., 195
markets: central planning and, 14, 16; defined, 1, 4, 13; division of knowledge and, 159–60; externalities and, 17–21, 125; failure of, 125–26, 139–44, 147–48, 153; forces of, 121–22, 132–34, 140–46; incentives and, 14–15; intrinsic values and, 154; noncooperative behavior and, 69–71; prices and, 16, 23, 163, 167; private property rights and, 14–15; rent seeking and, 14; self-love and, 70–71; specialization and exchange and, 15–17; values and, 158–61. *See also* environmental problems, public lands
Marshall, Alfred, 37, 50, 51n1
Martin, K. O., 294
Martin v. Reynolds Metals, 92
McCabe, Kevin, 57, 71, 74, 76, 78–80

McCaffery, Edward J., 241
McCay, Bonnie J., 284, 295
McChesney, Fred S., 14, 24, 176, 177
McCormick, Charles T., 174
McDonald v. Associated Fuels, 92
McDonald's, 140–41
McIlwain, Charles, 319
McKean, Roland N., 9, 24
McLaren, John P. S., 109
McNeil, Kent, 98
Mead Corporation, 139–40
Mealy, Linda, 60
Meckling, William, 194
Meguire, Philip C., 40
Meiners, Roger E., 3–4, 16, 22, 23, 26, 78,123, 208, 342
Meltzer, Allan H., 24
Menell, Peter S., 209
Meux's Brewery v. London Electric Lighting, 90, 95
Miner v. Gilmour, 99
Ministère de l'Environnement (Quebec), 307
Mitchell, William C., 315
Mithen, Steven, 63–65
Morriss, Andrew P., 172
Mowbray, K., 59
Mueller, Dennis C., 315
Munyali, Bevan, 274

Nader, Ralph, 197
National Oceanic and Atmospheric Administration, 156, 180
National Park Service, 189, 211n8, 265, 279
natural resource damage assessment rules (NRDAs), 179–80
Nature Conservancy, 235
Nedelsky, Jennifer, 90, 111
Nelson, Robert H., 179
Nepisiquit Real Estate and Fishing v. Canadian Iron, 98
Netting, Robert, 284
Nirvana Fallacy, 195, 203
Niskanen, William A., 315, 332
Nordhaus, William D., 40
North, Douglass C., 3, 9, 38, 39, 40

Norton, Seth, 3, 146, 342
nuisance. *See* common law

Oberg, K., 288, 289
O'Connor, Sandra Day, 223
Oesterle, Dale A., 188, 191–92
Office of Management and Budget, 145
Oil Pollution Act of 1990, 157, 179, 180
Olson, R. L., 288
Ontario Ltd. v. Huron Steel Products, 96
Ophuls, W., 283
Organization for Economic Cooperation and Development, 132
Orlando, Michael, 188
Ostrom, Elinor, 3, 8, 160, 284–86
Owen, Bruce M., 109

Pacific Lumber, 202, 215nn38–39, 251–52
Pareto-enhancing moves, 153
Peacock, F. Gregory, 301, 302
Pearse, Peer H., 98
Pejovich, Svetozar, 37, 41
Percy, David R., 98
Perkins, Clive, 276–78
Perrings, Charles, 45
Pimentel, David, 45
Pinker, Steven, 59
Pigou, A. C.: *Economics of Welfare* of, 121; externalities and, 120, 123–32, 147–48; false simplicity of, 120–21,128–29, 148–49; intellectual influence of, 121, 122 (figure 5.1); market failure and, 125–26, 139–40; social cost theory of, 120; taxes of, 120, 129–32; transaction costs and, 126; welfare theory of, 2, 18, 31n5, 121
Poindexter, Georgette C., 190
Political Economy Research Center (PERC), xii, 339
Pompe, Jeffrey J., 133, 146–47
Portney, Paul R., 156, 157
Potter, Charles, 268

preferences, 5–6
Pride of Derby v. British Celanese, 99
private property protection: constitutional choices and, 320, 329–32;
Congress and, 320; democratic
governance and, 315–16; dual security and, 332–33; endangered
species and, 321; federal domination and, 332–33; Fifth Amendment and, 333; "good" governance
and, 317–19, 334; liberal democracy and, 319–21; market pricing
and, 322–29; Ninth Amendment
and, 333; *ordnungstheorie* and,
329–32; political pricing and,
322–29; Seventeenth Amendment
and, 332; Sixteenth Amendment
and, 332; social democracy and,
319–21; Supreme Court and, 331;
Tenth Amendment and, 333. *See
also* common law, property rights
Proctor & Gamble, 140
property rights: attenuated, 38, 42, 44;
in Canada. *See* Canadian property
rights; central planning and, 3–4;
communal ownership of, 8–9; defined, xi, 55; earned, 74–80; economic growth and, 37–38, 43–51;
economic system function and, 3;
Endangered Species Act and, 1–2,
224–25; endogenous, 39–40; environmental quality and, 37; environmental problems and, xi, 2,
3–4, 38, 45–49; erosion of,
104–12; evolutionary psychology
and, 66–69; exchange of, 15–16;
externalities and, 3; in existence
value, 171–73; experimental behavior and, 69–80; habitat protection and, 223, 233, 237–39,
243–44, 247–48; institutions and,
6–7, 12–13; markets and, 14–15;
measures of, 41–43, 44 (table 2.1);
morality and, 7; open access,
17–19; partitioned, 12, 38–39; private ownership of, 9–10; restora-

tion of, 112–13; rule of law and,
12, 43, 44, 149; specialization in
production and, 15; state ownership of, 11–12; trade and, 16;
transaction costs and, 12–13, 16;
transfer of, 9; usufruct, 10–11;
wealth-maximizing and, 38. *See
also* common law, community
fisheries management, habitat protection, markets, private property
protection, reciprocity, wildlife
management
public lands: agency problem and,
192–93; common-law treatment
of, 209–10; Congress and, 187,
196–97, 210, 212n11; forest management on, 188–89, 197, 201–2,
203, 215n44; government stewardship of, 188–89, 192–93, 196–97,
205, 210; grazing practices on,
187, 188, 211nn2–6, 212n15; interest groups and, 188, 189, 192,
196–99; markets and, 194–95;
mining on, 188, 191–92, 211n7;
national parks, 189, 208, 209,
211nn8–10; privatization of, corporate model for, 193–200; privatization of, arguments for, 191,
199–210, 212n16; privatization of,
objections to, 192, 200–210; property rights and, 209–10; sale of,
191–92; stakeholders and, 189–91,
209–10, 212n12

Radetzki, Marian, 37, 45
Rassenti, Stephen, 57, 71, 74
Rebelo, Sergio, 41
reciprocity: in chimpanzees, 57–59;
earned property rights and, 74–80;
evolutionary psychology and,
63–69; in human nature, 55–56; in
hunter-gatherer societies, 60–66;
negative, 57–58, 81; noncooperative behavior and, 69–71; origins
of human trade and, 59–60; personal exchange and, 71–74; positive, 58, 61–62, 81–82

Rehnquist, William, 223
Renna, P., 59
Resolution Trust Corporation, 191
Rettig, R. Bruce, 302
Revesz, Richard L., 177
Rex v. Pease, 106, 108
Rice, William R., 67
Riker, William H., 39
Rinehart, James R., 133, 146–47
riparian rights, 97–104, 113n4
Risk, R. C. B., 88, 111
Roberts v. Gwyrfai District Council, 103
Robinson, Jerome B., 303–4
Robinson, Judith, 177, 180
Romano, Roberta, 200
Rose, Carol M., 208
Routhier, Yannick, 307
Ruddle, Kenneth, 300
Rushkin, F. R., 284
Russell Transport v. Ontario Malleable Iron, 96, 97
Rutherford, Malcolm, 3

Sacks, Oliver, 69
St. Helen's Smelting v. William Tipping, 111
Sala-I-Martin, Xavier, 41, 49 (table 2.3)
Sanchez, Nicholas, 11
Sanera, Michael, 28, 30n1
Savin, N., 76, 78
Sax, Joseph L., 22
Scalia, Antonin, 223
Schlager, Edella, 284
Schumpeter, Joseph, 16, 163
Scott, Anthony, 2, 98, 290
Scott, John P., 67
Scully, Gerald W., 37, 40–41
Seabrook, Charles, 145
Sefton, Martin, 76, 78
Seligman, Joel, 197
Semaw, S., 59
Senedeker, Itai, 39
Sethi, Rajiv, 4–5
Shachat, Keith, 78–80
Sharpe, Robert, 90, 98

Shaw, Jane S., 28, 30n1
Shelfer v. London Electric Lighting, 90, 95
Shetland Fish Producers' Organization Ltd., 302
Short, Kevin MacEwen, 300–301
Siegan, Bernard H., 331
Sierra Club v. Department of Forestry and Fire Protection, 251–52
Sierra Club v. Morton, 177–78
Simmons, Randy T., 284, 315
Simon, Julian L., 45
Smith, Adam: contradictory views of, 56–57, 69, 80–82; division of labor and, 159; fascination with markets of, 126; *Theory of Moral Sentiments* of, 76, 81, 82n2; *Wealth of Nations* of, 56, 70, 71, 72, 81
Smith, Vernon L., 3, 7, 19, 39, 57, 71, 74, 76, 78–80, 319, 342
Solow, Robert C., 40, 180
Somanathan, E., 4–5
Southview Associates, Ltd. v. Bongartz, 230–31
Squire, L., 59
Spiegel, Menaham, 176
Spitzer, Matthew, 72, 74–76, 241
Stago, Phillip, 273
Stanford Research Institute, 141
Star v. Rookesby, 91
State Environmental Monitor, 140
Stollmeyer v. Trinidad Lake Petroleum, 100
Strobel v. Kerr Salt, 100, 102–3
Stubblebine, William C., 20–21, 124, 153
substitutability, 5
Sunaram, Anant K., 203
Sunstein, Cass R., 171, 177
Supreme Court, U.S.: compensation rules and, 246–47; existence value and, 178; existing use and, 244; ideological make-up of, 253n5; private property and, 331; *Sweet Home* decision and, 223–24, 225, 226, 240, 247, 253, 253n5; White

Mountain Apache Indian Reservation and, 274
Swaigen, John, 90

takings. *See* Endangered Species Act, U.S. Constitution
Taylor Grazing Act, 187, 211n3
Tennessee Valley Authority, 178
Thaler, Richard, 76
Thieme, H., 62
Thomas, Clarence, 223
Thomas, Stacie, 143
Thresher, Valerie, 275–76
Thurber, James, 67
Tiebout, Charles, 231
Tietenberg, Tom, 119–20
Tock v. St. John's Metropolitan Area Board, 95, 105, 112
Tollison, Robert D., 260–61
transaction costs: defined, 12; economic system function and, 3; eminent domain in, 246; environmental problems and, 2; institutions and, 12–13; trade and, 17–19; wealth-maximizing and, 38; wildlife management and, 261–66. *See also* Ronald N. Coase, A. C. Pigou
Trebilcock, Michael, 110
trespass. *See* common law
Tribe, Laurence H., 22
Trinidad Asphalt v. Ambard, 95
Trivers, R. L., 58
Tytler, Alexander, 315

Umbeck, John, 3, 9
Upper Chattahoochee Riverkeeper, 145
Usher, Dan, 315
utility, 155, 168, 170
Uzelac, Milan, 98

value: defined, 23; explicit, 158; market, 158–61. *See also* contingent valuation, existence value
Varty, Dave, 269–70
Vaughn v. Taff Vale Railway, 107, 108
Viner, Jacob, 56, 81

Wagner, Richard E., 4, 30, 112–13, 149, 170, 342–43
Wales, Leonard J., 191
Walker, James, 286
Walker v. McKinnon Industries, 97
Wall Street Journal, 43
Walter v. Selfe, 97
Warren, Charles, 320
Watts, Myles J., 187
Webber, Carolyn, 323
Wenders, John T., 273
Weston Paper v. Pope, 101
Whalen v. Union Bag & Paper, 101
White Mountain Apache Indian Reservation, 272–74
Wiedenbaum, Murray, 188
Wiener, Jonathan, 228
Wildavsky, Aaron, 323
wildlife management: Coasean theory and, 260–64, 266–67, 272, 279–80; damages and, 27–28, 249, 250–51, 259–60, 265, 266–67, 274–76, 279; of eagles, 260–61; of elephants, 28, 260, 274–76; of elk, 267–68, 272–74; free-rider problem and, 262, 263, 264; by government, 265–66, 273, 278–79; holdout problem and, 262, 263, 265; integration and, 261, 262, 263, 264–65, 272–78; and open-access, 259; private contracting and, 266–72, 280; property rights theory and, 260; reciprocal costs and, 261–66; in South Africa, 269–72, 276–78, 280; transaction costs and, 260, 261–66, 272, 280; of waterfowl, 268–69; of whales, 29; of wolves, 266–67, 280, 281n5; in Zimbabwe, 28, 274–76. *See also* community fisheries management, habitat protection
Wilkinson, Charles F., 188
Willett, Thomas D., 260–61
Williamson, Robert, 296, 298
Willig, Robert D., 241
Winter, Ralph, 110

World Bank, 47 (table 2.2), 49 (table 2.3), 50 (table 2.4), 128–29
World Wildlife Fund, 275
Wright, Chester W., 8

Yandle, Bruce, 2, 3, 12, 18, 21, 38, 74, 88, 90, 110, 174, 175, 343

Yellowstone National Park, 27–28, 265, 266, 279
Yoder, Jonathan, 11, 280
John Young and Company v. Banker Distillery, 99

About the Political Economy Forum
and the Contributors

The Political Economy Research Center (PERC) is a nonprofit research center located in Bozeman, Montana, that focuses on market solutions to environmental problems. For more than fifteen years, PERC has been a pioneer in recognizing the value of the market, individual initiative, and the importance of property rights and voluntary activity. This approach is known as the new resource economics or free market environmentalism. PERC associates have applied this approach to a variety of issues, including resource development, water marketing, chemical risk, private provision of environmental amenities, global warming, ozone depletion, and endangered species protection.

In 1989, PERC organized the first of an ongoing series called the Political Economy Forum aimed at applying the principles of political economy to important policy issues. The forum brings together scholars in economics, political science, law, history, anthropology, and other related disciplines to discuss and refine academic papers that explore new applications of political economy to policy analysis.

The chapters in this volume emanate from the Political Economy Forum held in June 1997, where eight papers were presented. Biographical information on the paper authors is listed below. They were joined by fifteen participants who commented on the papers and discussed numerous issues surrounding property rights and the environment. These participants were: Daniel K. Benjamin (PERC and Clemson University), Henry Butler (University of Kansas), Dennis Coyle (Catholic University of America), Barbara Curti (Nevada Farm Bureau), William Dennis (Liberty Fund Inc., Indianapolis), John Hosemann (American Farm Bureau Federation), David McClure (Montana Farm Bureau), Bobby McCormick (Clemson University), John Moorhouse (Wake Forest University), Seth Norton (Wheaton College), Jeffrey Rachlinski

349

(Cornell University), Lynn Scarlett (Reason Public Policy Institute), Danielle Smith (Canadian Property Rights Research Institute), Bill Stamp III (Schoharie, New York), and Richard Stroup (PERC and Montana State University). The papers by Richard Epstein, Donald Leal, and Seth Norton were added to the volume after the forum.

Terry L. Anderson is executive director of PERC, senior fellow at the Hoover Institution at Stanford University, and professor of economics at Montana State University. Anderson is the series editor of PERC's Political Economy Forum Series published by Rowman & Littlefield. (This book is the thirteenth volume in the series.) He is author, coauthor, or editor of twenty books, including *Free Market Environmentalism* and *Enviro-Capitalists: Doing Good While Doing Well*, and has published numerous articles in professional journals and popular publications. Anderson has been a visiting scholar at Oxford University, the University of Basel (Switzerland), Canterbury University (New Zealand), Stanford University, and Cornell University Law School. He holds a B.S. in business administration from the University of Montana and an M.S. and Ph.D. in economics from the University of Washington.

Donald J. Boudreaux became president of the Foundation for Economic Education in 1997. From 1992 through 1997, he was associate professor of law and economics at Clemson University, and from 1985 to 1989 he was assistant professor of economics at George Mason University. Boudreaux earned his Ph.D. in economics from Auburn University and his J.D. is from the University of Virginia. He has published articles in the *Wall Street Journal, Reason, Regulation, Supreme Court Economic Review*, and other popular and academic outlets.

Elizabeth Brubaker is the executive director of Environment Probe, a division of the Toronto-based Energy Probe Research Foundation. She is the author of *Property Rights in the Defence of Nature*. She has contributed chapters to four other books and has written extensively on water, fisheries, and other environmental issues.

William J. Carney is the Charles Howard Candler Professor of Law at Emory University. He teaches corporation and securities law and has published numerous articles on corporate and securities law topics. He has served as reporter and chairman of the business corporation law revision committee of the State Bar of Georgia. Prior to teaching, he practiced law in Colorado and represented various users of the public lands. He has a B.A. and LL.B. from Yale University and has been active in law and economics throughout his academic career.

Louis De Alessi received his Ph.D. in economics from UCLA in 1961. He has held tenure faculty positions at Duke University, George Washington University, and the University of Miami, where he is professor emeritus; he has enjoyed visiting appointments at several U.S. and foreign universities as well as been a consultant to various private and governmental organizations. He has published extensively on economic theory and its application, with special emphasis on the economic consequences of alternative institutional arrangements.

Richard A. Epstein is the James Parker Hall Distinguished Service Professor of Law at the University of Chicago, where he has taught since 1972. He served as editor of the *Journal of Legal Studies* and since 1991 has been an editor of the *Journal of Law and Economics*. His books include *Mortal Peril: Our Inalienable Rights to Health Care?*; *Simple Rules for a Complex World*; *Bargaining With the State*; *Forbidden Grounds: The Case Against Employment Discrimination Laws*; and *Takings: Private Property and the Power of Eminent Domain*. He has written numerous articles on a wide range of legal and interdisciplinary subjects.

Peter J. Hill is professor of economics at Wheaton College, where he holds the George F. Bennett Chair. He is a senior associate of PERC, and in addition to this book, has coedited five previous volumes of the Political Economy Forum Series. His research and articles, especially on the evolution of property rights in the American West, helped found the new resource economics which is the basis for free market environmentalism. He is coauthor, with Terry L. Anderson, of *The Birth of a Transfer Society* and, with Joseph L. Bast and Richard C. Rue, of *Eco-Sanity: A Common Sense Guide to Environmentalism*. As an economic consultant, he has worked with the Bulgarian government in its attempts to privatize agricultural lands. Hill has a B.S. from Montana State University and a Ph.D. from the University of Chicago.

Donald R. Leal is a senior associate of PERC. He is coauthor with Anderson of *Free Market Environmentalism*, which received the 1992 Choice Outstanding Academic Book Award, and *Enviro-Capitalists: Doing Good While Doing Well*. He is a contributing author in *Multiple Conflicts Over Multiple Uses, Taking the Environment Seriously*, and *Taking Ownership: Property Rights in Fisheries*. Over the last twelve years, Leal has published numerous articles on fisheries, water, recreation, oil and gas, timber, and federal land use policy. His articles have appeared in the *Wall Street Journal, New York Times,* and *Chicago Tribune,* as well as specialized journals. Leal's recent studies comparing federal and state management of public forests have fostered a new perspective on public land management. Leal has a B.S. in mathematics and an M.S. in statistics from California State University at Hayward.

Roger E. Meiners is professor of law and economics at the University of Texas at Arlington and a senior associate of PERC. His economics degrees are from Washington State University, the University of Arizona, and Virginia Tech; his law degree is from the University of Miami. Meiners has also been a faculty member of Texas A&M University, Emory University, and Clemson University and was a regional director for the Federal Trade Commission. His research focuses on common law and market solutions to environmental issues and on the economics of higher education. Meiners serves on the board of the Roe Foundation and Consumer Alert and has published several books, including *Taking the Environment Seriously* (with Bruce Yandle).

Seth W. Norton is Aldeen Professor of Business and Economics at Wheaton College. Author of a wide range of articles on industrial organization and business and economic institutions and practices, Norton has also taught at Washington University in St. Louis, the University of Michigan, and Illinois State University. His current research focuses on the effects of property rights and cultural conflicts on human well-being. He received his Ph.D. in economics, industrial organization, and finance from the University of Chicago.

Vernon L. Smith is Regents' Professor of Economics and research director of the Economic Science Laboratory at the University of Arizona. He received his bachelor's degree in electrical engineering from Cal Tech and his Ph.D. in economics from Harvard. He has authored or coauthored more than 150 articles and books on capital theory, finance, natural resource economics, and experimental economics. Smith is past president of the Public Choice Society, the Economic Science Association, the Western Economic Association, and the Association for Private Enterprise Education. He is a distinguished fellow of the American Economic Association and was elected a member of the National Academy of Sciences in 1995.

Richard E. Wagner received his Ph.D. in economics from the University of Virginia in 1966. He is currently the Holbert L. Harris Professor of Economics at George Mason University. His scholarly writings have covered a broad range of topics on matters of political economy and public policy and have resulted in some twenty books and monographs and more than one hundred articles in scholarly journals. Wagner is coeditor of the scholarly journal, *Constitutional Political Economy*, and is a member of the editorial boards of three other scholarly journals: *Public Choice*, the *Supreme Court Economic Review*, and the *Madison Review*.

Bruce Yandle is Alumni Distinguished Professor of Economics and Legal Studies at Clemson University and PERC Senior Associate. Yandle received an A.B. from Mercer University and a Ph.D. from Georgia State University. He served as senior economist on the President's Council on Wage and Price Stability and as executive director of the Federal Trade Commission. Yandle is the author of *Environmental Use and the Market, The Political Limits of Environmental Regulation*, and *Common Sense and Common Law for the Environment*. He is coeditor of *Taking the Environment Seriously* and editor of *Land Rights: The 1990s' Property Rights Rebellion*.